System Software Programming:
The Way Things Work

System Software Programming:

The Way Things Work

David L. Clarke
Donald Merusi

To join a Prentice Hall PTR Internet mailing list, point to
http://www.prehnhall.com/register

Prentice Hall PTR
Upper Saddle River, NJ 07458
http://www.prenhall.com

Library of Congress Cataloging-in-Publication Data

```
Clarke, David L.
System software programming : the way things work / David L. Clarke,
   Donald Merusi
      p.  cm,
   Includes index.
   ISBN 0-13-490558-X
   1. Systems programming (Computer Science). 2. Computer software.
  I. Clarke, David L. II. Merusi, Donald. III. Title.
QA76.66.C55  1997
005.4'2—dc21                                         97-19517
                                                         CIP
```

Editorial/production supervision: *Mary Sudul*
Cover design: *Bruce Kenselaar*
Cover design director: *Jayne Conte*
Manufacturing manager: *Alexis R. Heydt*
Marketing manager: *Stephen Solomon*
Acquisitions editor: *Michael Meehan*
Editorial assistant: *Barbara Alfieri*

©1998 Prentice Hall PTR
Prentice-Hall, Inc.
A Simon & Schuster Company
Upper Saddle River, New Jersey 07458

The publisher offers discounts on this book when ordered
in bulk quantities. For more information, contact:

Corporate Sales Department
PTR Prentice Hall
One Lake Street
Upper Saddle River, NJ 07458

Phone: 800-382-3419
Fax: 201-236-7141
E-mail (Internet): corpsales@prenhall.com

Product names mentioned herein are the trademarks or registered trademarks of their respective owners.

ISBN 0-13-490558-X

Printed in the United States of America

   10 9 8 7 6 5 4 3 2 1

Prentice-Hall International (UK) Limited, *London*
      Prentice-Hall of Australia Pty. Limited, *Sydney*
      Prentice-Hall Canada Inc., *Toronto*
      Prentice-Hall Hispanoamericana, S.A., *Mexico*
      Prentice-Hall of India Private Limited, *New Delhi*
      Prentice-Hall of Japan, Inc., *Tokyo*
      Simon & Schuster Asia Pte. Ltd., *Singapore*
      Editora Prentice-Hall do Brasil, Ltda., *Rio de Janeiro*

To Evelyn, Heather, Christopher, and Joshua
who encouraged me to undertake this project.
—Dave Clarke

For Jodi, who was always there for me.
—Don Merusi

TABLE OF CONTENTS

PREFACE

This book is intended to be used as a professional reference for developers and system programmers who are working in either the UNIX or the Win32 environment and need to know more about the underlying hardware and software that makes up their environment. It can also serve as a bridge for those who are migrating from one of these two environments to the other.

This book can also serve as a text for an upper level undergraduate or graduate computer science course on compiler design and related topics.

In this book, the reader is presented with a variety of commonly used computer system software components and concurrency mechanisms that form the environmental foundation of virtually every computer system used today. As a prerequisite to understanding the principles discussed in this book, the reader should have had some exposure to elementary data structures. Some experience with **C++** would be helpful since many of the programming examples discussed are written in **C++**. Appendix A provides a quick introduction to **C++** for those readers who feel they lack the required level of coding proficiency.

This book actually begins describing how a computer executes a program at the most rudimentary level, machine language. Chapter 1 discusses various aspects of machine language and describes its relationship to machine architecture. The Digital Equipment Corporation Alpha processor is used as a case study system in this chapter and Chapter 2.

Chapter 2 discusses software specification at the next higher level, assembler language. The reader is shown how assemblers actually facilitate the writing of machine language and allow programmers to specify very intimate control to the machine. The essentials of a one and two-pass assembler is presented. Symbol, expression and macro resolution is also discussed.

Chapter 3 discusses how the output of assembler language must be packaged and processed so that it can be executed in the memory of the computer. Here we discuss the basic principles involved in how the absolute and relative linking and loading of executable modules takes place. This chapter also discusses how software routine library references are resolved. Run-time, or dynamically linked libraries, another means by which programs make use of service libraries *on-the-fly*, are also discussed.

Chapter 4 introduces the reader to basic compiler theory. BNF and syntax diagrams are used to describe the language syntax. Two basic parsing methods are discussed, operator-precedence and recursive decent. For the semantic analysis phase and code generations steps, the reader is introduced to P-Code. P-Code is an intermediate representation of the machine code produced by the compiler and is machine architecture independent. A platform specific P-Code interpreter can then be used to process and run the P-Code instructions. In Chapter 6, the P-Code interpreter will be expanded to allow the reader to discover the rudiments of how concurrent programming can be accomplished. The P-Code interpreter concept used here is very similar to the Java Virtual Machine used to run Java™ applets and programs.

The goal of Chapter 5 is to design your own *Lil'Luxlyk* compiler. All the requisite information has been discussed in Chapter 4. Chapter 5 leads the reader through the design of the source language description using layers of syntax diagrams instead of BNF production rules. Syntax diagrams make it easier to visualize the desired format. Chapters 4 and 5 together form a reasonably complete course in compiler design.

Chapter 6 begins the discussion about concurrency. Basic concurrency primitives are discussed including coroutines, 2-process synchronization algorithms, Peterson's Solution, semaphores, monitors, messaging, and the rendezvous.

Chapter 7 is an overview of operating systems. Basic operating system principles are discussed including principles of scheduling, memory management, I/O interrupt processing and system resource allocation management.

Chapter 8 discusses concurrency and asynchronous process synchronization services available in two popular operating system environments, UNIX and the Win32® API. This chapter is a case study using an assortment of practical programming examples written for these environments.

Appendix A gives the reader an overview of the **C++** language. Appendix B lists the UNIX system synchronization and process and thread scheduling functions discussed in this book.

Both Digital UNIX and Solaris system services are listed. Appendix C lists the synchronization and process and thread scheduling functions available in the Win32 API. Appendix D lists the instructions with their format descriptions for the ICS computer system. Appendix E lists the core code for the Luxlyk compiler. Appendix F lists the entire code for the Full Bodied P-Machine.

SOFTWARE BUILDING BLOCKS CD CONTENTS

The CD accompanying this book includes many examples from this book as illustrated in Table P.1.

Table P.1

CD Contents

Directory	Contents
lilluxly	Contains the complete **C++** source code for the Lil'LuxLyk compiler of Chapter 5, Win32 executables, sample Lil'LuxLyk programs, and a complete set of macro definitions that translate P-Code output by the compiler into Intel 8086 assembler language.
luxlyk	Contains the complete **C++** source code for the LuxLyk compiler of Chapter 6, a Win32 executable, and a complete set of LuxLyk programs that demonstrate basic concurrency principals.
pmachine	Contains the complete **C++** source code for the P-Machine of Chapter 6 and a P-Code program, realtest.pcd, that illustrates some of the P-Machine instructions that are not output by the compilers.
concurre	Contains the **C** source code for the two Win32 threads examples from Chapter 8.

The **C++** programs in this book use the Standard Template Library, STL. It should be possible to use these sources with any compiler that is STL compliant, although some modifications may have to be made depending on the particular compiler. (For instance, many compilers cannot handle the new "namespace" statements yet.) A list of STL-compatible compilers (and the 'fixes' or adjustments that might be necessary) can be found on the following internet web page:

http://www.cyberport.com/~tangent/programming/stl/compatibility.html

ACKNOWLEDGMENTS

The authors would like to thank Niklaus Wirth, Peter Calingaert, and *Byte* magazine for granting us permission to expand on some of the concepts that they have published. We would also like to thank Richard Funk for allowing us to include his Intel PC-based PCODE.DEF macros on our CD. We also thank our editors, Mary Sudul and Mike Meehan, and all the other staff members at Prentice Hall who have assisted us in bringing this book to fruition. And, finally, we need to remember all of our past students who have contributed in one way or another to the material presented here, specifically Patrick Burton who contributed the programs in Chapter 8.

CHAPTER 1

Machine Language

appropriately $\qquad$ This chapter will discuss the lowest level of interpretation of a program, *machine language*. All software ultimately ends up as machine language; the rudimentary combination of 1s and 0s that represent data and instructions. First, we will discuss basic machine architecture representative of most computer systems today. We will then learn how information is stored in the computer and how that information is understood by the hardware as being instructions or data. As a case study system, we will examine the machine language environment of Digital Equipment Corporation's Alpha processor.

1.0 BASIC SYSTEM ARCHITECTURE

To appreciate how software is executed, one must first understand what basic components comprise computer systems:

- Central Processing Unit (CPU)
  - Logic Unit
  - Registers

- Memory

- Peripherals
  - Disks
  - Tape drives
  - Communication devices
  - Terminals

Figure 1.1 illustrates how these components are interconnected.

The *system bus* is the common communications path between the components. Notice that memory is treated as another peripheral device on the bus. Many systems are designed this way to allow for a more expedient memory access.

1

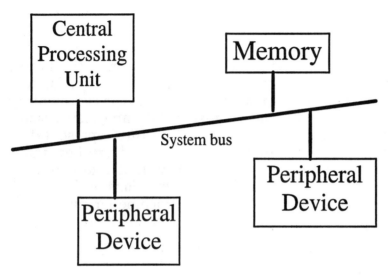

Figure 1.1
Basic machine architecture components.

When software is placed into the memory of the computer, the CPU can then begin executing the program. By using its *logic unit*, the CPU understands *machine language* and knows how to execute the various *instructions* that comprise the program. *Registers* are special locations that enable expedient storage and retrieval of information at the time a program is executed. Many computer instructions are designed to be used with registers, and every register has its own name designation such as R1 or R4. Register operations occur much faster than operations performed to memory. Depending on the machine, the number of registers will vary. Some machines have registers dedicated to a particular kind of data, such as integers (numbers without decimal points) or floating-point values (numbers with decimal points).

1.1 NUMBERING SYSTEMS

Before we look at how information is stored in the computer, you should have a comfortable understanding about the concept of numbering systems. A numbering system defines how many different numeric digits are required to represent a counting sequence before the digits have to be used over to maintain the counting sequence. We ordinarily use the **base 10** numbering system as part of our daily lives. In the base 10 numbering system, you have **10** different digits, **0 through 9**. After nine, you have to start to use the digits over again. Computers use different numbering systems to represent information. At the very lowest level, the system hardware uses **base 2**, the **binary** system. In base 2, you only have two digits, **0** and **1**. When we discuss machine language later in this chapter, we will revert to representing information in binary terms. The individual digits of the binary system are also referred to as *bits*. As we look at other numbering systems, we represent numbers in those bases in terms of groupings of bits. The rule is to use as many bits as are required to indicate the base value as a power of 2. For example, in the **octal**, or **base 8,** numbering system, since $2^3 = 8$, three bits are used to represent an octal digital. For **base 16**, also known as **hexidecimal**, $2^4 = 16$ where four bits are used to represent hexidecimal digits.

Base 16 allows you to specify much larger numbers than base 10 with fewer digits, a major consideration for computer memory storage. Since we have 16 digits in the hexidecimal numbering system, we need to add new digits after nine and use the letters of the alphabet **A through F**. Table 1.1 illustrates what values would be used to represent the numbers from 0 to 20 in four different numbering systems.

We will be using the hexidecimal and binary numbering systems in all subsequent discussions in this chapter. Hexidecimal is convenient for succinctly representing information, while binary is handy for illustrating field information and other kinds of bit-wise data breakdowns.

1.2 DATA FORMATS

Although computers do manipulate data in terms of bits, from a programming standpoint it is more convenient to deal with groups of bits. The **byte** is usually the smallest unit of information manipulated by machine instructions and is comprised of eight bits. Characters, such as letters of the alphabet, numbers, and other symbols, such as punctuation marks, are represented in terms of bytes. A half byte (four bits) is called a *nibble*.

Bytes are grouped together to form successively larger data types, as indicated in Table 1.2.

Table 1.1

The first twenty integers represented in base 2, 8, 10, and 16 respectively

Base 2	Base 8	Base 10	Base 16
0	0	0	0
1	1	1	1
10	2	2	2
11	3	3	3
100	4	4	4
101	5	5	5
110	6	6	6
111	7	7	7
1000	10	8	8
1001	11	9	9
1010	12	10	A
1011	13	11	B
1100	14	12	C
1101	15	13	D
1110	16	14	E
1111	17	15	F
10000	20	16	10
10001	21	17	11
10010	22	18	12
10011	23	19	13
10100	24	20	14

Table 1.2

Data types formed by combinations of bytes

# bytes	Resultant data type
2	Half-word
4	Word
8	Quadword

The data types are significant for understanding how a computer system *addresses memory*. Some computer systems are designed *byte addressable* and read or write memory one byte at a time. Other systems are unable to address memory at any smaller a resolution than a word. The CDC Cyber series machines were designed this way.

Because of the various numbers of bits required to represent the different data types described in Table 1.2, limitations exist in the size number that can be stored in such a memory location. We must also concern ourselves with representing negative as well as positive numbers. The generally accepted convention is to use the *most significant bit* (left-most) of the data to indicate the *sign* of the number. If this bit is set to one, the number is considered to be a negative value, and the remaining bits of the negative number are interpreted to be in *two's complement format.* To convert a positive number to a negative number in two's complement form, change all the one bits to zero bits and all the zero bits to one bits; this is also called *complementing* the value. Finally, add a binary one to the right-most bit of the complemented value. To change a negative number to its corresponding positive representation, perform the same procedure. Figure 1.2 illustrates the procedure.

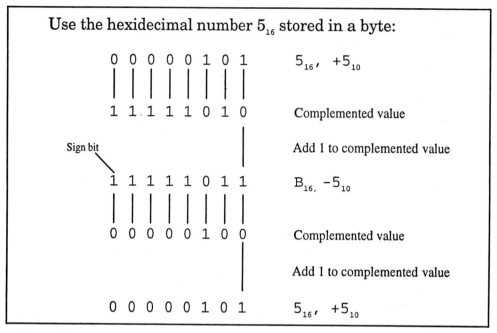

Use the hexidecimal number 5_{16} stored in a byte:

0 0 0 0 0 1 0 1 $5_{16},\ +5_{10}$

1 1 1 1 1 0 1 0   Complemented value

Sign bit   Add 1 to complemented value

1 1 1 1 1 0 1 1 $B_{16,}\ -5_{10}$

0 0 0 0 0 1 0 0   Complemented value

                          Add 1 to complemented value

0 0 0 0 0 1 0 1 $5_{16},\ +5_{10}$

Figure 1.2
Converting to and from two's complement.

Each of the data formats listed in Table 1.2 has limitations as to what magnitude range of integer values can be represented by the number of bits available. Floating-point numbers are stored in a completely different manner and will be discussed later in this chapter. Bits in a data field are numbered from left to right, starting with the highest number on the left. Therefore, the most significant bit (MSB) has the highest bit number in the field, and the least signifcant bit (LSB) has the lowest bit number. Table 1.3 lists the value ranges for the three integer data formats.

Table 1.3

Value ranges for three integer data formats

Data types	Bit format & Value range

Byte

7   0

-2^8 to $+2^8 - 1$

Half-word

15   0

-2^{16} to $+2^{16} - 1$

Word

31   0

-2^{32} to $+2^{32} - 1$

Quadword

63   0

-2^{64} to $+2^{64} - 1$

Most significant bit is sign bit.

Floating-point numbers are stored in a completely different manner. Most contemporary machines use two different formats to represent floating-point values. One format is particular to the machine architecture and the other is IEEE format. Because every system manufacturer has its own manner of representing floating-point numbers, the IEEE instituted a floating point number standard. Nevertheless, in general, most machine architectures store floating point numbers comprised of three parts:

1. Sign

2. Exponent

3. Fraction

The sign indicates whether the number is positive or negative, and the exponent and fraction are interpreted as follows:

$$.1\text{fraction} \times 2^{\text{Exp}}$$

The fraction is stored such that all of its digits are to the right of the decimal point. The exponent can be positive or negative and the sign of the exponent is expressed in *excess notation*. An exponent of zero is the excess value itself; an exponent value of +1 is the excess value plus one. For example, the Alpha processor uses excess-128 notation to express the exponent in VAX format floating-point numbers. An exponent of +1 is represented in the exponent field as 129_{10}. An exponent of −2 is represented in the exponent field as 126_{10}. The basic format of a typical floating point number is illustrated in Figure 1.3.

31	30 23	22 0
S	Exp.	Fraction

Figure 1.3
Generic floating-point number format; decimal point is between bits 23 and 22.

Depending on the precision of the floating-point number, the fraction may be larger than depicted in Figure 1.3. The exponent size may also vary. A consequence of converting a value from base 10 into internal floating-point representation (e.g., into hexidecimal/binary) is that the number cannot be accurately represented mathematically in its binary form. This inaccuracy is referred to as *loss of significance*. To minimize loss of significance, most computer systems *normalize* the fraction part. The fraction is aligned so that a one-bit always occurs immediately after the decimal point. Because this bit is always present, it is never displayed and is referred to as the *hidden bit*. When converting from internal floating point notation, remember to use this bit even though it does not appear as part of the number in the computer. Each bit of the fraction is computed as a power of two: $2^{-1} + 2^{-2} + 2^{-3}$ and so on. Let us now examine how to represent 12.34 in internal floating-point format. Figure 1.4 illustrates how this number would be represented internally by the computer according to the format in Figure 1.3. The sign bit is zero, indicating a positive value. The exponent field is +4, $84_{16} - 80_{16}$. Notice the use of the hidden bit to derive the fraction.

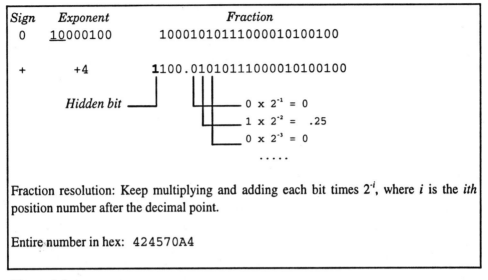

Figure 1.4
Floating point format for 12.34 according to the format described in Figure 1.3.

1.3 INSTRUCTION FORMATS

Machine instructions differ in size depending on system architecture and the nature of the instruction. Machine instructions are typically comprised of some or all of the following constituents:

- Operation code
- Register(s)
- Addressing mode specification
- Memory target address

Some instructions are comprised solely of an operation code (opcode) such as a HALT instruction. A HALT instruction has no need to reference memory or registers. It is simply a control mechanism to the computer to stop executing. Other instructions are used to move data from registers to memory or from one memory location to another. These kinds of instructions work with data in memory and therefore require the specification of a memory target address. The actual value that represents a memory target address can depend on the instruction *addressing mode*. These concepts are best understood by observing how some hypothetical machine instructions might appear. Programming directly in machine language is a lost art and rarely practiced today. However, during the late 1970s and early 1980s, programming such machines as the DEC PDP-11 frequently involved "fat-fingering" in instructions via the front console toggle switches.

1.4 THE IMAGINARY COMPUTER SYSTEM—ICS

Our hypothetical machine language runs on an imaginary computer called ICS, an acronym for *Imaginary Computer System.* It is appropriate to discuss some of the architectural details of ICS at this time. ICS contains 1 gigabyte of memory, 1 billion bytes, 16 32-bit wide integer (fixed-point) registers designated as R0 through R13, SP and PC, and 16 64-bit wide floating-point registers designated as F0 through F15. ICS uses R15 as the program counter (PC) to keep track of instruction execution and a 16-bit processor status word (PSW) to keep track of the state of the processor. ICS also uses R14 as a stack pointer (SP), which points to a linear storage area and has a particular orientation. When we refer to the *top of the stack*, we are referring to where SP is currently pointing. The ICS instruction set takes advantage of a stack information structure by providing a POP and PUSH instruction. When adding information to the stack, a PUSH instruction is used and when removing information, a POP is performed. The PUSH instruction adds data to the top of the stack while POP removes data from the top of the stack. An ICS word is 32 bits.

ICS is a RISC-based machine. A RISC, *Reduced Instruction Set Computer,* machine is designed to execute very simple instructions very fast. Because memory has become less of a premium resource today, it is thought that needing more instructions to represent a program is worth executing it faster; although it will require more memory compared to its non-RISC version. Machines through the 1980s were designed as CISC (*Complex Instruction Set Computer*) computers. Most instructions on a CISC machine perform elaborate operations. Perhaps the greatest example of a CISC machine is Digital Equipment Corporation's VAX computer. The VAX contained several very interesting instructions—one of the more noteworthy being

POLY. POLY is a machine instruction that actually performs an nth order polynomial evaluation! Here we have an incredible amount of functionality in a single machine instruction; however, the design trend into the nineties has migrated away from this kind of implementation as the RISC machines have taken over. Digital's successor to the VAX is the RISC-based Alpha processor. We will be reviewing various characteristics of the Alpha throughout this book.

1.5 ICS INSTRUCTION FORMATS

In an ICS computer, there are two instruction formats, *register-memory* and *register-register*. Figure 1.5 illustrates the basic field formats of a 48-bit (6 byte) register-memory and a 16-bit register-register instruction.

Register-Memory Instruction (RM type)

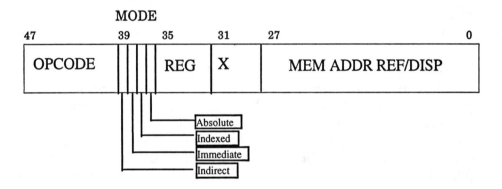

Register-Register Instruction (RR type)

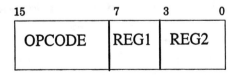

Figure 1.5
Instruction formats for the ICS computer.

If a particular instruction does not require a specific field, that field of the instruction is simply ignored. In an RM type instruction, the first field is eight bits wide and contains the instruction opcode. The next four bits contain the *mode* of the instruction. The mode controls the nature of how the instruction target is addressed in memory. The mode field contents are described in Table 1.4.

Table 1.4

Meaning of *mode* field in an ICS instruction

Mode field value	Addressing style	Target address (TA)
Bits 39—36 = 0	PC-relative	TA ← Displ. + (PC)
Bit 39 = 1	Indirect	TA ← [Displ. + (PC)]
Bit 38 = 1	Immediate	Literal value
Bit 37 = 1	Indexed	TA ← [Displ.+ (PC)] + (X)
Bit 36 = 1	Absolute	TA ← Displacement

The next two series of 4-bits fields indicate what general purpose register (REG) and what index register (X) may be used in the instruction. The X field contains zeros if no index register is used. The next 28 bits are used to accommodate the memory reference/displacement field. Most addressing on the ICS machine is performed *PC-relative*. For PC-relative addressing, these 28-bits will contain a signed value in the range -2^{27} to $+2^{27} - 1$. As the computer executes the current instruction, the *program counter*, or PC, is always pointing to the *next instruction address*. Therefore, if the instruction currently being executed is at address 10000_{16} and is an RM type, the PC is pointing to address 10006_{16}. Suppose the target address of the instruction is at location 14000_{16}. The memory address displacement field will contain the value $3FFA_{16}$, $10006_{16} + 3FFA_{16} = 14000_{16}$. The displacement value will remain unchanged no matter where a program is loaded in memory. This characteristic is key to making the code *relocatable*.

Indirect addressing refers to using the displacement as a pointer to the actual target address. The initial target address is computed PC-relative, as described above. The resultant address contains another address, which is now used as the target address. Using the above address as an example, suppose location 14000_{16} contains the value 21000_{16}. If indirect addressing were being used, the target address used would be 21000_{16}.

If the mode bits are set to *immediate (literal) mode*, addressing is not an issue. The signed value represented in the displacement field is used as a number typically loaded into a register. Literal mode is a convenient way of working with constants.

If the mode bits are set to *absolute addressing*, the displacement field is considered an unsigned value designating a specific address in memory.

If the mode bits are set to *indexed mode,* one of the 16 general purpose registers is specified as an *index register.* The target address is computed by adding the contents of the index register to the PC plus any displacement. Indexed mode requires a particular assembler language syntax and is convenient for manipulating data arrays.

RR type instructions can involve one or two registers. Some RR instructions may only specify one register, such as the **clear register** instruction (CLR), while other RR instructions can specify two registers, such as the **load register** instruction (LOADR). For single register RR instructions, the REG2 field is ignored.

1.6 THE DEC ALPHA PROCESSOR

The Digital Equipment Corporation Alpha processor contains 32 64-bit integer (R0 through R31) and floating-point (F0 through F31) registers. Both R31 and F31 always read as zero. Four floating point types are supported; VAX F_floating, IEEE single precision (32 bit), VAX G_floating, and IEEE double precision (64-bit).

The Alpha has four instruction formats, all 32 bits in length, as depicted in Figure 1.6.

31	26 25	21 20	16 15		5 4	0	
Opcode		Number					PALcode Format
Opcode	RA		Disp				Branch Format
Opcode	RA	RB		Disp			Memory Format
Opcode	RA	RB	Function			RC	Operate Format

Figure 1.5
The Alpha processor instruction formats.

The *operate format* instruction uses three registers. R_A and R_B are used as source registers, while the result is stored in R_C. Conditions differ depending on whether floating point or integer numbers are involved. For floating-point operations, R_A and R_B are the source, R_C receives the result. The function field is used to contain an 11-bit extended opcode. For integer operations, R_A and R_B can be used as the source, or an 8-bit literal value can be involved. The R_B field and 4-bits worth of the function field are used to specify a literal value. The other 7-bits worth of the function field are used to specify an extended opcode.

The *memory format* instructions are load-and-store instructions. Memory format instructions are used to move longwords or quadwords between register Ra and memory. Register Rb plus a signed 16-bit displacement is used to compute the target address.

The *branch format* instructions are actually conditional branches. Register Ra is tested and a 21-bit PC-relative longword address displacement is used to determine the target address. The return address from subroutine calls is placed into register Ra.

The *PALcode format* instructions are exclusive to the Alpha. PAL stands for *Privileged Architecture Library* and refers to a set of subroutines that are specific to a particular Alpha-supported operating system. You can think of PALcode as similar to BIOS code in the PC environment. PALcode is like firmware that streamlines rote operating system functions such as context switching and memory management. The Alpha can be set to use PALcode for OpenVMS, Digital UNIX (formerly OSF/1), and Windows NT. PALcode can be invoked by either hardware or software.

Table 1.5 Floating-point types supported by the Alpha

Type	Range	# decimal digits precision
VAX F_floating	$.294 \times 10^{-38}$ to $1.7 \times 10^{+38}$	7
VAX G_floating	$.29 \times 10^{-38}$ to $1.7 \times 10^{+38}$	16
VAX D_floating	$.56 \times 10^{-308}$ to $0.9 \times 10^{+308}$	15
IEEE S_floating	1.175×10^{-38} to $3.40 \times 10^{+38}$	7
IEEE T_floating	2.33×10^{-308} to $1.79 \times 10^{+308}$	15

The VAX floating-point forms use a hidden-bit, while the IEEE floating-point forms do not use a hidden bit. Table 1.6 illustrates special conditions defined for the IEEE floating-point forms.

Table 1.6 Special conditions represented by IEEE floating-point number forms on the Alpha

Sign	Exponent	Fraction	Interpretation
x	All 1s	$\neq 0$	$\pm$ NaN (not a number)
x	All 1s	0	$\pm \infty$
0	0	$\neq 0$	+ Denormal
1	0	$\neq 0$	− Denormal
0	0	0	+ 0
1	0	0	− 0
x	~ 1s or 0s	x	Finite

The NaN bit pattern exists in two forms, *signaling* and *quiet*. A signaling NaN (initial fraction bit is 1) is used to provide values to uninitialized variables, while the quiet NaN (initial fraction bit is 0) is used to diagnose invalid data and results. Signaling NaNs can generate an arithmetic exception, while a quiet NaN can propagate through a series of arithmetic operations without incurring an exception. *Denormal* refers to an IEEE bit pattern that represents a number whose value lies between zero and the smallest finite number.

The in-memory representation of these floating-point numbers differ from their in-register representation. The floating-point load instructions are responsible for certain bit reordering. Consider the VAX F_floating format. Figure 1.7 illustrates the layout of a VAX F_floating number in memory.

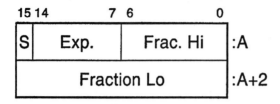

Figure 1.6
VAX_F floating-number format.

Two floating point values specified in FORTRAN:

```
DATA A/3.1415/
DATA B/.26E13/
...
```

Internal representation of two VAX F_floating point values:

```
0E564149    ⇒    3.141500
57055517    ⇒    0.2600000E+13
```

Figure 1.7
A VAX F_floating number in memory and sample numbers

The exponent for a VAX F_floating-point number in memory is 8 bits. Figure 1.7 illustrates how a VAX F_floating is stored in a floating-point register.

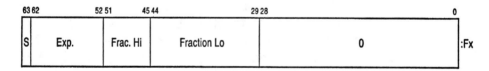

Figure 1.8
A VAX F_floating number in a floating-point register.

A VAX F_floating number in a floating-point register has an 11-bit exponent. This larger exponent makes this number comparable to a VAX G_floating number and can be used in subsequent calculations with VAX F_floatng or VAX G_floating numbers. VAX G_floating numbers are stored similarly, except the exponent remains unchanged, whether in memory or in a floating-point register.

IEEE floating-point numbers are stored according to the ANSI/IEEE 754-1985 specification, which defines four floating-point number formats. As with the VAX floating numbers, IEEE floating point numbers are stored differently in memory than they are stored in floating-point registers. Figure 1.9 illustrates how a single precision IEEE floating-point number appears in memory.

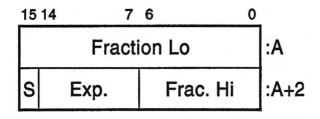

Figure 1.9
A single precision IEEE floating-point number in memory.

Notice how the sign, exponent, and high-order fractional portion are in the second word. Figure 1.10 illustrates how a single precision IEEE floating-point number is stored in a floating-point register.

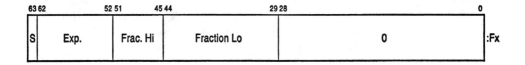

Figure 1.10
A single precision IEEE floating-point number in a floating-point register.

The Alpha has a 64-bit program counter and four sets of registers; *integer, floating-point, lock,* and *optional.* Floating-point number behavior on an Alpha is controlled by setting control bits in the FPCR, the *floating point control register*. The FPCR can be set to control rounding and trap behavior.

There are two lock registers per processor associated with certain load-and-store instructions—the *lock_flag* and *locked_physical_address* registers. These instructions are important for coordinating memory access in a multiprocessor configuration. These lock flags can be used to create the effect of a critical section. Use of these instructions are beyond the scope of this book.

An interesting result of the Alpha architecture is the manner in which arithmetic traps are handled. Because of the pipeline nature of instruction processing on the Alpha, arithmetic traps, such as underflow and overflow, are imprecise and are delivered many instructions from the point at which the trap was triggered. It is the responsibility of the programmer to explicitly test for the possibility of a trap condition. On the assembly language level, a TRAPB *trap barrier* instruction can be used. When an instruction triggers a trap, all subsequently executed instructions are called the *trap shadow*. The extent of the trap shadow is controlled by a TRAPB instruction. There are specific rules for writing a program that must execute in the trap shadow, such as no register must be used more than once as a destination register.

1.7 WRAP-UP AND FURTHER READING

Machine language is where the "bits meet the hardware." Every computer program, no matter in what language it is written, must be translated into machine language before it can be executed by the CPU. This chapter discusses machine language with respect to a hypothetical RISC machine environment called ICS (Imaginary Computer System). ICS was designed to contain properties generally found in most contemporary computer systems. Comprehending machine language requires understanding both instruction and data formats. Data can be in the form of integer or floating point numbers. Floating point numbers have always been architecture specific. Today, most computer manufacturers recognize both their own proprietary format and the IEEE format. The Digital Equipment Corporation Alpha processor was discussed as the case study system in this chapter.

For more in-depth reading about the architecture of the Alpha processor, the reader is urged to obtain a copy of the *Alpha Architecture Handbook,* published by Digital Equipment Corporation, EC-H1689-10. [Beck 1997] is one of the few academic texts available that discusses this topic. For a good overview of machine design and architecture, consult [Jordan 1996]. For those interested in the Sun SPARC technology, [Catanzaro 1991] is a good reference.

REFERENCES

[Beck 1997] Beck, Leland L., *System Software: An Introduction to Systems Programming 3rd Edition*, Reading, MA: Addision Wesley, 1997.

[Catanzaro 1991] Catanzaro, Ben J., *The SPARC Technical Papers*, published by Springer Verlag, 1991.

[Jordan 1996] Jordan, Harry F., Miles Murdocca and Vincent P. Heuring, *Computer Systems Design and Architecture*, published by Benjamin/Cummins, 1996.

CHAPTER 2

Assembler Language

This chapter will discuss assemblers, assembler language, and how they are used to facilitate programming in machine language. An assembler is a system software utility used to translate assembler language into machine code. We will discuss a basic two-pass assembler and an assembler language that runs on the ICS computer.

2.0 ASSEMBLER LANGUAGE BASICS

A program written in assembler is comprised of a series of statements containing computer instructions and associated arguments.

2.1 ASSEMBLER STATEMENT COMPONENTS

Most contemporary assemblers, such as the ICS assembler, use statements containing fields as depicted in Figure 2.1. A robust assembler would not restrict the fields to the position numbers specified.

1	10	18	30
label	opcode	arguments	//comments

Figure 2.1
Assembler statement fields with starting position numbers.

The *label* field is used to define the following:

1. Names for storage locations.
2. Branch points.

If neither a storage location is defined nor a branch point specified, the label field is left blank and the assembler statement is comprised of the opcode and any associated arguments. Names in the label field of the ICS assembler language are comprised of from 1–8 alphanumeric characters, letters, and numbers, and no special characters such as question marks, blanks, commas, or exclamation points. Also, the ICS assembler is case insensitive, so the labels MERUSI and Merusi are equivalent.

The *opcode field* is where the instruction mnemonic is specified. A collection of opcode mnemonic names is available to specify for different instructions. Appendix D contains the complete list of instruction opcodes for ICS. The instruction field can also contain a *pseudo-instruction* or *assembler directive*. Pseudo-instructions appear as instructions but are not translated into machine code. Pseudo-instructions are *commands to the assembler* and will be discussed later in this chapter.

The *arguments field* contains parameters appropriate for the instruction opcode. Some instructions require a register, a target address, or both.

The two // denote the beginning of a comment field. Anything that appears after these two symbols are not interpreted by the assembler. A comment field can begin anywhere on an assembler statement. Figure 2.2 illustrates the use of the comment field.

```
        LOAD   R1,TEMP      //Load the contents of TEMP into R1
LOOP    ADD    R3,ONE       //Increment the contents of R3 by 1
        TR     R2           //Test the contents of R2
        STORE  R5,WORK      //Save contents of R5 into WORK
```

Figure 2.2
Sample ICS assembler statements.

2.1.1 PSEUDO-INSTRUCTIONS

Pseudo-instructions (assembler directives), as mentioned in the previous section, are commands to the assembler. The pseudo-instructions used with the ICS assembler are listed in Table 2.1.

Figure 2.3 illustrates using some ICS assembler pseudo-instruction statements.

Table 2.1 ICS Assembler Pseudo-Instructions

Pseudo-Instruction	Meaning
BEGIN	Define the beginning of an assembler program
BYTE	Reserve memory storage for a byte constant
RESB	Reserve a byte of memory storage
WORD	Reserve memory storage for a word constant
RESW	Reserve a word of memory storage
END	Define the end of an assembler program
GLBDEF	Define a global symbol
EXIT	Exit program (performs a special RET instruction)

The BEGIN pseudo-instruction appears in the instruction field of the first line of an ICS assembler program. A BEGIN statement has the following format:

```
label          BEGIN
```

The label field defines the module name and is assumed to be a global definition. When the assembler sees a BEGIN statement, it starts the location counter at zero.

The RESW, RESB, BYTE, and WORD pseudo-instructions are used to reserve storage, as illustrated in Figure 2.3.

```
WORK    RESW    5           //Reserve five words
FIVE    WORD    5           //Reserve a word for constant number 5
STRING  RESB    10          //Reserve 10 bytes
NAME    BYTE    "MERUSI"    //Reserve storage for this character string
```

Figure 2.3
Sample ICS storage pseudo-instruction usage.

The END statement is used to indicate the last line of an as-
sm. The format of an END statement is as follows:

        END   [label]

The label field is not always required and is used to specify at what point execution is to begin in the program (also
called the *transfer point*). Logically, there is only one transfer
point in a program, so if a program is comprised of a collection of
assembler program modules, only one of the modules would
have a label specified on its END statement.

The GLBDEF statement is used to define symbols utilized in
the current program module and defined in another. GLOBAL
statements create records used by the linker/loader and are described in more detail in Chapter 3.

2.1.2 THE LOCATION COUNTER

The *location counter* is a value used by an assembler to keep
track of storage by maintaining a relative offset. This offset is
initialized to zero when the assembler begins processing the first
statement of the program, which is usually the BEGIN statement. As each program statement is processed, the location
counter is incremented to indicate the displacement produced by
that statement. For instance, each ICS instruction statement
encountered will cause the location counter to increment by two
or six, depending on whether it is an RM or RR type. If a
pseudo-instruction is encountered, such as an RESW 5, the location counter is incremented by 20 (five words of four bytes each).
The current location counter is always the offset from the beginning of a program module. Every program module begins at
zero. The value of the location counter has ramifications for how
PC-relative addressing is performed. The assembler has no idea
at which memory address a program will be loaded at execution
time. Because the location counter is always the same offset
relative to zero, its role in the computation of the target address
is always valid. When the assembler computes the target address displacement field in an instruction, it uses the value of
the location counter of the next instruction (in essence, the *program counter* or PC) to compute the displacement. Figure 2.4

shows a short segment of an ICS assembler program with location counter values.

Line No.	*Location Counter*	*Instruction Statement*		
001	0000	SAMPLE	BEGIN	
002	0000		LOAD	R1,TWO
003	0006		MUL	R1,TWO
004	000C		STORE	R1,ANSWER
005	0012		EXIT	
006	0014	TWO	WORD	2
007	0018	ANSWER	RESW	1
008	001C		END	

Figure 2.4
Sample ICS assembler program with location counter.

2.2 FORMATTING INSTRUCTIONS

Let us now take the short program portrayed in Figure 2.4 and produce the representative machine code.

Line 1 is the pseudo-instruction BEGIN. Pseudo-instructions do not get translated into machine code, they are commands to the assembler itself. BEGIN is telling the assembler the global name of this program is SAMPLE and to start the location counter at zero.

Line 2 is the first instruction to be translated. The opcode for the LOAD instruction is 01_{16}. Register 1 is specified and the address mode is PC-relative. Figure 2.5 illustrates how the fields of the ICS instruction are composed. The address mode field is 0 to indicate PC-relative. The register field is set to 1 and the address displacement field is set to C_{16}. The address field value is determined as follows:

TA   –   PC   =   Displacement
0014_{16} – 0006_{16} = $000C_{16}$

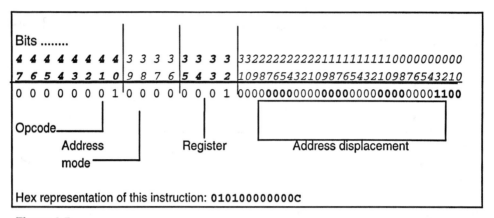

Figure 2.5
ICS instruction field composition for a LOAD instruction from the program in Figure 2.4.

The target address (TA) is at offset $000C_{16}$. The PC at the time of the translation of the LOAD instruction is 0006. The offset to the target address is therefore $000C_{16}$.

Line 3 is a multiplication instruction and is composed in a similar manner. Since the LOAD instruction is six bytes long, the location counter is incremented accordingly.

The STORE instruction on **Line 4** begins six bytes later, followed by the pseudo-instruction EXIT. Notice that the location counter does not adjust past the EXIT instruction because EXIT is a command to the assembler. No memory is allocated to pseudo-instructions.

Lines 6 and **7** define two memory locations—TWO, one word of memory contains a value of 2, and four bytes later, ANSWER, one word of storage.

2.3 THE TWO PASS ASSEMBLER

An assembler processes an assembler language program in two passes. The first pass is used to construct a *symbol table*. The symbol table contains a list of all the *labels* (see Figure 2.1) and their associated *location counter values*. The symbol table is used in the second pass where instructions are actually formatted and *object code* is produced.

The first pass scrutinizes each statement, determining how much the location counter should be adjusted. Instructions will always cause the location counter to be incremented by two or six. Pseudo-instructions, such as RESW and RESB will cause the location counter to be adjusted according to how much storage is specified in the operand field. When a label is recognized as a character string in the first eight positions of a program statement, it is placed into the symbol table along with the current location counter value. This process continues until all of the program statements have been read through.

Pass two starts to read the program again from the beginning. When a machine instruction is recognized, it is formatted. The appropriate opcode is derived for the instruction mnemonic. The addressing mode and register usage is determined. If the operand is a label referring to a memory location (storage or branch point), the symbol table is consulted. The subject label is found with its associated location counter value. Now the assembler is able to compute the appropriate displacement for the target address.

Pass one and pass two can be described by encapsulated code that appears in Figures 2.6 and 2.7.

```
DO [Read a program statement until EOF] {
CASE (Operand ) {
    BEGIN:
            LOCCTR = 0;
            Break;
    An instruction:
            If label exists, place label into symbol table
            w/current location counter value;
            If RM type, LOCCTR = LOCCTR + 6;
            If RR type, LOCCTR = LOCCTR + 2;
            Break;
    RESB:
            If label exists, place label into symbol table
            w/current location counter value;
            LOCCTR = LOCCTR + value in operand field;
            Break;
    RESW:
            If label exists, place label into symbol table
            w/current location counter value;
            LOCCTR = LOCCTR + value in operand field * 4;
            Break;
```

```
BYTE:
        If label exists, place label into symbol table
        w/current location counter value;
        LOCCTR = LOCCTR + 1 or length of string;
        Break;
WORD:
        If label exists, place label into symbol table
        w/current location counter value;
        LOCCTR = LOCCTR + 4;
    }
}
```

Figure 2.6
Basic logic for assembler first pass.

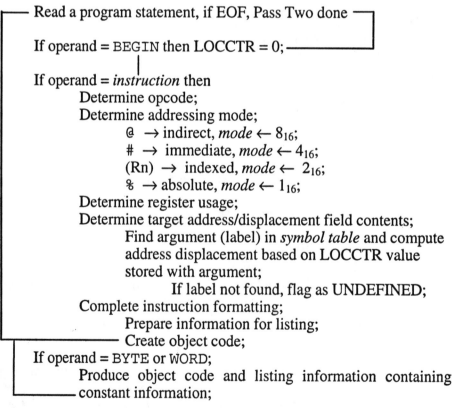

Figure 2.7
Basic logic for assembler pass two.

The symbol table is the only output from pass one. The symbol table is needed by Pass 2 to determine label reference displacements. Some error conditions can also be caught during pass one, such as finding an illegal instruction or pseudo-instruction. Figure 2.8 is a more elaborate example of an ICS assembler language program that computes the total of the first 100 integers.

One other important table that is required by the assembler during both Pass 1 and Pass 2 is the OPCODE table. This table contains all the instruction mnemonics, the associated opcode value, and the instruction type. The assembler uses this information during Pass 1 to determine how much to adjust the location counter. During Pass 2, the OPCODE table is again consulted to obtain the opcode value itself and the beginning of the assembly of the instruction into machine code. The OPCODE table is provided by the system manufacturer and is not something composed by the assembler.

LOCCTR		INSTRUCTION		MACHINE CODE
000	SAMPLE	BEGIN		
000	START	LOAD	R0,KTR	010000000038
006		CLR	R1	0D01
008		CLR	R2	0D02
00A	LOOP	ADD	R2,INTEGER	030200000036
010		LOAD	R3,INTEGER	010300000030
016		ADD	R3,ONE	030300000026
01C		STORE	R3,BUFFER(R1)	02210000002C
022		ADD	R1,#6	034100000006
028		SUB	R0,ONE	040000000014
02E		TR	R0	0F00
030		BNE	LOOP	0C00FFFFFFD4
036		STORE	R2,ANSWER	02020000000E
03C		EXIT		
03E	KTR	WORD	100	64
042	ONE	WORD	1	1
046	INTEGER	WORD	1	1
04A	ANSWER	WORD	1	1
04E	BUFFER	RESW	100	
1DE		END	START	

Figure 2.8
ICS assembler program that sums the first one-hundred integers.

2.4 OBJECT CODE

The output from the assembler is *object code*. Object code is the result of the translation of the assembler instructions into a form that the computer can understand. As we will see in Chapter 4, there is another system program that can produce object code, the compiler.

The assembler writes the object code as a series of records into a disk file. These records contain information for the linker/loader that describe how the object code is to be loaded into memory.

The records are distinguished by a single letter character code found in the first byte position, as illustrated in Table 2.2.

Table 2.2 Object File Records

1st position character	Type of record	Record Description
H	A *header* record	Contains entry point name and length of this program module **H⋏name⋏length**
G	A *global* record	Contains names of globally defined symbols and their locations **G⋏name1⋏loc1⋏name2⋏loc2 . . .**
E	An *end* record	Indicates end of object code; also indicates at what address to start executing a program **E⋏[startaddress]**
O	An *object* record	Contains object code and where it is to be loaded; as much as will fit in a record **O⋏location⋏code**
C	A *change* record	Global address modification **C⋏offset ± value**

The object code produced from the program illustrated in Figure 2.8 is depicted in Figure 2.9.

H▴SAMPLE▴01D8

O▴000000▴010000000038▴0D01▴0D02▴030200000036▴010300000030

O▴000016▴030300000026▴02210000002C▴034100000006▴040000000014

O▴00002E▴0F00▴0C00FFFFFFD4▴02020000000E▴1300

O▴00003E▴00000064▴00000001▴00000001▴00000001

E▴START▴000000

Figure 2.9
Sample object code for the ICS program from Figure 2.8. Spaces (▴) in O-records are meant for readability and not required by the linker/loader.

This sample object code does not illustrate all possible object code records. Chapter 3 discusses linker/loaders in more detail.

2.5 THE ALPHA OPENVMS MACRO-64 ASSEMBLER

Macro-64 is the assembler used to assemble native Alpha machine instructions under the OpenVMS operating system. The Macro-64 assembler will also assemble native VAX instructions since all of the unprivileged OpenVMS instructions are implemented in PALcode. These PALcode instructions are required to support running OpenVMS on an Alpha.

The program depicted in Figure 2.10 does not do anything other than contain a variety of instructions to demonstrate the fundamentals we have discussed in this chapter. A typical Macro-64 assembler program is divided into three sections, a *linkage section*, a *code section,* and a *data section.* All in-memory address references are performed through a *base register*. A base register contains an address anchor point from which all memory references are determined. It is convenient to think of PC-relative addressing as a "moving base register" style of addressing with the PC acting as the base register. An assembler needs base register information both at *assembly time* and at *run-time*. At assembly time, the contents of the base register are unknown since we do not know where we will be loaded into memory. The assembler is given enough information to determine address locations relative to the base register that will still work at run time. The .base assembler directive is giving the assembler this information for assembly time. What is not obvious from looking at the program in Figure 2.10 is where the base register is established at run time. This action is performed within the $-macro $code_section.

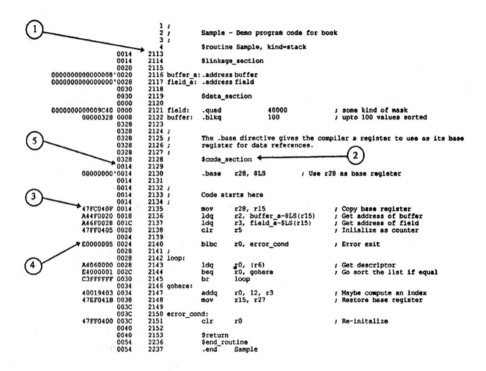

Figure 2.10
A sample Alpha OpenVMS Macro-64 listing.

Notice how the location counter value changes for each section while the line numbers maintain a constant progression. Several items in figure 2.10 have been identified by circled numbers:

① The line numbers abruptly jump from 4 to 2113. This is due to the amount of code that is part of the $routine macro.

② The $code_section macro defines the beginning of where the program actually starts. Notice how the $code_section macro does not cause the location counter to change since it is an assembler directive. Also notice that the location counter does change because of the new section, 0328 to 0014. The location counter does not start at zero for the new section because of code that is part of the $code_section macro requiring 20 bytes.

③ This is the machine code for the mov instruction on line 2135. This is a form of an operate type (see Alpha instruction formats described in Chapter 1) of Alpha instruction. This instruction has four fields, three registers, an opcode, and a function mask.

```
mov r28, r15
```

```
47FC040F
```

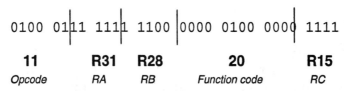

0100 01|11 111|1 1100 |0000 0100 000|0 1111

11	R31	R28	20	R15
Opcode	RA	RB	Function code	RC

R31 always reads zero; R28 is the source register and R15 is the target register. The function code field value of 20 refers to a specific PALcode instruction that must be executed to make this instruction work. This instruction is native mode VAX and must be emulated on the Alpha.

④ The Branch-If-Low-Byte-Clear instruction will branch to location error_cond if the low-order byte of R0 is not set to one. The field breakdown of this instruction is as follows:

```
E0000005
```

1110 00|00 000|0 0000 0000 0000 0000 0101

38	R0	5
Opcode	RA	Displacement

The field format of an Alpha branch instruction is described in Chapter 1. The interesting field is the displacement that is computed PC-relative. However, you
have to multiply it by four to get to the target address.
Therefore, consider $5 \times 4 = 16_{16}$. The displacement to er-
ror_cond, which is at 003C, is computed as follows:

```
0003C   =   0014              + 0028
error_cond   branch displacement   PC at time of
location     times four            blbc
```

⑤   Here we have the location counter. Notice how it changes
between the different sections and how it changes from
instruction to instruction. Assembler directives have no
effect on the location counter.

2.6 MACRO PROCESSING

Some assemblers provide a mechanism that facilitates writing
common sequences of code. Although macro processing has its
roots in assembler language, it is found in many other high-level
languages, such as C. Why would you code a macro instead of a
subroutine? Macros have one advantage over writing subroutines and can be used to make very sophisticated decisions about
how to generate source code. Macros can contain conditional
logic and even perform logical-IF tests. For the sake of simplicity, assembler laguage will be used here to discuss how macro
processing works.

Macro processing requires the use of several assembler directives that help define the macro as follows:

```
MACRO       macro-name, macro-arg1 . . .
....
....
Body of macro
....
....
MEND
```

The MACRO command defines the macro prototype and any associated arguments that may be processed by this macro. Proceeding the MACRO command are the instructions comprising the common sequence of code for which this macro is written. The macro definition is terminated by the MEND statement.

Macro processing adds another pass to our assembler language processing. Macro processing is performed before Pass 1. Therefore, all macro definitions must appear at the beginning of the program. Because the macros are going to be expanded within the source code of the program, the assembler must understand what macros are available before it starts processing the program during Pass 1. Once all the macros are recognized, the assembler goes through the source code and expands the macros with the associated arguments wherever the macro is used. The macro processing phase basically generates a new version of the source code with all of the macro expansions in place.

Let us now look at how a macro can be used. Assume that we need the ability to decrement the contents of a specific memory location by one. When the result of the decrementation becomes zero, location MASTER must be incremented by one. On the ICS machine, this operation requires the execution of several instructions. Rather than write the required instruction sequence over and over again, we will write a macro called DTI (Decrement-Test-Increment) as follows:

```
     MACRO DTI,LOC
     LOAD       R0,LOC
     INCR       R0
     STORE      R0,LOC
     TR         R0
     BGT        ?1
     LOAD       R0,MASTER
     INCR       R0
     STORE R0,MASTER
?1
     MEND
```

The ?1 represents a *dynamic label*. If a macro contains a branch point like this, subsequent expansion of DTI would result in a multiply defined symbol. By using a dynamic label, everytime DTI is expanded, a different symbol is generated in place of the ?1. A sample expansion of DTI is shown in a program fragment in Figure 2.11.

```
DEMO            BEGIN
//
// Macro definition follows
//
                MACRO   DTI,LOC
                LOAD            R0,LOC
                INCR            R0
                STORE           R0,LOC
                TR              R0
                BGT             ?1
                LOAD            R0,MASTER
                INCR            R0
                STORE           R0,MASTER
?1
                MEND
//
// Program starts here ...
//
000     ....
//
// First expansion of DTI
//
```

LOC	Source Statement		Object Code
00C		DTI	MYLOC	
00C+		LOAD	R0,MYLOC	0100000001EE
012+		INCR	R0	1900
014+		STORE	R0,MYLOC	0200000001E6
01A+		TR	R0	0F00
01E+		BGT	LBLX0001	0A0000000010
022+		LOAD	R0,MASTER	0100000001DE
028+		INCR	R0	1900
02C+		STORE	R0,MASTER	0200000001D4
032+	LBLX001			
		CLR	R2	0D02
		....		

```
                //
                // Second expansion of DTI
                //
        03E             DTI     MYLOC
        03E+            LOAD    R0,MYLOC        0100000001BC
        044+            INCR    R0              1900
        046+            STORE   R0,MYLOC        0200000001B4
        04C+            TR      R0              0F00
        050+            BGT     LBLX0002        0A0000000010
        054+            LOAD    R0,MASTER       0100000001AC
        05A+            INCR    R0              1900
        05E+            STORE   R0,MASTER       0200000001A2
        064+    LBLX002
                        CLR     R3              0D03
                        ....
        200     MYLOC   RESW    1
        206     MASTER  RESW    1
                        ....
                        END     BEGIN
```

Figure 2.11
A sample expansion of DTI.

2.7 WRAP-UP AND FURTHER READING

This chapter introduced assembler language by describing one for our hypothetical ICS computer. Although assembler language programming is less practiced today, understanding how an assembler works helps to understand how computers work. Assemblers facilitate writing machine language and historically have given programmers an unequivocal degree of control of their data. Studying assemblers is also the first step into learning the next level of writing high-level language programs and understanding compilers.

The output from a program assembler is object code. The object code is written to a file and is subsequently interpreted by another system program, the linker/loader. The linker/loader is the utility that actually loads the program into memory and starts its execution. The macro processing facility was also discussed as a means of writing common occurrences of source code in a less tedious fashion.

Beck [Beck 1997] is a good source for describing assembler language in a hypothetical machine environment. For assembler language programming in the IBM PC environment [Norton 1993] and [Jones 1991] are highly recommended. A good introductory book about assembler language programming can be found in [Duntemann 1992]. For the Microsoft Windows environment, a good book is [Kauler 1993], which discusses object-oriented and low-level systems programming in assembly language. Finally, [Sebesta 1991] is a good reference for structured assembler language programming on the VAX.

REFERENCES

[Beck 1997] Beck, Leland L., *System Software: An Introduction to Systems Programming 3rd Edition*, Reading, MA: Addison Wesley, 1997.

[Norton 1993] Norton, Peter, and John Socha, *Assembly Language for the PC 3rd Edition*, published by Brady, 1993.

[Jones 1991] Jones, D.S., *80X86 Assembly Programming*, published by Oxford University Press, 1991.

[Duntemann 1992] Duntemann, Jeff, *Assembly Language: Step-by-Step*, New York, NY: John Wiley & Sons, 1992.

[Kauler 1993] Kauler, Barry, *Windows Assembly Language & Systems Programming: Object Oriented & Low-Level Systems Programming in Assembly Language for Windows 3.X*, Englewood Cliffs, NJ: Prentice Hall, 1993.

[Sebesta 1991] Sebesta, Robert W., *VAX: Structured Assembly Language Programming*, published by Benjamin/Cummings, 1991.

CHAPTER 3

Linkers and Loaders

This chapter will discuss linkers and loaders, the utilities that take object code and prepare it for execution in memory. Certain kinds of address resolution must still be performed within the object code, including references to absolute addresses and entry points to external routines.

The term *linking* refers to the act of integrating the object code with the appropriate information to make a runnable program image. The term *loader* refers to the utility that actually inserts the program image into memory and begins its execution.

3.0 LINKER/LOADER BASICS

A program does not exclusively perform PC-relative addressing. Sometimes it is necessary to address something at an absolute location or at a location whose address is unknown until execution time. A PC-relative address reference will work no matter where a program is loaded in memory since the relative offset is always correct. However, a reference to a subroutine or function located in another program module is not known until all of the object code is situated in memory. The same is true for references made to system library routines. In contemporary operating system environments, shared libraries are maintained in memory and not included as part of the object code. References to them are dynamically resolved at load time. This action keeps the size of the program file to a minimum and puts the responsibility of address resolution on the program image loader. Dynamically loaded modules will be discussed in a later section.

A two-pass linker/loader is discussed in this chapter. For the sake of simplicity, we will include the loading function with our linker as part of the second pass. The linker passes perform the following basic actions:

Pass 1 Read the object file produced by the assembler, look for *global* records, and insert the label names and their associated location counter values into a symbol table.

Pass 2 Reread the object code, load it into memory at a location prescribed by the operating system, and resolve any in-memory address references to global symbols by using the symbol table constructed in Pass 1; any *change records* are also processed during this phase.

3.1 OBJECT FILE PROCESSING

The program from Figure 2.1 has been enhanced to include global references (see Figure 3.1). A small subroutine, ADDINT, has been created to demonstrate new object file records that we have not seen previously—*change records*. Change records must be generated to instruct the linker on how to resolve the addressing of various components defined in one program module and used in another. Change records are generated by the assembler when it realizes that a reference is being made to such a symbol.

LOCCTR		INSTRUCTION		MACHINE CODE
	// Main routine			
	//			
000	SAMPLE	BEGIN		
000		GLBDEF	INTEGER,ONE,INDEX,BUFFER	
000	START	LOAD	R0,KTR	010000000024
006		CLR	R2	0D02
008		STORE	R2,INDEX	020200000000
00E	LOOP	ADD	R2,INTEGER	030200000022
010		CALL	ADDINT	120000000000
016		SUB	R0,ONE	040000000012
01C		TR	R0	0F00
01E		BNE	LOOP	0C00FFFFFFEA
024		STORE	R2,ANSWER	02020000000E
028		EXIT		

```
02A         KTR        WORD  100           64
02E         ONE        WORD  1             1
032         INTEGER    WORD  1             1
036         ANSWER     WORD  1             1
03A         BUFFER     WORD  100
1CA                    END   START


         // Subroutine ADDINT
         //

000         ADDINT     GBLDEF INTEGER,ONE,BUFFER
000                    LOAD   R1,INDEX      010100000020
006                    LOAD   R3,INTEGER    010300000000
00C                    ADD    R3,#1         034300000001
012                    STORE  R3,BUFFER(R1) 022310000000
018                    ADD    R1,#6         034100000006
01E                    STORE  R1,INDEX      020100000002
024                    RET                  1300
026         INDEX      RESW   1
02A                    END
```

Figure 3.1
Sample ICS program demonstrating the use of an external routine.

A change record has the following format:

`Coffset±value`

The letter **C** is in the first byte position. Immediately following the letter **C** is the *offset in bytes* into this program module where the address resolution is to take place. The *value* amount represents the magnitude of the adjustment and can be added to or subtracted from the designated location. The value is derived from the global symbol table, as we will see in the next section.

A *global record* will also be generated on behalf of the GBLDEF pseudo instruction. A **G** record has the following format:

`Gsymbol▲value ...`

This record can contain more than one global symbol definition. If there are any symbols listed after a GBLDEF pseudo-instruction which never appear in a label field in a module, no **G** record will be created for the symbol. The value amount following the symbol name is the offset in the program module at which this symbol is defined.

Figure 3.2 illustrates object code that is produced for the program depicted in Figure 3.1.

```
H▴SAMPLE▴0001CA
G▴INTEGER▴000032▴ONE▴00002E▴BUFFER▴00003A
O▴000000▴010000000024▴0D02▴0202FFFFFFF2▴030200000022
O▴000010▴1200FFFFFFEA▴040000000014▴0F00▴0C00FFFFFFEA
O▴000024▴02020000000E▴1300▴000064▴000001▴000001▴000001
C▴000008+INDEX
C▴000008-SAMPLE
C▴000010+ADDINT
C▴000010-SAMPLE
E▴000000
```

> Underlined items represent the −
> **B** values

```
H▴ADDINT▴00002A
G▴INDEX▴000026
O▴000000▴010100000020▴0103FFFFFFF4▴034300000001▴02231FFFFFE8
O▴000018▴034100000006▴020100000002
C▴000006+INTEGER
C▴000006-ADDINT
C▴000012+BUFFER
C▴000002-ADDINT
E
```

Figure 3.2
Object code for ICS program depicted in Figure 3.1 with −B distances indicated.

Figure 3.2 illustrates the use of change records. Two address adjustments are required at 00008 and 00010 in SAMPLE and two change records are required for address adjustments at offset locations 000006 and 000012 in module ADDINT. The address adjustments specified by change records are assumed to be at the beginning of an ICS address field. Also, notice that routine entry point labels are automatically considered to be global symbols.

Figure 3.3 illustrates how the modules depicted in Figure 3.1 are situated into memory and how execution of routine ADDINT takes place from being called in module SAMPLE. The address of where module SAMPLE is loaded into memory (A) is provided by the linker. Since the linker knows the size of module SAMPLE, it also knows where the subroutine ADDINT will be loaded. The return address from ADDINT is understood by the assembler since this is a PC-relative address.

An H record is produced indicating the value of the global symbol for the entry point of the ADDINT routine (see Figure 3.2). Notice from Figure 3.3 that the entry point location is not exactly at the beginning address of where ADDINT is loaded into memory. The entry point for a subroutine is not necessarily at the beginning of the module, therefore it is represented by the value Y in the diagram. In our current example, the offset for ADDINT happens to be 0. Offset values such as this are given in a G record, but when the symbol is defined by an H record, the value is 0. We want to be able to use PC-relative addressing when calling routine ADDINT from SAMPLE. The PC-relative address offset is manifested by D. Mathematically, it is apparent that D can be obtained by subtracting C from Z. C represents the current program counter value at the time the CALL ADDINT routine is being executed. The distance Z is determined by the linker since it knows the load address of the beginning of the ADDINT module (X) and the load address of the entry point of ADDINT from the H record (Y). The value C is not immediately available and must be computed by using two other values—A, the load address of SAMPLE known by the linker, and B, the PC value relative to the beginning of SAMPLE and known by the assembler, hence D = Z − A − B. This equation is demonstrated by the change records in Figure 3.2 for SAMPLE where the distance of Z is added to location 10 while distance A is subtracted from location 10. Distance −B is already inserted by the assembler and is part of the object records. −B is the 2's complement value of the PC of the instruction following the instruction making the reference.

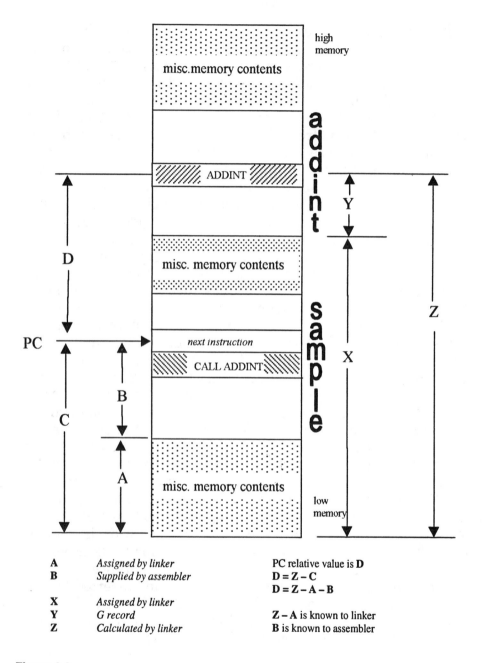

A	*Assigned by linker*		PC relative value is **D**
B	*Supplied by assembler*		**D = Z − C**
			D = Z − A − B
X	*Assigned by linker*		
Y	*G record*		**Z − A** is known to linker
Z	*Calculated by linker*		**B** is known to assembler

Figure 3.3
How the assembler and linker prepare modules SAMPLE and ADDINT for execution in memory; illustration is specifically for accessing routine ADDINT from SAMPLE.

Figure 3.4 shows the logic of Pass 1 and will help you better understand the use of object file records. It uses two functions: SST (*Search Symbol Table)* and IST (*Insert into Symbol Table)*. Function SST is a Boolean function, returning true or false depending on whether the symbol passed as an argument is found in the global symbol table. Function IST inserts the symbol and its associated argument value into the global symbol table.

```
Get load address from operating system: OSLOADADDR;
Set CURLOADADDR ← OSLOADADDR;
{
    Read MODULENAME and MODULELEN from H record;
    Set CURLOADLEN ← MODULELEN;
    If (SST(MODULENAME)) then
        COUT << "Duplicate global symbol";
    else
        IST(MODULENAME, CURLOADADDR);
    while (No "E" record){
        CASE(Recordtype){
            'D':
                for(Each symbol on "G" record){
                    If(SST(MODULENAME)) then
                        COUT << "Duplicate global symbol";
                    else
                        IST(SYMBOLNAME,
CURLOADADDR+Value_from_D_rec);
            default:
                continue;
            esac}
        }
        CURLOADADDR += MODULELEN;
}
```

Figure 3.4
Linker/loader Pass 1.

Once the global symbol table is established, global address references can be resolved and the object code can be loaded into memory. Pass 2 contains the logic used to perform this action and is illustrated in Figure 3.5.

```
Set CURLOADADDR ⬅ OSLOADADDR;
Set STARTADDR ⬅ OSLOADADDR;
while (Read from object file until EOF) {
    CURMODEULELEN ⬅ Length from "H" record;
    While (No "E" record found){
        CASE (RecordType){
            'O': Place object code into memory at
                CURLOADADDR + Value from "O" record;
                break;
            'C': If (SST(MODULENAME)) then
                Change address in memory at CURLOADADDR +
                "C" record value ⬅ Value from symbol table;
                else
                        COUT << "Undefined symbol";
                break;}
            }
        If(Address on "E" record)
                STARTADDR ⬅ CURLOADADDR + "E" record value;
            CURLOADADDR ⬅ CURMODULELEN;
    }
    Jump to location specified by STARTADDR;
}
```

Figure 3.5
Linker/loader Pass 2.

Let us assume the operating system is loading the program from Figure 3.1 at location 1000 (all addresses are in hexidecimal). The global symbol table would appear as in Figure 3.6.

```
SAMPLE      1000
    ONE         1028
    INTEGER     102C
ADDINT      1034
```

Figure 3.6
The global symbol table for the program in Figure 3.1.

The main output from Pass 1 is the global symbol table (GSTAB), sometimes called a *load map*. It is possible that if the program calls routines or functions defined in other libraries, the associated symbols will remain unresolved at the end of Pass 1. At this point, the linker begins searching for unresolved symbol names in various library files. Some of these library files are searched by default, while others must be explicitly specified. If a symbol is still not located after this step, the linker will produce a diagnostic message indicating it is undefined and the link will fail. The following sections discuss library searching in more detail.

How does the linker/loader resolve addresses between a collection of independent modules? Consider the sample ICS code segments that appear in Figure 3.7. The assembler will format the instruction or directive with as much information as it knows. PROGA, KTRA, and ONEA are defined locally, while TWOB and THREEC are defined externally.

```
        // PROGA
0000    PROGA  BEGIN
               GBLDEF KTRA,ONE
               ....
0010           LOAD   R2,KTRA              01020000000A
               ....
0020    KTRA   WORD   ONEA+TWOB-THREEC     00000024
0024    ONEA   WORD   1                    00000001
0028           END


        // PROGB
0000    PROGB  BEGIN
               GBLDEF TWOB,KTRA
               ....
0024           LOAD   R2,KTRA              011200000000
               ....
0036    TWOB   WORD   2                    00000002
003A           END


        // PROGC
0000    PROGC  BEGIN
               GBLDEF THREEC
               ....
0030           LOAD   R2,KTRA              011200000000
               ....
0042    THREEC WORD   3                    00000003
0046           END
```

Figure 3.7
Sample independent ICS modules to demonstrate address resolution.

The object code produced for these three modules allows for KTRA to be appropriately referenced between all three. Figure 3.8 illustrates the object code produced for the modules from Figure 3.7.

```
H▲PROGA▲000028
G▲KTRA▲00000020▲ONEA▲00000024
O▲01020000000A▲00000024▲00000001
C▲000020+TWOB
C▲000020-THREEC
E

H▲PROGB▲00003A
G▲TWOB▲00000036
O▲011200000000▲00000002
C▲000026+KTRA
E

H▲PROGC▲000046
G▲THREEC▲00000042
O▲011200000000▲00000003
C▲000032+KTRA
E
```

Figure 3.8
Object code for code fragment from figure 3.7.

Assume the operating system loads our code fragment starting at location 2000. Our global symbol table would appear as follows:

```
PROGA      2000
   KTRA      2020
   ONEA      2024

PROGB      2028
   TWOB      205E

PROGC      2062
   THREEC    20A4
```

How is the reference to KTRA in all three of these modules resolved? In PROGA no address adjustment for KTRA is necessary at the LOAD instruction and PC-relative addressing is used. However, two references must be resolved for the contents of KTRA—TWOB and THREEC. Therefore, the contents of memory location 2020 must be adjusted. The reader should be aware that the content of KTRA is actually an address and not constant information. Constants were specified just to make the object code more interesting! Therefore, the content of location KTRA (2020) is computed with the change records as follows:

ONEA   TWOB   THREEC   Value at KTRA (2020)
2024 + 205E - 20A4   = 1FDE

In PROGB, the reference to KTRA is absolute; notice the absolute addressing mode bit set in the LOAD instruction. The assembler understands that the value of KTRA is unavailable and that it must be provided at link/load time. PROGB requires an address adjustment at location 204E, the beginning of the address field of the LOAD instruction when it is loaded into memory. The value 2020 is placed here. The same mechanism is applied to PROGC where the reference to KTRA is absolute and the address is placed at location 2092, the address field of the LOAD instruction in PROGC.

3.2 LIBRARY SEARCHING AT LINK TIME

Many routines called by a program are found in libraries that are either provided by the user or made available by the operating system environment. Most linkers will execute a default transparent search of a set of libraries that contain most of the commonly called routines. These routines, such as math functions or other rudimentary routines, allow a programmer to obtain information such as the time of day. These library searches are performed at the end of Pass 1. Some of the library routines themselves also have global symbols that must be resolved by the linker performing an iterative search until all symbols are resolved. The library files are designed to expedite the search. Rather than searching through every byte of the library file, it is only necessary to review the *library file header*, usually found at the beginning of the file. The header contains all the information the linker needs to know to conduct its symbol search. For each routine found in the library file, the following information is found:

THE ROUTINE NAME	GLOBAL SYMBOLS ...	LOCATION IN FILE

The user has the option of specifying object file names directly to the linker:

```
cc proga rtn1 rtn2 sqrt -lthread -lmylib ...
```

It is possible to specify your own version of a system routine. As shown above, a personalized version of the sqrt routine could be incorporated into the program proga. Since the sqrt global symbol has been resolved, the linker will not pursue looking for sqrt in the other libraries.

3.2.1 DYNAMIC ADDRESS RESOLUTION

Many system service and library call references are resolved at execution time. These libraries reside in memory as a permanent part of the system environment and are shared by all running processes that reference them. On some systems, these libraries are referred to as *run-time libraries* (RTLs). Since these modules are not made part of the program, certain steps must be taken to make the module available at run time.

At the point in the program where a call is made to the library routine, a special call is made to the operating system. This special call is more like a *transfer* that involves executing special instructions that cause the library routine to be executed. The code involved in the transfer takes care of the following:

- What RTL is being called.
- What arguments are being passed.

How does the linker understand when to call a system RTL routine? As with all the other unresolved symbols at the end of Pass 1, the RTLs are searched. Once an RTL routine is identified, the hook is planted into the object code to make the call to the operating system for the specific routine. What is typically "called" in the operating system is a dispatcher. The dispatcher interprets the calling code and transfers control to the appropriate RTL routine.

3.3 THE OPENVMS LINKER

3.3.1 STRONG AND WEAK GLOBAL SYMBOLS

The linker in the OpenVMS operating system has an interesting way of resolving certain kinds of symbols. The linker deals with *weak* and *strong* global symbols. These two types of symbols are processed differently. If a symbol has been defined as strong, all libraries and input modules are thoroughly checked for its definition. A value of zero is assigned to all unresolved symbols. If a symbol has been defined as weak, the linker is not as thorough in resolving it and will not search all input modules and libraries. A value of zero will be returned for an unresolved weak reference, but no error message is produced. The exception to this rule is if a strong symbol reference is found in the same module as the weak reference. In this case, the linker will pursue resolving the weak reference as a strong one. The ability to define symbols as weak or strong facilitates testing programs. Typically, portions of code are evaluated and then gradually enhanced. Quite often, many symbol definitions do not exist during the early stages of building a program.

3.3.2 CREATING PROGRAM IMAGES

The runnable entity on an OpenVMS system is an image. When the user makes a request to run a particular program, an image file is read from disk and placed into memory by the image activator. The linker, RUN command, and image activator perform the role of our linker/loader discussed in this chapter.

The linker identifies all the program sections of an image (PSECTs) and classifies them according to specific attributes. These attributes refer to such characteristics as whether this image is write protected, if it is defined globally, or if it is execute-only. There are many other attributes too numerous to discuss here. The linker alphabetically combines program sections into image sections. The linker then attempts to allocate memory in terms of these image sections, which are aligned on CPU-specific boundaries (VAX or Alpha). Each program section is assigned a virtual address relative to the beginning address of its respective image section.

The linker further combines the image sections into clusters that are representative of the paging environment of OpenVMS. Program paging under OpenVMS occurs in terms of a cluster that may represent several virtual pages worth of memory. When a page fault occurs, a cluster's worth of the program is brought into memory. Faulting more than one page at a time streamlines a paging memory environment.

3.3.3 RUN-TIME LIBRARY SYMBOL RESOLUTION

Run-time library (RTL) symbol resolution in OpenVMS is accomplished by using *symbol vectors*. Symbol vectors are part of the RTL itself and are comprised of two quadwords. These quadwords contain different information depending on whether they refer to a program module, data, or constant. For a program module, the quadword pair points to the entry point of the RTL routine. In the program image, two quadwords are also reserved as a linkage pair. The linkage pair is updated at runtime with the address of the RTL routine. The code in the image is designed to refer to the calling entry point of the RTL routine from the linkage pair. Figure 3.9 illustrates the relationship of the RTL and the program.

3.3.4 OPENVMS ALPHA OBJECT LANGUAGE

This section describes the object language for OpenVMS on an Alpha processor. The object record types are amazingly similar to the hypothetical ones we discussed earlier in this chapter. Table 3.1 lists the record types and their ICS counterparts.

Table 3.1 DEC Alpha object language records compared to ICS object language records

Alpha Object Record	Alpha Object Record Type	ICS Object Record	ICS Object Record Type
Header	HDR	Header	H
End-of-Module	EOM	End	E
Global symbol directory	GSD	Define	D
Global symbol directory	GSD	Change	C
Text information and relocation	TIR	Text	O
Debugger information	DBG	N/A	N/A

The ICS linker/loader did not provide any option for debugger information. The order of the records in an AXP object module is mandatory and must appear as follows:

Main Module HDR record(s)

Language Name HDR record(s)

Other HDR record(s)

GSD(s)

TIR(s)

EOM

The AXP Object Language recognizes seven types of headers! Discussion of all of them is beyond the scope of this book; however, three types of headers besides the *main module header* and the *language processor name header* are:

- Copyright header
- Maintenance status header
- Title text header

All of these headers contain an ASCII text name of the type of information the header contains. For example, the language processor header contains the language name and version of the compiler that created the object module.

The GSD records consist of a main record portion followed by one of up to nine different GSD *subrecords*. These subrecords describe such characteristics as whether the GSD record is for a vectored or sharable program symbol definition. The GSD records also fulfill the role of the *change record* in ICS. A GSD record will contain the symbol name, location of the symbol's use in the program section, and what address adjustment is to take place.

TIR commands perform more than T records do in ICS. TIR records can manipulate the linker's stack or initialize storage in an image. The linker stack contains data entries 64-bits wide and is involved in how the linker initializes certain areas of an image. For example, pages of an image file are guaranteed to be zero unless otherwise specified by a compiler. The stack manipulation is quite extensive and the linker has a respectable repertoire of operations that can be performed. For more extensive information about the OpenVMS linker, consult the *OpenVMS Linker Utility Manual.*

3.4 WRAP-UP AND FURTHER READINGS

After an assembler translates all of the source statement into object code, the linker/loader must take that information and make it executable in memory. When several independent program modules are involved, some symbols are defined in one program module and referenced in another. The linker/loader must perform some kind of symbol address resolution. The algorithm used by the linker/loader is a 2-pass style just like the assembler. Pass 1 builds the external symbol table while Pass 2 loads the object code into memory and makes the necessary inter-program module symbol address adjustments. Finally, the chapter discussed dynamic linking with respect to the OpenVMS Run-Time Library environment.

Information about linkers and loaders is generally available as part of the manual set from the manufacturer. However, [Beck 1996] provides a good academic discussion about the principles of linkers and loaders.

REFERENCES

[Beck 1996] Beck, Leland L., *System Software: An Introduction to Systems Programming*, Reading MA.: Addision Wesley, 1996.

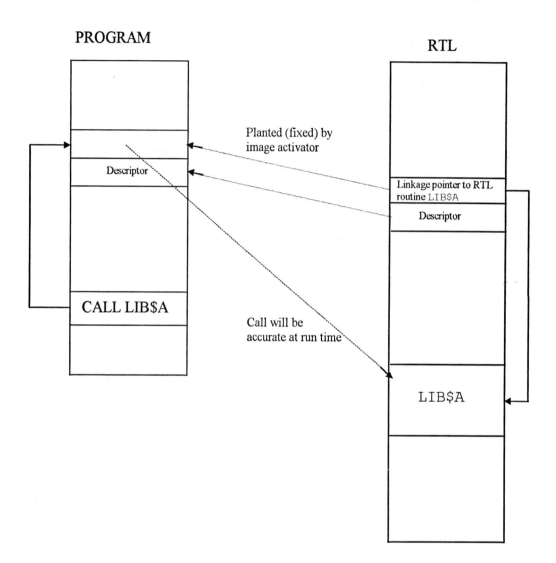

Figure 3.9
How run time linkage works for RTLs in an OpenVMS system.

CHAPTER 4

Basic Compiler Theory

Today, most application programs are written in a compiler language instead of an assembler language. Just as assembler language is easier to comprehend than machine language, compiler language is easier to understand than assembler language. In addition, a compiler language can be made to work on a wide range of processors instead of just being applicable to a single one. Part of the reason that compiler code is easier to understand is that assembler code is written in a language that resembles the way the machine 'reads' the instructions, while compiler code is written in a manner that looks somewhat like natural language. In this way, it should be easier for *us* to "read" it.

If you look at the previous paragraph, you'll notice that it mentions "language" quite often. *Language* is an important issue in understanding compilers. Therefore, this chapter will start out with an examination of language itself. After this, we will look more closely at the specific concerns of a *compiler language*. Next, we will peek inside the "black box" of a compiler and attempt to see how it translates from a language we can understand into a language the computer can understand. This will lead into the next chapter, where we will create an actual compiler for a simple language.

4.1 BASIC LANGUAGE CONCEPTS

We have used language for most of our lives. In high school we studied *grammar*. If you're like me, most of that has become stale; therefore, we need to review some definitions:

- A *grammar* is a formal description of a language.

- A *language* is a notational system for communication.

- A *sentence* is a collection of language symbols that are arranged according to the basic precepts of grammar.

- *Syntax* is the study of the "form" or structure of a language. More explicitly, it is the study of the form of sentences that are *valid* in the language.

- *Semantics* is the study of the "meaning" of (valid) sentences written in the language.

The above definitions work for spoken languages as well as compiler languages. With compiler languages, however, there are some additional definitions that we should consider.

- An *algorithm* is a recipe for specifying a computation. This implies an <u>abstract</u> description of how to solve a problem.

- A *program* is a <u>concrete</u> representation of a given algorithm in a programming language.

- A *programming language* is a special notational system for the communication of programs.

- *Translation* is the transformation of a program in one language into an equivalent program in another language.

- *Interpretation* is the performance of the algorithm that a program represents.

Compilers, assemblers, and linkers are *translators*. That is, they give us other forms of the same program. As an example, a **FORTRAN**, **COBOL**, or **Pascal** compiler translates a program written in its respective language into an equivalent program in the assembler language for the target machine. This is in turn translated by an assembler program into a machine language form of the program that will run on the given processor. In all of these translations, the basic algorithm of the program is not changed. Only the representational form is changed.

Programs such as **BASIC** and **APL** are *interpreters*. They actually execute the algorithm designed into their source program and produce answers. In fact, the only way to get answers from *any* program is to run it through an interpreter.

This poses a bit of a problem. If compilers and assemblers only translate a program into a different form, and the only way to get answers is with an interpreter, how do we get answers from compiled programs? The answer is that the hardware of the computer serves as the interpreter.

4.2 METHODS OF DEFINING THE SYNTAX OF A LANGUAGE

A programming language is usually defined as a *set* (i.e., a collection) of four things:

- A set of *"terminals"* or completely defined elements belonging to the language. Terminals are the basic *alphabet* of the language.
- A set of *"non-terminals"* or constructions that need to be further defined within the language. Non-terminals are sometimes called *"syntactic classes."*
- A set of *"production rules"* that define how non-terminals can be constructed out of a combination of terminals and non-terminals.
- A *"starting symbol"* that indicates an *initial* production rule that defines the entire language.

The word "symbol" is often used to refer to both terminals and non-terminals. However, the word "token" is used to refer to terminal symbols only.

Defining a language requires a notational system to express the production rules of that language. There are two notational systems in general usage—BNF and syntax graphs. We shall examine both of these.

4.2.1 BNF

BNF stands for "Backus Naur Form" or, in some texts, "Backus Normal Form." In this notation, terminals are written as they are seen (e.g., "BEGIN" or ":="). Non-terminals are usually enclosed in < >'s (e.g., "<expression>"). A production rule is expressed as a non-terminal followed by "::=" followed by the definition of the non-terminal. (Some books use "→" instead of "::=" when writing production rules. Either of these symbols may be read "...can be formed from...")

Many words in a natural (i.e., spoken) language have more than one definition. Likewise, there are also times when a non-terminal may be defined several different ways. When this happens, the symbol '|' is used to separate the choices in the BNF production rule. The '|' symbol should be interpreted as an exclusive; that is, only one choice is possible at a time. (A different choice may be made at a later occurrence of the symbol.)

The following notation is used to indicate that the object **z** is to be repeated at least **i** times but no more than **j** times. If **i** is omitted, it is assumed to be 0. When **j** is omitted, it is assumed to be infinite.

$$\{z\}_i^j$$

Actually, the above symbol is an extension to the normal BNF definition. It is used to avoid *recursive* definitions, that is, defining a symbol in terms of itself. As an example, a <term> could be defined as follows:

<term> ::= <term> * <factor> | <factor>

Notice that the symbol being defined also appears in the definition. In fact, it is the first symbol to appear in the definition. This situation is known as *left recursion*. Quite often, left recursion is not desirable. The problem can be avoided by rewriting the definition as follows:

<term> ::= <factor> { * <factor> }

BNF definitions of a language are very concise and exact. On the other hand, the definition is often hard to visualize.

The following sequence of (recursive) BNF productions defines an assignment statement.

<assign> ::= *ident* := <expr>
<expr> ::= <expr> + <term> | <expr> – <term> | <term>
<term> ::= <term> * <factor> | <term> / <factor> | <factor>
<factor> ::= *ident* | *numb* | (<expr>)

Unless otherwise specified, the first production rule in a list like the one above is the *starting symbol*. In this case, for example, all valid assignment statements start with the first production rule.

The *ident* and *numb* tokens are unique. All other tokens always consist of the same characters. For instance, the **Pascal** assignment operator is always comprised of the ':' and the '=' characters. Identifiers are represented by various combinations of letters and digits. Each different combination represents a unique identifier. Rather than considering each identifier to be a separate terminal symbol, the fact that the symbol is an identifier is considered sufficient to call it a terminal. Thus, *ident*, which represents *any* identifier, is considered to be a terminal. Likewise, all numbers are represented by the *numb* terminal.

4.2.2 SYNTAX DIAGRAMS

The other popular method of defining a language is easier to visualize, but tends to take quite a lot more space. This method is known as *syntax diagrams*.

The easiest way to understand syntax diagrams is to study how they can be created from BNF productions. The conversion is accomplished by adhering to the following rules:

1. Terminals are drawn

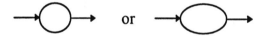

2. Non-terminals are drawn

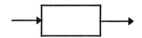

3. $<A> ::= <X_1> \mid <X_2> \mid ... \mid <X_n>$ is drawn

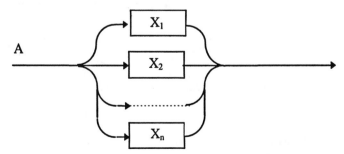

4. $\langle A \rangle ::= \langle X_1 \rangle \langle X_2 \rangle \dots \langle X_n \rangle$ is drawn

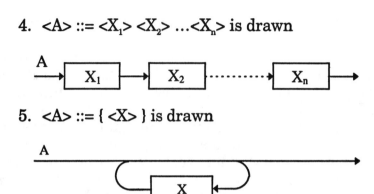

5. $\langle A \rangle ::= \{ \langle X \rangle \}$ is drawn

Syntax diagrams for the assignment statement are shown in Figure 4.1. These diagrams are produced from production rules in which left recursion has been eliminated.

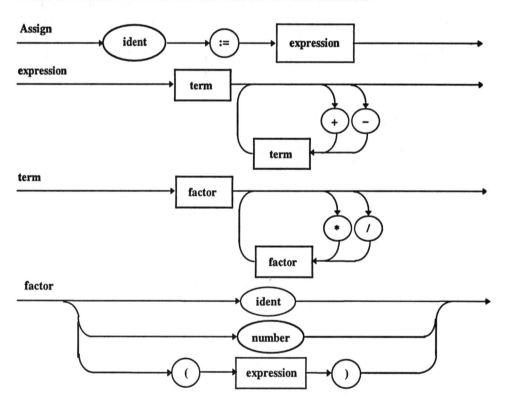

Figure 4.1
Syntax Diagrams for an assignment statement.

4.3 DIAGRAMMING THE STRUCTURE OF A PROGRAM

Another important syntax diagramming technique is that of showing the structure of an entire program or part of a program. This differs from syntax diagrams in that the latter are a model for all the possible ways that tokens may be combined. The new diagrams show how a specific sequence of tokens are combined. This new type of diagramming technique is known as *parse tree diagrams.*

The idea is to begin with the *starting symbol* as the root of the tree. This is expanded into one of its possible forms (based on the production rule). Each non-terminal resulting from this expansion is further expanded until all branches end with terminal symbols. The trick, of course, is to have these final terminals match those of the target program or statement. It may sometimes be easier to start at the terminals and work our way backwards up to the starting symbol.

The diagram for "A := B + C * (D – E)" is shown in Figure 4.2. It is based on the previous BNF production rules.

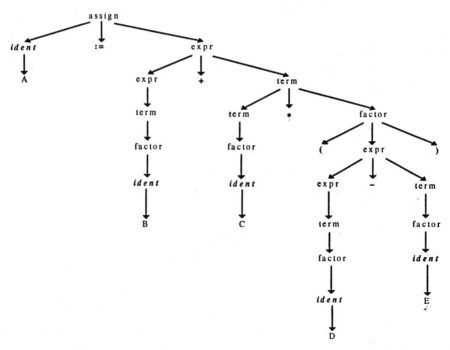

Figure 4.2
Parse tree for the expression "A := B + C * (D – E)".

In this diagram, the starting symbol is "<assign>". This is expanded into "*ident* := <expr>". The "*ident*" is the identifier *A*. The "<expr>" is expanded into "<expr> + <term>", one of the three possible choices. Now the "<expr>" is expanded through a series of choices until it resolves into the identifier *B*. The process of expanding non-terminals continues until all we have left are terminal symbols of the expression. It might be helpful to try expanding the diagrams yourself based on the description in this paragraph.

An important property of the parse tree is that it shows us the order in which the arithmetic operations must be performed. Basically, the last operations that we diagrammed are the first ones that must be done—or, from another point of view, we could work from the bottom of the diagram upwards. This way the operations are performed as we encounter them. The first arithmetic operation to be performed is $D - E$. This agrees with the algebraic rule that anything in parentheses is evaluated first. Next is to multiply C times the previous result. This agrees with the rule that multiplication is performed before addition. Next, we add B to the product and, finally, we assign the sum to A.

The parse tree is an important concept for compiler construction. As we shall soon see, most compilers create an internal form of the parse tree as part of their translation process.

The parse tree also lets us see something else about how a compiler operates. As was mentioned in the previous paragraph, the compiler creates an internal form of the parse tree. There are two basic ways for a compiler to do this—compilers are divided into two families based on the method chosen.

In the description above on how the parse tree for the expression "$A := B + C * (D - E)$" was constructed, I started at the top, that is, with the starting symbol, and worked down from there. At each step down, I had to find one of the current symbol's possible expansions that agreed with the sequence of input tokens. This procedure continued until I reached the bottom of the tree; that is, the terminal symbols. Compilers that work in a similar way are said to use a *top-down* parsing technique.

The other technique is to take the terminal symbols and try to group them together into progressively more sophisticated symbols until we eventually arrive at the starting symbol. We use the production rules backwards. That is, we find a sequence of symbols that matches one of the definitions on the right side of a production rule and we replace them all with the symbol on the left side of the rule. Compilers that work this way are said to use a *bottom-up* parsing technique. This, by the way, is the more traditional method used in writing a compiler. It is able to create compilers for more complicated languages than top-down compilers are capable of. (On the other hand, top-down compilers are easier to write and understand. We shall be using the top-down technique for the compiler design in the next chapter.)

Our example of a parse tree, Figure 4.2, only diagrams a single assignment statement. Although it is possible to diagram a complete program, this is seldom done. Think of how much room such a diagram would take. On the other hand, single statements are often diagrammed to demonstrate various aspects of compiler design. This will be seen from time to time in the ensuing sections of this chapter.

4.4 A PEEK INSIDE THE COMPILER

In this section, we will take successively deeper looks into the black box of a compiler to get a better idea of what goes on inside. First we look at the black box from the outside as shown in Figure 4.3.

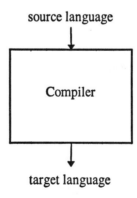

Figure 4.3
Outer view of the black box known as a Compiler.

A compiler translates a source language into a target language. We must therefore be concerned with two languages—

source and target. With compilers, the source language is the specific language for the compiler. The target language of the compiler is usually *object* code. In this form, it can be linked with other object modules (if necessary) to create an executable program.

We need to look a little deeper to get an idea of how the compiler translates between the languages.

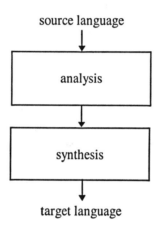

Figure 4.4
The two basic steps of compilation.

The compiler divides the compilation process into two actions: *analysis* and *synthesis*. The analysis section "analyzes" the source language. That is, it tears the source code apart and tries to understand it. Once it has successfully torn it apart, the synthesis section "synthesizes" the target language. This means that it puts the program together in the new form. What is not shown in Figure 4.4 is the fact that the basic algorithm of the program must be kept in some internal form in-between the analysis and synthesis sections. We saw in the previous section that a parse tree can be used to represent the structure and meaning of the program. The form that the compiler uses for its internal representation of the program is usually based on the parse tree.

There is another form of internal representation used in some compilers. It is known as P-Code. The name comes from the fact that this representation is meant to resemble the machine code for a **p**seudo machine. P-Code is very general and makes it easy to transition between the source language and the target language. (More on this later.)

To get a clearer idea of how the compiler does its analysis and synthesis, we must look one level deeper. See Figure 4.5.

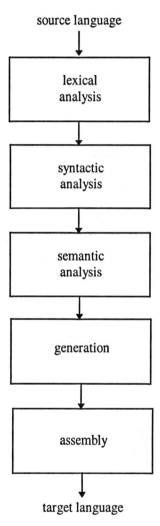

Figure 4.5
The principal compiler building blocks.

The analysis action of Figure 4.4 is performed by the three stages of lexical analysis, syntactic analysis, and semantic analysis. Likewise, the synthesis action is accomplished by the generation and assembly stages.

The input source code is actually a stream of characters fed into the compiler. The *lexical analysis* stage of the compiler searches for combinations of characters that make up the terminals, or *tokens*, of the language. These are passed on to the next stage as a stream of tokens. The lexical analysis stage is often called the *scanner*.

The *syntactic analysis* stage inputs the tokens and attempts to combine them into valid statements in the language, based on the production rules of the grammar. The *semantic analysis* stage determines the meaning of these statements and converts them into an internal representation that preserves this meaning. As mentioned before, this internal representation is usually based on the parse tree structure or on P-Code. These two stages are often thought of as a single element, known as the *parser*. This is the term that I shall usually use.

Up to this point, the structure of the code is machine independent. The algorithm originally contained in the source code is now saved in the internal representation. Neither the source code nor the internal representation depends on machine architecture. The *generation* stage of the compiler, however, converts the internal representation into a machine dependent form that may closely resemble the assembler language of the target computer.

The *assembly* stage of the compiler translates the machine dependent form into actual machine code, that is, into *object* code. At this point, the compiler has completed its objective.

We shall now take a closer look at the various stages.

4.5 LEXICAL ANALYSIS

The input to the lexical analysis stage is an unstructured character stream. The output of the lexical analyzer is a stream of tokens that identify basic elements of the language. The types of basic elements include:

- keywords
- identifiers
- constants
- operators
- punctuation

Tokens are usually expressed as ordered pairs. For instance, each token contains two pieces of information. Various sources choose to place different information into these two token fields. One form is:

< type, index >

Type identifies the basic element (from the previous list) and *index* indicates an index in a table. In this format, there is one table for each of the basic elemental forms. For instance, the *keyword* table could contain entries for BEGIN, CALL, CONST, and the like. A token to represent the keyword "CONST" would contain a *type* that referenced the keyword table and an *index* that indicated the entry in the table where the specific reference to "CONST" is to be found.

Another form is:

< symbol type, string >

In this form, each token has its own *symbol type*. Typical examples include **beginSym**, **callSym**, and **constSym**. There are also symbol types for operators and punctuation. All of these are completely defined by the symbol type code. There are two special symbol types: **ident** and **number**. Each of these can represent an almost unlimited number of variations. In this case, the specific variation is recorded in the *string* field of the token. Thus, the identifier "gcd" is represented by **<ident**, "gcd">** and the number "12345" is represented by **<number**, "12345">**. Although the other symbol types do not need the string part of the token definition, it doesn't hurt to include it. Therefore, the token for the assignment operator might be defined as **<becomes**, ":=">**.

There is not much difference in the appearance of keywords and identifiers. The sequence of characters "BEGIN" may be a keyword in some languages while the string "BEGUN" could be an identifier. Generally, keywords do not contain numeric digits but identifiers often do. This, however, does not tell us much about how the lexical analyzer can distinguish between the two. Sometimes things are not quite what they seem. Take a look at the following FORTRAN statement:

```
DO 33 I = 1. 25
```

The writer of this piece of code most likely meant to type:

```
DO 33 I = 1, 25
```

Unfortunately, the comma and period are located right next to each other on the keyboard. It's an easy mistake but can be an expensive one. A statement very much like this one was part of the program in a Venus probe. The first time the statement was executed, the probe was in deep space. This resulted in the complete loss of the probe at an estimated value of 1.6 billion dollars.

A FORTRAN lexical analyzer might assume that both statements are "DO" statements based on the initial characters. This works out well for a while, as it scans the succeeding characters. However, it runs into a problem when it encounters the period in the first statement. This just does not belong in a "DO" statement. Rather than flag this as an error, the lexical analyzer backs up and tries to see if there are any correct alternatives.

With a few exceptions, the typical FORTRAN lexical analyzer ignores spaces. This changes the first statement into:

```
DO33I=1.25
```

This is a valid "assignment" statement in the language. The FORTRAN compiler goes even farther. If the programmer has not defined an identifier, such as "DO33I," the compiler will define it for the neglectful programmer. In this case, the initial letter of the symbol is used to assign a type of "real" to the identifier,[1] which works well with the assigned value of 1.25. As a result, an undesired variable is assigned a bogus value and an intended loop is **not** executed 25 times.

FORTRAN has another interesting difficulty. The following is an "IF" statement (assuming "I" is defined as a "logical" variable):

```
IF ( I ) J = 5
```

---

[1] In FORTRAN, the initial letters I through N are reserved for integers.

The next statement assigns a value to an indexed variable:

```
IF ( I ) = 5
```

In this case, "I" is more likely an integer, and "IF" is the indexed variable.

The FORTRAN lexical analyzer has problems distinguishing identifiers from keywords. Many languages of more recent development avoid these problems by following two rules:

1. Spaces are **not** to be ignored. Therefore "DO 33 I" and "DO33I" cannot be the same.

2. "Reserve" all keywords—that is, forbid their use as an identifier. A single table can be used to hold all of the reserved words (i.e., keywords). If a token that begins with a letter is found in the table, it must be a keyword, otherwise, it's an identifier.

Other tokens are easier to determine. A string of digits is a number. Punctuation and operators are made up of easily recognized characters ("=") or character pairs (":="). The only real difficulty is when several tokens begin with the same character ("<", "<=", "<>"). The lexical analyzer has to examine the second character to determine the actual token type. If this character is part of the token (e.g., the "=" in "<=") the lexical analyzer now has the complete token. However, if the next character is not part of the token, for instance, if something other than "=" or ">" follows a "<", then the initial character is the complete token and the character read by the lexical analyzer is either white space or the first character of the next token. The question now becomes, "How do we handle this extra character?" Most lexical analyzers are either designed to deliberately read one character ahead for each token or to have some mechanism for returning the extra character to the input stream so that it can be read again when searching for the next token.

4.6 THE PARSER

The two stages of syntactic analysis and semantic analysis are often thought of as a single unit called the *parser*. I will use this representation to describe the combined syntactic and semantic operations.

The input to the parser is the stream of tokens generated by the lexical analyzer. The "output" of the parser is some form of intermediate representation of the program's intention. This internal depiction may take various forms:

- The "tree form" is the traditional method. It is usually rendered as a table that is often called a *node table*. Each entry in the table contains two operator tokens and one operation token. Thus, the table entry is an ordered triplet of ordered pairs—quite an ungainly data structure. (Some node tables contain a third operand token that is meant to indicate where to store the result of the operation on the other two operands.)

- P-Code is a more recent development. This form represents the program as if it were written in an assembler language for a **p**seudo–machine (hence the name "P-Code"). At least one microprocessor has been built that executes one form of P-Code as if it were the native language of the machine. This shortens the overall compilation time since some of the generation and assembly codes can be omitted.

An additional "output" of the parser is a *symbol table*. Most programming languages actually contain two sections. One of these is the expression of the program's algorithm that results in the internal representation previously mentioned. The other part is a *declarations* section where constants, variables, and other symbols are defined. These latter declarations result in the symbol table where each entry lists the symbol and its attributes. The attributes characterize such things as: how the symbol is used (constant, variable, procedure, etc.); the data type (integer, real, etc.); the organization (e.g. array); and, possibly, the relationship of this symbol to other symbols in the program.

Both of these "output" tables are never actually output by the compiler (with the possible exception of P-Code that can be executed on an actual machine). Instead, these tables are used by the later compiler stages to produce their output.

4.6.1 PARSING TO TREE FORM

As mentioned above, the "tree form" is usually represented as a table. This section will give a brief description of what is in the table. Once the actual form is shown, a simplified form shall be provided that helps clarify later examples that will be using the node table. The alternative to the node table is generating P-Code. This will be demonstrated with the compiler development in the next chapter.

The node table consists of multiple entries that represent the various nodes and leaves in the tree form of the expression or statement. Each entry has three or four fields. One of these fields is an operation and the others are operands. Each entry in the four-field form can specify a binary operation performed on two of the operands with the result being stored in a location indicated by the third operand. Quite often, this third operand refers to a temporary storage area. The three-field form of the table describes a binary operation performed on two operands. The result is implied by the entry itself. When a later node in the table needs to refer to the result, it points back to the node where the operation was performed. I will use this form in the following narrative.

The operands are represented by tokens. Since tokens can be expressed in several ways, we must decide on a consistent form to be used at this time. Since we are using a table to represent the parse tree, the < *type, index* > form of the token is a good choice. In this form, the *type* represents a table where the token is defined and the *index* is the number of the entry in the table where it can be found. Typical tables might include a keyword table, a combined operator/punctuation table, and a symbol table. Entries in the first two tables are constant and defined by the language. These tables can be populated before compilation begins. The entries in the symbol table are variable and depend on the program being compiled. This table is filled in as the compiler encounters the symbols in the source code.

For the time being, let's assume that the mathematical operations (i.e., +, −, *, and /) are located in the first four entries of the operator/punctuation table respectively, and that the assignment operator is the fifth entry in the table. Likewise, let's assume that the first five entries in the symbol table define the symbols *A*, *B*, *C*, *D*, and *E*. This means that the token for the plus sign is *<operator, 1>*, assignment is *<operator, 5>*, and the symbol *B* is expressed by the token *<symbol, 2>*.

The assignment statement:

$$A := B + C * (D - E)$$

would expand into the following node table (Table 4.1):

Table 4.1

Node Table for the Expression "A := B + C * (D − E)"

node index	operation	operand 1	operand 2
1	<operator, 2>	<symbol, 4>	<symbol, 5>
2	<operator, 3>	<symbol, 3>	<node, 1>
3	<operator, 1>	<symbol, 2>	<node, 2>
4	<operator, 5>	<symbol, 1>	<node, 3>

You will notice several entries that refer to the node table itself. For instance, entry two refers to entry 1 of the node table. The reference is generally interpreted as "use the result of node table entry number i as the current operand." In particular, node table entry two says to multiply (i.e., *<operator, 3>)* symbol *C* (i.e., *<symbol, 3>)* by the results of entry one (i.e., *<node, 2>)* of the node table. The result of this operation is then referenced in node entry number three.

Overall, the node table in its present form is rather hard to read. This is caused by the way the tokens are written. It is not very obvious that "*<operator, 1>*" really means "+" or that "*<symbol, 1>*" is the symbol *A*. A simplified form of the table is recommended to avoid the problem of reading it in its present form. In this form, the operator tokens are replaced by the actual character or characters (i.e., +, −, *, /, :=). Symbol tokens are replaced by the symbol itself. Finally, a reference to entry i of the node table is indicated by the symbol N_i. The previous node table becomes:

Table 4.2

Simplified Node Table for the Expression "A := B + C * (D − E)"

node index	operation	operand 1	operand 2
1	−	D	E
2	*	C	N_1
3	+	B	N_2
4	:=	A	N_3

   This form is much more readable. It is easy to see that the first entry represents the "D − E" operation. I will be using this form in future examples.

   It is worthwhile comparing Table 4.2 with Figure 4.2. In the discussion of Figure 4.2 I mentioned how it was possible by working upwards from the bottom of the parse tree diagram, to determine the order in which the mathematical operations are to be performed. The same order can be seen in Table 4.2. This is important. It means that the indicated statement can be evaluated by "executing" the nodes in the order in which they appear in the table. Now we only have one problem, "How does the parser determine this order?"

   This is truly the heart of the matter. Various methods have been introduced over the years. I will just cover one example, namely, parsing by operator precedence.

4.6.2 PARSING BY OPERATOR PRECEDENCE

This section gives a basic overview of the steps that must be followed when parsing by operator precedence.

   The first thing we must do in this method is to convert our production rules into *reduction rules*. This is done by placing each of the possible alternative definitions for a non-terminal on a separate line. The assignment statement is expressed by the following reduction rules:

```
<assign> ::= ident := <expr>
<expr> ::= <expr> + <term>
<expr> ::= <expr> – <term>
<expr> ::= <term>
<term> ::= <term> * <factor>
<term> ::= <term> / <factor>
<term> ::= <factor>
<factor> ::= ( <expr> )
<factor> ::= ident
```

The arrangement of the non-terminals in these reduction rules is designed to comply with the rules of mathematical precedence that state that anything inside of parentheses is evaluated first, then the multiplication and division operations are performed, and finally the addition and subtraction operations are done. This order is called *operator precedence*.

The next activity in this method is to define the relationship between pairs of terminals. There are three basic relationships:

1. The relation $L < R$ exists between two terminals, L and R, if there is a reduction rule containing the sequence ...Lx... where x is a non-terminal that derives into a reduction rule in which R is the <u>left</u>-most terminal. ("*Derives*" means that several cycles may need to be made through the reduction rules before the desired rule containing R is obtained.)

2. The relation $L = R$ exists between two terminals, L and R, if there is a reduction rule containing the sequence ...LxR...where x is either a non-terminal or is missing.

3. The relation $L > R$ exists between two terminals, L and R, if there is a reduction rule containing the sequence ...xR... where x is a non-terminal that derives into a reduction rule in which L is the <u>right</u>-most terminal.

These relations are best understood by looking at sample parse trees for the language. This is done in Figure 4.6. In this figure, terminal tokens are represented by uppercase letters, and non-terminals are shown as lowercase letters. In addition, the symbols L and R are specifically used to show that they appear to the *left* or to the *right* of the other token.

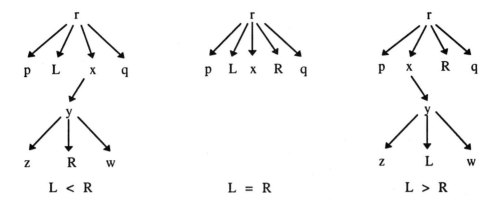

Figure 4.6
Parse trees for the relations "L < R", "L = R", and "L > R".

In the diagrams for "$L < R$" and "$L > R$", the non-terminal x derives into a rule that contains another non-terminal y. This in turn derives into another rule that contains the desired terminal. In actuality, it may take more or less steps to reach the target terminal. The important thing to remember here is that, although this token is <u>more</u> than one level below the root node, the other token is <u>exactly</u> one level below the root node. (Of course, with the "$L = R$" relation, both tokens are exactly one level below the root.)

It would be a mistake to read "<", "=", or ">" as "is less than," "is equal to," or "is more than." These relational operators have a slightly different meaning when used to show the relationships between program tokens. A better reading might be "has less precedence then", "has the same precedence as", or "has more precedence than".

Now we are ready for the next step, which is creating the operator precedence table. This table maps all of the possible relations between L and R tokens. There are many combinations of tokens to be concerned with. Working with only the reduction rules can be quite complex. The easiest way to examine these relationships is to draw sample parse tree diagrams and look for patterns like those shown in Figure 4.6. It may take several test diagrams to get all of the combinations. In addition, we must realize that some LR combinations are just plain impossible for the set of reduction rules we are working with.

Figure 4.7 can be used to derive many of the necessary relationships for our set of reduction rules.

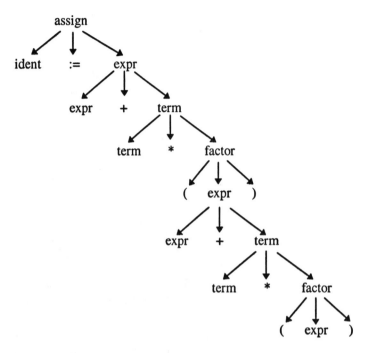

Figure 4.7
Parse tree diagram used to discover precedence relationships.

Using *assign* as the root node, we can see such relations as ***ident*** = ":=", ":=" < "+", ":=" < "*", and ":=" < "(". Trace down the tree until you reach the first *factor* node. Using this node as the root, we can find many more relationships: "(" = ")", "(" < "+", "(" < "*", and "(" < "(", as well as "+" > ")", "*" > ")", and ")" > ")". It is possible to expand this list by substituting "–" for "+" or "/" for "*". However, to find the relationships between "+" and "–" or between "*" and "/" would require drawing some different parse trees.

Once all the relationships have been determined, they are arranged in a precedence table. This table has a row for each *L* token and a column for each *R* token. The *LR* relationship is put in the table where the *L* row intersects the *R* column. Any entry in the table that does not show a relationship symbol is not possible in the language and should be treated as an error.

The precedence table for our assignment grammar is shown in Table 4.3.

Table 4.3

Precedence Table for Assignment Statement

left token	:=	+	−	right token *	/	(	)	ident
:=	<	<	<	<	<			<
+	>	>	<	<	<		>	<
−	>	>	<	<	<		>	<
*	>	>	>	>	<		>	<
/	>	>	>	>	<		>	<
(	<	<	<	<	<		=	<
)	>	>	>	>	>		>	
ident	=	>	>	>	>		>	

There are two additional pseudo–tokens that are often used when parsing statements, "⊢" and "⊣", which stand for "beginning of statement" and "end of statement" respectively. It is necessary to assign precedence relations to these two symbols. These can be summarized as follows: "⊢" < *anything*, and *anything* > "⊣". In addition, the special case "⊢" = "⊣" indicates that we are done.

We are now ready to do the actual parsing by operator precedence. This is done using a *stack*. Initially, the stack only contains the beginning of the statement symbol, "⊢". Then, statement tokens are read, one at a time. As each token is read, the relation between the top of stack token and the input symbol is determined. What is done next depends on this relationship:

- If the relation between the token at the top of the stack and the input symbol is either < or =, then the input to-ken is *shifted* onto the stack. This means that the token is removed from the input and placed on the stack where it becomes the new top of stack symbol.

- If the relationship between the top of stack and the input symbol is **>**, then the stack is *reduced* down to the next **<** relationship on the stack. Assume *stack₁* is the token at the top of the stack, *stack₂* is the next token down on the stack, and *input* is the input token. We will observe the following relations: $stack_2 < stack_1 > input$. The token inside the angle brackets is the one that must be reduced. (NOTE: in some cases, the "=" relation occurs instead of "<".)

Reduction can take one of three forms:

1. If the token inside the angle brackets is an ***ident***, then it is reduced to a "non-terminal." For instance, if the identifier should be the symbol **A**, then it will be reduced to the non-terminal **n_A**. Since the relationships are only between tokens, reducing the ***ident*** to a non-terminal removes it from consideration when testing how the top of stack relates to the input token.

2. If the token inside the angle brackets is an operation such as "**+**" or "*****", it will be surrounded by two "reduced identifiers." The whole thing in the angle brackets looks like < **n_A + n_B** >. This will be reduced to an entry in the node table. The *operand* in this case would be "**+**" and the operands are the symbols **A** and **B**. The resulting node table entry is indicated by the symbol **N_i**, which is considered to be a non-terminal.

3. A special case exists when "**)**" is the token between the angle brackets. In this case, the whole sequence looks like "**(** = **)**" > .... The reduction is made by simply removing both the "**(**" and the "**)**" from the stack.

    After each reduction, the new token on the top of the stack is compared with the input symbol. This will continue until the input symbol is finally shifted onto the stack. At this point, the next input symbol is read and compared with the stack. This continues until all the input symbols are processed.

    Table 4.4 shows the results of applying these directions to the assignment statement "A := B + C * (D − E)". The stack is shown in the first column by expanding towards the right as new items are shifted onto it. The second column shows the new tokens being considered one at a time. The third column shows the relations between the top tokens on the stack and the input symbol. The last column tells whether the relationship requires a shift or a reduce operation. Those reduce operations that produce a node table entry are shown in uppercase, (i.e., REDUCE).

Table 4.4

Parsing "A := B + C * (D – E)" by Operator Precedence			
Stack	**Next Token**	**Relation(s)**	**Shift / Reduce**
$\vdash$	A	$\vdash < A$	shift
$\vdash A$	:=	$\vdash < A > :=$	reduce
$\vdash n_A$		$\vdash < :=$	shift
$\vdash n_A :=$	B	$:= < B$	shift
$\vdash n_A := B$	+	$:= < B > +$	reduce
$\vdash n_A := n_B$		$:= < +$	shift
$\vdash n_A := n_B +$	C	$+ < C$	shift
$\vdash n_A := n_B + C$	*	$+ < C > *$	reduce
$\vdash n_A := n_B + n_C$		$+ < *$	shift
$\vdash n_A := n_B + n_C *$	(	$* < ($	shift
$\vdash n_A := n_B + n_C * ($	D	$(< D$	shift
$\vdash n_A := n_B + n_C * (D$	–	$(< D > -$	reduce
$\vdash n_A := n_B + n_C * (n_D$		$(< -$	shift
$\vdash n_A := n_B + n_C * (n_D -$	E	$- < E$	shift
$\vdash n_A := n_B + n_C * (n_D - E$	)	$- < E >)$	reduce
$\vdash n_A := n_B + n_C * (n_D - n_E$		$(< - >)$	REDUCE
$\vdash n_A := n_B + n_C * (N_1$		$(=)$	shift
$\vdash n_A := n_B + n_C * (N_1)$	$\dashv$	$(=) > \dashv$	reduce
$\vdash n_A := n_B + n_C * N_1$		$+ < * > \dashv$	REDUCE
$\vdash n_A := n_B + N_2$		$:= < + > \dashv$	REDUCE
$\vdash n_A := N_3$		$\vdash < := > \dashv$	REDUCE
$\vdash N_4$		$\vdash = \dashv$	done

The first REDUCE operation produces the node table entry "– $D\ E$". It is listed as N_1. It is used as an operand in the second REDUCE operation. The second node table entry is "* $C\ N_1$".

The third node table entry is "$+ B N_2$". The final one is "$:= A N_3$". These should be compared with Table 4.2.

This exercise has shown one of the many ways that an assignment statement can be parsed. Of course, assignment is only one of the many statements that must be handled by a compiler. Fortunately, the operator precedence paradigm can be expanded to handle other tokens. Thus, it is possible to construct a precedence table that contains tokens like IF, THEN, WHILE, and other keywords. This is much more complex than the assignment statement development that we just looked at. In fact, it is beyond the scope of this book. Instead, in the next section, we shall examine another parsing method that is more straightforward.

There are other methods that make use of tabular methods. Most of these are not easy to develop manually. On the other hand, they lend themselves quite easily to automation. One of the most familiar of these is the combination of **LEX** and **YACC**. Anyone interested in automatic compiler generation should look into these programs.

4.7 TOP-DOWN PARSING

What we've looked at so far belongs to the class of compiling known as "bottom-up parsing." As mentioned before, bottom up parsing is characterized by trying to assemble groups of tokens together into increasingly more complicated collections until a major non-terminal (i.e., "starting symbol") has been detected. From now on, I shall be working with another class of parsing known as "top-down parsing." With top-down parsing, we start with the "starting symbol" and work our way down to the tokens. It turns out that this approach lends itself to compilers that can be created manually instead of relying on automated techniques. Ultimately, this will give us a better picture of what goes on inside a compiler.

One characteristic of top-down parsing is that it is *goal oriented*. In order to start at the top and work down to the input tokens, there must be a way to direct the activity. Consider, for instance, that we must start at a rather vague "starting symbol" and end up matching a very specific set of tokens. Because of this, we need a grammar that supplies clues to the parser so that at each decision point in the process, the parser always has direction on how to proceed. This is why many languages start each statement with a distinct keyword. When the compiler sees the IF keyword, it is able to establish a goal of assembling an *if statement*. There may be additional clues within the if statement development that provide additional guidance, such as whether there is an *else clause* or not. There is one noticeable exception to the leading keyword requirement. The *assignment statement* begins with a leading **ident** instead of a keyword.

An additional characteristic of top-down parsing is that it often uses recursion to perform the parsing operation. There is no need to design special tables like the ones used in bottom-up parsing. (Some top-down parsers may use tables, but this is not the norm.) The recursive top-down parser usually does not produce an explicit node table. Instead, it will be seen that the node table is implied in the recursive call sequence.

The top-down parser code can be written almost directly from the syntax diagrams.

- The parser code calls the lexical analyzer to get the next token.
- If a keyword is expected, you compare it with the token that was just read. (Quite often, this token is saved in one form or another to be used later in generating the compiler output.)
- If a non-terminal is expected, it is handled by calling a procedure with the same name as the non-terminal.
- Alternative choices are handled by a sequence of **if / else** statements. The current token is used in this selection process. This means that any procedure that handles a non-terminal *begins* with the current token.
- Loops within the syntax diagram are implemented with a **while** statement.

Using the considerations suggested above, the assignment statement syntax diagrams of Figure 4.1 could be rendered with the following code sample:

```
void assign()
{
  save_token();
  get_next_token();
  if (symbol_type == becomesym)
  {
```

```
      get_next_token();
      expression();
    }
  }

void expression()
{
  term();
  while (symbol_type == plus ||
      symbol_type == minus)
  {
   save_token();
   get_next_token();
   term();
  }
}

void term()
{
  factor();
  while (symbol_type == times ||
      symbol_type == slash)
  {
   save_token();
   get_next_token();
   factor();
  }
}

void factor()
{
  if (symbol_type == ident ||
    symbol_type == numb)
  {
   save_token();
   get_next_token();
  }
  else if (symbol_type == left_paren)
  {
   get_next_token();
   expression();
   if (symbol_type == right_paren)
     get_next_token();
  }
}
```

In this simplified code segment, the call to the lexical analyzer is made by 'get_next_token()' and the token is saved for later usage by 'save_token()'. This code assumes the *symbol type, string>* token form.

Let's examine how this works with the input assignment statement "A := B + C * (D – E)".

A separate section of code, not shown here, reads the first token, (i.e., "A"), recognizes that it is an ***ident***, and calls the assign() procedure. Assign() saves the identifier "A" to be used by the output generator. It then reads the next token, confirms that it is the expected ":=", gets the next token, (which is the first token of an expression), and then finally calls the expression() procedure.

Expression() calls term(), hich calls factor(). This procedure notes that "B" is an identifier and saves it and reads the next token ("+"). It then returns to the term() procedure. Since the current token is neither "*" nor "/", term() returns to the expression() procedure. The "+" token *is* expected by expression(). It saves the token away, reads the next one, and calls term() again.

Term() calls factor(). Factor() saves the "C" token, reads the next token, and returns to term(). The current token is now "*", which is an expected token. Term() saves it, reads the next token, and calls factor() a second time.

Factor() detects a "(" token. Therefore, it gets the next token and calls expression(). It should be noted that this is a recursive call.

Expression() calls term() and term() calls factor(). Factor() sees that the current token is an identifier, "D", saves it, gets the next token, "–", and returns to term(). Since this is not one of the two tokens that term() expects, it returns to expression(). Expression() saves the "–", reads the next token, and calls term() again. Term() calls factor(). Factor() saves the final identifier, "E", and reads the next token, which is the ")" expected by expression(). At this point, one after another, all the procedures return to the one that called them. Along the way, expression() is satisfied to detect the expected right parenthesis and reads the next token. Eventually, after all of the returns, we end up in the assign() procedure that started the whole process.

This sequence of procedure calls is much easier to follow if we make a diagram of the distribution. Such a diagram is shown in Figure 4.8.

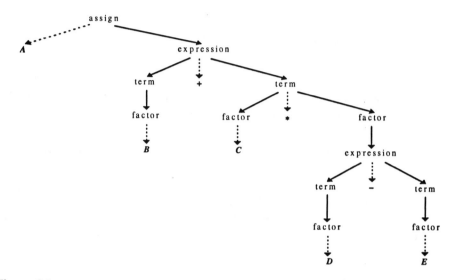

Figure 4.8
Calling sequence for the expression "A := B + C * (D – E)".

In this diagram, the solid arrows show the calling sequence, and the dashed arrows show the tokens that have been saved by the various procedures. It should be noted that some tokens, such as ":=" and the parentheses, are not required for the output generation and are therefore not saved.

If you compare this diagram with Figure 4.2, you will see that the basic information of the parse tree has been preserved. This illustration has shown that top down parsing techniques can reproduce the information in the parse tree without the use of tables. Furthermore, this can be done with fairly straight-forward code. Of course, many topics have been left out, such as handling statements other than assignment, handling error conditions, and generating the output translation of the input source code. On the other hand, these topics were not covered in the section on bottom-up parsing either. These topics and others shall be covered in the rest of this chapter and in the next. I shall, however, restrict my discussion to how they are handled by a top-down parser.

4.8 Error Recovery

The sample assignment parser of the previous section was rather naive. It assumed that the source code had no errors. The closest we got to any concept that there might be anything other than correct syntax is in statements such as:

```
if (symbol_type == becomesym)
{
  get_next_token();
  expression();
}
```

This statement only knows what to do when the symbol type *is* a becomesym. It says nothing about what to do when some other token is detected. A useful compiler must have some sort of approach to incorrect syntax. Two things must be done when an invalid symbol is input: it must *report the error* and it must try to *get back into sync*.

This last requirement needs some explanation. Top-down parsing was previously described as being "goal oriented." Once the parser determines the type of statement it expects to parse, it has certain expectations at various points along the line. For instance, at one point, it may expect an identifier, number, or left parenthesis; at another point, it might expect some type of arithmetic operator. When an error occurs, the parser can no longer count on its expectations, or you might say, it no longer knows what to expect. The parser is "out of sync" with the expectations necessary to fulfill its goal. It needs to get back in sync, that is, it must get back into a state where it knows what to expect. *Our* goal now is to come up with an algorithm that helps the parser get itself back into sync.

Let's try to determine what the parser should do for an IF statement. We shall use the following syntax diagram:

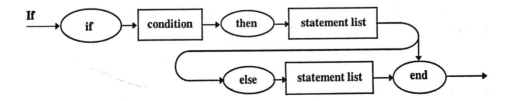

The following is a valid IF statement[2]:

```
IF (A = B) THEN C := D ELSE E := F END
```

Let's add an error and try to decide what to do to get things back in sync:

```
IF (A == B) THEN C := D ELSE E := F END
```

The error is in the "condition" non-terminal where an "==" is used instead of a valid "=". The question is, "where do we get back in sync?" A glance at the syntax diagram suggests that if an error is found in a non-terminal, the best place to get back in sync is at the next terminal token. In this case, we could skip everything until we reach the THEN token. Thus, the first rule for getting back in sync is:

- Skip everything until you reach the next expected terminal symbol.

Now let's mess things up a bit more. Assume the author of this statement is more familiar with **C** or **C++** and is having trouble converting to a new language. This explains why the "==" was used. This person might easily make another mistake by confusing the syntax with **C**. There is no THEN keyword in **C**, therefore the statement might erroneously be written:

```
IF (A == B) C := D ELSE E := F END
```

Unfortunately, the next expected keyword is no longer present to synchronize on. In this case, the best thing to do is skip everything until we find one of what I call "a set of *panic* tokens." It turns out that this is a dynamic set. The elements in the set change from time to time depending on the current syntax and other things. Whatever tokens are used at the end of a program, subroutine, or statement are normally part of the set.

---

[2] Note: Parentheses around a <condition> are accepted in **LuxLyk** but not in **Lil'LuxLyk**. Both of these compilers will be discussed in later chapters. The parentheses are used here for clarity, especially in the last example where the THEN keyword is omitted.

While parsing an IF statement, the ELSE token might be placed in the set of panic symbols before the <condition> is parsed.

The second rule of resynchronizing is:

- Skip everything until you reach the next panic symbol.

In our example, this would cause the parser to skip everything until it comes across the ELSE token. In other cases, the token that stops the search might be the keyword END or, perhaps, a semicolon.

Now try to imagine a situation in which IF statements are nested within other IF statements. If an error is found deep within this nesting, the parser starts skipping until it detects a token that satisfies one of the two resynchronizing rules. The token used may belong to one of the outer IF nestings. Thus, although the parser believes it is back in sync, it actually is not. As it continues to scan through the code, the parser will find new sections that just plain don't meet its expectations. This is because things are really not in sync. The parser will continue to produce additional error messages. This could easily continue until the end of the source code. Have you ever received pages of error listings resulting from a single missing semicolon? Hopefully, it is now less of a mystery why this happens. When the error-handling routine synchronizes on the wrong token, it acts more like an error injector than an error fixer.

4.9 STORAGE ALLOCATION: THE P-MACHINE

At this point, we have covered almost everything we need to know about the analysis part of the compiler. Now is the time to start looking at the synthesis section.

The analysis section was characterized by being machine independent, that is, the source code should be able to run on any machine. In the synthesis section, we must become more concerned with the target machine. There are two major concerns here. First, the output of the compiler *must* run on the target machine. Second, we really would like the compiler to run on *many* different machines; that is, we want to make it available to as large an audience as possible. Sometimes these two concerns seem to be pulling in opposite directions. How do we make the compiler efficient on a particular processor as well as portable to many different processors?

There are several approaches to this problem, including:

- Rewrite the synthesis section of the compiler for each processor.
- Produce the output in another language that *is* portable, such as **C**, then compile that form.
- Produce code for a pseudo machine. This code can be turned fairly easily into assembly language for the target machine.
- Produce code for a pseudo machine and then create the pseudo machine in software. If the pseudo-machine code is built into the synthesis part of the program, we have an interpreter, not a compiler.

We shall examine all but the first approach in the next chapter. I shall illustrate all these approaches using the pseudo machine abstraction. Therefore, we need to begin looking into pseudo machines. There are many different implementations of a pseudo machine. The one that I shall use is based on one that appeared in Wirth[3] [Wirth 1976] and later in *Byte Magazine*[4] [Chung 1978].

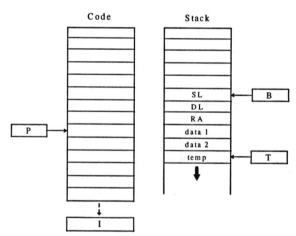

Figure 4.9
Architecture of the P-Machine Lite.

[3] *Algorithms and Data Structures = Programs* by Wirth, Nicklaus, ©1976. Adapted by permission of Prentice Hall, Inc., Upper Saddle River, NJ.
[4] *Byte Magazine*, September 1978. Adapted with permission. © by McGraw-Hill Companies, Inc.

One of the major concerns of the target machine is how to allocate storage. The pseudo machine (i.e., P-Machine) helps us towards this end. We first define storage for the P-Machine and then apply the model to the target machine.

Our basic P-Machine has four registers and two types of storage: **Stack** and **Code**.

The **Stack** memory segment stores all of the data used by the program that is running. As its name implies, it uses a stack architecture (although it is implemented as a large array). All data in this basic P-Machine are integers. Character data are also represented as integers, rather than in the smaller "byte" format. The **T** register points to either the last local variable for the current P-Code procedure (if no temporary data is on the **Stack**) or the last temporary data item pushed onto it (if temporary data is on the **Stack**). "**T**" stands for "top of stack" even though it appears on the bottom in the diagram. The **B** register gets its name from the fact that it points to the "base" of the stack frame that corresponds to the current P-Code procedure. The stack frame contains the following:

- *SL* (Static Link)—pointer to the stack frame of the procedure within which the current procedure is nested in the source code. This pointer is used to enforce the "scope rules" of the compiler.
- *DL* (Dynamic Link)—pointer to the stack frame of the procedure that called the present procedure. This pointer is used to replace the **B** register value when returning from the current procedure.
- *RA* (Return Address)—contains the return address, that is, the address of the P-Code instruction following the one that called the current procedure. This address is used to replace the **P** register value when returning from the current procedure.
- *data* (local data)—contains all of the variables that are local to the current procedure.
- *temp* (temporary data)—contains any values pushed on the **Stack** while executing P-Code instructions.

The **Code** memory segment contains the P-Code instructions. The next instruction to be executed is pointed to by the **P** register. As an instruction is to be executed, the **Code** contents pointed to by the **P** register are fetched into the **I** register and the

P register is incremented. After this, the instruction in the **I** register is executed. The *fetch/execute* cycle continues until the contents of the **P** register become zero (indicating a return from the main program). The execution of each instruction depends on its *fct* code, as shown by the pseudo-code in the following table:

Table 4.5

P-Machine Lite: the Basic P-Machine Instruction Set

FCT	LEV	ADR	Description
LIT	0	num	**inc**(T); Stack[T]←num;
OPR	0	0	T←B–1; P←Stack[T+3]; B←Stack[T+2];
"	0	1	Stack[T]← – Stack[T];
"	0	2	**dec**(T); Stack[T]←Stack[T]+Stack[T+1];
"	0	3	**dec**(T); Stack[T]←Stack[T]–Stack[T+1];
"	0	4	**dec**(T); Stack[T]←Stack[T]*Stack[T+1];
"	0	5	**dec**(T); Stack[T]←Stack[T]/Stack[T+1];
"	0	6	Stack[T]←Stack[T]⊗1;
"	0	7	**dec**(T); Stack[T]←Stack[T]%Stack[T+1];
"	0	8	**dec**(T); if Stack[T]=Stack[T+1] then Stack[T]←1 else Stack[T]←0;
"	0	9	**dec**(T); if Stack[T]≠Stack[T+1] then Stack[T]←1 else Stack[T]←0;
"	0	10	**dec**(T); if Stack[T]<Stack[T+1] then Stack[T]←1 else Stack[T]←0;
"	0	11	**dec**(T); if Stack[T]≥Stack[T+1] then Stack[T]←1 else Stack[T]←0;
"	0	12	**dec**(T); if Stack[T]>Stack[T+1] then Stack[T]←1 else Stack[T]←0;
"	0	13	**dec**(T); if Stack[T]≤Stack[T+1] then Stack[T]←1 else Stack[T]←0;
LOD	lev	adr	**inc**(T); Stack[T]←Stack[**base**(lev)+adr];
STO	lev	adr	**dec**(T); Stack[**base**(lev)+adr]← Stack[T+1];
CAL	lev	adr	Stack[T+1]←**base**(lev); Stack[T+2]←B; Stack[T+3]←P; B←T+1; P←adr;
INT	0	num	T←T+num;
JMP	0	adr	P←adr;
JPC	cnd	adr	**dec**(T); if Stack[T+1]=cnd then P←adr;
CSP	0	0	**inc**(T); **read_char**(Stack[T]);
CSP	0	1	**dec**(T); **write_char**(Stack[T+1]);
CSP	0	2	**inc**(T); **read_int**(Stack[T]);
CSP	0	3	**dec**(T); **write_int**(Stack[T+1]);

Table 4.5 *(Continued)*

NOTES:

- "%" is the MOD operator.
- "⊗" is the logical AND operator.
- **inc**() and **dec**() are built-in functions that increment or decrement their parameter by one count.
- **base**(lev) is a built-in function that traces down *lev* levels of the static link path.
- **read_xxx**() and **write_xxx**() are built-in functions that read or write the form that their name implies.

All instructions in the P-Machine contain three fields. The first field is the *fct* or "function" code. It corresponds to the opcode field in machine language. The second and third fields are the *lev* (level) and *adr* (address) fields. They have different roles depending on the *fct* code. These various roles are defined in the *description* field of Table 4.5. This description may be thought of as the microcode for the instruction. The "built-in" functions that are mentioned in the notes of the table can be thought of as microprocedures built into the "hardware" of the P-Machine that performs the indicated function.

Now let's take a look at the individual *fct* codes.

The "LIT" P-Code is used to push integer constants onto the top of the **Stack**. The constant value is contained in the *adr* field of the instruction.

The "LOD" P-Code is used to push integer variables onto the top of the **Stack**, while the "STO" P-Code is used to pop integers off from the top of the **Stack** and store them in their appropriate variable locations. The address of the variable is represented by the *lev* and *adr* fields of the instruction as follows: *lev* tells how many levels to trace down the *Static Link* path to find the base of the stack frame that contains the data and *adr* is an offset from that location to the desired data item.

Operations on the **Stack** contents are performed by the "OPR" P-Codes. The specific operation is determined by the *adr* field. Some OPR functions, such as *negate* (OPR 0, 1), only operate on the top integer on the **Stack**. These operations do not modify the **T** register, they just modify what the **T** register points to. Other OPR functions, such as *add* (OPR 0, 2), operate on the top *two* integers of the **Stack**. These operations usually do change the **T** register. You can think of it as if the top two values are popped off the **Stack**, the operation is performed on them, and the result is pushed back onto the **Stack**.

The "JMP," "JPC," and "CAL" P-Codes are used to modify the execution order of the program's instructions. JMP causes an unconditional jump to the **Code** location indicated by the *adr* field. The JPC instruction is a conditional jump to the **Code** location indicated by the *adr* field. The jump will only be made if the value on the top of the **Stack** matches the condition code in the *lev* field. Usually the condition code is a 0 (for *false*) or a 1 (for *true*). The comparison value is always popped off the **Stack** by the JPC instruction. The final order-modifying instruction is CAL. It is used to call a procedure. A procedure call is different from a jump in that a special *stack frame* is set up for the new procedure. This stack frame contains data that is specific to the procedure's local environment. This environment contains the return address, special linkage pointers like the static link, and local variables declared within the procedure. As usual, the *adr* field of the P-Code instruction holds the **Code** location on where to transfer. The *lev* field in this instruction is used to make sure that the static link is set to the right value.

The "INT" instruction is used to increment the **T** register. The *adr* field contains the value by which the register is to be incremented. (Negative increments are permissible.) When the CAL instruction creates the new stack frame, it moves the **B** register to point to the new static link. It does not modify the **T** register. The **T** register remains pointing to the location just before where the **B** register is now pointing. Normally, the first statement executed by the procedure will be an INT instruction that moves the **T** register over the static link, dynamic link, return address, and any local variables.

The remaining P-Codes are the "CSP" instructions. CSP stands for "call special procedure." These instructions perform special functions for the P-Machine; in particular, the ones shown here are used for input and output. The specific type of I/O to be performed is indicated by the *adr* field. Input operations will input from the *standard input* and push the new value on the stack. The standard input is usually the keyboard, although it could be redirected to a file. Output instructions will pop a value off the stack and output it to the *standard output*, usually the screen.

4.10 STORAGE ALLOCATION: THE STACK FRAME

Now we have to look more closely at the stack frame. Our goal is to see how it enforces the scope rules of the language. Of course, this means we must first examine the concept of scope rules.

Let's assume we have a main program with variables **x**, **y**, and **z**. Since they are the program's variables, they shall be global to all other procedures. Assume that the main program also contains a single procedure named **B**. Procedure **B** contains local variables **u**, **v**, and **w**. It also contains a nested procedure named **C**. Procedure **C** contains local variables **r**, **s**, and **t**.

When discussing nested procedures like this, it is easiest to express relationships in terms of levels. The body of the main program and its variables are said to be at level zero. Any procedure directly contained in the main program is said to be *defined* at level zero. The body of this procedure and its local variables are said to be at level one. Any procedure nested within this procedure is also defined to be at level one; however, its variables and body are at level two. This method of enumerating levels continues for each procedure nested within another one. Note carefully that the body and local variables of a procedure are always located one level higher than the level at which the procedure itself is defined.

Our main program with nested procedures **B** and **C** can be diagrammed as follows:

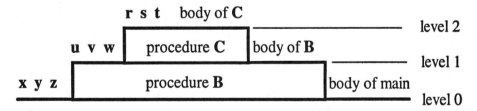

Figure 4.10
Levels in a nested program.

The body and variables for the main program are shown residing at level 0. In addition, procedure **B** sits on level 0. This is to demonstrate that the procedure is defined at this level. Its body, variables, and nested procedure are situated on top of the step that represents procedure **B**. This indicates that they are defined at level one. Likewise, although procedure **C** is defined at level 1, its body and variables are at level 2.

Now let's start looking at how the **Stack** develops as the program runs. As the main program starts running, the **Stack** is initialized, as shown below on the left:

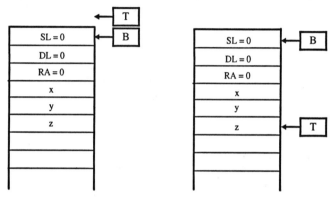

Figure 4.11
Main program stack frame initially and after main program's INT instruction.

The **B** register is set to point to the first location in the **Stack**. The **T** register actually points to the location before the **Stack**. Initial values of zero are given to the static link (SL), dynamic link (DL), and return address (RA). The last zero is important. Whenever there is an OPR 0, 0 instruction is executed and the return address value is placed into the **P** register. In all other cases, the return address will point somewhere in the actual **Code**, which means the value will be non-zero. A return from the main program will put a zero in the **P** register. This is how the P-Machine recognizes the end of the program and terminates.

The first instruction executed by the main program or a procedure will be an INT instruction that increments the **T** register by three plus the number of local variables. This causes the **T** register to point to the last local variable. The action for our main program with three variables is shown in Figure 4.11 on the right hand side.

The variables local to the main program are accessible at an offset from the **B** register. For instance, in Figure 4.11, **x** is offset by three locations, **y** is offset by 4, and **z** is offset by 5.

So far, everything is straightforward. Now, let's make it more interesting. Assume the main program calls procedure **B**. This will cause a new stack-frame for procedure **B**. One of the major concerns when transferring to a procedure's code is how to return to the caller at the end of the procedure. Since the **P** register is incremented after each fetch instruction, at the time of the call, the **P** register is pointing to the location following the CAL instruction. This is the location where we need to return. The question is where to store this value. With the P-Machine, the answer is on the **Stack** in the "return address" field in the new stack frame.

The **B** register is defined as pointing to the stack frame for the current procedure. This means that the register must be changed to point to the new stack frame. It no longer can point to the caller's stack frame. Again, we must worry about how to restore the register's value when we return from the new procedure. The solution is to save the old **B** register value in the dynamic link of the new stack frame. When returning from the procedure, we simply place this value back into the **B** register. The name dynamic link is used to indicate that this linkage shows the sequence in which one procedure has called the next at run-time. It is possible to determine the calling history by tracing up the dynamic link. We must remember, however, that the basic purpose for the dynamic link is to return the **B** register to the proper location when returning from the current procedure. The main purpose is NOT to establish a history of procedure calls, but that *is* a definite byproduct.

Once again, the first instruction of the new procedure (i.e., procedure **B**) is an INT that moves the **T** register from where it was left by the CAL instruction (i.e., pointing to the end of the calling code's stack frame) to where it should be (i.e., pointing to the last local variable of the new procedure). The increment is three plus the number of local variables. The "three" is required so that the register steps over the three locations that hold the static link, dynamic link, and return address.

Figure 4.12 shows the final result. The arrow from the dynamic link of the new procedure to the static link of the calling procedure (or program) is meant to show that it points to where the **B** register pointed to before the call was made.

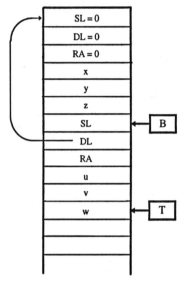

Figure 4.12
The stack after the main program calls procedure B and after the T register is incremented.

As was true for the main program, the variables that are local to procedure **B** are accessible as an offset from the new stack frame pointed to by the **B** register.

Now let's make it more interesting again. Let's assume that procedure **B** calls procedure **C**. Once again, a new stack frame is created. The new return address is saved in the stack frame. The location previously pointed to by the **B** register is saved in the new stack frame's dynamic link. The **B** register is modified to point to the new stack frame.

As usual, the first instruction of procedure **C** is an INT that moves the **T** register from where it was left by the CAL instruction (i.e., pointing to the end of the **B**'s stack frame) to where it should be (i.e., pointing to the last local variable of procedure **C**). As before, the increment is three plus the number of local variables. One of the purposes for this adjustment of the **T** register is to make room on the **Stack** for the local variables. The variables that are local to procedure **C** can be accessed at offsets from the **B** register.

Figure 4.13 shows the final result of all these actions.

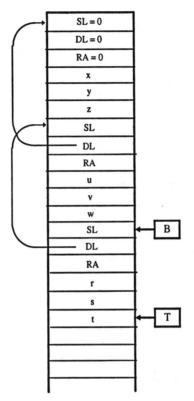

Figure 4.13
The stack after the procedure B calls procedure C and the T register is incremented.

Now we can start talking about variables that are not local to the current procedure. It will help to look at Figure 4.10. It corresponds to the **Stack** layout in Figure 4.13. Since procedure **C** has just been called, we are executing in the body of **C**. The local variables are **r, s,** and **t.** As was mentioned before, these variables can be accessed directly from the **B** register. Whenever a reference is made to a variable that is not local to the procedure, the compiler will try to find the variable in the next level down. If the variable can't be found there, the compiler will search in the next level below that. Of course this terminates when the compiler reaches level zero. Assume the variable being searched for is found at a particular level. If a variable of the same name also exists at an outer nesting (i.e., lower level), the inner occurrence (i.e., higher level) is used. As long as two variables with the same name are at different levels, they are not multiply defined. This protocol for searching through successively outer nesting levels is generally referred to as the scope rules. The rules tell us which variables are available from any given place in the program. One more rule must be mentioned; although we can search into lower levels, we are NEVER permitted to search into even higher levels than those at which we are presently operating.

How do we access these external variables? A quick glance at Figure 4.13 might lead us to think that the dynamic link could be used. For instance, from the body of procedure **C**, the variables **u**, **v**, and **w** are one level down and the variables **x**, **y**, and **z** are two levels down. (This can be seen in Figure 4.10.) Figure 4.13 shows that variables **u**, **v**, and **w** are one step down the dynamic link and **x**, **y**, and **z** are two steps down. There seems to be a great correspondence here.

Sometimes, things are just too good to be true. This is one of those times.

Assume that procedure **C** makes a recursive call to procedure **B**. This will set up another stack frame. As usual, the dynamic link of this stack frame points to the stack frame of the procedure that called the new one. In this case, the link for this instance of procedure **B** will be pointing to the frame for procedure **C**. If it were true that the dynamic link pointed to the external variables one level down, then procedure **C** would be one level below procedure **B**. A glance at Figure 4.10 will show you that this is not true. The main program is one level down from procedure **B**.

We need another approach. Let's take a longer look at Figure 4.10. Notice that the relationships between the procedures and the variables do not change; they are static. What we need is a pointer that always represents these static relationships. Well, that's why the remaining link in the stack frame is called the static link.

Next, we need a technique for determining where the static link should point while the new stack frame is created. The dynamic link pointed to the correct place when the main program called **B**, and when **B** subsequently called **C**. Obviously, the static link should point to the same place in these cases. Where we ran into trouble was when we made a recursive call.

We need a way to tell the difference between a recursive call and the earlier type of call. It turns out that *level difference* supplies the clue. The body of the main program is said to be at level 0. (Refer to Figure 4.10.) Its variables are also at level 0. Not only that, but procedure **B** is *defined* at level 0. When a call is made from the main program to procedure **B**, the level difference between where we are and where we want to go is zero.

$$\begin{array}{r} \text{level from which we are making the call} = \quad 0 \\ \underline{- \text{ level at which the destination is } \textit{defined} = \quad 0} \\ 0 \end{array}$$

When this level difference is zero, the static link of the new stack frame will point to the stack frame of the caller.

On the other hand, recursive calls will have a non-zero level difference. The body of procedure **C** is at level 2. Procedure **B** is defined at level 0. When procedure **C** calls **B**, we have a level difference of 2.

$$\begin{array}{r} \text{level from which we are making the call} = \quad 2 \\ \underline{- \text{ level at which the destination is } \textit{defined} = \quad 0} \\ 2 \end{array}$$

When the level difference is non-zero, instead of pointing to the caller's stack frame, we trace down the caller's static link a number of steps equivalent to the level difference. The static link of the new stack frame must point to the location where our trip down the caller's static link ended. For instance, when **C** calls **B**, two steps down, **C**'s static link will end up pointing to the main program's stack frame. This means that the static link of the new stack frame for procedure **B** will point to the main program's stack frame. This is as it should be. One level down from the body of **B** is the main program. The **x**, **y**, and **z** variables of the main program are one step down the static link from the new stack frame for procedure **B**.

The CAL P-Instruction is used to make a procedure call. The *lev* field of this command will contain the level difference as calculated above. The P-Machine will use this value to tell how many steps to take down the caller's static link to find the location that the static link of the new stack frame must point. Of course, when the level difference is zero, the static link points directly to the caller's stack frame, (i.e., zero steps down the caller's static link).

Our final stack frame is shown in Figure 4.14.

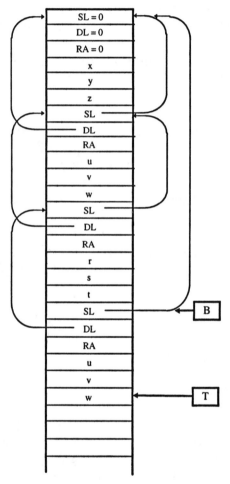

Figure 4.14
The stack after procedure C calls procedure B, showing both static and dynamic links.

All variables external to a given procedure are accessed by the static link. Each LOD and STO instruction contains a level difference value in the *lev* field. This level difference value is calculated in much the same way as the same field was determined in the CAL instruction. For instance, if an instruction in the body of procedure **B** refers to variable **x**, which is local to the main program, the calculation is as follows:

$$\begin{array}{r} \text{level of the body of code we are presently at} = 1 \\ \underline{- \text{ level at which the target variable is } \textit{defined} = 0} \\ 1 \end{array}$$

This value tells how many steps we must go down the static link to find the stack frame containing the desired variable. Once we reach the proper level, the variable can be found at an offset from where the final link is pointing. For instance, the variable **x** is at an offset of three. This value goes in the *adr* field of the LOD or STO instruction. If the variable is local, the *lev* field will be 0. The value in the *adr* field in this case represents the offset from the location pointed to by the **B** register.

We have mentioned in the discussion above that the LOD, STO, and CAL instructions all require a mechanism for tracing down the static link. If you examine the notes attached to Table 4.5, you will see a built-in function named **base**(*lev*). This can be interpreted as microcode built into the P-Machine to trace down the static link by the proper number of steps (as dictated by the *lev* field in the P-Instruction). This is how the P-Machine is able to handle local and external variables and make normal and recursive procedure calls.

4.11 A SYMBOL TABLE

Compilers use a symbol table to save information about all the identifiers used in a program. The symbol assigned to the identifier is stored in a field known as *name*.

Besides the symbolic name itself, the table must contain additional information about the symbol. The form of this information is often somewhat dependent on both the source code and the target processor. The previous section has shown us that in our target processor, the P-Machine, it is very important to know at which source code level a symbol is defined. Therefore, our symbol table will store this information in a field known as *level*.

In addition, for a variable definition, the table contains an offset from the beginning of the appropriate stack frame to where the particular identifier is stored. In the case of a procedure definition, the symbol table will indicate where the procedure begins in the **Code** segment. For constant definitions, the value assigned to the constant will be kept in the symbol table. All of these values will be kept in a field known as *value*.

One additional piece of information should be kept in the symbol table. Our table contains definitions for constants, variables, and procedures. Each of these will most likely be handled differently by the compiler. Notice for instance, that each has a different meaning for the value in the *value* field. To handle this diversity, the symbol table will contain another field that defines whether the symbol is a constant, variable, or procedure name. This will be known as the *kind* field.

These four fields, *name*, *kind*, *level*, and *value*, are the basic fields that our symbol table needs to handle variable definitions.

4.12 PRODUCING THE TARGET CODE

In this section, we shall examine the P-Code that must be generated to perform many of the routine operations of a program. We will start by looking at assignment statements (which we've covered to some extent already) and then look at some other types of statements.

Note: Many of the examples that follow use an abbreviated form of P-Code: *lev* fields that are always "0" are omitted, the *lev* and *adr* fields for variables are replaced by the variable symbols themselves, and the *adr* fields of OPR and CSP instructions are replaced by appropriate mathematical symbols or other helpful notations.

4.12.1 ASSIGNMENT STATEMENTS

Assignment statements are accomplished on the P-Machine by pushing the proper constants or variables on the **Stack** and performing arithmetic operations on the element(s) at the top of the **Stack**. The final result is popped off the **Stack** and placed in the assignment variable's location. Of course, the pushes and **Stack** operations must be done in the correct order to get the right result.

Constant values are pushed onto the **Stack** using the LIT P-Instruction. If the constant is expressed as a symbol in the symbol table, the value in the *adr* field of the instruction comes directly from the *addr* field in the symbol table. If, however, the constant is expressed as a numeric value, the *adr* field of the instruction will be this numeric value.

The assignment statement, "*A := B + C * (D - E)*" would be performed by the following P-Code:

```
LOD   B
LOD   C
LOD   D
LOD   E
OPR   -
OPR   *
OPR   +
STO   A
```

The sequence of OPR instructions was suggested during our study of top-down parsing. In Figure 4.8, the subtraction operation is closest to the bottom. This indicates that it should be done first. Likewise, working up the parse tree will give us the multiplication and addition operations in that order. Refer to Section 4.7 if you need to review this area. There will be more coverage in the next chapter of exactly how this code is generated.

The last operation in an assignment statement is the STO instruction. We will encounter other statements that require an *expression* in their production rule (i.e., syntax diagram). The only difference between a simple expression and an assignment statement is that an expression does not end with an STO instruction. Instead, the result of the expression is left on the top of the **Stack**.

4.12.2 INPUT AND OUTPUT STATEMENTS

One of the statements that requires an expression is the write statement. This is seen in Figure 4.15.

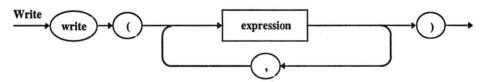

Figure 4.15
Syntax diagram for a typical write statement.

A write statement such as "WRITE(B + C * (D – E))" would produce the following P-Code:

```
LOD   B
LOD   C
LOD   D
LOD   E
OPR   -
OPR   *
OPR   +
CSP   Write_int
```

where the CSP instruction pops an integer of the top of **Stack** and writes it to the standard output. The integer is, obviously, the result of the expression inside of the parentheses.

A read statement is used to read values from the input and stores them into a variable's location. The syntax diagram is shown in Figure 4.16.

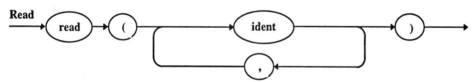

Figure 4.16
Syntax diagram of a typical read statement.

A read statement such as "READ(A)" would produce the following P-Code:

```
CSP   read_int
STO   A
```

where the CSP instruction reads an integer from the standard input and pushes it onto the **Stack**.

It is instructive to compare the P-Code that is generated for the assignment statement with the combined P-Code generated for the output and input statements.

4.12.3 CONDITIONAL STATEMENTS

The last type of statement we shall study here shall be the conditional statements. This type of statement is used to change the flow of control within the program. An if statement allows the program to go to one of two possible locations depending on a specific condition. The while statement causes the program to repeat a section of code as long as some designated condition remains true.

The syntax diagram (Figure 4.17) for a simple IF statement could be:

Figure 4.17
Syntax diagram for a simple IF statement.

You will notice that this simple if statement does not have an else clause. That's okay; this form will get the point across. You may also notice that, although the statement has three terminal symbols (i.e., keywords), it has two non-terminals. These non-terminals are a bit of a problem. These areas can contain unique code depending on the intended usage of the statement. We don't know what will be put there. When we attempt to list the P-Code produced by the if statement, the best we can do is use a skeletal form that shows where the code for these non-terminals would go—without attempting to show any specific code.

The concept behind this form of the IF statement is that it controls whether the statements in the "statement list" are executed depending on the value of the "condition." We can assume that the condition is a special kind of expression that leaves a *conditional value* on the top of the **Stack**. Normally, a value of zero is interpreted as meaning "false." Various values are used for "true." Some compilers use +1, others use –1. I will assume that *any* non-zero value is "true."

The mechanism that is used to make the IF statement work is the JPC instruction. The JPC statement compares the value of its *lev* field with the conditional value on the top of the **Stack** and branches over the statement list if they are the same. The conditional value is popped off the **Stack** in the process. The important consideration is to determine which conditional value to use in the JPC instruction. We are supposed to execute the statement list if the conditional value is true—that means that we should skip over the list if the condition is false.

The skeletal form of the IF statement is:

```
    ---      ---        ! P-Code for
    ---      ---        ! the condition
    ---      ---        ! section.
    JPC      0,L1       ! skip if false.
    ---      ---        ! P-Code for
    ---      ---        ! the statement
    ---      ---        ! list section.
L1:
```

I have used the label, L1, to indicate the destination of the JPC statement. Most compilers would just place the actual address in the JPC statement instead of using the label. On the other hand, labels make it easier for us to follow the generated P-Code.

The remaining conditional statement that I will cover at this time is the while statement (illustrated in Figure 4.18). The syntax diagram for a while statement has exactly the same structure as the if statement.

Figure 4.18
Syntax diagram for a while statement.

The major difference between the two statements is that the while statement repeats the statement list section as long as the condition is true. This requires a slight change in the skeletal model for the generated P-Code. The JPC still performs its jump on a false condition. However, at the end of the statement list, we must jump back to the beginning of the condition evaluating P-Code. This requires an unconditional JMP instruction at the end of the statement list section. We also will use another label for the JMP instruction. The skeletal model for the while statement is as follows:

```
L2: ---      ---      ! P-Code for
    ---      ---      ! the condition
    ---      ---      ! section.
    JPC      0,L1     ! skip if false.
    ---      ---      ! P-Code for
    ---      ---      ! the statement
    ---      ---      ! list section.
    JMP      L2       ! try it again.
L1:
```

4.13 WRAP-UP AND FURTHER READING

This chapter has examined many of the basic concepts of compiler design. The bulk of the information has been on parsing techniques. After this, we looked at the P-Machine that we will be using as a target machine. We ended by examining some of the specific forms of generated code. In the next chapter, we will put much of this together and develop an actual compiler.

A few books are listed here for additional reading. For those interested in further study in compiler design, the [Aho 1988] text is suggested. The treatment of operator precedence parsing found in this chapter is modeled on [Calingaert 1979]. The P-Machine is described in [Wirth 1976] and further developed in [Chung 1978].

REFERENCES

[Aho 1988] Aho, Alfred V., Ravi Sethi, Jeffrey D. Ullman, *Compilers, Principals, Techniques, and Tools*, Reading, MA: Addison–Wesley Publishing Company, 1988.

[Calingaert 1979] Calingaert, Peter, *Assemblers, Compilers, and Program Translation*, New York, NY: Computer Science Press, 1979, pp. 142–150.

[Chung 1978] Chung, Kin-Man, Herbert Yuen, "A 'Tiny' Pascal Compiler," *Byte Magazine*, September, 1978, pp. 58–65; 148–154.

[Wirth 1976] Wirth, Niklaus, *Algorithms + Data Structures = Programs*, pp. 331–347. Englewood Cliffs, NJ: Prentice Hall, Inc., 1976.

CHAPTER 5

Compiler Case Study: Designing the Lil'LuxLyk Compiler

The goal of this chapter is to design our own compiler. We have just about everything we need at this time. We have an insight into top-down parsing by recursive descent. We have the description of the target machine. What we don't have is a description of the source language. It's time to satisfy that need. We will do this in layers using syntax diagrams. Syntax diagrams are used instead of BNF production rules because they make it easier to visualize the desired format. Once we define the language, which we shall call *Lil'LuxLyk*, we will proceed with designing the compiler.

5.1 THE LIL'LUXLYK LANGUAGE

Figure 5.1 shows the overall or top-level view of a Lil'LuxLyk program. The primary goal of this level is to define symbols. The diagrams for the actual code of the program will be given at a lower level.

A program is made up of a *block* terminated by a period. It should be noted that the main program is the only block to end with a period. Procedure blocks are terminated by a semicolon.

Each block is made up of two sections—the *declaration* section is where all of the user symbols are defined and placed in the symbol table; the *body* section is where the actual algorithm of the program is written.

Constants, variables, and procedures can be defined in any order in the declarations section. Constants are introduced by the keyword CONST. The keyword is followed by the *constant declaration* section. Several constants can be introduced by a single constant declaration section. The constants are declared by a symbolic name followed by a "=", a numeric value, and ending with a semicolon. Variables are introduced by the keyword VAR. This keyword is followed by a *variable declaration* section. Several variables may be defined here by separating their symbolic names by commas and terminating the list with a semicolon. Procedures are introduced by the keyword

111

PROCEDURE. This is followed by the *procedure declaration* section. Only one procedure can be defined in each procedure declaration. It is declared as a symbolic name followed by a semicolon followed by a block and terminated with a semicolon.

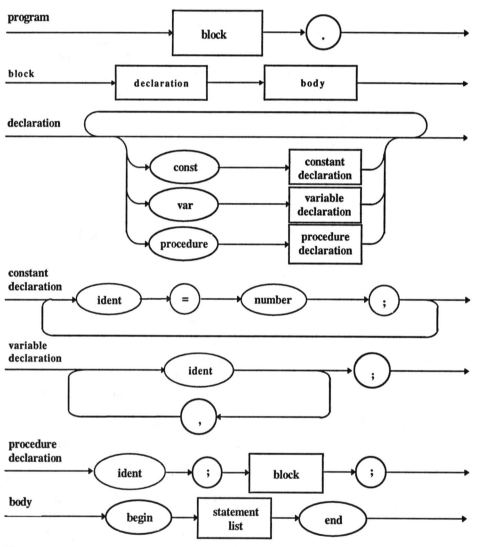

Figure 5.1
Diagram of the top level Lil'LuxLyk syntax.

The body begins with the keyword BEGIN. It is followed by a *statement list* that is terminated with the END keyword. The statements are shown in Figure 5.2.

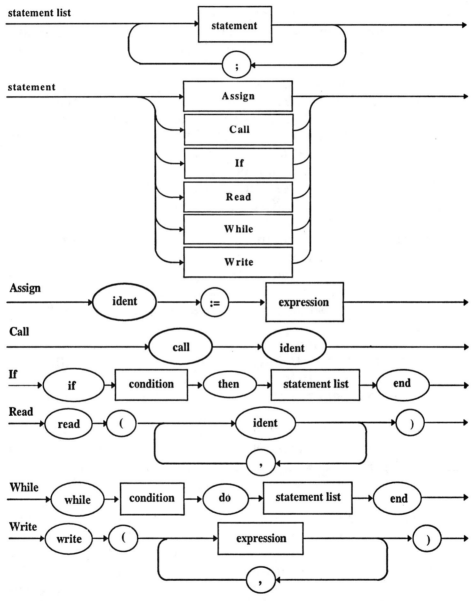

Figure 5.2
Syntax diagrams of the Lil'LuxLyk statements.

The statement list is made up of a series of individual statements separated by semicolons. Valid statements in the Lil'LuxLyk language include *assign, call, if, read, while,* and *write.*

The assign, or assignment, statement consists of an *ident* or identifier followed by ":=" followed by an *expression.* The result of the expression will be stored in the location associated with the identifier.

The call statement starts with the keyword CALL followed by an identifier that is the name of the procedure being called.

The if statement begins with the keyword IF. This is followed by a special kind of expression known as a *condition.* The condition produces a value of either false (i.e., 0) or true (i.e., anything but 0). The condition is followed by the THEN keyword. This is followed by a statement list terminated by an END keyword. The objective of the if statement is to skip over the statement list if the result of the condition is false.

The read statement begins with the keyword READ followed by a left parenthesis. Next comes a list of identifiers separated by commas and terminated with a right parenthesis. The purpose of the read statement is to read values entered from the keyboard and store them in the variables associated with the identifiers in the list.

The while statement has a form much like that of the if statement, except that it begins with the keyword WHILE and uses the DO keyword instead of THEN. The purpose of the while statement is to repeat the statement list as long as the condition remains true.

The write statement begins with the keyword WRITE followed by a left parenthesis. Next comes a series of expressions separated by commas and terminated with a right parenthesis. The purpose of the write statement is to evaluate each expression in the list and output the result to the computer screen.

We still need to examine the expression and condition syntax. They are shown in Figure 5.3. We have seen a form of the expression syntax in the previous chapter. Our new form is slightly more robust in that an expression may be introduced by a unary plus or minus. An additional enhancement to the expression syntax is the use of "%" between factors to signify module division.

Condition is a new construction that we haven't seen before. A condition can come in one of three forms. The first results in a value of true if its accompanying expression is odd. The second form is a single expression. The third form compares the values of two expressions and returns a true or false depending on the type of relational operation used to compare the results.

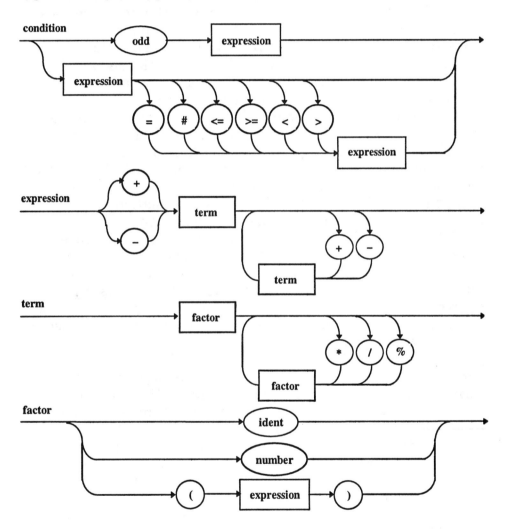

Figure 5.3
Syntax diagrams of the Lil'LuxLyk expressions.

5.2 THE BASIC STRUCTURE OF THE COMPILER

In the previous chapter, we learned that many compilers create a node table that represents the source program. The task of creating a data structure for this table could be quite an effort in itself. Instead, I shall use the *class* construction of **C++** to build the table rather painlessly. We will build the table using a single class called *ParseNode*; it represents any of the non-terminals in the syntax diagrams. In fact, all of the non-terminals in the previous syntax diagrams shall be represented by a distinct class. All of these individual classes, however, shall inherit the basic ParseNode class. Any non-terminal definition that contains other non-terminals in its syntax diagram will contain analogous ParseNodes within its corresponding class definition. As the source code is parsed, these inner ParseNodes will be expanded (recursively), eventually recreating the fundamental node table. Some non-terminal definitions contain choices between multiple terminal symbols, such as the choice between a plus or a minus between terms in an expression. This information will also be saved in the private section of the class definition.

The node table is built while parsing the source code. The ParseNode class for each non-terminal has a member function called Parse, which is called to parse that particular non-terminal. When the `Parse` member function reaches a point in its syntax definition that refers to another non-terminal, it will create a new ParseNode for that construction, save the object in its private area, and then call its Parse function to continue parsing the source. After the new Parse function has finished parsing the code appropriate to its syntactic definition, it returns control to the function that called it. In this way, bit by bit, the complete node tree structure is built up. At the end, we have a structure very much like the one in Figure 4.8.

Once the complete node table has been created, we need to generate code from it. The ParseNode class has an additional member function, `Generate`, that performs this role. Each ParseNode generates the P-Code specific to itself. From time to time it will call the Generate function of any of the ParseNodes embedded within its private area. Of course, this must be done at the proper time in order to generate the correct output code. The timing is determined by the original syntax of the source. In due time, this process produces the complete output code.

Thus, the two major member functions of every ParseNode correspond to the two phases of compiling, namely, analysis and synthesis.

After the description above, it's time to actually look at the ParseNode. The fundamental ParseNode class definition is shown in Figure 5.4.

```
class ParseNode                     // the basic parse tree node
{
public:
                ParseNode()  {}     // Constructor
    virtual     ~ParseNode() {}     // Destructor
    virtual void Parse()     {}     // Parse the source code for this node
    virtual void Generate()  {}     // Generate the output code for the node
};
```

Figure 5.4
The fundamental ParseNode class.

As was mentioned above, any non-terminal definition that contains other non-terminals in its syntax diagram will contain analogous ParseNodes within its corresponding class definition. For most classes, the number of references is explicit. The *StatementList* class, however, collects an indeterminate number of individual *Statements* together. The Parser must gather all of these ParseNodes together so they can later be passed to the Generate function. They must be kept in the same order that they appeared in the source. A queue comes to mind. We could create our own queues when we need them, but there is an easier way. We shall use a library of standard containers.

The ISO and ANSI communities have proposed the use of the Standard Template Library (i.e., STL) for just this sort of situation. We can use the STL to create a queue of pointers to ParseNodes. This is defined as shown in Figure 5.5.

```
#include <queue>                    // defines a queue
#include <list>                     // ...used by the queue

typedef queue<ParseNode *, list<ParseNode *> > parseQ;
```

Figure 5.5
Definition of the queue used to contain ParseNodes.

The typedef statement defines a new *data type* named "*parseQ*." This new type is a queue of pointers to objects of the ParseNode class. STL queues are called adapters, which means they are built on top of other containers. This queue is made from a list. That is why there is a reference to "list" in the definition of parseQ.

We need several other basic definitions before we can get started. We will be parsing *Tokens* so we need to know what they look like. We also need to have some idea of how new tokens are obtained when needed. For now, we shall just look at the definitions. We shall examine the implementations later. Tokens are defined in Figure 5.6.

```
enum TokenType { //  generic symbols:
                noToken, Ident,     Number,
                //  keyword symbols:
                beginSym, callSym,  constSym,  doSym,    elseSym, endSym,
                ifSym,    oddSym,   procSym,    readSym,  thenSym, varSym,
                whileSym, writeSym,
                //  punctuation symbols:
                Plus,     Minus,    Times,     Slash,    Percent,
                Equal,    notEqual, lessEqual, Less,     Greater,
                grtrEqual,
                Becomes,  Period,   Comma,     Semicol,  lParen,  rParen
            };

struct Token
{
  TokenType  Token;             // enumerated type of the Token
  string    *Value;             // character string for this Token
};

class Symbol
{
public:
            Symbol();             // Lex analyser constructor
  Token    *getNewSymbol();       // returns the next Token
  Token    *getSymbol();          // returns the same Token again
  void      Message(char *str);   // writes error message
};
```

Figure 5.6
Definition of Lil'LuxLyk Tokens, TokenTypes, and the lexical analyzer.

TokenType is basically an enumeration of the various types of tokens used by the compiler. This allows us to refer to the tokens by name instead of by numbers, which would be hard to remember. A *Token*, itself, is a structure that consists of two fields. The first tells the TokenType of the token. The second one records the specific string of characters that makes up the token.

The lexical analyzer is provided by a class named *"Symbol."* I have omitted the private data from the class definition for the present time. The important thing about the Symbol class is that it has two member functions. The "getNewSymbol" function returns the next token in the source code. The "getSymbol" function returns the current token. We will soon find that this is necessary. There is also a "Message" function to provide output messages to the user. These messages will automatically contain a reference to the line number in the source code.

The highest level of parsing classes (which we shall examine first) is primarily concerned with storing user defined symbols in a symbol table. Therefore, we must look at the definition of the *SymbolTable* class. This is done in Figure 5.7.

```
class SymbolTable
{
public:
        SymbolTable();              // constructor

   void Enter    (string     name,   // symbol being entered in table
                  TokenType  kind,   // type of symbol (e.g. Constant...)
                  int        level,  // nesting level of symbol
                  int        value,  // value of the symbol
                  int        tx);    // index location for storing in table

   int  Position(string      name,   // symbol begin sought
                 int         tx);     // index to search down from

   int  Examine (string     &name,   // symbol at location
                 TokenType  &kind,   // kind of symbol
                 int        &level,  // nesting level of symbol
                 int        &value,  // value of symbol
                 int         tx);    // table index to examine

   int  FixValue(int         value,  // new value for the table entry
                 int         tx);     // index of entry to be modified
};
```

Figure 5.7
Definition of the Lil'LuxLyk symbol table.

Once again, I have left out the Private data section of the class definition. Note that most of the member functions have parameters for the four fields of a symbol table entry mentioned in Section 4.11: *name*, *kind*, *level*, and *value*. Entries are placed into the table sequentially. Each entry has an index number associated with it that shows where in this sequence the entry is located. A new parameter in all of the member functions, *tx*, tells where to place or find the entry in the sequence. The `Enter` function enters a single definition into the symbol table at index location tx. The `Position` function returns the index to where in the symbol table before index tx the symbol "name" can be found. The `Examine` function returns the field values from a specific index location in the table. Finally, the `FixValue` function is used to modify the value at a specific entry in the table.

Before symbols get into the symbol table, they go through the Parser. They are detected by the Parse function and are stored by the Generate function. The symbols and the related information must be saved in some form to be passed between the two functions. This form is a structure known as *DeclObj*. A glance at the syntax diagrams shows us that several symbols may be collected at one time. This means that we often need a container to hold them as they pass between the Parse and Generate functions. For this we use another queue called the *declQ*. The declaration structure and queue are defined as shown in Figure 5.8.

```
struct DeclObj                          // the basic identifier definition
{                                       // (holds definition temporarily)
    string          name;               //     name of symbol
    TokenType       kind;               //     type of variable (const, var)
    int             level;              //     nesting level of the symbol
    int             n_value;            //     numeric value of the symbol
    string          value;              //     string form of the number
};

typedef queue<DeclObj *, list<DeclObj *> > declQ;
```

Figure 5.8.
Definition of the DeclObj and the declQ.

Although the top level classes are primarily responsible for creating the symbol table, they will generate a small amount of code. There must be a class defined to hold the code that gets generated. This class, called *Code*, is shown in Figure 5.9. As usual, the private data is not presented at this time. Its member functions are quite similar to SymbolTable. There is an `Enter` function to save individual instructions. Instructions are stored sequentially and the index is maintained by the Code class itself. The Enter function returns the location of the next free code location by its `cx` parameter. The `Fetch` function retrieves the instruction at a specific location. The `FixValue` function is used to modify the address value at a specific location. The `CurrentLoc` function returns the location where the next instruction will be stored.

Coupled with the Code class is the *FunctType* enumeration that defines the various P-Code operation codes.

Another companion class is called *Level*. It is used to keep track of the nesting level of Lil'LuxLyk procedures within other procedures. It has member functions that allow us to increment and decrement the value of the level. It also has a member function to get the current level from the class.

```
enum FunctType  { OPR, LIT, LOD, STO,   CAL, INT, JMP, JPC, CSP  };

class Code
{
public:
            Code();                         // constructor
    void    Enter       (FunctType  fct,    // type of function (e.g. OPR...)
                         int        level,  // nesting level of code
                         int        value,  // value of the code
                         int        &cx);   // location for next instr
    int     Fetch       (FunctType  &fct,   // type of function
                         int        &level, // nesting level of instr
                         int        &value, // value of code
                         int        cx);    // code location to examine
    int     FixValue    (int        value,  // new value for the instr
                         int        cx);    // location of instr to be modified
    int     CurrentLoc();                   // return current location
};

class Level
{
public:
            Level();                        // constructor
    void    inc();                          // raise the nesting level
    void    dec();                          // lower the nesting level
    int     get();                          // get the nesting level
};
```

Figure 5.9
The Lil'LuxLyk Code and Level classes.

We are now ready to examine the top level of the compiler.

5.3 PARSING THE TOP LEVEL

The technique for writing the code for the `Parser` member functions can almost be stated as "look at the syntax diagram and write code to describe it." This is typified by the *Program* class. For instance, compare the Parse function in Figure 5.10 with the syntax diagram in Figure 5.1.

```
Symbol *Sym;              // lex analyser
Code    code;             // code ADT
Level   level;            // nesting level

class Program:     public ParseNode      // The Program (i.e., root) Node
{
    Block          *block;
public:
                    Program();
    virtual void    Parse();
    virtual void    Generate();
};

Program::Program()      // The Program (i.e., root) Node
{  Sym = new Symbol();   }

void  Program::Parse()
{
    Token  *token;

    block = new Block;
    block->Parse();
    block->Generate();
    delete block;

    token = Sym->getSymbol();
    if (token->Token != Period)
        Sym->Message("'.' expected");
}
```

Figure 5.10
The Lil'LuxLyk Program class.

The first part of Figure 5.10 is the definition of the Program class. Notice that it inherits the ParseNode class. The syntax diagram for "program" shows that it contains a non-terminal "block." Therefore, a (pointer to a) Block ParseNode is included in the private section of the Program class definition. This approach will be used in future ParseNodes as well; that is, the private data will contain ParseNodes for each non-terminal found in the syntax diagram that corresponds to the class being defined.

There is a constructor and two member functions in the public part of the Program class definition.

The code for the constructor is the next item in Figure 5.10. (It is the function `Program::Program`.) The lexical analyzer must be globally accessible to all parsing functions. The only action of the Program constructor is to create a new instance of the Symbol class. All Parser functions can now reference *Sym* to get tokens. There are two other global classes shown in Figure 5.10, *code* and *level*. These are initialized differently and do not need to be instantiated by the Program constructor.

The code for the `Program::Parse` function demonstrates the general method used in these top level parser functions; that is, whenever a non-terminal is encountered in the syntax diagram, a new instance of a corresponding class is created and its Parse and Generate functions are called. Once this is complete, the instance of the class may be deleted. In this case, the *Block* class is the one so used. After this, the Program parser checks to make sure that the current token is a Period. At this point, our Parser has, in effect, parsed the complete program and stored all of its P-Code.

Oddly enough, the `Program::Generate` function will be the last function that we shall examine.

Now we shall look at the development of the Block class. We need to keep track of some more information at this point, that is, where in the symbol table to store the next symbol and, in the case of variables, what the offset from the **B** register is for the variable. Within a particular class, *dx* will keep track of the **B** register offset and *tx* will keep track of the table index. In some cases it will be necessary to keep track of the initial value that tx had upon first constructing an instance of the class. In this case, the variable *tx0* will be used. One or more of these variables will be passed as parameters to the constructor. Their values will be saved in the private data of the class as *dsp_x*, *tbl_x*, and *tbl_x0*, respectively. The Parse and Generate functions will modify one or more of these values. The updated values will be returned by a member function called `Update_x`. This will be seen in the code for the Block class. Most of the rest of the top level parsing classes that we shall see from now on shall have the Update_x member function in addition to the constructor, Parse, and Generate.

The Block class is shown in Figure 5.11. The constructor saves the current values of tbl_x and tbl_x0. It sets dsp_x to 0.

The Block::Parse function parses the two non-terminals indicated in the syntax diagram, that is, the declaration section and the body section.

```
class Block:        public ParseNode  // The Program or Procedure Block Node
{
    Declaration     *declar;
    Body            *body;
    int             tbl_x, tbl_x0;    // index into symbol table
    int             dsp_x;            // base register offsets
    int             pcd_x;            // index into code area
public:
                    Block(int  tx = 0);
    virtual void    Parse();
    virtual void    Generate() { }
    virtual void    Update_x(int &tx,  int &dx);
};

Block::Block(int  tx)
{
    tbl_x = tx;     tbl_x0 = tx;
    dsp_x = 0;
}

void  Block::Parse()
{
    Token       *token;

    code.Enter (JMP, 0, 0, pcd_x);
    symbolTable.FixValue ( pcd_x - 1,   tbl_x0 );

    if (level.get() > 0)
    {
        token = Sym->getNewSymbol();
        if (token->Token != Semicol)  Sym->Message("`;' expected");
    }

    declar = new Declaration(tbl_x);
    declar->Parse();
    declar->Generate();
    declar->Update_x(tbl_x, dsp_x);
    delete declar;

    body = new Body(tbl_x, dsp_x, tbl_x0);
    body->Parse();
    body->Generate();
    body->Update_x(tbl_x, dsp_x);
    delete body;
}

void  Block::Update_x(int &tx,  int &dx)
{   tx = tbl_x;     dx = dsp_x;   }
```

Figure 5.11
The Lil'LuxLyk Block class.

The Parse function also contains one of the two cases where code is generated in the Parse code. The reason is that the JMP instruction just *has* to be generated before anything may be generated by the declaration or body sections located within the Parse function. (It is possible to avoid generating in the parser code by defining a dummy class that gets called at the same location in the parser. In this dummy class, the Parse section will do nothing and the Generate section will generate the JMP statement.) The generated P-Code will contain the JMP statement at the point where the block for the body of a Lil'LuxLyk program or one of its procedures is first encountered in the source code input to the compiler. This jump will point to the place in the P-Code where the first instruction of the body for that section is stored. Unfortunately, the location is not known when the jump is stored, so a zero is used in the address field that will be corrected later when the location becomes known. The location of the jump instruction is saved in the symbol table. This is used to point back to the instruction when it is time to correct its address.

A glance at the syntax diagrams shows that blocks for procedure declarations will be preceded by a semicolon while the block for the main code is not. This difference is handled by the if statement towards the beginning of the Block::Parse code.

The `Block::Generate` function is empty. All the necessary generation is to be done by the two ParseNodes in the Block class.

The `Block::Update_x` function returns the latest values of tbl_x and dsp_x. These values get modified when the Block parser calls the Declaration parser.

The *Declaration* class is responsible for parsing all of the various declarations in a Lil'LuxLyk program or procedure. It is shown in Figure 5.12. All of the effort of this class is done by the `Declaration::Parse` function, which does little more than dispatch to another declaration class that does the actual work.

```
class Declaration: public ParseNode     // The Declaration Dispatcher
{
    ConstDeclar   *constDeclar;
    VarDeclar     *varDeclar;
    ProcDeclar    *procDeclar;
    int            tbl_x;
    int            dsp_x;
public:
                   Declaration(int  tx);
    virtual void   Parse();
    virtual void   Generate() { }
    virtual void   Update_x(int &tx,  int &dx);
};

Declaration::Declaration(int  tx)
{
    tbl_x = tx; // table storage index
    dsp_x = 3;  // base offset value (leave room for SL, DL, & RA)
}

void  Declaration::Parse()
{
    Token      *token;
    TokenType  sym;

    token = Sym->getNewSymbol();    sym   = token->Token;
    while ( dclr_beg_sym.contains(sym) )
    {
        switch (sym)
        {
            case constSym:
                constDeclar = new ConstDeclar(tbl_x, dsp_x);
                constDeclar->Parse();    constDeclar->Generate();
                constDeclar->Update_x(tbl_x, dsp_x);
                delete constDeclar;
                break;
            case varSym:
                varDeclar   = new VarDeclar(tbl_x, dsp_x);
                varDeclar->Parse();       varDeclar->Generate();
                varDeclar->Update_x(tbl_x, dsp_x);
                delete varDeclar;
                break;
            case procSym:
                procDeclar  = new ProcDeclar(tbl_x, dsp_x);
                procDeclar->Parse();     procDeclar->Generate();
                procDeclar->Update_x(tbl_x, dsp_x);
                delete procDeclar;
                break;
        }
        token = Sym->getSymbol();    sym   = token->Token;
        if ( ! (  dclr_beg_sym.contains(sym)
               || stmt_beg_sym.contains(sym)
               || sym == Ident) )   // ident also begins a statement
        {   //        try to get back in sync
            Sym->Message("Declaration or statement expected");
            while ( ! ( dclr_beg_sym.contains(sym)
                     || stmt_beg_sym.contains(sym)
                     || sym == Ident
                     || sym == Period || sym == Semicol) )
            { token = Sym->getNewSymbol();    sym   = token->Token;  }
        }
    }
}

void  Declaration::Update_x(int &tx,  int &dx)
{ tx = tbl_x;    dx = dsp_x;  }
```

Figure 5.12
The Lil'LuxLyk Declaration class.

There is, however, one major thing that the Parse function does do. The function consists of a major loop that searches for a CONST, VAR, or PROCEDURE token. Once found, it creates an instance of the appropriate class to parse and generates entries in the symbol table. At the end of the loop, the function gets the next symbol from the source code. It should be either one of the declaration introducing keywords, CONST, VAR, or PROCEDURE, or it should be the BEGIN token that begins the source code of the program or procedure body. (It is also possible that the author of the code started the body code off with a statement. This is not a good idea, but we must check for it.) If one of the expected tokens is not found, the code in this function searches additional symbols looking for a valid token. The error recovery concepts discussed in Section 4.8 are put into practice at this point. Two special classes are used in the error recovery here, *dclr_beg_sym* and *stmt_beg_sym*. The contains(sym) method of these two classes returns "true" if the sym parameter is one that introduces a declaration or a statement respectively.

The *ConstDeclar* class, shown in Figure 5.13, is used to declare constants and place them in the symbol table.

```
class ConstDeclar: public ParseNode      // Node for declaring constants
{
    declQ           *constants;
    int             tbl_x;
    int             dsp_x;
public:
                    ConstDeclar(int tx,  int dx);
    virtual void    Parse();
    virtual void    Generate();
    virtual void    Update_x(int &tx,  int &dx);
};

ConstDeclar::ConstDeclar(int tx,  int dx)
{
    constants = new declQ;
    tbl_x = tx;   dsp_x = dx;
}

void  ConstDeclar::Parse()
{
    Token       *token;
    TokenType   sym;
    DeclObj     *constDef;

    token = Sym->getNewSymbol();   sym   = token->Token;
    do
    {
        if (sym == Ident)
        {
            constDef = new DeclObj;
```

```
        constDef->name  = *token->Value;
        constDef->kind  =  constSym;
        constDef->level =  level.get();
        token = Sym->getNewSymbol();            sym   = token->Token;
        if (sym == Equal || sym == Becomes)
        {
            if (sym == Becomes)  Sym->Message("Replace `:=' by `='");
            token = Sym->getNewSymbol();        sym   = token->Token;
            if (sym == Number)
            {
                constDef->value = *token->Value;
                constants->push(constDef);
                token = Sym->getNewSymbol();    sym   = token->Token;
            }
            else
                Sym->Message("Number expected");
        }
        else
            Sym->Message("`=' expected");
        }
    else
        Sym->Message("Identifier expected");
    if (sym == Semicol)
    {   token = Sym->getNewSymbol();            sym   = token->Token;   }
    else
        Sym->Message("`;' expected");
    }
    while (sym == Ident);
}

void  ConstDeclar::Generate()
{
    DeclObj     *constDef;
    int          numb;

    while ( ! constants->empty() )
    {
        constDef = constants->front();
        constants->pop();

        numb = atoi(constDef->value.data());

        symbolTable.Enter(constDef->name, constDef->kind, constDef->level,
                          numb,              ++tbl_x);
        delete constDef;
    }
    delete constants;
}

void  ConstDeclar::Update_x(int &tx,  int &dx)
{  tx = tbl_x;    dx = dsp_x;   }
```

Figure 5.13
The Lil'LuxLyk Constant Declaration class.

The ConstDeclar::Parse member function looks for the
following sequence of tokens: first an identifier, followed by an
equals sign, followed by a number, and terminated by a semicolon. If these tokens are found, the identifier's string value is

saved in a DeclObj structure, along with a "kind" of *constSym*, the current level, and the string of digits associated with the number. There are error messages in the routine if the expected tokens are not found where they are expected. There is also a warning message if an assignment token, ":=", is used instead of the equals token. Once all the required fields have been filled in, the DeclObj structure is placed on the *constants* queue. The function cycles back looking for another occurrence of the required sequence of tokens. The loop continues until a token is found that does not match what is expected at the beginning of the sequence, that is, an identifier.

The `ConstDeclar::Generate` member function removes the DeclObj structures from the queue one at a time. As each structure is removed, its value string is converted to an integer and entered into the symbol table along with the name, kind, and level fields. The tbl_x index is used to define where in the symbol table the entry will be stored. It is incremented before each insertion. The final value of tbl_x is obtained by the `ConstDeclar::Update_x` function. It is fed to the next declaration class accessed so that the storage sequence remains in order.

```
class VarDeclar:  public ParseNode      // Node for declaring variables
{
    declQ         *variables;
    int           tbl_x;
    int           dsp_x;
public:
                  VarDeclar(int tx,  int dx);
    virtual void  Parse();
    virtual void  Generate();
    virtual void  Update_x(int &tx,  int &dx);
};

VarDeclar::VarDeclar(int tx,  int dx)
{
    variables = new declQ;
    tbl_x = tx;    dsp_x = dx;
}

void  VarDeclar::Parse()
{
    Token      *token;
    TokenType  sym;
    DeclObj    *varDef;

    token = Sym->getNewSymbol();             sym   = token->Token;
    do
    {
       if (sym == Ident)
       {
          varDef = new DeclObj;
```

```
                varDef->name  = *token->Value;
                varDef->kind  =  varSym;
                varDef->level =  level.get();
                token = Sym->getNewSymbol();     sym   = token->Token;
                variables->push(varDef);
            }
            else
                Sym->Message("Identifier expected");
            while (sym == Comma)
            {
                token = Sym->getNewSymbol();     sym   = token->Token;
                if (sym == Ident)
                {
                    varDef = new DeclObj;
                    varDef->name  = *token->Value;
                    varDef->kind  =  varSym;
                    varDef->level =  level.get();
                    token = Sym->getNewSymbol();  sym   = token->Token;
                    variables->push(varDef);
                }
                else
                    Sym->Message("Identifier expected");
            }
            if (sym == Semicol)
            {  token = Sym->getNewSymbol();       sym   = token->Token;  }
            else
                Sym->Message("`;' expected");
        }
        while (sym == Ident);
    }

void  VarDeclar::Generate()
{
    DeclObj  *varDef;

    while ( ! variables->empty() )
    {
        varDef = variables->front();
        variables->pop();

        symbolTable.Enter(varDef->name,  varDef->kind,   varDef->level,
                          dsp_x++,        ++tbl_x);
        delete varDef;
    }
    delete variables;
}

void  VarDeclar::Update_x(int &tx,  int &dx)
{  tx = tbl_x;    dx = dsp_x;   }
```

Figure 5.14
The Lil'LuxLyk Variable Declaration class.

The code for the Lil'LuxLyk *VarDeclar* class, shown in Figure 5.14, is much simpler than the constant declaration class. The VarDeclar::Parse function looks for a sequence of identifiers separated by commas and terminated by a semicolon. As each identifier token is found, its string value is inserted into a DeclObj structure along with a "kind" of *varSym* and the current nesting level. The structures are each placed in the *variables* queue. This continues until the semicolon is found.

The `VarDeclar::Generate` member function removes the DeclObj structures from the queue one at a time. As each is removed, its symbolic name, kind, and level are placed into the symbol table. The value field of the table entry is supplied by the dsp_x variable. This value represents the offset from the **B** register to the variable being stored in the table. The value of dsp_x was initially set to three by the Declaration constructor. (This allows room for the static link, dynamic link, and return address on the runtime stack.) Dsp_x is incremented after each variable is entered into the symbol table so that the variables are stored in successive locations on the stack. The tbl_x index is used exactly the same way it was in the constant declaration class.

The *ProcDeclar* class is shown in Figure 5.15. It is a much more complicated Lil'LuxLyk class than the other declaration classes. Part of this complexity is due to the fact that it involves a recursive call to the Block class. To really understand what ProcDeclar does, one must re-examine the earlier classes all over again.

```
class ProcDeclar: public ParseNode     // Node for declaring procedures
{
   Block          *procedure;
   int            tbl_x;
   int            dsp_x;
public:
                  ProcDeclar(int tx,  int dx);
   virtual void   Parse();
   virtual void   Generate()  { }
   virtual void   Update_x(int &tx,  int &dx);
};

ProcDeclar::ProcDeclar(int tx,  int dx)
{  tbl_x = tx;   dsp_x = dx;   }

void  ProcDeclar::Parse()
{
   Token      *token;
   TokenType  sym;

   token = Sym->getNewSymbol();    sym   = token->Token;
   if (sym == Ident)
   {
     symbolTable.Enter(*token->Value, procSym, level.get(), 0, ++tbl_x);

     level.inc();
     procedure = new Block(tbl_x);
     procedure->Parse();
     procedure->Generate();
     level.dec();
```

```
   }
   else
      Sym->Message("Identifier expected");
   token = Sym->getSymbol();        sym   = token->Token;
   if (sym == Semicol)
   {  token = Sym->getNewSymbol();   sym   = token->Token;  }
   else
      Sym->Message("`;' expected");
}

void  ProcDeclar::Update_x(int &tx,  int &dx)
{  tx = tbl_x;    dx = dsp_x;  }
```

Figure 5.15
The Lil'LuxLyk Procedure Declaration class.

ProcDeclar::Parse looks for the identifier that names the procedure being declared. It then enters this name into the symbol table using a "kind" of *ProcSym* and the current nesting level. ProcDeclar is the other top level class where generation is done within the Parse member function. This is because the procedure name must be entered before its local variables and they will be entered when the Block class is called. Before this call is made, however, the nesting level is incremented. All variables local to the procedure will be defined at one level higher than the procedure's definition. The current value of tbl_x is passed to the new instance of Block. Thus, the constants, variables, and procedures local to this procedure shall be entered consecutively from our current location in the symbol table. The table index used for these table entries will be the tbl_x that is private to the new instance of Block. When the parser returns from that instance of Block, that index disappears and the current tbl_x value becomes the table index again. All of the procedure's local symbol definitions are no longer part of the table. This is very significant. It means that the procedure's symbols are only defined while we are parsing the block for the procedure (or any procedures nested within it). These symbols are not accessible from the lower (or outer) level because they are not in the symbol table. This agrees with access concepts shown in Figure 4.10. One other important action must coincide with the return from the Block class, that is, the nesting index must be decremented back to its former value.

It is instructive to look back at the code for the Block class and see what it does with respect to the procedure being declared. The first thing it does is generate a "JMP" instruction. After this, it places the address of the JMP instruction into the value field of the procedure's entry in the symbol table. It then proceeds to parse the declaration and the body of the procedure.

The *Body* class is the only Figure 5.1 diagram that we haven't examined yet.

```
class Body:        public ParseNode       // The Program or Procedure Body
(Node)
{
    ParseNode       *statementList;
    symSet          *untilSyms;
    int             tbl_x, tbl_x0;
    int             dsp_x;
    int             pcd_x;
public:
                    Body(int tx,  int dx,  int tx0);
    virtual void    Parse();
    virtual void    Generate();
    virtual void    Update_x(int &tx,  int &dx);
};

Body::Body(int  tx,  int  dx,  int  tx0)
{  tbl_x = tx;    tbl_x0 = tx0;    dsp_x = dx;   }

void Body::Parse()
{
    Token       *token;
    TokenType   sym;

    token = Sym->getSymbol();          sym    = token->Token;
    if (sym == beginSym)
    {  token = Sym->getNewSymbol();    sym    = token->Token;   }
    else
        Sym->Message("`BEGIN' expected");

    untilSyms = new symSet;
    untilSyms->insert(endSym);
    statementList = new StatementList(untilSyms, tbl_x);
    statementList->Parse();
    delete untilSyms;

    token = Sym->getSymbol();          sym    = token->Token;
    if (sym != endSym)
    {
        Sym->Message("`END' expected");
    }
    token = Sym->getNewSymbol();       sym    = token->Token;
}

void  Body::Generate()
{
    string      name;
    TokenType   kind;
    int         lev, val;

    code.Enter(INT, 0, dsp_x, pcd_x);

    symbolTable.Examine(name, kind, lev, val, tbl_x0);
```

```
    code.FixValue(pcd_x - 1, val);
    symbolTable.FixValue(pcd_x - 1, tbl_x0);

    statementList->Generate();

    code.Enter(OPR, 0, 0, pcd_x);
}

void  Body::Update_x(int &tx,  int &dx)
{   tx = tbl_x;    dx = dsp_x;  }
```

Figure 5.16
The Lil'LuxLyk Procedure Declaration class.

As shown in Figure 5.16, the `Body::Parse` function is fairly straightforward. Basically, it looks for the BEGIN keyword, a statement list, and the END keyword. We will be looking at the statement list in the next section, but one matter can be addressed now. Statements will keep track of the symbols that can be used to resynchronize the parser whenever errors are detected. Since this statement list is terminated by the END keyword, *endSym* is the resynchronizing symbol. It is passed to the `StatementList` class in a special class called a *symSet*. Usage of the symSet will be covered in the next section.

Some very important actions are performed by the `Body::Generate` function. To start with, an "INT" instruction is entered into the Code class. The INT instruction is the first instruction in the body of either the main program or a procedure. Figure 4.11 showed how this is used for the main program. Before any program code is run, the **T** register points to a space above the actual **Stack**. The purpose of the INT instruction is to move the **T** register to point to the space reserved for the main program's last local variable. In a similar manner, before any procedure code is run, the **T** register points to the location just before the stack frame of the new procedure. The INT instruction is again used to make **T** point to the space reserved for the last variable that is local to the procedure. The dsp_x variable is the same one that was used to store the variables in the symbol table. It was initially set to three and incremented each time that a variable was entered in the table. It is therefore the right number of locations for the **T** register to move. That is why it is used in the statement that enters the INT instruction into the Code.

At the beginning of the Block that this Body belongs to, a JMP instruction was placed in the Code. Its purpose was to direct the P-Machine to the P-Code belonging to the Body. At that time, we did not know where the code would begin (the code for nested procedures could fall between the original JMP and the INT that we just entered). Now that we are at the beginning of the Body, we can go back and fix the JMP instruction. Tbl_x0 is the index in the symbol table where the information about the procedure (or main program) was initially stored. We "Examine" the entry at this index to find out where the JMP instruction was placed in the Code. We then fix the value at that location to make it point to the location in Code of the INT instruction. Since the INT instruction is the true beginning of the body, not the JMP instruction, we next go back to the symbol table and fix its value field to point to the INT instruction also. These last two updates are made by using the `FixValue` method of the appropriate class.

The P-Code for the statement list is generated next. This is followed by an "OPR 0 0" (i.e., return) instruction. This completes the P-Code for the body.

By now, you may be wondering why the JMP instructions are needed. The main program JMP is fairly easy to grasp. Since declarations precede the body and procedures are part of the declarations, the body of the main program is the last code generated by the compiler. Since execution begins at the first location in the code, we need a way to instantly direct the computer to the main code. The initial JMP does this for us. Now we need an explanation for the other JMP instructions.

Assume we have a main program with a nested procedure named **B**. Assume also that **B** has a nested procedure named **C**. The code for **C** will come first in the P-Code, followed by the code for **B**, and finally, the code for the main program. Assume that the main program calls **B**, **B** calls **C**, and **C** calls **B** recursively. (This is exactly the sequence shown in Figure 4.14.) The P-Code that would be generated for this sequence is shown in Figure 5.17. Do not try to run this P-Code program, it tends to run out of **Stack** quickly. A more complete program would include conditional statements that would eventually interrupt the recursive loop.

```
0        JMP     0    9        ! jump to main program
1        JMP     0    6        ! jump to procedure B
2        JMP     0    3        ! jump to procedure C
3        INT     0    6        ! beginning of procedure C
4        CAL     2    1        !    call to procedure B
5        OPR     0    0        ! end of procedure C
6        INT     0    6        ! beginning of procedure B
7        CAL     0    3        !    call to procedure C
8        OPR     0    0        ! end of procedure B
9        INT     0    6        ! beginning of main program
10       CAL     0    6        !    call to procedure B
11       OPR     0    0        ! end of main program
```

Figure 5.17
P-Code for a very simple program.

When the main program calls **B**, the code for **B** has already been stored. The CAL instruction can therefore reference the procedure body directly (i.e., location 6). Likewise, procedure **B** can call the **C** procedure directly because the code for **C** has also been previously stored. However, when **C** attempts to call **B** at location 4, the code for **B** has not yet been stored. This forward reference problem is solved by having the call refer back to the appropriate JMP instruction instead. (It's easier to back-fix the single JMP instruction than it would be to attempt to fix all of the CAL instructions that might possibly be referencing the procedure.) The JMP instruction at location 2 is not used in the present example. There are no forward references to procedure **C**; therefore, no CAL instructions have to refer back to the JMP instruction that jumps forward to **C**.

The CAL instruction at location 4 demonstrates another important point. The value in the level field is two. In the other CAL instructions, the level field is zero. Section 4.10 explained why recursive calls, such as the one at location 4, will have a non-zero value in the level field. Here we see some code where this is the case. In the next section, we shall see how the level field is actually calculated.

5.4 PARSING THE STATEMENTS

Statement parsing is slightly different than top level parsing. In the top level code we were primarily concerned with storing symbols in the symbol table. We desired to put the symbols into the table in the order they were received. The best way to do this turned out to be to immediately follow the call to the Parse function by a call to the Generate function. This was also true of the statement list of the procedure or main code body. That is, once we had completely parsed the body, we went back and generated the *complete* P-Code for the body. Since the generation for all statements is done all at once at the end, we do not have to call Generate immediately after Parse for each individual statement. In fact, we *should not* call it immediately. For any given Lil'LuxLyk statement, the parsing and generation may be separated by a considerable period of time.

The fundamental *Statement* class is shown in Figure 5.18.

```
class Statement:  public ParseNode          // The General Statement Node
{
   ParseNode     *statement;
   symSet        *untilSyms;
   int           tbl_x;
   int           dsp_x;
   int           pcd_x;
public:
                 Statement(symSet *UntilSyms, int tx);
                 ~Statement();
   virtual void  Parse();
   virtual void  Generate();
};

Statement::Statement(symSet *UntilSyms, int tx)
{
   untilSyms = new symSet(*UntilSyms);
   tbl_x = tx;
}

     Statement::~Statement()
{  delete untilSyms;  }

void   Statement::Parse()
{
   Token     *token;
   TokenType sym;

   token = Sym->getSymbol();            sym = token->Token;
   if (sym == beginSym)
   {
      Sym->Message("delete `BEGIN'");
      token = Sym->getNewSymbol();    sym = token->Token;
   }
   switch (sym)
   {
      case Ident:
         statement = new assignStatement(untilSyms, tbl_x);
         break;
      case callSym:
         statement = new callStatement(untilSyms, tbl_x);
         break;
      case ifSym:
         statement = new ifStatement(untilSyms, tbl_x);
         break;
      case readSym:
```

```
            statement = new readStatement(untilSyms, tbl_x);
            break;
        case whileSym:
            statement = new whileStatement(untilSyms, tbl_x);
            break;
        case writeSym:
            statement = new writeStatement(untilSyms, tbl_x);
            break;
        default:      // fubar, try next symbol (this one is no good!)
            Sym->Message("Improper symbol beginning statement");
            statement = NULL;
            token = Sym->getNewSymbol();    sym = token->Token;
        return;
    }
    statement->Parse();
    token = Sym->getSymbol();              sym = token->Token;
    if ( ! ( stmt_beg_sym.contains(sym)
          || dclr_beg_sym.contains(sym)
          || untilSyms->contains(sym)
          || sym == Ident  // Ident also begins a statement
          || sym == Period || sym == Semicol) )
    {
        Sym->Message("Improper symbol before statement");
        //          try to get back in sync
        while ( ! ( stmt_beg_sym.contains(sym)
                 || dclr_beg_sym.contains(sym)
                 || untilSyms->contains(sym)
                 || sym == Ident
                 || sym == Period || sym == Semicol) )
        { token = Sym->getNewSymbol();    sym = token->Token;  }
    }
}

void   Statement::Generate()
{
    if (statement != NULL)
    {
        statement->Generate();
        delete statement;
    }
}
```

Figure 5.18
The fundamental Lil'LuxLyk Statement class.

All statement constructors are passed two parameters. The first is the error resychronizing set mentioned in the previous section. We will look at it some more as we examine the various statements. The other parameter is the index of the next free location in the symbol table. This value will be used to look up symbols in the symbol table.

`Statement::Parse` is basically a dispatcher. It examines the initial token and calls the constructor for the corresponding statement class. For instance, the CALL token implies that the *callStatement* should be parsed, likewise, an IF token infers an *ifStatement*. Top-down parsing is goal-oriented; the statement parser code is where the goal is determined. This selection is done by a `switch` statement in the parser. Once the choice has been made and the constructor instantiated by the `new` command, the chosen statement is parsed. One of the powerful attributes of **C++** is used here. Since all statements inherit the ParseNode class, it is possible to define "ParseNode" as the type of whatever statement class is selected. However, when the Parse member function is called, the Parse function for the chosen class is called rather than the "virtual" Parse function of the ParseNode class. This helps to simplify the code somewhat; a separate call to parse the selected statement class would otherwise be necessary in each `case` of the `switch` statement.

While parsing the selected statement, we might run into an error in the syntax. If the statement's parser can't handle the problem effectively it will eventually return to the fundamental statement parser of Figure 5.18. Statements without any errors will also return to the fundamental statement parser. The next section of the Statement::Parse function is used to recover from any possible errors that may have been encountered. There are a limited number of tokens that we can reasonably expect to follow a statement. These include a semicolon, any keyword that begins a statement, or an identifier that begins an assignment statement. If we find one of these, we're probably in good shape. Under some error conditions in the statement just parsed, we may end up with a panic token such as the period at the end of a program, a token that begins a declaration, or one of the tokens passed to Statement::Parse by the UntilSyms symSet. If the current token is one of these, the resynchronizing was most likely done in the statement just parsed. This would mean we're back in good shape. However, if the current token is neither one of the expected tokens nor one of the panic tokens, we are out of sync. Therefore, after first writing an error message, we start searching until we find a member of either of these two groups of tokens.

As can be seen from the discussion above, this fundamental statement parser performs two purposes. First, it determines a goal and dispatches to the proper class to parse the statement, and second, it handles any error recovery that may be necessary *after* the statement has been parsed.

The `statement::Generate` function simply calls the Generate function of the ParseNode to which the parser dispatched. The actual code generation will be done in the function *called* by Statement::Generate.

An enlargement of the basic statement class is found in the *StatementList* class. It collects several statements together into a single unit. The statements are separated by semicolons and terminated by an expected keyword. The concluding keyword is passed in the UntilSyms argument of the constructor. In this case, the meaning of the argument's name becomes clear. The parser continues to collect statements *until* it finds one of the UntilSyms tokens. The StatementList class is shown in Figure 5.19.

```
class StatementList: public ParseNode      // A Compound Statement
{
    parseQ          *statements;
    symSet          *untilSyms;
    int              tbl_x;
    int              dsp_x;
    int              pcd_x;
public:
                    StatementList(symSet *UntilSyms, int tx);
                    ~StatementList();
    virtual void    Parse();
    virtual void    Generate();
};

StatementList::StatementList(symSet *UntilSyms, int tx)
{
    statements = new parseQ();
    untilSyms  = new symSet(*UntilSyms);
    tbl_x = tx;
}


    StatementList::~StatementList()
{
    delete statements;
    delete untilSyms;
}

void    StatementList::Parse()
{
    ParseNode *statement;
    Token     *token;
    TokenType  sym;

    statement = new Statement(untilSyms, tbl_x);
    statement->Parse();
    statements->push(statement);
    token = Sym->getSymbol();               sym    = token->Token;
    while ( sym == Semicol
            || stmt_beg_sym.contains(sym))
    {
        if (sym != Semicol)
```

```
            Sym->Message("insert `;'");
        else
        { token = Sym->getNewSymbol();  sym   = token->Token;  }
        statement = new Statement(untilSyms, tbl_x);
        statement->Parse();
        statements->push(statement);
        token = Sym->getSymbol();          sym   = token->Token;
    }
}

void   StatementList::Generate()
{
    ParseNode *statement;

    while ( ! statements->empty() )
    {
        statement = statements->front();
        statements->pop();
        statement->Generate();
        delete statement;
    }
}
```

Figure 5.19
The Lil'LuxLyk StatementList class.

The `StatementList::Parse` function follows the syntax diagram fairly closely. As previously mentioned, this class uses a parseQ to store all of the statements in the list. As each statement is detected, a ParseNode is created for it and its Parse function is called. The ParseNode is then placed on the queue. As long as the semicolons that separate statements are detected following the latest statement, the parser attempts to read a new statement. If the semicolon is not found, the parser checks to see if the token is one of the keywords that introduce a statement. If it is one of these, the parser assumes that the programmer erroneously left out the semicolon and outputs a warning message. If the concluding token is neither a semicolon nor an initial statement keyword, the parser assumes it is one of the expected UntilSym tokens and returns. It is actually up to the function that called StatementList::Parse to verify this final token.

`StatementList::Generate` pops statement ParseNodes off the queue and calls their Generate functions. This continues until the queue is empty.

Now that we've covered the generic statement forms, we can look at the specific statement classes. The first statement we will look at is the assignment statement. The *assignStatement* class is shown in Figure 5.20.

```
class assignStatement:  public ParseNode   // Assignment Statement Node
{
    Expression     *expression;
    symSet         *untilSyms;
    TokenType       typ;
    int             lev, val;
    int             tbl_x;
    int             dsp_x;
    int             pcd_x;
public:
                    assignStatement(symSet *UntilSyms, int tx);
                    ~assignStatement();
    virtual void    Parse();
    virtual void    Generate();
};

assignStatement::assignStatement(symSet *UntilSyms, int tx)
{
    untilSyms = new symSet(*UntilSyms);
    tbl_x = tx;
}

    assignStatement::~assignStatement()
{
    delete untilSyms;
}

void    assignStatement::Parse()
{
    Token      *token;
    TokenType  sym, kind;
    string     name;
    int        pos;

    token = Sym->getSymbol();                sym = token->Token;
    pos   = symbolTable.Position(*token->Value, tbl_x);
    if (pos == 0)
    {
        Sym->Message("Undefined variable");
        expression = NULL;
    }
    else
    {
        symbolTable.Examine(name, kind, lev, val, pos);
        if  (kind == varSym)
        {
            token = Sym->getNewSymbol();     sym = token->Token;
            if (sym != Becomes)
                Sym->Message("`:=' expected");
            else
            { token = Sym->getNewSymbol();  sym = token->Token;  }
            expression = new Expression(untilSyms, tbl_x);
            expression->Parse();
        }
        else
        {
            Sym->Message("Assignment to non-variable");
            expression = NULL;
```

```
      }
    }
}
void   assignStatement::Generate()
{
   if (expression != NULL)
   {
      expression->Generate();
      delete expression;
   }
   code.Enter(STO, level.get() - lev, val, pcd_x);
}
```

Figure 5.20
The Lil'LuxLyk Assignment statement.

The `assignStatement::Parse` function is called when an identifier is detected. The first thing that is done is to check to see if the identifier is in the symbol table and is a variable (we can't assign values to a constant or a procedure). In the process, it reads the identifier's level and address values, that is, *lev* and *val*, from the symbol table and saves them in the private area of the class so that it can be passed to the generator routine. Next, the parser reads the next token and verifies that it is the assignment operator. Finally, an instance of the Expression class is created and its Parse function is called. All of this follows from the syntax diagram.

The `assignStatement::Generate` function generates the code for the Expression by calling its Generate function. Once this is done, a STO instruction is entered into the Code. The level difference is calculated by subtracting the *lev* value (obtained by the Parse function) from the current level (obtained from the Level class). The address value comes directly from the *val* that was obtained by the Parse function. These actions result in P-Code generation similar to that shown in Section 4.12.1.

The *callStatement* class is called when the fundamental statement class detects a CALL keyword. The syntax diagram shows that the only other token in the call statement is an identifier. The `callStatement::Parse` function shown in Figure 5.21 verifies that this next token is indeed an identifier, and that it has been defined as a procedure name. Likewise, the `callStatement::Generate` function enters a CAL instruction into the code. The address field of the instruction comes directly from the symbol table. The level field is calculated as the difference between the current level and the level field from the symbol table.

```
class callStatement: public ParseNode     // Call Statement Node
{
    ParseNode       *procedure;
    symSet          *untilSyms;
    int             lev, val;
    int             tbl_x;
    int             dsp_x;
    int             pcd_x;
public:
                    callStatement(symSet *UntilSyms, int tx);
                    ~callStatement();
    virtual void    Parse();
    virtual void    Generate();
};

callStatement::callStatement(symSet *UntilSyms, int tx)
{
    untilSyms = new symSet(*UntilSyms);
    tbl_x = tx;
}

    callStatement::~callStatement()
{
    delete untilSyms;
}

void    callStatement::Parse()
{
    Token       *token;
    TokenType   sym, kind;
    int         pos;
    string      name;

    token = Sym->getNewSymbol();            sym = token->Token;
    if (sym != Ident)
    {
        Sym->Message("Ident expected");
        procedure = NULL;
    }
    else
    {
        pos  = symbolTable.Position(*token->Value, tbl_x);
        if (pos == 0)
        {
            Sym->Message("Undefined variable");
            procedure = NULL;
        }
        else
        {
            symbolTable.Examine(name, kind, lev, val, pos);
            if (kind != procSym)
            {
                Sym->Message("call to non-procedure");
                procedure = NULL;
            }
            else
            { token = Sym->getNewSymbol(); sym = token->Token;  }
```

```
      }
   }
}

void   callStatement::Generate()
{
   code.Enter(CAL, level.get() - lev, val, pcd_x);
}
```

Figure 5.21
The Lil'LuxLyk Call statement.

The most complex statement so far is the if statement. The *ifStatement* class is shown in Figure 5.22. This class is called by the fundamental statement class when the IF keyword is found. This class is complicated by having two non-terminals that are concluded by different keywords and by having what amounts to a forward reference in the generated code. The constructor takes care of the need for two sets of terminating symbols by saving the UntilSyms passed to it in two separate symSets, *untilSyms* and *endSyms*. In ifStatement::Parse, untilSyms is used to follow the call to parse the condition. The expected *thenSym* is inserted into untilSyms along with the less probable *doSym* and *endSym*. If a doSym is detected after parsing the condition, the Parse function warns the user to replace DO with THEN. In this case, the endSym is used as a "panic" stopping symbol. The end-Syms symSet is used to follow parsing the statement list. In this case, endSym is the expected token. After parsing the list, ifStatement::Parse makes sure that the next token truly is the expected END.


```
class ifStatement: public ParseNode        // If Statement Node
{
   Condition      *condition;
   ParseNode      *statementList;
   symSet         *untilSyms;
   symSet         *endSyms;
   int            tbl_x;
   int            dsp_x;
   int            pcd_x;
public:
                  ifStatement(symSet *UntilSyms, int tx);
                  ~ifStatement();
   virtual void   Parse();
   virtual void   Generate();
};

ifStatement::ifStatement(symSet *UntilSyms, int tx)
```

```
{
   untilSyms = new symSet(*UntilSyms);
   endSyms  = new symSet(*UntilSyms);
   tbl_x = tx;
}

    ifStatement::~ifStatement()
{
   delete untilSyms;
   delete endSyms;
}

void  ifStatement::Parse()
{
   Token     *token;
   TokenType  sym;

   token = Sym->getNewSymbol();      sym = token->Token;
   untilSyms->insert(thenSym);
   untilSyms->insert(doSym);
   untilSyms->insert(endSym);
   condition = new Condition(untilSyms, tbl_x);
   condition->Parse();
   token = Sym->getSymbol();         sym = token->Token;
   statementList = NULL;
   if (sym == thenSym || sym == doSym)
   {
      if (sym == doSym)
         Sym->Message("Replace `DO' with `THEN'");
      token = Sym->getNewSymbol();   sym = token->Token;
      endSyms->insert(endSym);
      statementList = new StatementList(endSyms, tbl_x);
      statementList->Parse();
      token = Sym->getSymbol();
      sym   = token->Token;
      if (sym == endSym)
      {  token = Sym->getNewSymbol();  sym = token->Token;  }
      else
         Sym->Message("`END' expected");
   }
   else
      Sym->Message("`THEN' expected");
}

void  ifStatement::Generate()
{
   int       cx1;

   condition->Generate();
   delete condition;
   code.Enter(JPC, 0, 0, pcd_x);
   cx1 = pcd_x - 1;
   if (statementList != NULL)
   {
      statementList->Generate();
      delete statementList;
   }
   code.FixValue(code.CurrentLoc(), cx1);
}
```

Figure 5.22
The Lil'LuxLyk If statement.

The `ifStatement::Generate` function first calls the generate function for the condition non-terminal. It then enters a "JPC 0 0" instruction into the Code. The Enter call returns the next free location in the Code (i.e., the *pcd_x* parameter). *Cx1* is made to point to the JPC instruction by subtracting 1 from the pcd_x value. After calling the generate function for the statement list, ifStatement::Generate goes back and changes the address in the JPC statement to the current location, that is, the location of the next instruction after the statement list of the if statement. The cx1 variable is the way that the generate function takes care of the forward reference required by the JPC instruction. It is used to remember the location of the JPC so that it can be corrected when the destination is known.

The *readStatement* class is much simpler than the previous one. The syntax diagram shows that it consists primarily of a series of identifiers separated by commas and terminated by a right parenthesis. It turns out that, since these are terminals not non-terminals, the untilSyms set is not required. On the other hand, we do need a queue to place the identifiers in. The constructor creates a new instance of the declQ for this purpose.

The readStatement class is shown in Figure 5.23.

```
class readStatement: public ParseNode     // Read Statement Node
{
    declQ           *varList;
    int             tbl_x;
    int             dsp_x;
    int             pcd_x;
public:
                    readStatement(symSet *UntilSyms, int tx);
                    ~readStatement();
    virtual void    Parse();
    virtual void    Generate();
};

readStatement::readStatement(symSet *UntilSyms, int tx)
{
    varList   = new declQ;
    tbl_x = tx;
}

    readStatement::~readStatement()
{ delete varList;   }

void    readStatement::Parse()
{
    Token       *token;
    TokenType   sym, kind;
    int         lev, val, pos;
    string      name;
```

```
    DeclObj    *variable;

    token = Sym->getNewSymbol();                      sym = token->Token;
    if (sym != lParen)
        Sym->Message("`(' expected");
    else
    {
        do
        {
            token = Sym->getNewSymbol();              sym = token->Token;
            if (sym != Ident)
                Sym->Message("Ident expected");
            else
            {
                pos = symbolTable.Position(*token->Value, tbl_x);
                if (pos == 0)
                    Sym->Message("Undefined variable");
                else
                {
                    symbolTable.Examine(name, kind, lev, val, pos);
                    if (kind != varSym)
                        Sym->Message("Read to non-variable");
                    else
                    {
                        variable = new DeclObj();
                        variable->level    = lev;
                        variable->n_value = val;
                        varList->push(variable);
                    }
                    token = Sym->getNewSymbol();   sym = token->Token;
                }
            }
        }
        while (sym == Comma);
        if (sym != rParen)
            Sym->Message("`)' expected");
        else
        {  token = Sym->getNewSymbol();               sym = token->Token;  }
    }
}

void    readStatement::Generate()
{
    DeclObj    *variable;
    int         lev, val;

    while ( ! varList->empty() )
    {
        variable = varList->front();
        varList->pop();
        lev = variable->level;
        val = variable->n_value;
        code.Enter(CSP,                   0,        2, pcd_x);
        code.Enter(STO, level.get() - lev,     val, pcd_x);
        delete variable;
    }
}
```

Figure 5.23
The Lil'LuxLyk Read statement.

The readStatement::Parse procedure makes sure that a left parenthesis follows the READ token. Then it starts collecting identifiers and placing them in the queue. This continues as long as commas separate the identifiers. The parse procedure then checks that the final token is the right parenthesis.

The readStatement::Generate procedure pulls all of the identifiers out of the queue and generates two P-instructions for each. The first is a "CSP 0 2" that reads integers from the standard input, and the second is an STO instruction that pops the value off the stack and stores it. The *lev* and *val* fields from the symbol table are used. As usual, the level difference is the value actually placed in the instruction.

Before we examine the *whileStatement* class, take a look at Figure 5.2. The syntax diagram of the while statement has the same form as the if statement. The only difference is that the initial keyword is WHILE instead of IF, and the DO keyword follows the condition instead of THEN. For this reason, the WhileStatement::Parse function looks fairly similar to the corresponding code from the if statement class. About the only difference is that using THEN instead of DO is a less likely error; there is no warning in this parse method.

Likewise, WhileStatement::Generate is also similar to the corresponding function in the if Statement class. The P-Code for the while statement ends with a JMP statement that brings control back to the condition code. This is handled in the generate method by introducing a new code index, *cx2*. This is set to the current code location before the condition code is generated. At the end of the statement list, the JMP statement is generated that points back to the location saved in cx2.

The whileStatement class is shown in Figure 5.24.

```
class whileStatement:  public ParseNode    // While Statement Node
{
   Condition      *condition;
   ParseNode      *statementList;
   symSet         *untilSyms;
   symSet         *endSyms;
   int             tbl_x;
   int             dsp_x;
   int             pcd_x;
public:
                   whileStatement(symSet *UntilSyms, int tx);
                   ~whileStatement();
   virtual void    Parse();
```

```
    virtual void   Generate();
};

whileStatement::whileStatement(symSet *UntilSyms, int tx)
{
    untilSyms = new symSet(*UntilSyms);
    endSyms   = new symSet(*UntilSyms);
    tbl_x = tx;
}

    whileStatement::~whileStatement()
{
    delete untilSyms;
    delete endSyms;
}

void    whileStatement::Parse()
{
    Token      *token;
    TokenType  sym;

    token = Sym->getNewSymbol();        sym   = token->Token;
    untilSyms->insert(doSym);
    untilSyms->insert(endSym);
    condition = new Condition(untilSyms, tbl_x);
    condition->Parse();
    token = Sym->getSymbol();           sym   = token->Token;
    statementList = NULL;
    if (sym == doSym)
    {
        token = Sym->getNewSymbol();        sym   = token->Token;
        endSyms->insert(endSym);
        statementList = new StatementList(endSyms, tbl_x);
        statementList->Parse();
        token = Sym->getSymbol();           sym   = token->Token;
        if (sym == endSym)
        {  token = Sym->getNewSymbol();  sym   = token->Token;  }
        else
            Sym->Message("`END' expected");
    }
    else
        Sym->Message("`DO' expected");
}

void    whileStatement::Generate()
{
    int    cx1;
    int    cx2 = code.CurrentLoc();

    condition->Generate();
    delete condition;
    code.Enter(JPC, 0,    0, pcd_x);
    cx1 = pcd_x - 1;
    if (statementList != NULL)
    {
        statementList->Generate();
        delete statementList;
    }
    code.Enter(JMP, 0, cx2, pcd_x);
    code.FixValue(pcd_x, cx1);
}
```

Figure 5.24
The Lil'LuxLyk While statement.

The only Lil'LuxLyk statement remaining is the *Write* class. It is similar to the read statement except instead of inputting values and storing them in the specified variables, the write statement evaluates expressions and outputs the values. This tends to simplify the parser code somewhat when compared to the read statement. The `writeStatement::Parse` function does not have to verify that the read variables are properly defined in the symbol table. Instead, it passes that task off to the expression parser. As each expression is encountered in the input source, an instance of an expression ParseNode is created, parsed, and then placed in a parseQ named *exprList* for later generation. This can be seen in the writeStatement class listing shown in Figure 5.25.

```
class writeStatement:  public ParseNode    // Write Statement Node
{
    parseQ          *exprList;
    symSet          *untilSyms;
    symSet          *endSyms;
    int             tbl_x;
    int             dsp_x;
    int             pcd_x;
public:
                    writeStatement(symSet *UntilSyms, int tx);
                    ~writeStatement();
    virtual void    Parse();
    virtual void    Generate();
};

void    writeStatement::Parse()
{
    Token       *token;
    TokenType   sym;
    Expression *expression;

    token = Sym->getNewSymbol();              sym   = token->Token;
    if (sym != lParen)
        Sym->Message("`(' expected");
    else
    {
        untilSyms->insert(Comma);
        untilSyms->insert(rParen);
        do
        {
            token = Sym->getNewSymbol();     sym   = token->Token;
            expression = new Expression(untilSyms, tbl_x);
            expression->Parse();
            exprList->push(expression);
            token = Sym->getSymbol();         sym   = token->Token;
        }
        while (sym == Comma);
        if (sym != rParen)
            Sym->Message("`)' expected");
        else
        { token = Sym->getNewSymbol();        sym   = token->Token;  }
```

```
     }
}

void   writeStatement::Generate()
{
   ParseNode *expression;

   while ( ! exprList->empty() )
   {
      expression = exprList->front();
      exprList->pop();
      expression->Generate();
      code.Enter(CSP, 0,   3, pcd_x);
      delete expression;
   }
   code.Enter(LIT, 0, 13, pcd_x);
   code.Enter(CSP, 0,  1, pcd_x);
   code.Enter(LIT, 0, 10, pcd_x);
   code.Enter(CSP, 0,  1, pcd_x);
}
```

Figure 5.25
The Lil'LuxLyk Write statement.

The writeStatement::Generate member function pops the individual expressions out of the exprList queue and calls their generate functions. This creates the P-Code that puts the expression's value on the stack. Next a "CSP 0 3" instruction is entered in the code. After all of the expressions have been handled, the function creates a series of P-Code instructions that will output a carriage return (i.e., ASCII 13) and a line feed character (i.e., ASCII 10). In Lil'LuxLyk, the write statement always terminates the current output line.

5.5 PARSING THE EXPRESSIONS

Parsing expressions is essentially an extension of parsing statements. Expressions and conditions are components of many of the statements we have just surveyed. Likewise, statements were themselves a component of a statement list. The processing is the same for these new components as it was for the earlier ones. That means we create an instance of the desired type of expression and call its Parse function. At a later time, we call its Generate function and create its corresponding P-Code.

The syntax diagrams of Figure 5.3 show that there are loops in which many terms or factors are parsed sequentially as long as they are separated by the proper operators. As was true in other loops, these terms and factors must be collected in some form of queue. Since there are several different types of non-terminals involved, as well as a multitude of possible separating operators, a special `struct` and queue are defined for this case. They are shown in Figure 5.26.

```
struct  SubExpr
{
   TokenType      operation;
   ParseNode      *operand;
};

// expr./term/factor queue
typedef queue<SubExpr *, list<SubExpr *> > subexprQ;
```

Figure 5.26
Definition of the queue used to contain subexpressions.

The first expression form to be developed is the *Condition* class. It is called by the if and while statements. The syntax diagram shows that the condition statement can take two paths. The first is introduced by the keyword ODD followed by a plain expression. The second is either a single expression or a pair of expressions separated by a relational operator such as *Equal*, *notEqual*, *Less*, and the like. The result of either of these paths should be either a false or a true value, that is, either zero or non-zero (usually one). The Condition class is shown in Figure 5.27.

```
class Condition:  public ParseNode          // Conditional Expression Node
{
   symSet         *untilSyms;
   symSet         *endSyms;
   subexprQ       *expressions;
   int            tbl_x;
   int            pcd_x;
public:
                  Condition(symSet *UntilSyms, int tx);
                  ~Condition();
   virtual void   Parse();
   virtual void   Generate();
};

Condition::Condition(symSet *UntilSyms, int tx)
{
   untilSyms   = new symSet(*UntilSyms);
   endSyms     = new symSet(*UntilSyms);
   expressions = new subexprQ;
   tbl_x = tx;
```

```
}

    Condition::~Condition()
{
    delete untilSyms;
    delete endSyms;
    delete expressions;
}

void  Condition::Parse()
{
    Token      *token;
    TokenType  sym;
    SubExpr    *subCond;

    token = Sym->getSymbol();              sym = token->Token;
    if (sym == oddSym)
    {
        subCond = new SubExpr();
        subCond->operation = oddSym;
        token   = Sym->getNewSymbol();     sym = token->Token;
        subCond->operand = new  Expression(untilSyms, tbl_x);
        subCond->operand->Parse();
        expressions->push(subCond);
    }
    else
    {
        untilSyms->insert(Equal);
        untilSyms->insert(notEqual);
        untilSyms->insert(lessEqual);
        untilSyms->insert(Less);
        untilSyms->insert(Greater);
        untilSyms->insert(grtrEqual);
        subCond = new SubExpr();
        subCond->operation = noToken;
        subCond->operand = new  Expression(untilSyms, tbl_x);
        subCond->operand->Parse();
        expressions->push(subCond);
        token = Sym->getSymbol();              sym = token->Token;
        if (  sym == Equal  ||  sym == notEqual  ||  sym == lessEqual
           ||  sym == Less   ||  sym == Greater   ||  sym == grtrEqual  )
        {
            subCond = new SubExpr();
            subCond->operation = sym;
            token   = Sym->getNewSymbol();     sym      = token->Token;
            subCond->operand = new  Expression(endSyms, tbl_x);
            subCond->operand->Parse();
            expressions->push(subCond);
        }
        else
        Sym->Message("Relational operation required");
    }
}

void  Condition::Generate()
{
    SubExpr *subCond;

    subCond = expressions->front();
    expressions->pop();
    subCond->operand->Generate();
    if (subCond->operation == oddSym)
    {
        code.Enter(OPR, 0, 6, pcd_x);
        delete subCond;
```

```
   }
   else
   {
      delete subCond;
      if ( ! expressions->empty() )
      {
         subCond = expressions->front();
         expressions->pop();
         subCond->operand->Generate();
         switch (subCond->operation)
         {
            case Equal:     code.Enter(OPR, 0,  8, pcd_x);  break;
            case notEqual:  code.Enter(OPR, 0,  9, pcd_x);  break;
            case Less:      code.Enter(OPR, 0, 10, pcd_x);  break;
            case grtrEqual: code.Enter(OPR, 0, 11, pcd_x);  break;
            case Greater:   code.Enter(OPR, 0, 12, pcd_x);  break;
            case lessEqual: code.Enter(OPR, 0, 13, pcd_x);  break;
         }
         delete subCond;
      }
   }
}
```

Figure 5.27
The Lil'LuxLyk Condition class.

In Condition::Parse(), if an *oddSym* token is detected, a new SubExpr structure, named *subCond*, is created, the oddSym token is saved as the operation, and an expression is created as the operand. The expression is then parsed. Finally, the subCond structure is pushed on the queue for generation at a later time.

In the absence of an oddSym, the Parse function creates a new subCond structure and stores a "*noToken*" symbol as the operation. A new expression is created as the operand and then parsed. The subCond structure is pushed onto the queue. Any one of the relational operations is expected after the expression. If it is encountered, another subCond structure is created and the relational operation is saved as the operation. Next, a new expression is created, parsed, and used as the operand field of the structure. Finally, the structure is added to the queue.

The Condition::Generate method pops the first subCond off the queue and generates the expression in the operand field. After that, it examines the operation field. If it's an *oddSym*, an "OPR 0 6" test for odd instruction is entered into the P-Code. If the operation was not *oddSym*, the Generate function attempts to pop additional subCond records off the queue. For each record retrieved, the expression pointed to by the operand field is generated, then an OPR instruction that corresponds to the operation field is entered into the P-Code. For example, if the operation is *Equal*, an "OPR 0 8" instruction is stored.

Next, we come to the *Expression* class itself. We previously saw a simplified form of the Parse method in Chapter 4. Now we shall look at the whole class in more detail. The Expression class is shown in Figure 5.28.

```
class Expression: public ParseNode          // Expression Node
{
    symSet          *untilSyms;
    subexprQ        *terms;
    int             tbl_x;
    int             pcd_x;
public:
                    Expression(symSet *UntilSymssym, int tx);
                    ~Expression();
    virtual void    Parse();
    virtual void    Generate();
};

Expression::Expression(symSet *UntilSyms, int tx)
{
    untilSyms = new symSet(*UntilSyms);
    terms     = new subexprQ;
    tbl_x = tx;
}


    Expression::~Expression()
{   delete untilSyms;    delete terms;   }

void  Expression::Parse()
{
    Token       *token;
    TokenType   sym;
    SubExpr     *subExpr;

    untilSyms->insert(Plus);
    untilSyms->insert(Minus);
    token    = Sym->getSymbol();            sym = token->Token;
    subExpr = new SubExpr;
    if (sym == Plus || sym == Minus)
    {
        subExpr->operation = sym;
        token = Sym->getNewSymbol();        sym = token->Token;
    }
    else
        subExpr->operation = noToken;
    subExpr->operand = new Term(untilSyms, tbl_x);
    subExpr->operand->Parse();
    terms->push(subExpr);
    token = Sym->getSymbol();               sym = token->Token;
    while (sym == Plus || sym == Minus)
    {
        subExpr = new SubExpr;
        subExpr->operation = sym;
        token    = Sym->getNewSymbol();    sym = token->Token;
        subExpr->operand = new Term(untilSyms, tbl_x);
        subExpr->operand->Parse();
```

```
                  terms->push(subExpr);
                  token    = Sym->getSymbol();          sym = token->Token;
          }
}

void  Expression::Generate()
{
    SubExpr    *subExpr;

    subExpr = terms->front();         terms->pop();
    subExpr->operand->Generate();
    if (subExpr->operation == Minus) code.Enter(OPR, 0, 1, pcd_x);
    delete subExpr;
    while ( ! terms->empty() )
    {
        subExpr = terms->front();     terms->pop();
        subExpr->operand->Generate();
        switch (subExpr->operation)
        {
            case Plus:    code.Enter(OPR, 0,  2, pcd_x);   break;
            case Minus:   code.Enter(OPR, 0,  3, pcd_x);   break;
        }
        delete subExpr;
    }
}
```

Figure 5.28
The Lil'LuxLyk Expression class.

Expression::Parse first checks to see if there is an initial plus or minus. If so, it saves the TokenType in the operation field of a *subExpr* structure; otherwise, it saves a noToken. Next, it creates a new instance of the Term class and parses it. The pointer to this new Term is saved in the operand field of the subExpr. The subExpr is then pushed onto a queue of terms. The function then looks to see if the next token is either plus or minus. If it is, another instance of the Term class is created, parsed, and saved (along with the plus or minus token) in a subExpr that is pushed on the queue. This continues until the next token is not a plus or minus.

Expression::Generate pulls the first subExpr off of the queue, generates the Term in its operand field, and then checks to see if the operation field contains a minus token. If it does, an "OPR 0 1" P-Code is entered into the code to negate what's on the run-time stack. Next, the function checks the queue. As long as there are more subExpr structures in the queue, one is removed, its Term is generated, and an "OPR 0 2" or "OPR 0 3" is entered into the code, depending on whether the operation field contained a plus or a minus token.

The *Term* class, shown in Figure 5.29, is very similar to the Expression class. A glance at Figure 5.3 shows why. The syntax diagrams are nearly the same.

```
class Term:  public ParseNode                  // Term Node
{
    symSet        *untilSyms;
    subexprQ      *factors;
    int           tbl_x;
    int           pcd_x;
public:
                  Term(symSet *UntilSyms, int tx);
                  ~Term();
    virtual void  Parse();
    virtual void  Generate();
};

    Term::Term(symSet *UntilSyms, int tx)
{
    untilSyms = new symSet(*UntilSyms);
    factors   = new subexprQ();
    tbl_x = tx;
}

    Term::~Term()
{
    delete untilSyms;
    delete factors;
}

void  Term::Parse()
{
    Token      *token;
    TokenType  sym;
    SubExpr    *subTerm;

    untilSyms->insert(Times);
    untilSyms->insert(Slash);
    untilSyms->insert(Percent);
    subTerm = new SubExpr;
    subTerm->operation = noToken;
    subTerm->operand   = new Factor(untilSyms, tbl_x);
    subTerm->operand->Parse();
    factors->push(subTerm);

    token = Sym->getSymbol();              sym = token->Token;
    while (sym == Times || sym == Slash || sym == Percent)
    {
        subTerm = new SubExpr;
        subTerm->operation = sym;
        token    = Sym->getNewSymbol();    sym = token->Token;
        subTerm->operand = new Factor(untilSyms, tbl_x);
        subTerm->operand->Parse();
        factors->push(subTerm);
        token    = Sym->getSymbol();       sym = token->Token;
    }
}

void  Term::Generate()
{
    SubExpr    *subTerm;
```

```
   subTerm = factors->front();
   factors->pop();
   subTerm->operand->Generate();
   delete subTerm;

   while ( ! factors->empty() )
   {
      subTerm = factors->front();
      factors->pop();
      subTerm->operand->Generate();
      switch (subTerm->operation)
      {
         case Times:    code.Enter(OPR, 0,  4, pcd_x);  break;
         case Slash:    code.Enter(OPR, 0,  5, pcd_x);  break;
         case Percent:  code.Enter(OPR, 0,  7, pcd_x);  break;
      }
      delete subTerm;
   }
}
```

Figure 5.29
The Lil'LuxLyk Term class.

Term::Parse creates an instance of the Factor class and parses it. The pointer to this Factor is saved in the operand field of a *subTerm* structure. A "noToken" is saved in the operation field. The subTerm is then pushed onto a queue of factors. The function then looks to see if the next token is an asterisk, slash, or percent sign. If it is, another instance of the Factor class is created, parsed, and saved (along with the latest operation token) in a subTerm that is pushed onto the queue. This continues until the next token is not an asterisk, slash, or percent sign.

Term::Generate pulls the first subTerm off of the queue and generates the Factor in its operand field. Next, the function checks the queue. As long as there are more subTerm structures in the queue, one is removed, its Factor is generated, and an "OPR 0 4", "OPR 0 5", or "OPR 0 7" is entered into the code depending on whether the operation field contained an asterisk, slash, or percent sign token.

The only remaining class is *Factor*. It is another recursive class, as seen in Figure 5.3. This is also the class where numbers and identifiers are recognized. This recognition is done by the Factor::Parse member function. This function also performs another important function. Factor is positioned at the bottom of the set of syntax diagrams. That makes it an optimum place to make sure that our source code is still synchronized with the proper syntax for the language. This is done in much the same way it was done in the Statement class. First, there are a limited number of tokens that can begin a factor, namely, identifiers, numbers, and a left parenthesis. If the current token is not one of these, we are out of sync and must search for one of them or a "panic token" to get back in sync. Second, the factor should be followed by one of the UntilSyms that were originally passed to the Factor constructor. If one of these is not detected, we are also out of sync and must search for a synchronizing token.

In-between these two tests, Parse does its primary work. It first looks at the current token and determines whether to parse an identifier, number, or another expression. In the process, it stores information in the class's private data area that will be used during code generation. If the token is an identifier, it is looked up in the symbol table. If the symbol's kind is a variable or a constant, the table's values are transferred to the class's data. If the token is a number, *kind* is set to constSym and *val* is set to the value of the number. In either of these cases, *expression* is set to NULL. In the final case where the current token is a left parenthesis, a new Expression is created and parsed. The expression variable is made to point to the new Expression and the kind variable is set to noToken.

Factor::Generate decides what to do based on the expression and kind variables. If the expression pointer is not NULL, the expression it points to is generated; if not, it examines kind. If kind is varSym, a "LOD lev val" is generated; otherwise, it generates a "LIT 0 val" where "lev" and "val" come from the class's private data.

The Factor class is shown in Figure 5.30. This completes all of the actual parsing and generating classes.

```
class Factor:  public ParseNode              // Factor Node
{
    symSet        *untilSyms;
    Expression    *expression;
    TokenType     kind;
    int           lev, val;
    int           tbl_x;
    int           pcd_x;
public:
                  Factor(symSet *UntilSyms, int tx);
```

```
                        ~Factor();
    virtual void   Parse();
    virtual void   Generate();
};

Factor::Factor(symSet *UntilSyms, int tx)
{
    untilSyms = new symSet(*UntilSyms);
    tbl_x = tx;
}

     Factor::~Factor()
{ delete untilSyms;    }

void  Factor::Parse()
{
    Token       *token;
    string      name;
    TokenType   sym;
    int         pos;

    token = Sym->getSymbol();                           sym    = token->Token;
    if ( ! (  fctr_beg_sym.contains(sym)
           || untilSyms->contains(sym)
           || sym == Period || sym == Semicol) )
    {
        Sym->Message("Improper symbol before factor");
        //           try to get back in sync
        while ( ! (  fctr_beg_sym.contains(sym)
                  || untilSyms->contains(sym)
                  || sym == Period || sym == Semicol) )
        {  token = Sym->getNewSymbol();                 sym   = token->Token;  }
    }
    if ( fctr_beg_sym.contains(sym) )
    {
        switch (sym)
        {
            case Ident:
                pos = symbolTable.Position(*token->Value, tbl_x);
                if (pos != 0)
                {
                    symbolTable.Examine(name, kind, lev, val, pos);
                    if  (kind == constSym || kind == varSym)
                    {  token = Sym->getNewSymbol();   sym    = token->Token;  }
                    else
                    {
                        Sym->Message("Constant or variable expected");
                        kind = noToken;
                    }
                }
                else
                {
                    Sym->Message("Undefined variable");
                    kind = noToken;
                }
                expression = NULL;
                break;
            case Number:
                kind = constSym;
                val  = atoi( token->Value->data() );
                token = Sym->getNewSymbol();            sym    = token->Token;
                expression = NULL;
                break;
            case lParen:
                kind = noToken;
```

```
               token = Sym->getNewSymbol();            sym   = token->Token;
               untilSyms->insert(rParen);
               expression = new Expression(untilSyms, tbl_x);
               expression->Parse();
               token = Sym->getSymbol();               sym   = token->Token;
               if (sym != rParen)
                  Sym->Message("`)' expected");
               else
               {  token = Sym->getNewSymbol();          sym   = token->Token;  }
               break;
         }
      if ( ! (  untilSyms->contains(sym)
                || sym == Period || sym == Semicol || sym == rParen) )
         {
            Sym->Message("Improper symbol after factor");
            //          try to get back in sync
            while ( ! (  untilSyms->contains(sym)
                      || sym == Period || sym == Semicol || sym == rParen) )
               {  token = Sym->getNewSymbol();          sym   = token->Token;  }
         }
      }
   else
   {  expression = NULL;     kind = noToken;   }
}

void    Factor::Generate()
{
   if (expression != NULL)
   {
      expression->Generate();
      delete expression;
   }
   else  if (kind == varSym)
      code.Enter(LOD,  level.get() - lev, val, pcd_x);
   else  // must be a constSym
      code.Enter(LIT,                 0, val, pcd_x);
}
```

Figure 5.30
The Lil'LuxLyk Factor class.

5.6 THE PARSER SUPPORT CLASSES

We have now seen all of the classes related to parsing the source code and generating the internal P-Code. It is now time to look at the support classes. We've seen definitions of most of these already. Now it's time to look at the implementation code.

The most important support classes relate to the symbol or token definitions. We saw the class definition in Figure 5.6. At that time the private data of the class were omitted. It is time to look at it and the implementation code. The Symbol class is shown in Figure 5.31.

```
#include <map>
#include <string>
typedef map <string, TokenType, less<string> > sym_dict;
typedef sym_dict::iterator                      location;

class Symbol
{
    static  sym_dict    keywords;
    static  string      line;
    static  int         filled;
    static  Token       *nextToken;
    static  int         lineno;
            char        getChar();
            void        ungetChar(char ch);
public:
                        Symbol();
            Token       *getNewSymbol();
            Token       *getSymbol();
            void        Message(char *str);
};

extern  ifstream in; // input source file

    sym_dict  Symbol::keywords; //  the `static' definitions
    string    Symbol::line;
    int       Symbol::filled = 0;
    Token     *Symbol::nextToken;
    int       Symbol::lineno = 0;

    Symbol::Symbol()      // constructor -- saves keywords in a dictionary
    {
    if (filled) return;
    keywords["BEGIN"]     = beginSym;
    keywords["CALL"]      = callSym;
    keywords["CONST"]     = constSym;
    keywords["DO"]        = doSym;
    keywords["ELSE"]      = elseSym;
    keywords["END"]       = endSym;
    keywords["IF"]        = ifSym;
    keywords["ODD"]       = oddSym;
    keywords["PROCEDURE"] = procSym;
    keywords["READ"]      = readSym;
    keywords["THEN"]      = thenSym;
    keywords["VAR"]       = varSym;
    keywords["WHILE"]     = whileSym;
    keywords["WRITE"]     = writeSym;
    filled = 1;

    nextToken = NULL;
    }

char Symbol::getChar()              // returns a single ch from the input
{
    char  ch, readLine[80];

    if (line.empty())               // read in new line (unless end of file)
    {
        lineno++;
        if ( in.getline(readLine, 80) )
        { line = readLine;   line += ' ';  }
        else
        {
            Message("Program ends too soon");
```

```
            exit(EXIT_FAILURE);
      }
   }
   ch   = line[0];                 // extract 'ch' from beginning of line
   line = line.remove(0, 1);
   return ch;
}

void Symbol::ungetChar(char ch)   // puts a ch back in the input stream
{
   string  prepend;

   prepend = ch;
   line    = prepend + line;      // add 'ch' back at beginning of line
}

Token *Symbol::getNewSymbol()     // returns the next Token from the input
{
   TokenType  tok;
   location   key;
   string     val;
   char       ch;

   if (nextToken != NULL)         // free up previous Token
      delete nextToken;
   nextToken = new Token;         // get space for new Token

   do
   {
      do ch = getChar();          // get a character
      while (ch > '\0' && ch <= ' ');  // skip white space
      val = ch;                   // convert character to a string

      if (ch == '\0')
         tok = noToken;
      else if (isdigit(ch))       // number
      {
         do
         {
            ch = getChar();
            if (isdigit(ch)) val += ch;
         }
         while (isdigit(ch));
         ungetChar(ch);    tok = Number;
      }
      else if (isalpha(ch))           // keyword or ident
      {
         do
         {
            ch = getChar();
            if (isalpha(ch) || isdigit(ch)) val += ch;
         }
         while (isalpha(ch) || isdigit(ch));
         ungetChar(ch);
         key = keywords.find(val);
         if (key != keywords.end())
            tok = (*key).second;
         else
            tok = Ident;
      }
      else if (ch == ':')             // special character pairs ...
      {
         ch = getChar();
         if (ch == '=')
         {   val += ch;    tok = Becomes;    }
```

```
               else
               {   ungetChar(ch); tok = noToken;     }
           }
           else if (ch == '<')
           {
               ch = getChar();
               if (ch == '=')
               {   val += ch;      tok = lessEqual;  }
               else if (ch == '>')
               {   val += ch;      tok = notEqual;   }
               else
               {   ungetChar(ch); tok = Less;        }
           }
           else if (ch == '>')
           {
               ch = getChar();
               if (ch == '=')
               {   val += ch;      tok = grtrEqual;  }
               else
               {   ungetChar(ch); tok = Greater;     }
           }
           else if (ch == '!')
           {
               ch = getChar();
               if (ch == '=')
               {   val += ch;      tok = notEqual;   }
               else
               {   ungetChar(ch); tok = noToken;     }
           }
           else if (ch == '+')     tok = Plus;  // single character tokens
           else if (ch == '-')     tok = Minus;
           else if (ch == '*')     tok = Times;
           else if (ch == '/')     tok = Slash;
           else if (ch == '%')     tok = Percent;
           else if (ch == '=')     tok = Equal;
           else if (ch == '#')     tok = notEqual;
           else if (ch == '.')     tok = Period;
           else if (ch == ',')     tok = Comma;
           else if (ch == ';')     tok = Semicol;
           else if (ch == '(')     tok = lParen;
           else if (ch == ')')     tok = rParen;
           else
           {
               tok = noToken;
               cerr << "Line # " << lineno << ": ";
               cerr << ch << " is not a valid character" << endl;
           }
       }
   while (tok == noToken);

   nextToken->Token = tok;
   nextToken->Value = new string(val);
   return nextToken;
}

Token *Symbol::getSymbol()              // returns the previous Token again
{   return nextToken;   }

void   Symbol::Message(char *str)
{   cerr << "Line # " << lineno << ": " << str << endl;   }
```

Figure 5.31
The Lil'LuxLyk Symbol class.

The Symbol class, also known as the Token Analyzer, uses a dictionary that maps character strings such as "BEGIN" into members of the TokenType enumeration, such as *beginSym*. The Standard Template Library, STL, is used to define the data structure that is the dictionary. The necessary STL header files are included by the first two lines of Figure 5.31. The dictionary type and an iterator into the dictionary are defined in the next two lines of the figure. This declaration is followed by a new definition of the Symbol class—including the private data. Several of the private variables are defined as static. This is so that even if there are multiple instances of the Symbol class, there will only be one instance of such important things as the input line of source code, the line number, the current token, and the dictionary itself. The private area also contains special member functions to read characters from the input source and to "put them back" into the input so they can be read again.

The implementation starts by declaring the static variables. Two of them are given initial values. The *lineno* is set to zero because no input lines have been read in yet. The *filled* variable is used to indicate whether the dictionary has been created yet. It is initially set to zero. The constructor, which comes next in the implementation, checks the filled variable. If it is still 0, the dictionary is created. The name of the dictionary is *keywords*. It is created by the series of assignment statements that follow in the constructor. Once the dictionary has been created, the filled variable is set to one; thus, any other calls to the constructor will return instantly without creating the dictionary again.

The Symbol::getChar private member function is used by the Lexical Analyzer to input individual characters. GetChar first checks to see if the *line* string is empty. If it is empty, a new line of the source is read into the string. The procedure then extracts the first character from the string and returns it to the calling routine. The Symbol::ungetChar private member function 'returns a character to the input' by simply placing it back at the beginning of the line string.

The Symbol::getNewSymbol function is the actual lexical analyzer. It skips over the spaces, tabs, and other 'white space' characters until it gets a usable character. It examines this character to determine what type of token it might be. There are several possibilities: It could be a number, an alphanumeric, or punctuation. If the first character is a digit, a string named *val* is initialized to contain the character and additional characters are input and appended to val until a non-digit is detected. The non-digit is returned to the input. The function then returns a Token that consists of the val string and a TokenType of *Number*.

If the initial character had been alphabetic, val is initialized to contain the character and additional characters are input and appended to val until a nonalphanumeric character is detected. This last character is returned to the input. The val string is looked up in the dictionary; if it is found, the corresponding TokenType from the dictionary is returned. If not found, the function returns a Token that consists of the val string and a TokenType of *Ident*.

All other tokens are punctuation of some type. Some of these may be made up of multiple characters. If the first character indicates that one of these is possible, additional characters are input to see if the token is in fact one of the multiple character tokens. If the additional character does not belong to one of these tokens, the last character is returned to the input as usual. The function returns a TokenType that depends on the characters that made up the detected token. In all cases, numeric, alphanumeric, or punctuation, the Token detected by this function is saved in the private data of the class. In this way, `Symbol::getSymbol` is able to return the current Token merely by accessing the current private value.

The final member function is `Symbol::Message` that outputs a string, *str*, to the standard error stream preceded by the current line number. This particular function is not too closely related to the Symbol class; the only reason it is located here is because the line number is maintained by the lexical analyzer.

A series of classes closely related to the Symbol class are the Symbol Set classes. These classes are used to define several sets of closely related tokens. One such set is the set of tokens that begin a statement, such as *ifSym*, *whileSym*, and so on. A more general Symbol Set is one that defines the tokens that might be expected to follow a non-terminal such as the "condition" in an if statement. The Symbol Set class is shown in Figure 5.32.

```
#include <set>
typedef set <TokenType, less<TokenType> > Sym_set;

class  symSet
{
    Sym_set  sym_set;
public:
          symSet()  {  }
    void  insert(TokenType  sym);
    int   contains(TokenType  sym);
};

void  symSet::insert(TokenType  Token)
{  sym_set.insert( Token );   }

int   symSet::contains(TokenType  Token)
{  return int( sym_set.find(Token) != sym_set.end() );   }


class  decl_beg_symbols
{
    Sym_set  decl_beg;
public:
          decl_beg_symbols();
    int   contains(TokenType  sym);
};

decl_beg_symbols::decl_beg_symbols()
{
    decl_beg.insert(constSym);    decl_beg.insert(procSym);
    decl_beg.insert(varSym);
}

int   decl_beg_symbols::contains(TokenType  Token)
{  return int( decl_beg.find(Token) != decl_beg.end() );   }

class  stmt_beg_symbols
{
    Sym_set  stmt_beg;
public:
          stmt_beg_symbols();
    int   contains(TokenType  sym);
};

stmt_beg_symbols::stmt_beg_symbols()
{
    stmt_beg.insert(beginSym);    stmt_beg.insert(callSym);
    stmt_beg.insert(ifSym);       stmt_beg.insert(readSym);
    stmt_beg.insert(whileSym);    stmt_beg.insert(writeSym);
}

int   stmt_beg_symbols::contains(TokenType  Token)
{  return int( stmt_beg.find(Token) != stmt_beg.end() );   }

class  fctr_beg_symbols
{
    Sym_set  fctr_beg;
public:
          fctr_beg_symbols();
    int   contains(TokenType  sym);
};

fctr_beg_symbols::fctr_beg_symbols()
{
    fctr_beg.insert(Ident);       fctr_beg.insert(Number);
    fctr_beg.insert(lParen);
```

```
}
int   fctr_beg_symbols::contains(TokenType   Token)
{   return int( fctr_beg.find(Token) != fctr_beg.end() );   }
```

Figure 5.32
The Lil'LuxLyk Symbol Set class.

The Symbol Set class uses the STL *set* definition. The first line of the figure imports the appropriate STL header file. The second line defines the set that will be used, basically a set of TokenTypes. The general *symSet* class allows each symbol to be entered into the set. For this reason, the constructor is empty and the class has a separate member function to `insert` the symbols. In all the other classes, the constructor preloads the desired symbols and there is no insert method. All of the classes, however, have a `contains` member function that returns "true" if the TokenType passed to it is in the set; otherwise, it returns "false." It should be noted that, within the implementation code for the various classes, "insert" and "contains" refer to calls to the STL set container itself.

Although its name, Symbol Table, may lead you to believe that it is closely related to the Symbol class, it is quite different. The Symbol class consists of the keywords that are predefined in the language. The Symbol Table is used to save those special symbols that are defined within the source code. We already saw the basic definition of the Symbol Table in Figure 5.7. The expanded form, including the implementation code, is shown in Figure 5.33.


```
struct TableEntry        // special type definition
{                        // used for dictionary storage
   string      Name;
   TokenType   Kind;
   int         Level;
   int         Value;
};

typedef map <int, TableEntry, less<int> > sym_tab;

class SymbolTable
{
   sym_tab   symbolTable;
  public:
        SymbolTable();              // constructor
```

```
    void   Enter    (string      name,    // symbol being entered in table
                     TokenType    kind,    // type of symbol (e.g. Constant...)
                     int          level,   // nesting level of symbol
                     int          value,   // value of the symbol
                     int          tx);     // index location for storing in table

    int    Position(string       name,    // symbol begin sought
                    int           tx);     // index to search down from

    int    Examine (string       &name,   // symbol at location
                    TokenType     &kind,   // kind of symbol
                    int           &level,  // nesting level of symbol
                    int           &value,  // value of symbol
                    int           tx);     // table index to examine

    int    FixValue(int          value,   // new value for the table entry
                    int           tx);     // index of entry to be modified
};

    SymbolTable::SymbolTable()
{
    TableEntry  entry;

    entry.Name  = "main";              // create dummy initial entry
    entry.Kind  = procSym;
    entry.Level = 0;
    entry.Value = 0;
    symbolTable[0] = entry;            // put in table
}

void  SymbolTable::Enter(string  name,   TokenType kind,    int level,
                         int      value, int       tx)
{
    TableEntry entry;

    symbolTable.erase(tx);            // remove, in case something's there

    entry.Name  = name;               // prepare the entry
    entry.Kind  = kind;
    entry.Level = level;
    if (kind == procSym)
       entry.Value = 0;
    else
       entry.Value = value;

    symbolTable[tx] = entry;          // put in table
}

int   SymbolTable::Examine(string &name,   TokenType &kind,   int &level,
                           int     &value, int        tx)
{
    TableEntry entry;

    if (symbolTable.find(tx) == symbolTable.end())
       return FALSE;
    else
    {
       entry = symbolTable[tx];       // pull from table
       name  = entry.Name;            // output its fields
       kind  = entry.Kind;
       level = entry.Level;
       value = entry.Value;
       return TRUE;
    }
}
```

```
int   SymbolTable::Position (string name,  int tx)
{
    TableEntry  entry;
    int         index = tx;

    entry = symbolTable[0];          // get current sentinel
    entry.Name = name;               // update its name
    entry.Level = 0;
    symbolTable.erase(0);            // remove current
    symbolTable[0] = entry;          // replace the sentinel

    index++;
    do                               // find most recent entry of symbol
    {
        index--;
        entry = symbolTable[index];
    }
    while (name != entry.Name);
    return index;
}

int   SymbolTable::FixValue (int value,  int tx)
{
    TableEntry  entry;

    if (symbolTable.find(tx) == symbolTable.end())
        return FALSE;
    else
    {
        entry = symbolTable[tx];     // get indicated entry
        entry.Value = value;         // update its value
        symbolTable.erase(tx);       // remove old entry
        symbolTable[tx] = entry;     // replace with new entry
        return TRUE;
    }
}
```

Figure 5.33
The Lil'LuxLyk Symbol Table class.

The Symbol Table consists of entries that are indexed sequentially. That is, each entry can be referenced by an integer value that tells where it is located in the table. The form of the *TableEntry* is shown at the beginning of Figure 5.33. It consists of fields for the *name*, *kind*, *level*, and *value* parts of a symbol definition. The typedef line in the figure defines the STL map or dictionary structure that is used to store the symbols. It shows that integers are mapped into individual TableEntries. The private area of the *SymbolTable* class contains an instance of this dictionary; it is known as the *symbolTable*.

The SymbolTable constructor creates a dummy TableEntry and places it at location zero. Location 0 serves two special purposes. In the first place, it points to the location in the Code where the main program section of the source code begins. The second purpose is to simplify the Position member function. This will be seen below.

The `SymbolTable::Enter` member function moves the entry values passed to it into a TableEntry structure and then stores this *entry* in the symbolTable as indicated by the *tx* parameter.

The `SymbolTable::Examine` member function first checks to see if an entry actually exists at the index indicated by the tx parameter. If it does, the entry is extracted from the table and the data in its fields are moved to the variables directed by the name, kind, level, and value parameters. The function returns a value of "true" in this case; otherwise it returns a "false."

The purpose of the `SymbolTable::Position` function is to find the location in the table of an entry whose name field has the same value as the parameter passed to it. The function starts at the index provided by the tx parameter and proceeds to lower entries until the matching entry is found. This type of search usually requires two tests. The first test is to see if the entry matches. If it doesn't, a second test is required to see if we have reached the bottom of the list. This function uses a different technique that requires only a single test. First it stores the desired name in the entry at location zero. Now when it searches downwards, it doesn't have to check to see if it reached the bottom. We are sure to find the entry. When it is found, the function returns the index at which it was found. A returned value of 0 indicates that the symbol was not in the table.

The `SymbolTable::FixValue` member function extracts the indicated entry from the table, replaces its value field with the value passed to it, and then puts the entry back into the table.

The *Code* class is similar to the Symbol Table class. The entries are a structure called PInstr instead of TableEntry and the Symbol Table's Examine function has been renamed Fetch. There is no Position function; instead, there is a new Member function called CurrentLoc. The Code class is shown in Figure 5.34.

```
#include <map>

enum FunctType  { OPR,      // operation
                  LIT,      // load immediate  (i.e., literal)
                  LOD,      // load value
                  STO,      // store value
                  CAL,      // call subroutine
                  INT,      // increment T register
                  JMP,      // jump  (unconditional)
                  JPC,      // conditional jump
                  CSP  };   // call special procedure

struct PInstr
{
    FunctType  fnctn;       // op_code of the instruction
    int        level;       // level (difference) value
    int        value;       // value of the instruction
};

typedef map< int, PInstr, less<int> > code_dict;

class Code
{
    static  code_dict  code;
    static  int        c_loc;
public:
          Code();                      // constructor
    void  Enter     (FunctType fct,    // type of function (e.g. OPR...)
                     int       level,  // nesting level of code
                     int       value,  // value of the code
                     int       &cx);   // location for next instr
    int   Fetch     (FunctType &fct,   // type of function
                     int       &level, // nesting level of instr
                     int       &value, // value of code
                     int       cx);    // code location to examine
    int   FixValue  (int       value,  // new value for the instr
                     int       cx);    // location of instr to be modified
    int   CurrentLoc();                // return current location
};

code_dict  Code::code;                 // the static variables
int        Code::c_loc;                //  "     "       "

Code::Code()                           // constructor
{ c_loc = 0;  }                        // set to beginning of dictionary

void Code::Enter (FunctType  fct, int  level, int  value, int &cx)
{
    PInstr  entry;

    entry.fnctn = fct;                 // load the entry
    entry.level = level;
    entry.value = value;
    code[c_loc] = entry;               // store entry in dictionary
    cx = ++c_loc;                      // return pointer to next entry
}

int Code::Fetch (FunctType &fct, int &level, int &value, int  cx)
{
    PInstr  entry;

    if (code.find(cx) != code.end())
    {
        entry = code[cx];              // get the entry
        fct   = entry.fnctn;           // extract the field values
```

```
        level = entry.level;
        value = entry.value;
        return TRUE;
    }
    else
        return FALSE;
}

int Code::FixValue (int value, int cx)
{
    PInstr  entry;

    if (code.find(cx) != code.end())
    {
        entry = code[cx];                  // get old entry
        entry.value = value;               // change the value
        code[cx] = entry;                  // store back in dictionary
        return TRUE;
    }
    else
        return FALSE;
}

int Code::CurrentLoc()
{  return c_loc;   }
```

Figure 5.34
The Lil'LuxLyk Code class.

　　　The first line of Figure 5.34 imports the STL map header file as before. This is followed by an enumeration that defines the names of all of the P-Code functions. After that, we finally have the definition of an entry in the Code, a "PInstr". Next comes the definition of the STL map used to store the Code. In this case, we are mapping an integer storage location into the P-Instruction (i.e., PInstr) stored at that location. An instance of this map is in the private area of the class; its name is *code*.

　　　This class varies somewhat from the Symbol Table class by the fact that it maintains control of where the next entry shall be placed. (In the Symbol Table, the tx parameter told where the entry was to be made.) The Code class maintains the current location by the private data variable named *c_loc* that is set to zero by the constructor. The present value is always output by the Code::Enter member function. It can also be obtained by calling the Code::CurrentLoc method. Other than these few changes, the implementation closely follows the Symbol Table code.

　　　The final Lil'LuxLyk class is *Level*. It has an integer in its private data that keeps track of the current procedure nesting level. The constructor sets this value to zero. There are member functions that increment or decrement the value and one that returns its current value. Static variables are used to ensure that only one instance of the current level is maintained. In addition, the *defed* variable is used to make sure that only the first instance of the Level class sets level to zero. The Level class is shown in Figure 5.35.

```
class Level
{
    static int   level;
    static int   defed;
  public:
          Level();                    // constructor
    void  inc();                      // raise the nesting level
    void  dec();                      // lower the nesting level
    int   get();                      // get the nesting level
};

int   Level::level;                   // the static variables
int   Level::defed = 0;               // "    "      "

Level::Level()
{
    if (defed)   return;
    level = 0;
    defed = 1;
}

void  Level::inc  ()     {  level ++ ;          }

void  Level::dec  ()     {  level -- ;          }

int   Level::get  ()     {  return (level);     }
```

Figure 5.35
The Lil'LuxLyk Level class.

5.7 A SIMPLE EXAMPLE

We shall now go through a rather short example to get a clearer idea of how the parser creates a ParseNode tree and how the P-Code is generated by the tree structure. We shall look at the compilation of the Lil'LuxLyk program shown in Figure 5.36.

```
VAR
    A, B, C, D, E;
BEGIN
    READ (B, C, D, E);
    A := B + C * (D - E);
    WRITE (A)
END.
```

Figure 5.36
A simple Lil'LuxLyk program.

The compiler's main program starts things off by creating an instance of the Program class and calling its Parse function. Program::Parse creates an instance of the Block class and calls its Parse function. Block::Parse generates a "JMP 0 0" at Code location 0 and then creates a Declaration ParseNode and calls its Parse function. This in turn sees the VAR token and creates a VarDeclar node. The Parse function of that class collects the symbol names "A," "B," "C," "D," and "E" in a declQ. After this, the Block::Parse function calls Declaration::Generate, which it turn calls VarDeclar::Generate. This function enters the variables from its queue into the Symbol Table. This completes the declarations for our simple program. The contents of the Symbol Table at this point are shown in Table 5.1.

Table 5.1

Initial Symbol Table

Entry #	Symbol	Kind	Level	Value
0	main	procSym	0	0
1	A	varSym	0	3
2	B	varSym	0	4
3	C	varSym	0	5
4	D	varSym	0	6
5	E	varSym	0	7

Entry 0 Value points to the JMP 0 0 instruction.

The Block::Parse function now switches over to parsing the body of the program. It creates an instance of the Body class and calls its Parse function. Body::Parse detects the BEGIN token in the source code, creates an instance of the StatementList class, and calls its Parse function. StatementList::Parse will detect the three statements, creating individual Statement ParseNodes for each, calling their Parse functions, and placing each node in its parseQ.

The first Statement::Parse sees the READ token and creates an instance of the readStatement class. Its Parse function collects the symbols named between the parentheses and places them in a declQ.

The second Statement::Parse notes that the current token is an identifier and creates an instance of an assignStatement. We have already seen how this assignment statement expands in Figure 4.8. Refer to Section 4.7 to review its development.

The third Statement::Parse function sees the WRITE token and creates an instance of the writeStatement class. Its Parse function creates ParseNodes to evaluate all the expressions between the parentheses, calls their Parse functions, and places them in its parseQ. In this case, there is only one expression. It resolves to a single term/factor/identifier, that is, the symbol "A."

At this point, all the Parse functions return until we get back to Body::Parse, which sees the END token and is satisfied by it. All tokens have now been read except the final period. It will not be examined until we finally return to the Program::Parse function. In between, we shall do all of the P-Code generation. The complete parse tree has now been completed. It would be helpful to look at it.

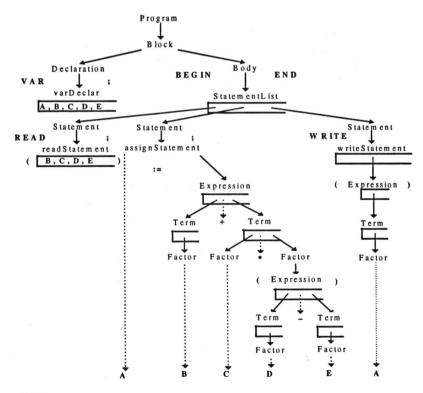

Figure 5.37
Calling sequence for the simple program.

The call sequence is shown in Figure 5.37. It shows quite a lot of information and therefore requires some explanation. For instance, I said several times in the previous paragraphs that one ParseNode created an instance of another ParseNode class. In all of these cases, the original node contains a pointer to the new node in its private data. This is how the parse tree is built. In the diagram, solid arrows point to the new node. Thus, we can see that the Program node created a Block node that in turn created two nodes—a Declaration node and a Body node. The VAR token shown below the Declaration node indicates that it directed Declaration to create the varDeclar ParseNode. It also shows where that particular token is actually used by a Parse function. You will find all of the other tokens of the source distributed around the diagram at the locations where they are used. For instance, the next sequence of tokens is "A, B, C, D, E." These are read by the varDeclar node and saved in a queue. You will see them located just below the varDeclar node inside of an open-ended box. This box is used to represent a queue; you will see them wherever an unknown number of items are collected in the private area of a class. Some tokens are shown sort of floating in space such as the ":=" and the left or right parenthesis. These free-floating tokens show where the tokens are parsed but not otherwise saved. Some other tokens contain information that must be saved. For instance, the arithmetic operations determine the type of OPR instruction that *must* be used. Therefore, information about these tokens is saved in the private area of the class. In addition, identifiers contain level and value information that must be used in either LOD or STO instructions. This too must be saved in the private area of the class. These saved tokens are represented by dotted arrows in Figure 5.37. It would be helpful to compare the diagram with the paragraphs preceding it that tell how the parse tree is created. Hopefully this will make the process clearer.

Now we are ready to see how the P-Code is stored. Recall that we left off where Body::Parse had detected the END token. From here, process control returns to the Block::Parse function that immediately calls Body::Generate.

Body::Generate puts an "INT 0 8" into the Code at location 1. It then goes back and modifies the address value of Code location 0 and Symbol Table entry 0 to point to the INT instruction at location 1. The corrected Symbol Table looks like Table 5.2.

Table 5.2

Corrected Symbol Table				
Entry #	Symbol	Kind	Level	Value
0	main	procSym	0	1
1	A	varSym	0	3
2	B	varSym	0	4
3	C	varSym	0	5
4	D	varSym	0	6
5	E	varSym	0	7

Entry 0 Value points to the INT 0 8 instruction.

Body::Generate calls StatementList::Generate that pulls the first statement off the parseQ and follows the Generate calls through to the readStatement class. Its Generate function creates a "CSP 0 6" and an STO instruction pair for each identifier in the declQ. This will load instructions into Code locations 2 through 9.

Eventually, all calls return back to StatementList::Generate again, which pulls the second Statement off the queue and follows the calls to Expression::Generate. It pulls the leftmost Term off the subexprQ and follows the Generate call path down to the "B" identifier. This enters a "LOD 0 4" instruction into the Code at location 10. The right-most Term involves another queue with multiple entries. The left-most Factor is the "C" identifier; it puts a "LOD 0 5" into location 11. In the same manner, "LOD" instructions for "D" and "E" are loaded into the next two locations. As we go back up the call path, the functions enter OPR P-Codes for subtraction, multiplication, and addition, respectively. When we finally get back to the assignStatement, it enters an "STO 0 3" to store the results of the expression at the location reserved for identifier "A."

Eventually, we get back to StatementList::Generate which pulls the last Statement out of the queue and follows it down to the writeStatement::Generate function that enters a P-Code to load "A" onto the stack and a "CSP 0 3" to write it out. This is followed by four instructions that output a carriage return character and a line feed character.

Once more, we return from one function to the other until we reach Body::Generate again. It outputs the "OPR 0 0" P-Code that is the final program return. A couple more function returns brings us to the point where Program::Parse checks for the final period. At this point, the complete program has been entered into the Code class. The final generated P-Code is shown in Figure 5.38.

0	JMP	0	1
1	INT	0	8
2	CSP	0	2
3	STO	0	4
4	CSP	0	2
5	STO	0	5
6	CSP	0	2
7	STO	0	6
8	CSP	0	2
9	STO	0	7
10	LOD	0	4
11	LOD	0	5
12	LOD	0	6
13	LOD	0	7
14	OPR	0	3
15	OPR	0	4
16	OPR	0	2
17	STO	0	3
18	LOD	0	3
19	CSP	0	3
20	LIT	0	13
21	CSP	0	1
22	LIT	0	10
23	CSP	0	1
24	OPR	0	0

Figure 5.38
P-Code for a simple program.

5.8 RUNNING THE PROGRAM

Now that our Lil'LuxLyk programs can be translated into their P-Code equivalent form, we still need to find a way to do something useful with them. What we really want to do is "run" the programs so that we can get answers. In Section 4.1, I pointed out that the only way that we can get answers is by interpreting the program. What we need to do is to find a way to interpret the P-Code. There are several ways that this can be done; some involve hardware and some involve software. Generally, the hardware solutions are faster. Some of the methods we could use are:

- Interpret the P-Code within the same program that did the conversion. In this form, the conversion program is an interpreter rather than a compiler.
- Output the P-Code in a form that can be run by another program that does the interpretation. This is the method that will be used in the study of basic concurrency. This approach is essentially the way Java™ works. A Java *class* file is a form of pseudo-code that is interpreted by the "Java Virtual Machine." Java can run on any platform that has an implementation of this machine. This makes it very portable.
- Translate the P-Code into another language that can be compiled on the given platform. This is one way that a language can be ported to a new platform. For instance, we will be able to port Lil'LuxLyk to any platform that has a **C** compiler.
- Translate the P-Code into assembler language for the target processor—assemble, link, and load it. In this case, the central processing unit is the interpreter. This way may not be portable, but it is often the most efficient.

I shall look at most of these approaches. I will not build an interpreter inside the present translator; however, this could be done quite easily. All the examples I shall show will produce some sort of output file that requires further processing. The Lil'LuxLyk compiler is accessed from a command line, for instance, from a DOS prompt. The command line will contain the name of the source file to be compiled. Unless otherwise specified, the output of the compiler will be sent to standard output (i.e., the screen). It is possible to redirect this output to a file. The following command would compile a source program named "simple.lll" and send its output to another file named "simple.pcd".

```
C:\> Lilluxly simple.lll >simple.pcd
```

We need some main program code that will access the file named in the command line and then call Program::Parse and Program::Generate. The output will be produced by the latter function. Code that will satisfy these requirements is shown in Figure 5.39.

```
#include <stdlib.h>
#include <string.h>
#include <iostream.h>
#include <fstream.h>

#include "Parser.h"                       // Parser class definition

    char      file_name[80];
    ifstream  in;                         // used by Lexical Analyser

int main(int argc,  char *argv[])
{
    Program  *program;

    if (--argc == 0)
    {
        cerr << "\n    usage:     LilLuxLy  <input file>\n" << endl;
        exit(EXIT_FAILURE);
    }
    else
        strcpy(file_name, *++argv);

    in.open(file_name);
    program = new Program;
    program->Parse();                     // parse the input program
    program->Generate();                  // produce the output
    delete program;
    in.close();

    return (EXIT_SUCCESS);
}
```

Figure 5.39
The Lil'LuxLyk main program.

Now we are ready to look at the Program::Generate code. As I said when we looked at Program::Parse, the Generate function would be the last one examined. Of all of the Generate functions, it is unique. By the time it executes, all of the P-Code has been entered into the Code class. It's up to the Program's Generate function to access that code and do something useful with it. We shall examine three different "useful" approaches.

The first approach that we shall look at is the simplest. We shall output the P-Code as readable text that can be input by another program that interprets it. The PMachine in the next chapter is one such program; in fact, the PMachine will execute files that this method produces. A version of Program::Generate that accomplishes our objective is shown in Figure 5.40.

```
void  Program::Generate()
{
   FunctType    fct;
   int          lev, val;
   int          done, i = 0;

   do
   {
      done = code.Fetch(fct, lev, val, i);
      if (done)
      {
         cout << i << '\t';
         switch (fct)
         {
            case OPR:    cout << "OPR";    break;
            case LIT:    cout << "LIT";    break;
            case LOD:    cout << "LOD";    break;
            case STO:    cout << "STO";    break;
            case CAL:    cout << "CAL";    break;
            case INT:    cout << "INT";    break;
            case JMP:    cout << "JMP";    break;
            case JPC:    cout << "JPC";    break;
            case CSP:    cout << "CSP";    break;
         }
         cout << '\t' << lev << '\t' << val << endl;
      }
      i++;
   }
   while (done);
   cout << endl;

   delete Sym;
}
```

Figure 5.40
A Program::Generate that outputs P-Code.

This particular form produces output that looks like the listing in Figure 5.38. Once more, we will be using this form of output with the LuxLyk compiler and the PMachine in the next chapter.

Next we shall look at a different form of Program::Generate. This one will produce a **C** program. The concept is to actually construct the PMachine in the **C** program that gets output. The output starts by declaring the stack and the registers. Next it prints out a function to simulate tracing down the static links to find a global variable. The main program that gets output begins by setting the return value to 0 in the main program's stack frame. After this, each P-Code instruction is translated into an equivalent **C** form, that is, one or more **C** statements that perform the operation intended for the P-Code. Some of these statements will have labels. "JMP" and "JPC" will be translated into "goto" statements that reference these labels. Return instructions, that is, "OPR 0 0", are more complex. They get the return address from the stack, but must branch to a switch statement that converts the numeric value into a label. After all P-Codes have been translated, the Generate function creates the switch statement. This form of Program::Generate is shown in Figure 5.41 and a sample output for our simple program is shown in Figure 5.42. All you have to do with the output **C** code is run it through a **C** compiler to get an executable program. In addition, it is possible to construct a PMachine by removing the "cout" part of the statements and just leaving the C statements themselves. The jump and return P-Codes can actually be handled easier then the way they are done in Generate.

```
typedef set    < int, less<int> > labelSet;

void  Program::Generate()
{
    FunctType    fct;
    int          lev, val, dim, siz;
    int          done, i = 0;
    string       name;
    TokenType    kind, typ;
    labelSet     labels;
    returnQ      returns;
    int          ret;

    labels.insert( 0 );      // always label location 0
    do    // find all the branch targets (for labels)
    {
        done = code.Fetch(fct, lev, val, i);
        if (done)
        {
            if (fct == CAL || fct == JMP || fct == JPC)
                labels.insert( val );
            if (fct == CAL)
                labels.insert( i + 1 );
        }
        i++;
    }
    while (done);
    cout << "\n#include <stdio.h>\n#include <stdlib.h>\n";
    cout << "#define  SSIZE 500" << endl;
    cout << "\nint  st[SSIZE];\nint  t = -1;\nint  b =  0;" << endl;
    cout << "\nint  base(int lev)\n{\n    int bt = b;" << endl;
    cout << "\n    while (lev > 0) {\n\tbt = st[bt];\n\tlev--;\n    }";
    cout << "\n    return bt;\n}" << endl;
    cout << "\nint main()\n{\n\tint  r;\n\n\tst[t+3] = 0;\n" << endl;

    i = 0;    // start over and produce output
    do
    {
        done = code.Fetch(fct, lev, val, i);
        if (done)
```

```
{
    if ( labels.find(i) != labels.end() )
        cout << 'L' << i << ":\t";
    else
        cout << "\t";
    switch (fct)
    {
        case OPR:   switch (val)
                    {
                        case 0:  cout << "t = b-1;  b = st[t+2];  "
                                      << "r = st[t+3];  goto retrn;"
                                      << endl;
                                 break;
                        case 1:  cout << "st[t] = - st[t];"
                                      << endl;
                                 break;
                        case 2:  cout << "st[t-1] += st[t--];"
                                      << endl;
                                 break;
                        case 3:  cout << "st[t-1] -= st[t--];"
                                      << endl;
                                 break;
                        case 4:  cout << "st[t-1] *= st[t--];"
                                      << endl;
                                 break;
                        case 5:  cout << "st[t-1] /= st[t--];"
                                      << endl;
                                 break;
                        case 6:  cout << "st[t] &= 1;"
                                      << endl;
                                 break;
                        case 7:  cout << "st[t-1] %= st[t--];"
                                      << endl;
                                 break;
                        case 8:  cout << "st[--t] = "
                                      << "st[t] == st[t+1];"
                                      << endl;
                                 break;
                        case 9:  cout << "st[--t] = "
                                      << "st[t] != st[t+1];"
                                      << endl;
                                 break;
                        case 10: cout << "st[--t] = "
                                      << "st[t] < st[t+1];"
                                      << endl;
                                 break;
                        case 11: cout << "st[--t] = "
                                      << "st[t] >= st[t+1];"
                                      << endl;
                                 break;
                        case 12: cout << "st[--t] = "
                                      << "st[t] > st[t+1];"
                                      << endl;
                                 break;
                        case 13: cout << "st[--t] = "
                                      << "st[t] <= st[t+1];"
                                      << endl;
                                 break;
                    };
                    break;
        case LIT:   cout << "st[++t] = " << val << ';' << endl;
                    break;
        case LOD:   cout << "st[++t] = st[base(" << lev
                         << ") + " << val << "];" << endl;
                    break;
```

```
        case STO:   cout << "st[base(" << lev << ") + "
                         << val << "] = st[t--];" << endl;
                    break;
        case CAL:   cout << "st[t+1] = base(" << lev
                         << ");  st[t+2] = b;  st[t+3] = "
                         << (i+1) << ";  b = t+1;  goto L"
                         << val << ';' << endl;
                    returns.push(i+1);
                    break;
        case INT:   cout << "t += " << val << ';' << endl;
                    break;
        case JMP:   cout << "goto L" << val << ';' << endl;
                    break;
        case JPC:   cout << "if (st[t--] == " << lev
                         << ") goto L" << val << ';' << endl;
                    break;
        case CSP:   switch (val)
                    {
                        case 0:  cout << "st[++t] = getchar();";
                                 break;
                        case 1:  cout << "putchar(st[t--]);";
                                 break;
                        case 2:  cout << "++t;  printf (\"> \");  "
                                      << "scanf(\"%d\", &st[t]);";
                                 break;
                        case 3:  cout << "printf(\"%d \", st[t--]);";
                                 break;
                    };       cout << endl;
                    break;
        }
    }
    i++;
    }
    while (done);

    cout << "\nretrn:\tswitch(r) {" << endl;
    cout << "\t    case 0:  goto finis;" << endl;
    while ( ! returns.empty() )
    {
        ret = returns.front();      returns.pop();
        cout << "\t    case " << ret << ": goto L" << ret << ';' << endl;
    }
    cout << "\t}\nfinis:\treturn (EXIT_SUCCESS);\n}" << endl;
    delete Sym;
}
```

Figure 5.41
A Program::Generate that outputs a C program.

```
#include <stdio.h>
#include <stdlib.h>
#define  SSIZE 500

int  st[SSIZE];
int  t = -1;
int  b =  0;

int  base(int lev)
{
    int  bt = b;

    while (lev > 0) {
        bt = st[bt];
        lev--;
    }
    return bt;
}

int main()
{
        int  r;

        st[t+3] = 0;

L0:     goto L1;
L1:     t += 8;
        ++t;   printf ("> ");  scanf("%d", &st[t]);
        st[base(0) + 4] = st[t--];
        ++t;   printf ("> ");   scanf("%d", &st[t]);
        st[base(0) + 5] = st[t--];
        ++t;   printf ("> ");   scanf("%d", &st[t]);
        st[base(0) + 6] = st[t--];
        ++t;   printf ("> ");   scanf("%d", &st[t]);
        st[base(0) + 7] = st[t--];
        st[++t] = st[base(0) + 4];
        st[++t] = st[base(0) + 5];
        st[++t] = st[base(0) + 6];
        st[++t] = st[base(0) + 7];
        st[t-1] -= st[t--];
        st[t-1] *= st[t--];
        st[t-1] += st[t--];
        st[base(0) + 3] = st[t--];
        st[++t] = st[base(0) + 3];
        printf("%d ", st[t--]);
        st[++t] = 13;
        putchar(st[t--]);
        st[++t] = 10;
        putchar(st[t--]);
        t = b-1;  b = st[t+2];  r = st[t+3];  goto retrn;

retrn:  switch(r) {
            case 0:  goto finis;
        }
finis:  return (EXIT_SUCCESS);
}
```

Figure 5.42
C Program produced for a simple program.

When running this form of the compiler, which produces a C program, it is important to enter the command line as follows:

```
C:\> Lilluxly simple.lll >simple.c
```

The last form that we shall look at is one that produces assembler language output. The output from the compiler will not look too much different from a simple listing of the P-Code, but the effect will be quite different. First, let's look at the new form of Program::Generate. It's shown in Figure 5.43.

```
typedef set   < int, less<int> > labelSet;

void  Program::Generate()
{
    FunctType   fct;
    int         lev, val;
    int         done, i = 0;
    string      name;
    TokenType   kind;
    labelSet    labels;

    labels.insert( 0 );      // always label location 0

    do    // find all the branch targets (for labels)
    {
        done = code.Fetch(fct, lev, val, i);
        if (done)
        {
            if (fct == CAL || fct == JMP || fct == JPC)
                labels.insert( val );
            if (fct == CAL)
                labels.insert( i + 1 );
        }
        i++;
    }
    while (done);

    i = 0;        // start over and produce output
    cout << "\n\tINCLUDE\tPCODE.DEF\t; p-code macro definitions\n" << endl;
    do
    {
        done = code.Fetch(fct, lev, val, i);
        if (done)
        {
            if ( labels.find(i) != labels.end() )
                cout << 'L' << i << ":\t";
            else
                cout << "\t";
            switch (fct)
            {
                case OPR:   cout << "OPR";   break;
                case LIT:   cout << "LIT";   break;
                case LOD:   cout << "LOD";   break;
                case STO:   cout << "STO";   break;
                case CAL:   cout << "CAL";   break;
                case INT:   cout << "MVT";   break;
```

```
                case JMP:    cout << "JUM";    break;
                case JPC:    cout << "JPC";    break;
                case CSP:    cout << "CSP";    break;
          }
          cout << '\t' << lev << ',' << val << endl;
      }
      i++;
   }
   while (done);
   cout << "\tTEXT\tENDS\t\t; required for 80x86 assembly" << endl;
   cout << "\tEND \tSTRT\t\t; end of program" << endl;

   delete Sym;
}
```

Figure 5.43
A Program::Generate that Outputs Code for Assembly Language.

The function starts out by examining all of the P-Codes to see which ones are the target of a jump or return instruction. The jump targets are found within the P-Code instruction itself. The return addresses are the locations following the call statements. When we output lines of P-Code during the next part of the function, we will place a label in front of any lines that have been determined to be targets. (The same sort of analysis was used in the Generator that produced a **C** program.)

The rest of the Generator function fetches each instruction out of the Code and writes it out to the standard output. There are a couple of changes made. Instead of writing "JMP" and "INT," the opcodes "JUM" and "MVT" are used instead. The original mnemonics happen to be used in various assembler languages. We will be attempting to supply a different meaning to our op codes. Therefore, to avoid confusion, we use different codes. There are other modifications. The line "INCLUDE PCODE.DEF" is placed at the beginning of the output and the lines "TEXT ENDS" and "END STRT" are placed at the end. We should use the following command line with this version of the compiler:

```
C:\> Lilluxly simple.lll >simple.asm
```

The ".asm" extension shown above should be replaced by whatever extension is expected by the assembler on whatever platform the code is targeted for.

The output of this version of Program:Generate is shown in Figure 5.44.

```
          INCLUDE PCODE.DEF      ; p-code macro definitions

L0:       JUM       0,1
L1:       MVT       0,8
          CSP       0,2
          STO       0,4
          CSP       0,2
          STO       0,5
          CSP       0,2
          STO       0,6
          CSP       0,2
          STO       0,7
          LOD       0,4
          LOD       0,5
          LOD       0,6
          LOD       0,7
          OPR       0,3
          OPR       0,4
          OPR       0,2
          STO       0,3
          LOD       0,3
          CSP       0,3
          LIT       0,13
          CSP       0,1
          LIT       0,10
          CSP       0,1
          OPR       0,0
          TEXT      ENDS          ; required for 80x86 assembly
          END       STRT          ; end of program
```

Figure 5.44
"Assembler Language" form of simple program.

This doesn't look too much different from the original listing of the P-Code program. The power of this approach is in the file named "PCODE.DEF," which gets included by the first line of the output "assembler code." The PCODE.DEF file contains a set of macro definitions and initialization code written in assembler language that converts the "P-Code" output into true assembler language. Of course, the PCODE.DEF file must be written anew for each different assembler language that we intend to use with our compiler.

Figure 5.45 shows a possible PCODE.DEF file for use with the DEC Alpha computer. There are a couple of changes that must be changed to get the Alpha assembler to accept this code. The first line must be charged to read as follows:

```
.INCLUDE    "PCODE.DEF"
```

and the last line must be changed to:

```
$end_routine    STRT
```

Once these changes are made, the PCODE.DEF file will be properly included in the P-Code file and the STRT routine will be properly delimited.

```
.title    P machine -- Basic architecture and macros for DEC Alpha

;     The following p-machine / real machine correspondences are made:

;              P -- Machine                    Real Machine
;        ===========================    ==============================
;        registers:
;           P - program counter         pc - program counter
;                                       sp - system stack pointer
;           T - top of stack pointer    r5 - top of stack pointer
;           B - base register           r4 - local base register
;                                       r3 - holds level difference
;                                       r2 - final base pointer
;                                       r1 - used in arithmetic ...
;                                       r0 -   ... calculations
;        SL, DL, RA saved on stack      RA saved on system stack
;                                       SL and DL saved on stack
;        able to traverse static link   procedure BASE used to
;                                              traverse the static link

;     Native code generation macros written for the DEC Alpha

.macro test    op, ?lbl1, ?lbl2
        CMP'op' (T)+, (T),   r22
        B'op'   r22, lbl1
        MOV     #1, (T)
        BR      lbl2
lbl1:   CLR     (T)
lbl2:
        .endm   test


.macro bse     lv, ad
   .if eq <lv>
        MOV     B, r2
   .iff
        MOV     #'lv', r3
        $CALL   BASE
   .endc
        .endm   bse
```

```
.macro bas     lv, ad
       bse     'lv', 'ad'
       SUBL    #'ad'*2, r2, r2
       .endm   bas


.macro put     x, y
       MOV     'x', -'y'(T)
       .endm   put


.macro LIT     lv, ad
       put     #'ad'
       .endm   LIT


.macro OPR     lv, ad
   .if idn <ad>,<0>
       MOV     B, T
       ADDL    #ArgStk+2, T, T
       MOV     -4(T), B
       $RETURN
   .endc
   .iif idn <ad>,<1>,    SUBL    R31, (T), (T)
   .iif idn <ad>,<2>,    ADDL    (T)+, (T), (T)
   .iif idn <ad>,<3>,    SUBL    (T)+, (T), (T)
   .iif idn <ad>,<4>,    MULL    (T)+, (T), (T)
   .iif idn <ad>,<5>,    $CALL   opr5
   .iif idn <ad>,<6>,    BIC     #-2, (T), (Y)
   .iif idn <ad>,<7>,    $CALL   opr7
   .iif idn <ad>,<8>,    test    NE
   .iif idn <ad>,<9>,    test    EQ
   .iif idn <ad>,<10>,   test    LE
   .iif idn <ad>,<11>,   test    GT
   .iif idn <ad>,<12>,   test    GE
   .iif idn <ad>,<13>,   test    LT
       .endm   OPR


.macro LOD     lv, ad
       bas     'lv', 'ad'
       put     ArgStk(r2)
       .endm   LOD


.macro STO     lv, ad
       bas     'lv', 'ad'
       MOV     (T)+, ArgStk(r2)
       .endm   STO
```

```
        .macro CAL      lv, ad
                bse     'lv', 'ad'
                put     r2, 2
                put     B,  4
                MOV     T,  B
                SUBL    #ArgStk+2, B, T
                $CALL   L'ad'
                .endm   CAL


        .macro INT      lv, ad
                SUBL    #'ad'*2, T, T
                .endm   INT


        .macro JUM      lv, ad
                JMP     L'ad'
                .endm   JUM


        .macro JPC      lv, ad
                CMPEQ   (T)+, #'lv',  r22
                BEQ     r22, L'ad'
                .endm   JPC


        .macro CSP      lv, ad
                $CALL   CSP'ad'
                .endm   CSP


        .macro TEXT     ends    ; not used for DEC Alpha
                .endm   TEXT


        .page
        ;       P - machine kernel written for the DEC Alpha computer

                $routine STRT, kind=stack,local=true,
                    data_section_pointer=true,
                    saved_regs=<r2,r3,r4,r5>

        B - R4                          ; Base register for P-machine
        T = R5                          ; Top-of-stack register for P-machine

                $linkage_section        ; BEGIN
                $code_section           ;
                .base   r27, $ls        ;
                mov     r27, r2         ;
```

```
        ldq     r3, $dp         ;
        .base   r3, $ds         ;
        .base   r2, $ls         ;
        MOV     #ArgStk, T      ;   T := 0;
        MOV     #-2, B          ;   B := 1;
        CLR     -2(T)           ;   S[T+1] := 0;
        CLR     -4(T)           ;   S[T+2] := 0;
        CLR     -6(T)           ;   S[T+3] := 0;
        $CALL   L0              ;   L0();  (* call p-code program *)
        $RETURN                 ; END.    (* return to O.S. *)


BASE:   MOV     B, r2           ; FUNCTION Base(1: INTEGER): INTEGER;
B1:     TST     r3              ;   VAR  b1: INTEGER;
        BLE     B2              ; BEGIN
        MOV     ArgStk(r2), r2  ;   b1 := B;
        DEC     r3              ;   WHILE 1 > 0 DO b1 := S[b1]; DEC(1)
        BR      B1              ;   END;      RETURN b1
B2:     $RETURN                 ; END;


        .=.+2000                ; Var
ArgStk:                         ;   S[500]: INTEGER;


        .extrn  CSP0, CSP1      ; External routines
        .extrn  CSP2, CSP3      ;   CSP0, CSP1, CSP2, CSP3,
        .extrn  OPR5, OPR7      ;   OPR5, OPR7,


                                ; (* P-code expansion follows *)
```

Figure 5.45
PCODE.DEF for the DEC Alpha computer.

Once this PCODE.DEF file is created, all you have to do is take the output from the compiler and feed it into the Alpha Macro 64 Assembler. It will include the PCODE.DEF file, which will expand all of the P-Code macro calls into actual assembler code. This must be linked with another assembler file that defines the special input and output routines, CSP0, CSP1, CSP2, and CSP3, and the divide and mod routines, OPR5 and OPR7. (The Alpha does not have a divide instruction.) The result is an executable program in the native machine language of the computer.

Note: A copy of PCODE.DEF written for the Intel 80×86 family of PCs is included on the CD-ROM. An assembler file that supplies the required CSP and OPR routines is also included.

5.9 WRAP-UP AND FURTHER READING

This chapter designed a complete compiler using top-down, recursive descent techniques. Using **C++** allowed object-oriented techniques to be used as well. Other books covering top-down design such as [Aho 1988] or [Wirth 1976] have not used object-oriented techniques. The result usually has both the parsing and generation done in the same piece of code. This is often harder to read because two things are going on at once. [Bergin 1994] is probably one of the earliest to cover compiler design using object-oriented techniques.

For those interested in a fully mature P-Machine, the Java Virtual Machine is described in [Lindholm 1997].

REFERENCES

[Aho 1988]   Aho, Alfred V., Ravi Sethi, Jeffrey D. Ullman, *Compilers, Principals, Techniques, and Tools*, Reading, MA: Addison–Wesley Publishing Company, 1988.

[Bergin 1994] Bergin, Joseph, *Data Abstraction: The Object-Oriented Approach Using C++*, New York, NY: McGraw-Hill, Inc., 1994.

[Lindholm 1997]   Lindholm, Tim, Frank Yellin, *The Java Virtual Machine Specification*, Reading, MA: Addison–Wesley Publishing Company, 1997.

[Wirth 1976]   Wirth, Niklaus, *Algorithms + Data Structures = Programs*, pp. 331–347. Englewood Cliffs, NJ: Prentice Hall, Inc., 1976.

CHAPTER 6

Elementary Concurrency and Synchronization Principles

In this chapter, we shall look at some basic principles of concurrency and process synchronization. This will serve as an introduction to topics that will be further elaborated on in later chapters. Here we shall examine the problems that can occur when two or more processes communicate or share common resources, and we will discuss several common solution systems. In the later chapters, we shall put these solution systems to practical use developing elements of an operating system.

There are several things that we require just to get started. We need to develop the concept of what concurrency is all about, then we will need a platform on which we can try out several test cases to discover the properties of a concurrent system. After we determine the properties, we shall be able to go on to developing several practical concurrent strategies. We will be able to try out these strategies on the same platform that we use to discover the basic properties. In later chapters, we will use some of these strategies on "real" platforms.

6.1 WHAT IS CONCURRENCY?

Concurrency implies two or more things happening at one time. In computer systems, the "things" are programs or parts of a program, and what is happening is that they are running. That means that we are concerned with two program units that are running at the same time. However, there is more involved than just that. If one program is calculating the thousandth digit of pi and another is compiling a Lil'LuxLyk program, the fact that they are both running at the same time is not very interesting. The situation only becomes interesting when the two program units share some common item, known as a *resource*. There are several things that may be considered resources. These include memory and I/O devices. On a single processor system, the central processing unit is also one of the resources that can be shared (in fact, it *must* be shared). For a long time, this single processor system was the rule; that's the way things were made. Nowadays, there are many systems that contain more than one processor. In these systems it is possible for different program units to run on separate processors.

A common name for these program units is *processes*. They can be either separate programs or individual parts of a single program that work together. I will use the name "processes" in this chapter. Later chapters will discuss the more recent concept of "threads."

Let's get back to what concurrency means. In a multiple processor system, it is easy for processes to run at the same time as they can each run on separate processors. In a single processor system, it is not possible for processes to truly run at the same time. Instead, each process is allowed to run for a period of time and then must yield to another process so that the new one gets its time on the processor. This method of letting each process execute a few instructions at a time is know as *interleaving*. Some textbooks give a special name to the type of concurrency that results from this interleaving of processes—it's called "pseudo-concurrency." It turns out, however, that the problems encountered and the resulting solutions are the same in either case. Therefore, I shall simply use the single word "concurrency" for either case. Thus, concurrency shall be described as multiple cooperating processes that either execute simultaneously on separate processors or are interleaved on a single processor.

6.2 A TEST PLATFORM

We will be investigating some the properties of concurrent programming. In order to do this we need a platform to perform the tests In the past, this test platform has not been easy to find For one thing, much of this material relates to special operating system functions that were concealed from most application programmers for fear of what might happen. ("Crashing" a multiuser system is not usually appreciated.) Another obstacle was that few languages in the past supported concurrency primitives, although that is presently changing. We shall avoid these problems by introducing a language that does support concurrency and running it on a pseudo-machine that has some simple built-in concurrency functions. Both parts of our solution are created out of software elements that we can examine. This will help develop a deeper understanding of all sides of the problem. With this knowledge in hand, we shall be ready to forge ahead into the study of actual operating system implementations, but first we must become acquainted with the elements of our test platform.

6.2.1 THE LUXLYK LANGUAGE

The language we shall be using is LuxLyk. I call it that because you're sure to see some constructions in it that "looks like" something you've seen in some more familiar language. Since it resembles several other languages, it is not hard to learn. You've already been using it. Lil'LuxLyk is a subset of LuxLyk. The top level syntax diagrams for the LuxLyk language are shown in Figure 6.1.

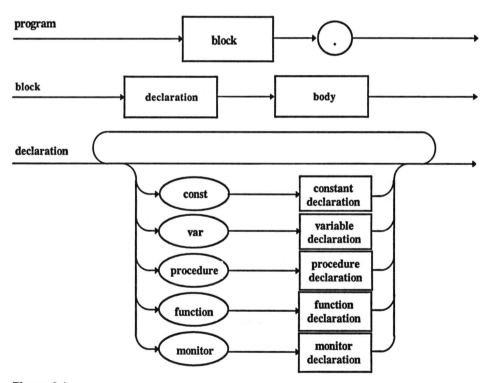

Figure 6.1

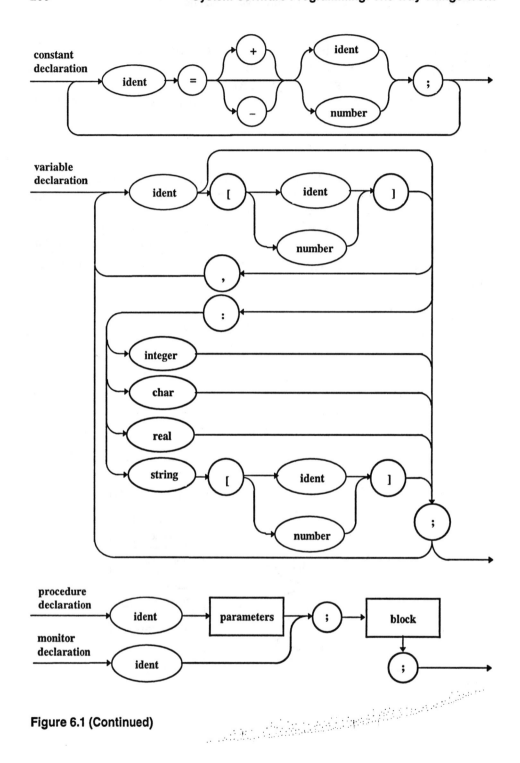

Figure 6.1 (Continued)

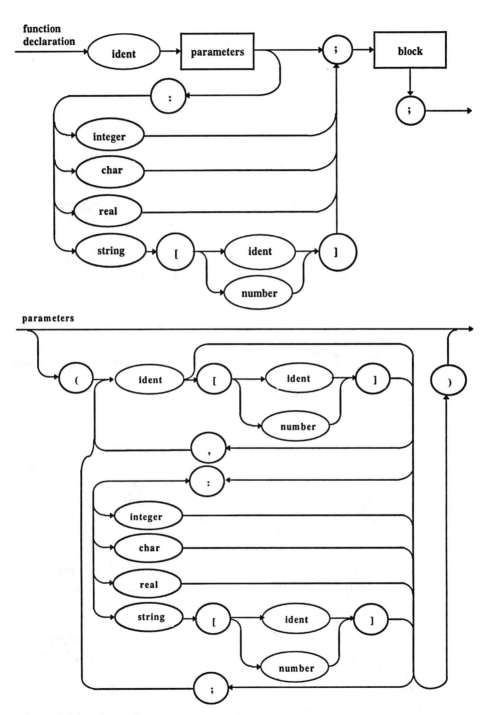

Figure 6.1 (Continued)

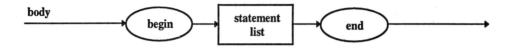

Figure 6.1
Diagram of the top level LuxLyk syntax.

You will notice that, besides the *const*, *var*, and *procedure* declarations of Lil'LuxLyk, we have two new ones. The *function* is similar to the procedure but has the added capability of being able to return a value. The monitor is a special construction used to support one kind of concurrency protocol. Obviously, we shall see more about it later.

The constant declaration is more robust. Not only can it be negative, but it can also refer back to a previously defined symbol. All constants, however, must be of integers.

Variables may now have *types* declared. The language has four predefined types: *integer, char, real,* and *string[...]*. It is also possible to omit the type declaration whenever integers are used. This allows Lil'LuxLyk code to be upwards compatible with the LuxLyk compiler. The string[...] is a special type. The value inside the square brackets must be a constant that defines the maximum number of characters in the string.

Array variables can also be employed. They are declared by placing the number of elements in square brackets after the variable's name. LuxLyk array indices always begin at zero. Note that an array of characters and an equally sized string are assignment compatible; one form may be copied into the other.

You can now pass values to a procedure or a function. The parameters are part of the declaration. Parameters are declared the same way as variables

Functions can return information of any singular type· If no type is declared then the default of integer is assumed. Arrays cannot be returned; however, the string is considered a singular type and can be returned.

Most of the rest of the upper level syntax can be understood by comparing it to the Lil'LuxLyk syntax and the descriptions in the previous chapter.

Now we shall turn our attention to the LuxLyk statements. They are diagrammed in Figure 6.2.

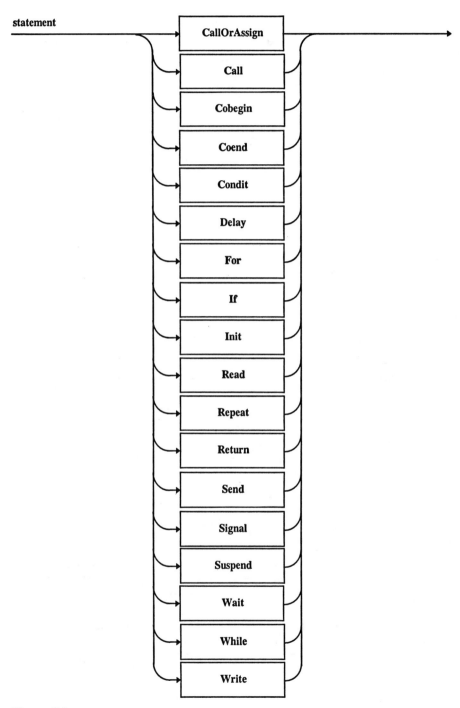

statement

- CallOrAssign
- Call
- Cobegin
- Coend
- Condit
- Delay
- For
- If
- Init
- Read
- Repeat
- Return
- Send
- Signal
- Suspend
- Wait
- While
- Write

Figure 6.2

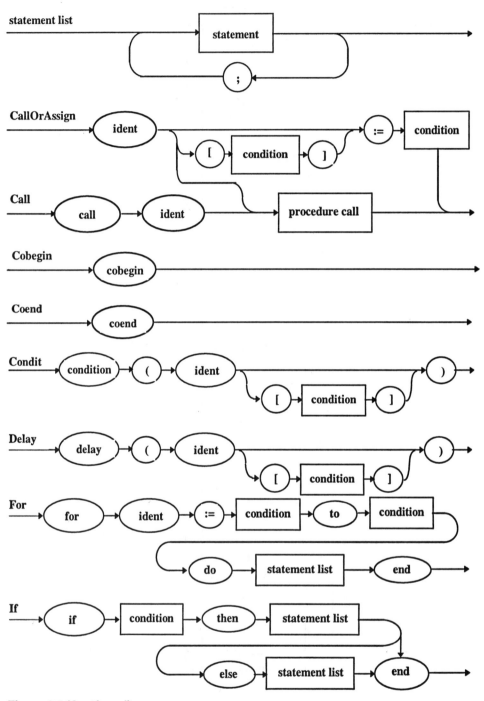

Figure 6.2 (Continued)

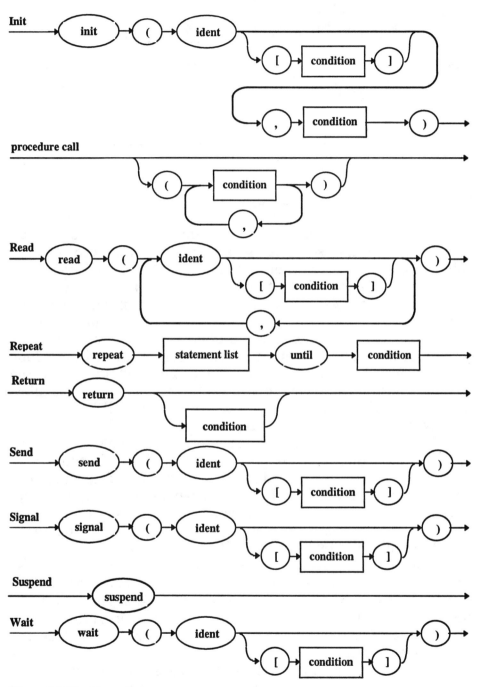

Figure 6.2 (Continued)

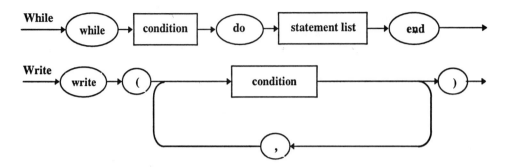

Figure 6.2
Syntax diagrams of the LuxLyk statements.

The LuxLyk compiler handles many more statements than Lil'LuxLyk did, and some of the old ones are enhanced. For one thing, the keyword CALL is optional before a procedure name. The compiler determines that the identifier is a procedure name, not a variable, by looking it up in the Symbol Table. The procedure name is now followed by a new non-terminal called "procedure call" in which the parameters are passed. The conception of what an "expression" is has been expanded to include Boolean expressions. This is designed, not just to satisfy the need for a condition in an if or while statement, but also to allow assignments like *"full := (count = max)"*. Full will be true (i.e., 1) only if count does equal max; otherwise, it will be false (i.e., 0). The incorporation of Boolean expressions makes condition more fundamental than expression. Therefore, all the places where "expression" was used in Lil'LuxLyk have been replaced by "condition" in LuxLyk. Note also, wherever a condition appears between square brackets following the name of an array variable, it indicates that a particular element is being referenced, as indicated by the value of the condition.

Other modifications include the addition of an optional *else* clause in the if statement and the addition of *for, repeat,* and *return* statements. The return statement is used to render a function's return value; however, it can be used to provide an early exit from a procedure. In the latter case, it should not be followed by a condition.

All of the other new statement types are used to support the concurrency issues built into our platform. We shall see more of them in the future.

Next we shall look at the Expression diagrams. They are shown in Figure 6.3.

The condition, expression, and term diagrams are pretty much the same as they were in Lil'LuxLyk, with the exception that logical operators (*and* and *or*) have been added. Things are different when we look at the factor diagram. It introduces a new level into the abstraction. The *atom* allows us to raise things to a power, that is, $atom^{factor}$.

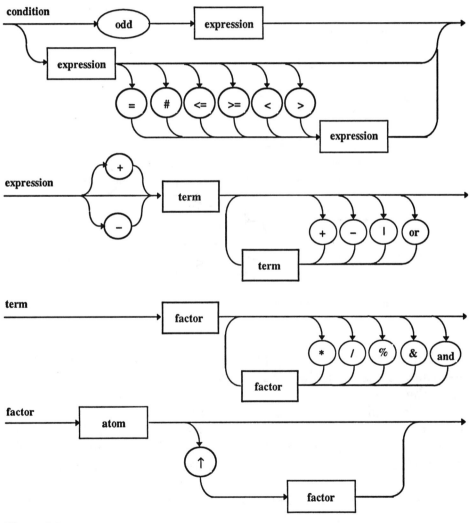

Figure 6.3

atom

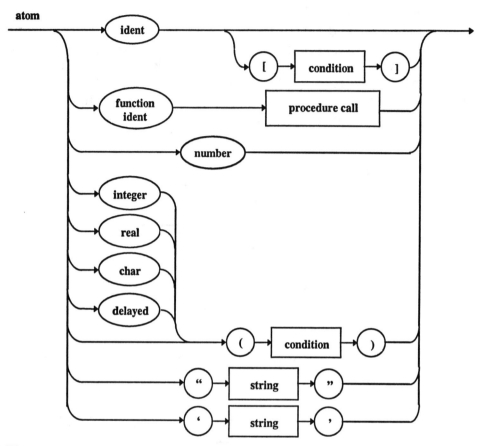

Figure 6.3
Syntax diagrams of LuxLyk expressions.

The atom structure is now the smallest subdivision of an expression. It assumes the place formerly held by the factor. Therefore, the atom diagram is where the numbers and identifiers appear. The identifier has been modified to allow individual array elements to be used. Two new items have been added: the *string constant* and the *function*. The string constant is made up of a series of characters surrounded by either matching single quotes or double quotes. User defined functions are indicated by their names followed by their list of parameters surrounded by parentheses. There are several built-in functions. The *integer*, *real*, and *char* functions are used for type casting. For instance, the integer function will convert characters or reals into integers. Likewise, char will change an integer into its equivalent ASCII character. LuxLyk does not have any implicit conversion; you must request all conversions explicitly. The remaining built-in function, *delayed*, will be used for concurrency later in this chapter.

6.2.2 THE P-MACHINE

In Section 4.9 we met the P-Machine for the first time. It had an instruction set that was sufficient for Lil'LuxLyk, but it is barely adequate for many of the advanced features of modern languages, and it is definitely not capable of any concurrency. Fortunately, the P-Machine is part of a family of processors. What we saw before is called the P-Machine/Lite. The top of the line processor is called the Full Bodied P-Machine, usually written as P-Machine / FB.

The architecture of the Full Bodied P-Machine is basically the same as the Lite version except for a few additions. For one thing, it is able to perform floating-point arithmetic. The *lev* field is used to tell the processor whether to execute a real or an integer operation. Since the Lite model, which only handled integers, used 0, a 1 is used for real. There is a special OPR code (i.e., 23) to convert between integer and real forms of the value on the top of the **Stack**. The lev field of the instruction tells the *type* of the top of **Stack** value *before* the operation is performed. There are also OPR instructions that do logical operations such as *and*, *or*, and *not*—these are used in the Boolean expressions. The P-Machine is able to shift left or right even though the LuxLyk compiler has no corresponding instructions. OPR numbers 19 through 21 are intended to be used by the for statement; however, LuxLyk doesn't use 20. Exponentiation is handled by OPR 0 22 and dynamic memory allocation is done by OPR 0 24. The latter operation returns a pointer to the new fragment of memory. It also requires an extra register, **H** (for heap pointer), in the extended P-Machine models. This instruction is very similar to the *new* statement of **C++**, but LuxLyk cannot duplicate the instruction since it does not handle pointer types. The operation *will* be used when we get into concurrency. The rest of the OPR functions, that is, 25 through 38, are used for concurrency.

The extended instruction set is shown in Table 6.1.

Table 6.1

P-Machine / FB: The Full Bodied P-Machine Instruction Set

FCT	LEV	ADR	Description
LIT	0	num	**inc**(T); Stack[T]←num;
OPR	0	0	T←B–1; P←Stack[T+3]; B←Stack[T+2];
"	0 or 1	1	Stack[T]← – Stack[T];
"	0 or 1	2	**dec**(T); Stack[T]←Stack[T] + Stack[T+1];
"	0 or 1	3	**dec**(T); Stack[T]←Stack[T] – Stack[T+1];
"	0 or 1	4	**dec**(T); Stack[T]←Stack[T] * Stack[T+1];
"	0 or 1	5	**dec**(T); Stack[T]←Stack[T] / Stack[T+1];
"	0	6	Stack[T]←Stack[T] ⊗ 1;
"	0	7	**dec**(T); Stack[T]←Stack[T] % Stack[T+1];
"	0 or 1	8	**dec**(T); if Stack[T]=Stack[T+1] then Stack[T]←1 else Stack[T]←0;
"	0 or 1	9	**dec**(T); if Stack[T]≠Stack[T+1] then Stack[T]←1 else Stack[T]←0;
"	0 or 1	10	**dec**(T); if Stack[T]<Stack[T+1] then Stack[T]←1 else Stack[T]←0;
"	0 or 1	11	**dec**(T); if Stack[T]≥Stack[T+1] then Stack[T]←1 else Stack[T]←0;
"	0 or 1	12	**dec**(T); if Stack[T]>Stack[T+1] then Stack[T]←1 else Stack[T]←0;
"	0 or 1	13	**dec**(T); if Stack[T]≤Stack[T+1] then Stack[T]←1 else Stack[T]←0;
"	0	14	**dec**(T); Stack[T]←Stack[T] ⊗ Stack[T+1];
"	0	15	**dec**(T); Stack[T]←Stack[T] ⊕ Stack[T+1];
"	0	16	Stack[T]← ¬ Stack[T];
"	0	17	Stack[T]←Stack[T]*2;
"	0	18	Stack[T]←Stack[T]/2;
"	0	19	**inc**(Stack[T]);
"	0	20	**dec**(Stack[T]);
"	0	21	**inc**(T); Stack[T]←Stack[T–1];
"	0 or 1	22	**dec**(T); Stack[T]←Stack[T] ↑ Stack[T+1];
"	0	23	Stack[T]←**float**(Stack[T]);
"	1	"	Stack[T]←**trunc**(Stack[T]);
"	siz	24	H←H–siz; **inc**(T); Stack[T]←H;
"	0	25	Initialize coprocessing
"	0	26	Start coprocessing
"	0	27	Suspend process
"	0	28	Define semaphore
"	0	29	Semaphore wait
"	0	30	Semaphore send
"	0	31	Define monitor condition
"	0	32	Monitor gate signal
"	0	33	Condition wait
"	0	34	Condition signal
"	0	35	Increment condition value
"	0	36	Decrement condition value
"	0	37	Get condition value
"	0	38	determine if processes are delayed by a condition
LOD	lev	adr	**inc**(T); Stack[T]←Stack[**base**(lev)+adr];
LODA	lev	adr	**inc**(T); Stack[T]←**base**(lev)+adr;
LODI	0	siz	T←T+siz; for i←0 to siz do Stack[T-i]←Stack[Stack[T–siz]+siz–i];
LODX	lev	adr	Stack[T]← Stack[**base**(lev)+adr+Stack[T]];
STO	lev	adr	**dec**(T); Stack[**base**(lev)+adr]← Stack[T+1];

Table 6.1 (Continued)

STOI	0	siz	T←T–(siz+2); for i←0 to siz do Stack[Stack[T+1]+i] ← Stack[T+2+i];
STOX	lev	adr	T←T–2; Stack[base(lev)+adr+Stack[T+1]←Stack[T+2];
CAL	lev	adr	Stack[T+1]←base(lev); Stack[T+2]←B; Stack[T+3]←P; B←T+1; P←adr;
PRC	lev	adr	Process create
INT	0	num	T←T+num;
JMP	0	adr	P←adr;
JPC	cnd	adr	**dec**(T); if Stack[T+1]=cnd then P←adr;
CSP	0	0	**inc**(T); **read_char**(Stack[T]);
CSP	0	1	**dec**(T); **write_char**(Stack[T+1]);
CSP	0	2	**inc**(T); **read_int**(Stack[T]);
CSP	0	3	**dec**(T); **write_int**(Stack[T+1]);
CSP	0	4	**inc**(T); **read_hex**(Stack[T]);
CSP	0	5	**dec**(T); **write_hex**(Stack[T+1]);
CSP	0	6	**inc**(T); **read_real**(Stack[T]);
CSP	0	7	**dec**(T); **write_real**(Stack[T+1]);
CSP	siz	8	T←T–(siz+1); **write_string**(Stack[T+1]);

Notes:

- "%" is the MOD operator.
- "⊗", "⊕", and "¬" are the logical AND, OR, and NOT operators.
- **inc**() and **dec**() are built-in functions that increment or decrement their parameter by one count.
- **base**(lev) is a built-in function that traces down *lev* levels of the static link path.
- **float**() and **trunc**() are built-in functions that convert between integer and real forms of the value at the top of the **Stack**.
- **read_xxx**() and **write_xxx**() are built-in functions that read or write the form that their name implies.
- "siz" is *one more than* the number of integers in the data structure.
- OPR 0 0 and CAL are handled differently for the lowest level of coprocessing.

The OPR codes are not the only ones where changes have been made. There are new LOD and STO forms. The list of CSP functions has been expanded to include hexadecimal numbers, real numbers, and strings. There is also a new kind of "call" code.

LODX and STOX are used for array operations on integers. An assignment like "$Y[i] := X[j]$" could be translated as follows:

```
LOD    i
LOD    j
LODX   X
STOX   Y
```

The LOD statements push the indices onto the **Stack**. The LODX uses the index value on the top of the **Stack** as an offset from the address of the X array to where the desired array element is located. Likewise, the STOX uses the index value on the Stack as an offset from the address of the Y array to the correct destination array element. A careful examination of the example code will show that during the STOX operation, the index value is *not* at the top of the **Stack**. The value to be moved is located there, and this is followed by the index.

Note: This example uses the same simplification used in Chapter 4, that is, the actual symbols are used instead of supplying the lev and adr fields. In succeeding examples, the simplifications will also omit lev fields that are usually zero and will replace the adr field of OPR instructions with appropriate mathematical symbols.

Real numbers, strings, and arrays do not take up the same amount of space on the **Stack** as integers. They cannot be operated on by the usual LOD, LODX, STO, and STOX P-Codes. Some additional ones are used.

The LODA command loads the actual address of the variable onto the **Stack**. The LODI command uses the address loaded by the LODA and moves the data at that location onto the **Stack**. In the process, it overwrites the address value. The number of bytes to be transferred (minus 1) is indicated in the "lev" field of the LODI command.

The STOI command uses the address loaded by the LODA and moves the data from the **Stack** to the indicated location. The number of bytes to be removed from the **Stack** (minus 1) is indicated in the "lev" field of the STOI command. The address value also gets removed during the transfer.

If X and Y are arrays of non-integer-sized elements (such as reals or strings) then an assignment like "$Y[i] := X[j]$" could be translated as follows:

```
LOD    i            !value of i
LIT    y_siz        ! size of Y array element
OPR    *            !  offset into Y to element i
LODA   Y            !address of Y
OPR    +            ! address of Y[i]
LOD    j            !value of j
LIT    x_siz        ! size of Y array element
OPR    *            !  offset into Y to element j
LODA   X            !address of X
OPR    +            ! address of X[j]
LODI   x_siz - 1    !load X[j] data of stack
STOI   y_siz - 1    !store at Y[i]
```

As you can see, it takes quite a lot more code to handle non-integers. The P-Code has to actually calculate the offsets into the arrays since they depend on the size of the elements in the array. LODX and STOX did the calculation automatically.

Among the other extended instructions are the new CSP commands. In addition to the original character and integer I/O, the supplementary forms will input or output hex and floating-point numbers, and one will output strings. The hex forms are not supported by the present LuxLyk compiler, but could be a useful extension (to anyone that feels so moved). The string will turn out to be quite useful in our future examples. There are two things that you must be aware of when using these CSP commands. First, the P-Machine automatically places a blank space after any numeric value such as an integer, a hex, or a floating-point value. This makes for fairly satisfactory output without having any format control in the LuxLyk language. Second, the compiler normally outputs a carriage return and line feed character at the end of each write statement. There is one exception: If the last item in the write statement parameter list is a single character, the carriage return and line feed characters are omitted. This deviation stems from a special case involving low-level I/O, such as cursor control escape sequences.

One more new command found in our extended P-Machine instruction set is the PRC command that appears in the same place that a procedure call would normally appear, but has the added functionality of being able to turn the procedure into a process. Of course, we will be looking into this command much more in the study of concurrency.

Although passing parameters to a procedure does not use any of the extended P-Machine instructions, it does use some new ideas that we should investigate. Here's how it's done. When parameters are passed to a procedure, the expressions in the parentheses (which represent the parameters) are evaluated *before* the CAL instruction. This means that when the called procedure begins execution, the parameter values appear on the **Stack** before the SL, DL, and RA fields of the stack frame. The **B** register will still point to the SL as before. In the same way that local variables are indicated as positive offsets from the **B** register, the parameters are indicated as negative offsets. Once the called procedure returns, it is the task of the calling code to remove the parameters from the **Stack**.

The following P-Code shows the typical expansion for a call such as "*CALL abc(x, y)*".

```
LOD    x              !push parameters
LOD    y              ! onto stack
CAL    abc            !call procedure
INT    -2             !remove parameters from stack
```

An additional situation to be considered is where the called procedure is actually a "function." In this case, the calling code must reserve room on the **Stack** for the "returned value" (i.e., RV) *before* evaluating the parameters. This means that the called procedure (i.e., function) sees it at a more negative offset than any of the parameters. The function must place the returned value in this location before it returns. (Notice that, after the parameters are popped off the Stack, the returned value is on the top; it is ready for storage or mathematical operations.) The following P-Code shows the typical expansion for an expression containing a function; the high-level language statement is "*z := add(x, y)*".

```
INT    1              !make room for returned value
LOD    x              !push parameters
LOD    y              ! onto stack
CAL    add            !call function
INT    -2             !remove parameters from stack
STO    z              !store the result
```

If the "add" function contains a statement like *"RETURN (Param1 + param2)"* (where "param1" and "param2" are the local parameter values), its P-Code expansion would be:

```
LOD   -2        !push passed parameter
LOD   -1        ! values onto stack
OPR   +         !add them
STO   -3        !store the result in
                ! the return value area
```

Figure 6.4 shows a portion of the **Stack** when a function with two parameters and two local variables is called:

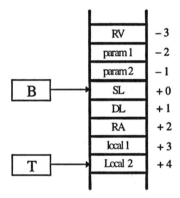

Figure 6.4
The P-Machine Stack with passed parameters and local variables.

The previous parameter passing examples have assumed integer parameters. To pass or work with any other type would require use of the LODA, LODI, and STOI commands.

LuxLyk always places a copy of the actual data onto the **Stack**. This is a method known as "pass by value"; that is, the actual value is passed to the procedure. There is another technique of passing parameters—this method is known as "pass by reference." In this approach, the address of the data is passed to the procedure instead of the data. The following shows the typical expansion for a call such as *"CALL swap(x, y)"*.

```
LODA   x                    !push parameters
LODA   y                    ! onto stack
CAL    swap                 !call procedure
INT    -2                   !remove parameters from stack
```

(**Note:** it is assumed that integers and addresses take the same space on the P-Machine **Stack**.) In this system, the procedure would push the parameter/address on the **Stack** with a LOD command and use it as if it had come from a LODA. This is not so unusual since the original parameter came from a LODA. The following could be the P-Code for a procedure that swaps the parameter values:

```
INT    4                    !make room for 1 local (temp)
LOD    -2                   !load address of x
LODI   0                    ! load value of x
STO    3                    !store in temp
LOD    -2                   !load address of x
LOD    -1                   !load address of y
LODI   0                    ! load value of y (size-1=0)
STOI   0                    ! store value at x
LOD    -1                   !load address of y
LOD    3                    !load value of temp
STOI   0                    ! store value at y
OPR    return               !return
```

It should be noted that, since this method uses the address of the parameters, when the procedure references one of them, it is referencing the actual variable. Thus, when it does an STOI, it changes the value of the *original variable* itself. Pass by value, on the other hand, can not affect the original variables since it's a copy of the variable that is passed to the procedure. Although this example has shown that the P-Machine can handle pass-by reference, the LuxLyk compiler only uses pass-by value.

Before we leave the discussion of the P-Machine platform, it would be helpful to get a bit of an idea on how the P-Machine works. A real processor consists of a loop that first fetches an instruction from memory and then executes the instruction. The P-Machine duplicates this functionality. A partial listing is shown in Figure 6.5.

```
do {
    if ( code->Fetch(I.fnctn, I.level, I.value, P++))  {
        switch (I.fnctn)  {
            case CAL:                          // CALl procedure
                stk[T+1] = base(I.level);
                stk[T+2] = B;        B = T + 1;
                stk[T+3] = P;        P = I.value;
                break;
            case LIT:                          // load LITeral
                stk[++T] = I.value;  break;

            •  •  •       •  •  •

        }
    }
} while (P > 0);
```

Figure 6.5
The Basic P-Machine Fetch and Execution cycle.

The code in the above listing has been simplified in several ways. For one thing, there is no error handling. (What if the Fetch returns a false?) Another simplification is the fact that most of the instructions have been omitted. What is left should give the general idea. Once the instruction is fetched, its opcode is examined and dispatched to an appropriate section of code by a switch statement. The section of code performs the operations indicated and then returns to the Fetch instruction. This loop continues until an OPR 0 0 command places a 0 into the P register. The only time that this should happen is when we return from the main program. A zero was purposefully placed in the main program's stack frame for this very reason.

At this point, we should know enough about the P-Machine to start looking into how it handles concurrency.

6.3 THE FIRST EXPERIENCES WITH CONCURRENCY

Most code written in LuxLyk runs sequentially, that is, one instruction at a time. The language allows several procedures to run at the same time, but this feature requires special language commands to "turn it on." Just like the tokens BEGIN and END surround the statements that make up the body of a program or procedure, the new tokens COBEGIN and COEND surround the calls to the procedures that are to be run concurrently. For instance, if we want proc1 and proc2 to run concurrently after passing them values of 4 and 3 respectively, we would write:

```
COBEGIN;
    proc1(4);
    proc2(3);
COEND;
```

Now we need to examine what the P-Machine does during process activation. First, we must discover the purpose of the **H** register that's been added to the Full Bodied P-Machine. At the opposite end of the data memory from the **Stack** is a region called the **Heap**. Just as the **T** register initially points above the **Stack**, the **H** register initially points below the **Heap**. Each time an OPR siz 24 command is executed, the **H** register moves up "siz" locations and the resulting value is pushed on the top of the **Stack**. The area between the old and new values of the **H** register is what's known as dynamic memory. The OPR command has allocated the area, and the value at the top of the **Stack** can be used as a pointer to this data. LuxLyk does not offer any pointer type, but it does use it internally for process activation.

Every LuxLyk / P-Machine process has two requirements. It has a data structure that defines the process's condition, and it has its own private stack. The data structure is called the "process Control Block" or PCB. It consists of fields that hold what the contents of the processor's main registers should be the next time that the process starts to run. The private stack is the area allocated by the OPR siz 24 command. The environment for a process is defined by its PCB and by its stack. Each process, including the main program, will have its own PCB and stack. The main program is the one that originally starts running in the **Stack**. It activates the other processes and then sits back and waits until they are finished. The P-Machine has a special PCB structure, known as *main*, to hold the main program's environment while it waits. Only one process can run at a time in the P-Machine. The other processes may be ready to run, but only one can have access to the P-Machine's registers. The other processes, or rather, their PCBs, wait in a special queue called the *ready* queue. We are now ready to study the actual way that processes are created.

The COBEGIN ...COEND sequence above will be translated by the LuxLyk compiler into the following P-Code.

```
OPR   1000   24
OPR   0      25
LIT   0      4
PRC   0      2        ! location of proc1
OPR   1000   24
OPR   0      25
LIT   0      3
PRC   0      25       ! location of proc2
OPR   0      26
```

Let's look at what each of these instructions does.

The first OPR 1000 24 allocates 1000 integer locations from the **Heap**, adjusts H accordingly, and places a pointer to the allocated memory on the top of the **Stack**. This allocated memory will be the stack for process 1.

The OPR that follows creates a new PCB and places the current contents of **T** minus 1 into the T field of the PCB. This value is only temporary and will be replaced when the process is completely defined. Next, the value at the top of the **Stack** minus 1 is placed into the **T** register. The T register now points one location above the new process's stack. The *active_processes* value is also incremented by this OPR.

The LIT 0 4 command pushes 4 onto the new process's stack. **T** will point to this value.

The PRC 0 2 instruction creates a stack frame on the new process's stack. The static link points to the outer nesting level's stack frame as usual. The dynamic link receives the current value of **B**. The return address is set to −1. This is used to catch invalid process terminations. The temporary value previously saved in the PCB's T field is now retrieved and saved in a local variable for later use. The P field is set to the value of the address field from the PRC command, that is, the location of proc1. The B field becomes the current **T** value plus 1. Finally, the current **T** value is copied into the PCB's T field. Now that the PCB is complete, it is pushed onto the ready queue. Once the PCB has been queued, the previously saved T value is copied to the **T** register so that it points back to the main or system **Stack**.

The next four instructions set up the second process, proc2, in the same way as above and places its PCB in the ready queue.

Finally, the OPR 0 26 puts the current values of **P**, **B**, and **T** into the "main" PCB structure, pulls a PCB off the ready queue, copies its environmental fields into the **P**, **B**, and **T** registers, and enables concurrency by setting *concur* to 1. Since a queue is "first in, first out," the process pulled from the queue should be process 1. It has just been given possession of the processor's registers, so it is the currently running process. The second process is waiting in the ready queue for its turn, and the main program is waiting in "main" for the two processes to terminate. The current situation is shown in Figure 6.6.

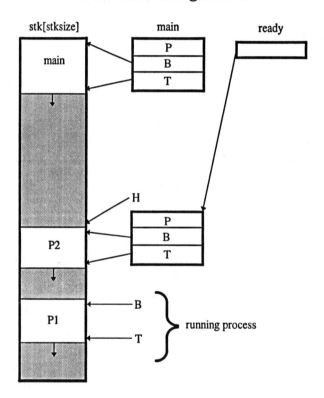

Figure 6.6
P-Machine / FB Stack partitioning and process activation.

Once the processes are queued up, as described and shown above, the P-Machine will start interleaving the processes in the ready queue. In an attempt to simulate the way a real processor schedules processes, each process on the P-Machine is given a random amount of time to run. This randomness is modified somewhat by the fact that commands must be allowed to complete before being switched out. The P-Machine achieves this by placing a small piece of code into the fetch/execute cycle just after the execution section. This new part uses a random number generator to determine when it is time to switch the processes. If it decides that it's time, the current contents of the **P, B,** and **T** registers are saved in the running process's PCB and the Process Control Block is placed in the ready queue. After this, a PCB is removed from the ready queue, and its contents are placed into the **P, B,** and **T** registers. This new process is now running on the processor. This simple method of scheduling processes is called "round robin." It is a fair method but not necessarily the most effective. More practical scheduling algorithms will be discussed in the next chapter.

The P-Machine code for context switching is shown in Figure 6.7.

```
do {
    if ( code->Fetch(I.fnctn, I.level, I.value, P++))  {
    switch (I.fnctn)  {

            • • •     • • •

    }
    if (concur)                              // context switch
    {
        int r = int( rand() % 16384 );
        int d = (16383 + chance) / chance;
        if (r / d >= chance - 1)
        {
            proc->Put(P, B, T, level);
            ready->push(proc);
            proc = ready->front();
            ready->pop();
            proc->Get(P, B, T, level);
        }
    }
    }
} while (P > 0);
```

Figure 6.7
The P-Machine / FB context switch.

As mentioned earlier, processes that have no interaction are not very interesting—at least not for our study. The easiest way to get these processes to interact is to have them share a variable in common memory. Variables local to the main program are global to all procedures; therefore, this is where we usually place our common variables. Just because a variable is shared does not necessarily make it interesting. If all the processes do is *read* the common variable, there's not really any interaction. The following LuxLyk program, in Figure 6.8, has two processes that share the "a" variable, but both read it.

```
(* no_fun.ll  --  just two processes doing their own thing *)
VAR a, b, c;
PROCEDURE proc1(x); BEGIN  b := a * 5 / x END;
PROCEDURE proc2(x); BEGIN  c := a * 2 / x END;
BEGIN
    a := 24;
    COBEGIN;
        proc1(4);
        proc2(3);
    COEND;
    WRITE(a, b, c)
END.
```

Figure 6.8
An uninteresting concurrent LuxLyk program.

The name of this program is "no_fun.ll". The "no_fun" part comes from the fact that it is no fun in a concurrent sense. The '.ll' extension stands for Lux_Lyk. The program is compiled with the following command:

    C:\> LuxLyk no_fun.ll >no_fun.pcd

The output of the compiler is redirected to a file named "no_fun.pcd" where the '.pcd' stands for P-Code. The P-Code is executed by the following command:

    C:\> PMachine no_fun.pcd

This same basic sequence must be followed for each LuxLyk program. When this particular program is run, it always outputs the same result, "24 30 16". Like I said, it's not much fun. If you start with the fact that the main program assigns a value of 24 to "a" before starting the concurrent processes and then look at the simple equations in the two procedures, you will see that the final results are just what you would expect.

Now let's look at a program where both processes *write* to the common variable. The program in Figure 6.9 is exactly that.

```
(*    process.ll  --  a concurrent program with a problem    *)
VAR   count;     (* this global variable is the critical data *)
PROCEDURE Proc ( max );
    VAR  i;
    BEGIN
        FOR i := 1 TO max DO
            count := count + 1
        END
    END;
BEGIN
    count := 0;
    Proc (  5 );              (* run processes sequentially *)
    Proc ( 10 );
    WRITE( count );
    count := 0;
    COBEGIN;
        Proc (  5 );          (* run processes concurrently *)
        Proc ( 10 );
    COEND;
    WRITE( count )
END.
```

Figure 6.9
A concurrent program with a problem.

This program has a single procedure that is used by each process. The procedure increments the shared variable, *count*, by the number passed to it. The incrementing is done by a simple for loop. The beginning of the main program sets count to zero and then calls the procedure twice (sequentially) passing values of 5 and 10 respectively. It then prints out the final value of count. The output value here is always 15, which is what you would expect. Next, it repeats the same sequence except the two processes are run concurrently (by the simple expedient of adding COBEGIN and COEND statements). The results may surprise you. Instead of always getting 15, you usually get 12, but you often will see other values like 10, 11, 13, 14 , or 15. We normally like to have our programs be predictable. This does not qualify. At this point, we need to do find two things: what went wrong and how to make it predictable again.

If we think about how the processes are interleaved, we'll begin to get an idea of what went wrong. Consider the following scenario:

Process 1	**Process 2**
load *count* on stack (= 0)	- - -
- - -	load *count* on stack (= 0)
load 1 on stack	- - -
- - -	load 1 on stack
add top of stack (= 1)	- - -
- - -	add top of stack (= 1)
store stack value in *count*	- - -
- - -	store stack value in *count*

Notice that, although both processes have completed one cycle of the loop, the value of count has only gone up by one. The sequence shown here is a one-for-one interleaving; each process gets to execute exactly one instruction. It is possible to force the P-Machine into this one-for-one interleaving by using an option in the command as follows:

```
C:\> PMachine -1 no_fun.pcd
```

The number 1 tells the P-Machine that there should be 1 chance in 1 that the processes shall be switched; a value of 2 says that there should be 1 chance in 2 that the processes shall switch. You can experiment with higher values also. If no value is given, the P-Machine defaults to 2.

When forced into one-for-one interleaving, the answer will always be 10. This is because the two processes complete their first five cycles in perfect synchronization as shown above, with the net result of only raising count to five. The second process then completes its last five cycles alone. This adds five more to the value of count, bringing it up to ten. When a little bit of randomness is added, it is possible for one process to get more than one cycle in to the other's single cycle, or at least one process can get far enough ahead that it stores its value of count just before the other process loads the value. In rare cases, a result of 15 is possible, but this value should always be the result, not the exception. We need to make the answer always come out right.

6.4 THE PRINCIPLES OF CONCURRENCY

In the previous section we found that when two processes both write to a variable in common memory, the results are not predictable. In this section, we shall make several attempts at developing an algorithm that guarantees that the program produces a correct or consistent result. First, we must look at the life of a process.

A process goes through several stages in its lifetime. It goes through some initialization code when the process is first called. Normally, this stage is not repeated. After that, the process goes into a cycle or program loop. Unlike sequential programs that are expected to produce a correct result and exit, in operating systems and real-time programming the process should never exit its loop. (A *stopped* operating system is an operating system that has *crashed*.) Therefore, in this section, we shall worry about processes stopping. Our primary concern will be that, if one process stops, it should have no effect on any other processes.

Within the process loop, there will be one section of code that accesses the shared resource and another section of code where the process is working on other things. We call the section that accesses the shared resource the *critical section* or *region*. I like to call the other section the "rest of the story," but it's usually called the *remainder*. The best way to make sure that the program produces a consistent or correct result is to make sure that only one process is in its critical region at a time. This is known as *mutual exclusion*. We're going to have to add some additional code to this loop to guarantee the mutual exclusion of the critical region. We will need some code before the critical region that makes sure that it is safe for this process to enter the critical code and, at the same time, make sure that the other process cannot enter its critical region. We also need some code after the critical section that allows the other process to enter its critical region now that this process has finished using the region. The section of code before the critical region is known as the *pre-protocol*; the code that follows it is called the *post-protocol*. From the above description, it can be seen that the lifetime of a process consists of the following sections of code:

- Initialization
- Pre-protocol
- Critical section
- Post-protocol
- Remainder

No process should ever terminate in its critical section. This is because when one process is in the critical region, no other process can enter. If one process terminates in the region, the other would be permanently blocked. Since the system is in a state of transition during the protocol sections, it is just as bad for a process to terminate in its protocol regions. The only valid place for a process to terminate is during its remainder section.

Figure 6.10 shows two processes—their program loops—and their respective code sections.

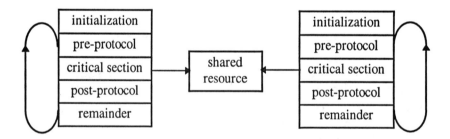

Figure 6.10
Two communicating processes showing their sections and the shared resource.

We shall now try to develop a working protocol. Along the way, we shall discover most of the pitfalls that complicate concurrent programming. Figure 6.11 shows our first attempt.

```
VAR  inCount, turn;
PROCEDURE Proc1;
    VAR  i, j;
    BEGIN
        j := 0;
        FOR i := 1 TO 100 DO
            (*  pre-protocol  *)
            WHILE turn = 2 DO SUSPEND END;
            (*  critical region  *)
            inCount := inCount + 1;
            WRITE("Process 1 in critical region");
            IF inCount = 2 THEN
                WRITE("violation of critical region");
                RETURN
            END;
            inCount := inCount - 1;
            (*  post-protocol  *)
            turn := 2;
            (*  remainder  *)
            WRITE("Process 1 has left critical region");
            j := j + 1;       (* the process killer *)
            IF j = 50 THEN RETURN END
        END
    END;
PROCEDURE Proc2;
    VAR  i, j;
    BEGIN
        j := 0;
        FOR i := 1 TO 100 DO
            (*  pre-protocol  *)
            WHILE turn = 1 DO SUSPEND END;
            (*  critical region  *)
            inCount := inCount + 1;
            WRITE("Process 2 in critical region");
            IF inCount = 2 THEN
                WRITE("violation of critical region");
                RETURN
            END;
            inCount := inCount - 1;
            (*  post-protocol  *)
            turn := 1;
            (*  remainder  *)
            WRITE("Process 2 has left critical region");
            j := j + 1;       (* the process killer *)
```

```
            IF j = 75 THEN RETURN END
        END
    END;
BEGIN
    inCount := 0;    turn := 1;
    COBEGIN;
        Proc1;
        Proc2;
    COEND
END.
```

Figure 6.11
First attempt at a concurrent protocol.

This example also shows the technique we shall be using to test these attempts. Instead of an endless loop, a for loop with a large upper limit is used. This will keep things going long enough to test our protocol attempts.

The common variable, *inCount*, is also used to test for failure to achieve mutual exclusion. As a process enters the critical region, it increments inCount. It then checks to see if the value is equal to 2. This would indicate both processes are in the region and we have failed to achieve mutual exclusion. As a process leaves the region, it decrements the value of inCount.

In the remainder section of the loop, we have a process killer. The variable j is set to 0 in the initialization section and incremented each time the process enters the remainder. Once the value reaches a specific value, the process executes a return statement, which effectively terminates the process.

Our protocol uses another shared variable named *turn*. We are attempting to protect one shared variable by using another. That should warn us that there may be problem. The protocol works as follows. Turn can take on values of either 1 or 2. It is set to 1 by the main program. A value of 1 means that proc1 may enter its critical region and 2 allows proc2 in. Proc1 will be the first one in. As it leaves, it sets turn to 2 so that proc2 may enter. Likewise, proc2 sets turn back to 1 as it leaves the critical region. (In this kind of setup, where two processes transfer back and forth between themselves, the processes are known as *coroutines*.) If a process wishes to enter the critical region but finds that it is the other process's turn, it will execute a

SUSPEND command. This has the effect of putting the process to sleep. The SUSPEND command is handled in the P-Machine by placing the current process on the ready queue and activating another process from the ready queue.

There are two problems with this protocol. The first one is that the processes are forced into strict alternation. If one of the processes is much faster than the other, it will be held back by the slower process.

The second problem is much worse. Assume that process 1 terminates. If process 2 is not yet in its critical region, it can enter once because the first process sets turn to 2. As process 2 leaves the critical region, it sets turn back to 1. Process 1 has terminated, so it will never set turn back to 2. Process 2 will, therefore, not be able to get back into the region. One of the requirements of a concurrent system is that if one process terminates, it should not affect any other process. This principle has not been complied with here. When one process died, the other process was as good as dead. It can't proceed. We say that this attempt failed due to a lack of *liveness*. Liveness is one of the measures we use to see if a concurrent program is "correct." Therefore, we call liveness one of the two *correctness properties*.

Our next attempt fails due to a lack of the other correctness property.

Our first attempt failed because the second process was counting on the first process to change the mutual control variable, but this could never happen when the first process terminated. It seems like a reasonable idea to use two variables, one for each process. Since sharing is a problem, each process will have its own control variable that only it can write to. The process can set the variable to 1 when it is safe for the other process to enter the critical region and to 0 when it is about to enter the region itself. Each process could inspect the other process's control variable to decide if it can enter the critical area. If the value is 1, it can enter; otherwise, it must wait. The code for process 1's protocol sections are shown in Figure 6.12. The other process would reverse the references to C1 and C2.

```
(*  pre-protocol  *)
WHILE C2 = 0 DO SUSPEND END;
C1 := 0;
(*  critical region  *)

      .  .     .  .  .
(*  post-protocol  *)
C1 := 1;
```

Figure 6.12
Protocol for the second attempt.

Before either process starts, that is, before the COBEGIN, the main program must set both C1 and C2 to 1. Otherwise, neither process will be able to get started. This looks like a reasonable evolution from the previous attempt. This attempt has a fatal problem also. If we run it with strict alternation of processes, we would see the following sequence:

- Process 1 checks C2 and sees that it is 1, that is, safe to go into the critical region.
- Process 2 checks C1 and sees that it is 1.
- Process 1 sets C1 to 0.
- Process 2 sets C2 to 0.
- Process 1 enters the critical region.
- Process 2 enters the critical region.

If you run this program on our platform with the –1 option, you will not see a message that there's a violation of the critical region. This is due to the same problem that caused the program in Figure 6.9 to give incorrect results; each process loads the in-Count variable, increments it, and compares it to two in perfect synchronization. The result is that neither process detects the fact that both processes are in the critical region. If you use a higher option value when running the program, you will be more likely to see the error message.

This attempt fails to enforce the mutual exclusion principle that is supposed to keep the resource safe. For this reason, we say that this attempt fails due to the lack of *safety*. Safety is the second correctness property.

So now we must make another try. It seems that checking the other process's control variable and then clearing our own was not a good approach. It left the door open for the other process to sneak in. Perhaps it would be a better approach to say first that we were going to attempt to enter the critical region, and the other process had better keep out. (Sounds like a fairly proactive approach, if I do say so myself.) We accomplish this by reversing a couple of lines in the code. This is shown in Figure 6.13.

```
(*  pre-protocol  *)
C1 := 0;
WHILE C2 = 0 DO SUSPEND END;
(*  critical region  *)
     .   .   .      .   .   .
(*  post-protocol  *)
C1 := 1;
```

Figure 6.12
Protocol for the third attempt.

Now we stake our claim first and then go to see if the other process's control variable will let us proceed. If not, we wait until it says we can proceed. But, this waiting is the problem. With strict alternation of processes, we will have the following sequence:

- Process 1 sets C1 to 0.
- Process 2 sets C2 to 0.
- Process 1 waits for C2 to become 1.
- Process 2 waits for C1 to become 1.

You may notice that these processes will wait a long time. In fact, they could wait forever. In this case, both processes are locked out even though neither process has terminated. There is a special name for this lack of liveness; it is called *deadlock*.

To get a better understanding of deadlock, let's look at a totally different field. Popular legend has it that there was a law written in Kansas that stated that "when two trains approach each other at a crossing, they shall both come to a full stop and neither shall start up until the other has gone." Picture a place where two train tracks cross. The critical region is the small square where the two tracks intersect. If one train going North and another going West should approach the intersection at the same time, the Kansas law would have them both stop with no way of starting up again (unless one suddenly blew up). This is a classic example of deadlock.

It turns out that this example furnishes us with our next attempt. Try changing just two words so that the law becomes "when two trains approach each other at a crossing, they shall both come to a full stop and neither shall *go forward* until the other has gone." If one train should back up, the other train could proceed across the intersection. Our next attempt will use this same concept. If the processes see that they are both trying to enter the critical section, they can drop their claim for the right to enter the critical region by setting their control variable to 1, waiting a while, and then trying again (by setting the variable to 0). While they've dropped their claim, the other process could enter the region. If you run this program, you'll see that it has a better chance of progressing. On the other hand, if both processes are in perfect sync as they back off, wait, and then try again, they will continually block each other. It is only when a bit of randomness is introduced into the picture that things have a chance of working. Since this situation has a chance of getting out of the blocking condition, we call this situation *lockout* instead of deadlock.

The fourth attempt is shown in Figure 6.13.

```
(*  pre-protocol  *)
C1 := 0;
WHILE C2 = 0 DO
    C1 := 1;
    SUSPEND;
    C1 := 0;
END;
(*  critical region  *)
    .   .    .   .
(*  post-protocol  *)
C1 := 1;
```

Figure 6.13
Protocol for the fourth attempt.

It's beginning to seem like each attempt to fix the problems of the previous attempt just gives us new problems. Fortunately, a person named Dekker was able to figure out how to combine the first and fourth attempts into a final solution. It satisfies both the liveness and safety requirements. Dekker's algorithm is shown in Figure 6.14.

As you can see, turn is only examined if the other process's control variable says that it is attempting to enter its critical region. That means, of course, that the other process is still alive. If the turn variable indicates that it is the other process's turn (to enter the critical region), this process will back off, that is, set its control variable to 1 for a period of time so that the other process may proceed. Turn is used here to avoid the problem of the previous attempt, where both processes backed off at exactly the same time. Dekker's algorithm makes sure that only one process backs off, not both.

Although the post-protocol still sets turn to select the other process as it did in the first attempt, it also sets its control variable to 1. That way, even if this process should terminate in the remainder section of its code, the outer while loop of the other process will skip right over the check on the turn variable. This prevents the liveness failure we experienced in the first attempt.

```
(*  pre-protocol  *)
C1 := 0;
WHILE C2 = 0 DO
    IF turn = 2 THEN
        C1 := 1;
        WHILE turn = 2 DO SUSPEND END;
        C1 := 0
    END
END;
(*  critical region  *)
    .  .  .    .  .  .
(*  post-protocol  *)
C1   := 1;
turn := 2
```

Figure 6.14
Protocol for Dekker's Algorithm.

As you can see, the simple one-line pre- and post-protocols of the first attempt have become very much more complicated—the price we have to pay to get it to work. On the other hand, once one person comes up with an idea, someone else can improve it. The resulting shorter form is known as Peterson's solution. It is shown in Figure 6.15.

```
(*  pre-protocol  *)
C1 := 0;
turn := 1;
WHILE (turn = 1) AND (C2 = 0) DO
    SUSPEND
END;
(*  critical region  *)
    .  .  .    .  .  .
(*  post-protocol  *)
C1 := 1;
```

Figure 6.15
Peterson's solution.

Although it is shorter, it is still quite complex. Another consideration is that what we have looked at so far has just had two processes. The complexity practically doubles when an additional process is added. The standard operating system does not know how many processes to expect, but the total number is not so important as the fact that the number is very large. Therefore, Dekker's algorithm and Peterson's solution are not considered practical. The study leading up to their design was beneficial in showing us what problems are encountered in concurrent programming. They also showed that solutions are possible. All modern operating systems today use some other protocol mechanism to enforce mutual exclusion. The protocol used depends on the hardware architecture and on the compiler implementation. There are several general protocols that are used in various popular environments. We shall examine some of these in the rest of this chapter. We must be aware that the actual implementation depends on the hardware and operating system. Some of this will be described in the following chapters.

In the meantime, we will use the P-Machine to get an idea of how the implementation might work on a real processor.

6.5 SEMAPHORES

Remember the Kansas law about two trains meeting at a crossing? Well there's an even worse situation. During the last century, thousands of miles of railroad track were laid across the continent. In order to reduce the total cost, most of this was done as a single track. Although we find one lane in each direction to be necessary on our highways, the railroads used a single track for both directions. This became a problem when more than one locomotive shared the track. Odds are that sooner or later they would be approaching each other from opposite directions. A method to avoid collisions had to be developed. Their solution was the original semaphore.

Here's how it works. At places along the track where trains are expected to meet, special (pairs of) sidings are provided. An electrical switch is placed slightly before each siding. This switch is connected to a signal system near the opposite siding. When a train going in one direction crosses over the switch, the signal on the distant siding warns any trains going in the opposite direction of the oncoming train. The second train pulls into the siding to avoid being hit. After the first train passes, a second switch puts the signal into the all-clear position. The second train backs out of the siding and proceeds on its way. The way that the switches were wired had to be clever enough to manage the situation where both trains crossed the switch at the same time. Basically, one switch was given preference, that is, it overrode the other switch. The railroad semaphore system is shown in Figure 6.16.

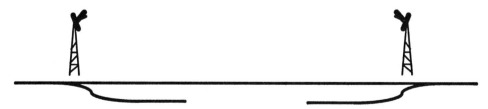

Figure 6.16
The original semaphore system.

The software version of the semaphore borrows quite heavily from the railroad image. The shared track corresponds to the shared variable that must be made safe. The only way to do this in either case is to ensure mutual exclusion. When one train discovers that another train is using the track, it must wait on a siding. The software semaphore protocol has a WAIT function that must be called before entering the critical region. If the WAIT function determines that another process is in the critical region, it causes the calling process to wait on a queue until the area is free. When the other train is leaving the area, it sends a signal that all is clear. The software semaphore protocol has a SEND function that signals that another process may enter the critical section. At that time, one of the processes waiting on the queue is extracted so that it may take its turn in the region.

The software queue functions quite well as a siding, but the semaphore protocol allows other data structures to be used as long as the method of removing processes is fair. "Fair" in this case means that once a process has been placed in the "siding," eventually it will be extracted. Alternate data structures include stacks and sets. If a set is used, a fair extraction method would have to be developed.

There is one other function used in the P-Machine's version of the semaphore protocol. The SEMAPHORE procedure is used to define and initialize a semaphore structure. It turns an integer variable into a pointer to a semaphore structure. This structure consists of the "waiting" queue and a count that tells how many more SENDs than WAITs have been called. It is possible, however, to give an initial value to this count.

The LuxLyk/P-Machine implementation of the semaphore protocol is described in Figure 6.17.

SEMAPHORE(semaphore_variable, initial_value)
- Create a new Semaphore and place its pointer into the next free entry in the semaphore array of the P-Machine. The Semaphore constructor automatically creates an empty queue and has the Semaphore's "waiting" field point to this queue. It also presets the "count" field to 0.
- Place the index number of the semaphore array element into the semaphore_variable.
- Assign the initial_value to the Semaphore's "count" field.

WAIT(semaphore_variable)
- Determine the actual Semaphore indicated by the index value contained in the semaphore_variable.
- IF a previous SEND was sent (i.e., 'count' > 0)
    1. Decrement "count" by one.
    2. Return—that is, continue current process.
- ELSE IF ready queue is empty
    DEADLOCK
- ELSE
    1. Put current process on the Semaphore queue.
    2. Remove a process from the ready queue and transfer to it.

SEND(semaphore_variable)
- Determine the actual Semaphore indicated by the index value contained in the semaphore_variable.
- IF any processes are waiting on the Semaphore queue
    1. Put current process on the ready queue.
    2. Remove a process from the semaphore queue and transfer to it.
- ELSE
    1. Increment "count" by one.
    2. IF ready queue is not empty
        - Put current process on the ready queue.
        - Remove a process from the ready queue and transfer to it.

Figure 6.17
The LuxLyk / P-Machine Semaphore protocol.

SEMAPHORE, WAIT, and SEND are built-in procedures in LuxLyk. Each translates into a specific P-Machine command.

The SEMAPHORE call loads the semaphore_variable and initial_value onto the stack and then calls "OPR 0 28". The P-Machine has an internal array of pointers to Semaphores. The Semaphore is basically a structure that contains a count field and a queue to hold Process Control Blocks. The OPR code finds the next available free element in the pointer array, creates an instance of a Semaphore, and places its pointer in the array element. The index of the array element is placed in the semaphore_variable and the initial_value is placed into the count field of the Semaphore. When the OPR has finished, the semaphore_variable points indirectly to the Semaphore and can be accessed by the WAIT and SEND commands. These LuxLyk commands first push the semaphore_variable on the stack and then call OPR 0 29 for WAIT or OPR 0 30 for SEND. The code for these P-Codes follows the descriptions in Figure 6.17 quite closely. The complete P-Machine code can be found in Appendix F for those who want a better look at the code. The diagram of the collection of data structures required to make semaphores function is shown in Figure 6.18.

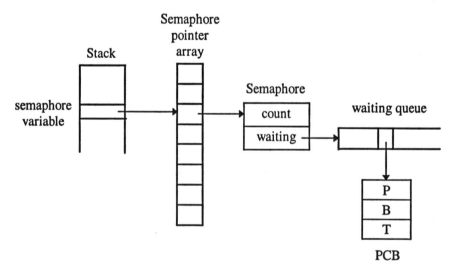

Figure 6.18
The Semaphore data structures.

As you can see, the Semaphore comes with quite a collection of data structures. Now let's put semaphores back in our first concurrent program, the one with the problem. Figure 6.19 shows the modified version.

```
(*     process_s.11 -- a concurrent program with semaphores   *)
VAR count;     (* this global variable is the critical data *)
    OK;        (* the semaphore variable *)
PROCEDURE Proc ( max );
   VAR  i;
   BEGIN
      FOR i := 1 TO max DO
         WAIT(OK);
         count := count + 1;
         SEND(OK)
      END
   END;
BEGIN
   count := 0;
   SEMAPHORE( OK, 1 );
   COBEGIN;
      Proc (  5 );
      Proc ( 10 );
   COEND;
   WRITE( count )
END.
```

Figure 6.19
The concurrent program with a Semaphore added.

The SEMAPHORE command initializes the semaphore with an initial value of 1. Unless this is done, the first time a process encounters a WAIT instruction, it will be queued. We need an initial "send" to get things started. This semaphore will only take on count values of 0 and 1. For this reason, it is called a binary semaphore. Its primary use in this form is to allow many processes to share a single resource—control just sort of ping-pongs from one process to the next.

Another form of the semaphore is the "general" or "counting" semaphore. It is used to keep track of how many more SENDs there have been than WAITs. It is most often used when data is buffered between two processes. Buffering tends to speed up some programs. Consider a system that can read 60 cards per minute and can print out 60 lines per minute. If we try to list cards using a standard sequential program that first reads data from a card, prints the data on the printer, and then goes back to read the next card, we will find that the system only puts out 30 lines per minute. The read takes a second and the write takes another second—the total time is 2 seconds. Therefore, the cycle can only be executed 30 times per second. If, instead, we have two processes and a buffer, we can run at 60 lines per minute. One process reads a card and puts the data in a buffer. The other process takes data from the buffer and prints it out. Since buffer operations take hardly any time, both processes run at one second per cycle. Thus the system throughput is 60 lines per minute. Figure 6.20 shows a typical buffered program.

```
CONST  max = 4;                  (* buffer size (quite small) *)
       newline = 10;             (* ASCII new-line character  *)
VAR    buff[max],                (* the buffer itself         *)
       inpos, outpos,            (* buffer position pointers  *)
       chPresent, spPresent;     (* general semaphores        *)
PROCEDURE deposit(x);
    BEGIN
        WAIT(spPresent);
        buff[inpos] := x;
        inpos := (inpos + 1) % max;
        SEND(chPresent)
    END;
FUNCTION  fetch;
    VAR  x;
    BEGIN
        WAIT(chPresent);
        x := buff[outpos];
        outpos := (outpos + 1) % max;
        SEND(spPresent);
        RETURN x
    END;
PROCEDURE producer;
    VAR  ch: CHAR;
    BEGIN
        REPEAT
```

```
                READ(ch);
                deposit( INTEGER(ch) )
        UNTIL    INTEGER(ch) = newline
    END;
PROCEDURE consumer;
    VAR  ch: CHAR;
    BEGIN
        REPEAT
            ch := CHAR( fetch() );
            WRITE('*');
            WRITE(ch)
        UNTIL    INTEGER(ch) = newline
    END;
BEGIN
    inpos  := 0;
    outpos := 0;
    SEMAPHORE(chPresent, 0);
    SEMAPHORE(spPresent, max);
    COBEGIN;
        producer;
        consumer;
    COEND
END.
```

Figure 6.20
A buffered program using Semaphores.

This program uses a circular buffer. *Inpos* keeps track of where the next character will be placed in the buffer. Likewise, *outpos* keeps track of where the next character may be taken from. It is important in this system that we don't put in more characters than we have room for or take out more characters than have been placed in the buffer. To deal with these requirements, we use two counting semaphores: one to keep track of how much space is left in the buffer and one to keep track of how many characters are in it. The first semaphore is initialized to the size of the buffer. The other is initialized to zero.

The program consists of two processes. The producer reads from the standard input and deposits the characters in the buffer. The consumer fetches data from the buffer and writes out each character with a "*" in front of it.

Deposit and fetch are the procedures that actually operate on the buffer. They are the ones that reference the two semaphores. Fetch WAITs on the *spPresent* semaphore for space to be present in the buffer. Once it's available, the procedure places its character in the buffer, increments the inpos pointer, and does a SEND on the *chPresent* semaphore to indicate that another character is in the buffer. Figure 6.17 shows that a call to WAIT decrements the semaphore's value of count and a call to SEND increments the value. The semaphores addressed by the deposit procedure have effectively decremented the count of spaces in the buffer and incremented the number of characters in it. Looking at the fetch function will show that exactly the opposite happens.

There is something else that should be noticed in this example. Although the placement of the WAITs and SENDs look like Figure 6.19, where they surrounded the critical region, this system is more complex. The WAIT for a particular semaphore is in (the procedure called by) one process and the SEND is in the other. What we actually have here are two processes using the semaphore to communicate. The correct handling of the information received from this communication is what enforces mutual exclusion of the critical resource.

When you run this program, you may be surprised that the characters are not output by the consumer process as soon as you type a character. This is because the operating system has its own buffer. All the characters you type in are buffered until you hit the carriage return. At that point, the operating system feeds the characters to the program as fast as it can request them. The result is that when you finish typing your line, the program produces its output on the next line. (Just for fun, run this program and enter the letters "MASH".)

Now we are ready to look at another practical protocol.

6.6 MONITORS

Monitors are a more sophisticated concurrency protocol than the semaphore. The monitor philosophy includes the concept of encapsulation. This means that the critical data structure and the functions that handle it are all contained in the same unit. If you consider the buffer program of Figure 6.20, the data structure is the buffer and the functions are deposit and fetch. A closer look will reveal that the initialization of the pointer and control variables was done in the main program. With monitors, the initialization code is done in the containing unit where it belongs. A rewrite of the buffer program using monitors is shown in Figure 6.21.

```
CONST   max = 4;                  (* buffer size (quite small) *)
        newline = 10;             (* ASCII new-line character  *)
MONITOR buffer;
    VAR     buff[max],            (* the buffer itself         *)
            inpos, outpos,        (* buffer position pointers  *)
            n,                    (* fullness indicator        *)
            notempty, notfull;    (* monitor conditions        *)
    PROCEDURE deposit(x);
        BEGIN
            IF n = max THEN
                DELAY(notfull)
            END;
            buff[inpos] := x;
            inpos := (inpos + 1) % max;
            n := n + 1;
            SIGNAL(notempty)
        END;
    FUNCTION  fetch;
        VAR  x;
        BEGIN
            IF n = 0 THEN
                DELAY(notempty)
            END;
            x := buff[outpos];
            outpos := (outpos + 1) % max;
            n := n - 1;
            SIGNAL(notfull);
            RETURN x
        END;
    BEGIN                         (* body of buffer monitor    *)
        inpos  := 0;
        outpos := 0;
        n      := 0;
        CONDITION(notempty);
        CONDITION(notfull)
    END;                          (* end of buffer monitor     *)
```

```
PROCEDURE producer;
    VAR  ch: CHAR;
    BEGIN
        REPEAT
            READ(ch);
            deposit( INTEGER(ch) )
        UNTIL   INTEGER(ch) = newline
    END;
PROCEDURE consumer;
    VAR  ch: CHAR;
    BEGIN
        REPEAT
            ch := CHAR( fetch() );
            WRITE('*');
            WRITE(ch)
        UNTIL   INTEGER(ch) = newline
    END;
BEGIN
    COBEGIN;
        producer;
        consumer;
    COEND
END.
```

Figure 6.21
A buffered program using monitors.

As you can see, this monitor program is quite similar to the
semaphore version, but there are some differences. Let's take a
look at some of the more obvious ones. Instead of the WAIT and
SEND operators, the monitor uses DELAY and SIGNAL. You
will also notice that the DELAY is embedded in an if statement.
Unlike the semaphore WAIT function, the DELAY function does
not have a conditional test built into it to determine if the process should be placed on a queue. It is the responsibility of the
programmer to make that decision. Therefore, this program uses
the variable n to keep track of the number of characters in the
buffer. The monitor cannot keep track of the count by itself; basically, the monitor has no memory. On the other hand, the parameters passed to the DELAY and SIGNAL procedures are
called "conditions." Recall that the parameters passed to WAIT
and SEND were called semaphores. The semaphores were ini-

tialized by the SEMAPHORE command. The conditions are initialized by the CONDITION statement. You will notice that the condition is not set to an initial value the way semaphores were. This is further evidence of the fact that conditions do not have any memory. What "not having any memory" ultimately means is that if a call is made to SIGNAL when there are no waiting processes, the next DELAY executed will have no way of knowing about the previous SIGNAL; it leaves no trace. That is why the code within the monitor's functions must track this information on its own.

The initialization is done in what corresponds to the body of the monitor. The functions that access the monitor's data (i.e., deposit and fetch) look like they are simply nested within the monitor; however, they can be accessed by processes (such as producer and consumer). I call them *access procedures*. The internal data of the monitor, however, is hidden from the view of external procedures.

The differences are more than skin deep. There is a mutual exclusion requirement on the whole monitor itself. This means that only one process can be *active* within the monitor at a time, although several inactive ones can exist on the queues attached to the conditions. In addition, the monitor protocol insists that the inactive processes must be re-activated in a first come first served order. The semaphore only required that the process activation be fair. Queues are about the only acceptable container for processes in a monitor.

Monitors are simulated by semaphores on the LuxLyk and P-Machine platform. There is a hidden semaphore used just to enforce mutual exclusion on the monitor itself; I call it the *gate* semaphore. At the beginning of the initialization in the body of the monitor, the LuxLyk compiler automatically inserts P-Code equivalent of a "SEMAPHORE(gate, 1)" statement. Directly after the "INT" P-Code at the beginning of any access procedure, the LuxLyk compiler inserts a "WAIT(gate)" command into the P-Code. Neither of these references to gate will be seen in the source code, but they *do* end up in the generated P-Code.

Each condition in the monitor is simulated by a Condition structure that includes a semaphore, a pointer to the gate, and a count that is used to indicate if any processes are waiting on the condition. Since this structure requires a reference to the gate, the reference is passed to it during initialization. The compiler automatically inserts this reference into the P-Code generated by the CONDITION statement. This reference is also not seen in the source code, but it does end up in the generated P-Code.

The P-Machine has an array of pointers to Conditions. During the execution of the CONDITION statement, instances of the Semaphore and Condition structures are created. The Condition is made to point to the Semaphore and to the previously created gate Semaphore. The condition_variable passed to CONDITION is given the index of the element in the Condition pointer array that points to Condition that was just created. Figure 6.22 is a diagram of a monitor with a single condition defined.

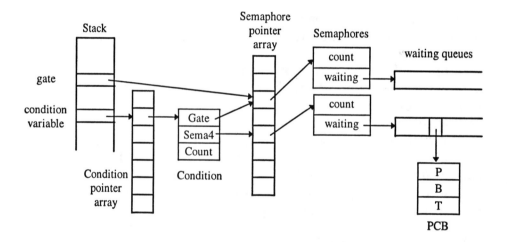

Figure 6.22
The monitor data structures.

The P-Machine supplies additional P-Codes to work with the semaphores associated with conditions. OPR 0 31 is the one that creates the Condition structure itself. OPR 0 32 performs a SEND to the gate associated with a condition. OPR 0 33 and 34 perform WAIT and SEND operations on the semaphore linked with a condition. OPR 0 35 and 36 increment and decrement the count that is associated with a condition. OPR 0 37 pushes onto the **Stack** the value of the count associated with the condition.

The LuxLyk compiler changes calls to DELAY and SIGNAL into sequences of P-Code that use these new OPR commands. It turns out that it is easier to describe these expansions as if they were written in a higher level language.

A call to "DELAY(condition_variable)" expands as:

```
INCR(condition_variable);
SEND(gate);
WAIT(condition_variable);
DECR(condition_variable);
```

The expansion of a "SIGNAL(condition_variable)" command is more complicated. The P-Code expansion actually consists of an if statement.

```
IF (condition_variable.count > 0) THEN
    SEND(condition_variable)
ELSE
    SEND(gate)
END
```

where condition_variable.count is the value of the count in the Condition structure.

Again, the Luxlyk compiler does this conversion behind the scene. The source code needs only to contain the DELAY or SIGNAL call, and the P-Code equivalent to the high-level code is generated.

Our present buffered program transfers one character at a time. By adding another pair of procedures we can transfer a whole string at a time. You might say that this is a message passing system. Figure 6.23 shows this program.

```
CONST   msgSize = 25;        (* max message size          *)
        max     = 4;         (* buffer size (quite small) *)
        newline = 10;        (* ASCII new-line character  *)
MONITOR buffer;
    VAR     buff[max],       (* the buffer itself         *)
            inpos, outpos,   (* buffer position pointers  *)
            n,               (* fullness indicator        *)
            notempty, notfull;  (* monitor conditions     *)
        PROCEDURE deposit(x);
```

```
        BEGIN
            IF n = max THEN
                DELAY(notfull)
            END;
            buff[inpos] := x;
            inpos := (inpos + 1) % max;
            n := n + 1;
            SIGNAL(notempty)
        END;
    FUNCTION  fetch;
        VAR  x;
        BEGIN
            IF n = 0 THEN
                DELAY(notempty)
            END;
            x := buff[outpos];
            outpos := (outpos + 1) % max;
            n := n - 1;
            SIGNAL(notfull);
            RETURN x
        END;
    BEGIN                      (* body of buffer monitor    *)
        inpos  := 0;
        outpos := 0;
        n      := 0;
        CONDITION(notempty);
        CONDITION(notfull)
    END;                       (* end of buffer monitor     *)
(*    channel definition  -- note, this is not a monitor    *)
    PROCEDURE sendMessage(msg[msgSize]: CHAR);
        VAR  i, len: INTEGER;
        BEGIN
            len := 0;          (* get length of message *)
            WHILE (msg[len] # CHAR(0)) AND (len < msgSize) DO
                len := len + 1
            END;
            deposit( len );
            FOR i := 0 TO len - 1 DO
                deposit(msg[i])
            END
        END;
    FUNCTION  receiveMessage: STRING[msgSize];
        VAR  i, len:        INTEGER;
             msg[msgSize]:  CHAR;
```

```
        BEGIN
            len := fetch;
            FOR i := 0 TO len - 1 DO
                msg[i] := CHAR( fetch )
            END;
            IF len < msgSize THEN
                msg[len] := CHAR(0)
            END;
            RETURN msg
        END;
(*    end of channel definition                          *)
PROCEDURE producer;
    VAR  message[msgSize]: CHAR;
         ch:                CHAR;
          i:                INTEGER;
    BEGIN
        i := 0;
        REPEAT
            READ(ch);
            message[i] := ch;
            i := i + 1
        UNTIL (i > msgSize) OR (ch = CHAR(newline));
        IF i <= msgSize THEN
            message[i - 1] := CHAR(0)
        END;
        sendMessage( message )
    END;
PROCEDURE consumer;
    VAR  message: STRING[msgSize];
    BEGIN
        message := receiveMessage;
        WRITE( message )
    END;
BEGIN
    COBEGIN;
        producer;
        consumer;
    COEND
END.
```

Figure 6.23
Message passing using channels.

I call this the channel model. The concept is that we have opened up a communication channel between the producer and the consumer processes and then passed messages through the channel. This program also shows how the LuxLyk STRING[...] data type is used as a return type for a function.

6.7 A MINI-RENDEZVOUS

With a little work, a modified form of a *rendezvous* can be created. The monitor was simulated in the P-Machine hardware by monitors. Now we will simulate a simple form of rendezvous in software using channels made from monitors. Normally, there are several "sender" processes and a single "receiver" process. Our simple form will only have one sender and one receiver.

Several properties are usually ascribed to the rendezvous:

- Two processes "meet" for a rendezvous. The first process to arrive must wait for the other.
- Only one transaction is negotiated per rendezvous.
- There is a two-way flow of data during the transaction.

The transaction that will be conducted in our rendezvous will be the passing of a message. The two way property requires a channel in both directions. Basically, we shall be passing the message in both directions. Our rendezvous program is shown in Figure 6.24.

```
CONST    msgSize = 50;        (* max message size          *)
         max     = 16;        (* buffer size (quite small) *)
         newline = 10;        (* ASCII new-line character  *)
MONITOR inBuffer;
    VAR     inBuff[max],       (* the inBuffer itself       *)
            inInpos, inOutpos, (* inBuffer position pointers *)
            inCnt,             (* fullness indicator        *)
            inNotEmpty, inNotFull; (* monitor conditions    *)
    PROCEDURE inDeposit(x);
        BEGIN
            IF inCnt = max THEN
                DELAY(inNotFull)
            END;
            inBuff[inInpos] := x;
            inInpos := (inInpos + 1) % max;
```

```
                    inCnt := inCnt + 1;
                    SIGNAL(inNotEmpty)
              END;
         FUNCTION  inFetch;
              VAR  x;
              BEGIN
                    IF inCnt = 0 THEN
                         DELAY(inNotEmpty)
                    END;
                    x := inBuff[inOutpos];
                    inOutpos := (inOutpos + 1) % max;
                    inCnt := inCnt - 1;
                    SIGNAL(inNotFull);
                    RETURN x
              END;
         BEGIN                      (* body of inBuffer monitor    *)
              inInpos  := 0;
              inOutpos := 0;
              inCnt       := 0;
              CONDITION(inNotEmpty);
              CONDITION(inNotFull)
         END;                       (* end of inBuffer monitor     *)
    (*    inChannel definition  -- note, this is not a monitor     *)
         PROCEDURE inSendMessage(msg[msgSize]: CHAR);
              VAR   i, len: INTEGER;
              BEGIN
                    len := 0;                 (* get length of message *)
                    WHILE (msg[len] # CHAR(0)) AND (len < msgSize) DO
                         len := len + 1
                    END;
                    inDeposit( len );
                    FOR i := 0 TO len - 1 DO
                         inDeposit(msg[i])
                    END
              END;
         FUNCTION  inReceiveMessage: STRING[msgSize];
              VAR   i, len:           INTEGER;
                    msg[msgSize]:     CHAR;
              BEGIN
                    len := inFetch;
                    FOR i := 0 TO len - 1 DO
                         msg[i] := CHAR( inFetch )
                    END;
                    IF len < msgSize THEN
```

```
                        msg[len] := CHAR(0)
                END;
                RETURN msg
        END;
(*    end of inChannel definition                              *)
MONITOR outBuffer;
    VAR      outBuff[max],          (* the outBuffer itself       *)
             outInpos, outOutpos,   (* outBuffer position pointers *)
             outCnt,                (* fullness outdicator        *)
             outNotEmpty, outNotFull;  (*  monitor conditions     *)
    PROCEDURE outDeposit(x);
        BEGIN
            IF outCnt = max THEN
                DELAY(outNotFull)
            END;
            outBuff[outInpos] := x;
            outInpos := (outInpos + 1) % max;
            outCnt := outCnt + 1;
            SIGNAL(outNotEmpty)
        END;
    FUNCTION  outFetch;
        VAR  x;
        BEGIN
            IF outCnt = 0 THEN
                DELAY(outNotEmpty)
            END;
            x := outBuff[outOutpos];
            outOutpos := (outOutpos + 1) % max;
            outCnt := outCnt - 1;
            SIGNAL(outNotFull);
            RETURN x
        END;
    BEGIN                (* body of outBuffer monitor    *)
        outInpos  := 0;
        outOutpos := 0;
        outCnt    := 0;
        CONDITION(outNotEmpty);
        CONDITION(outNotFull)
    END;                    (* end of outBuffer monitor    *)
(*   outChannel definition -- note, this is not a monitor    *)
    PROCEDURE outSendMessage(msg[msgSize]: CHAR);
        VAR   i, len: INTEGER;
        BEGIN
            len := 0;                        (* get length of message *)
```

```
                WHILE (msg[len] # CHAR(0)) AND (len < msgSize) DO
                    len := len + 1
                END;
                outDeposit( len );
                FOR i := 0 TO len - 1 DO
                    outDeposit(msg[i])
                END
            END;
        FUNCTION  outReceiveMessage: STRING[msgSize];
            VAR   i, len:              INTEGER;
                msg[msgSize]:      CHAR;
            BEGIN
                len := outFetch;
                FOR i := 0 TO len - 1 DO
                    msg[i] := CHAR( outFetch )
                END;
                IF len < msgSize THEN
                    msg[len] := CHAR(0)
                END;
                RETURN msg
            END;
    (*    end of outChannel definition                          *)
    (*    rendezvous definition                                 *)
        FUNCTION  call(inMessage: STRING[msgSize]): STRING[msgSize];
            VAR       outMessage: STRING[msgSize];
            BEGIN
                inSendMessage(inMessage);
                outMessage := outReceiveMessage;
                RETURN outMessage
            END;
        FUNCTION  accept:    STRING[msgSize];
            VAR   inMessage: STRING[msgSize];
            BEGIN
                inMessage := inReceiveMessage;
                RETURN inMessage
            END;
        PROCEDURE reply(outMessage: STRING[msgSize]);
            BEGIN
                outSendMessage(outMessage)
            END;
    (*    end of rendezvous definition                          *)
    PROCEDURE producer;
        VAR  inMsg[msgSize]: CHAR;
            outMsg[msgSize]: CHAR;
```

```
        ch:             CHAR;
        i:              INTEGER;
BEGIN
    i := 0;
    REPEAT
        READ(ch);
        inMsg[i] := ch;
        i := i + 1
    UNTIL (i > msgSize) OR (ch = CHAR(newline));
    IF i <= msgSize THEN
        inMsg[i - 1] := CHAR(0)
    END;
    WRITE( "producer sending  ", inMsg );
    outMsg := call( inMsg );        (* call for rendezvous *)
    WRITE( "producer received ", outMsg )
END;
PROCEDURE consumer;
    VAR  inMsg[msgSize]: CHAR;
         outMsg[msgSize]: CHAR;
         i:              INTEGER;
BEGIN
    inMsg := accept;                (* accept rendevous    *)
    WRITE( "consumer received ", inMsg );
    FOR i := 0 TO msgSize - 1 DO
        IF (inMsg[i] >= 'a') AND (inMsg[i] <= 'z') THEN
            outMsg[i] :=
                CHAR( INTEGER(inMsg[i]) -
                    INTEGER('a') + INTEGER('A') )
        ELSE
            outMsg[i] := inMsg[i]
        END
    END;
    WRITE( "consumer sending  ", outMsg );
    reply( outMsg )                 (* reply to rendezvous *)
END;
BEGIN
    COBEGIN;
        producer;
        consumer;
    COEND
END.
```

Figure 6.24
A mini-rendezvous made with monitors.

Having two channels reveals an interesting problem about the monitor. Although it is an encapsulation, it is not a true abstract data type. That is, it is not possible to have multiple instances of a monitor. To get two channels, we need two buffers, and that means we need two separate monitors. One monitor is for input to the sender process; the other is for output.

After the two monitors comes the code for the rendezvous functions. The `call` function is made by the sender to request a rendezvous. It starts the operation by sending a message to the receiver process. The receiver starts its part of the rendezvous by calling the `accept` function. This delivers the message to the receiver. The receiver will then call `reply` to complete its part of the rendezvous. This procedure sends a response back to the sender in the form of another message. The response is received by the sender in the form of a returned value from the "call" function. This completes the sender's side of the transaction. It is interesting to think about how the sender sees it. As far as it can tell, it called a function that returned a string. It doesn't realize all that went on between the call and the return.

The program itself is fairly straightforward. `Producer` is the sender process. It reads a line that is typed in and passes it to the sender. `Consumer` is the receiver process. It receives the message, converts it to uppercase, and sends this form back to the receiver. The sender types out the modified sentence. At this point the rendezvous has been completed by both processes.

The rendezvous shown here should give some idea of the concepts it involves. The rendezvous defined in the Ada programming language has much more functionality. For one thing, the receiver is able to "select" a rendezvous from any one of several sender processes. This makes it much more useful than our single sender version.

6.8 WRAP-UP AND FURTHER READING

This chapter started with a very brief description of what concurrency is all about. It then started to describe the platform that would be used to study the basic principles of concurrency. This involved a description of the Full Bodied P-Machine and the LuxLyk language. Examples were given of how advanced features, such as passing parameters or interleaving processes, were implemented on this platform. With this platform in hand, we began to examine the problems involved in concurrent programming. From these fundamental activities, we progressed to looking at several practical concurrency protocols that are in use in actual operating systems. This should prepare us for an examination of some of these operating systems in the following chapters.

A few books are listed here for additional reading. For those interested in rendering some of the P-Machine functions, such as passing parameters, the [Chung 1978] article is suggested. Semaphores can be found in [Dijkstra 1968]. Monitors were introduced in [Hoare 1974]. An excellent tutorial of concurrency can be found in [Ben-Ari 1990]. The Ada programming language (including the rendezvous) is defined in [DOD 1983].

REFERENCES

[Ben-Ari 1990] Ben-Ari, M., *Principles of Concurrent and Distributed Programming*, Englewood Cliffs, NJ: Prentice Hall, Inc., 1990.

[Chung 1978] Chung, Kin-Man, Herbert Yuen, "A 'Tiny' Pascal Compiler," *Byte Magazine*, September, 1978, pp. 58–65, 148–154.

[Dijkstra 1968] Dijkstra, E. W, "Co-operating Sequential Processes" in Genuys (ed.) *Programming Languages*, New York, NY: Academic Press, 1968.

[DOD 1983] U.S. Department of Defense, *The Ada Programming Language*, Washington, D.C.: U.S. Government Printing Office, 1983.

[Hoare 1974] Hoare, C. A. R., "Monitors: An Operating System Structuring Concept," *Communications of the ACM*, 17(10): 549–57, 1974.

CHAPTER 7

Operating Systems Overview

An operating system is a collection of software that makes computer hardware available, efficient, and convenient to a user. Operating systems act as resource managers by controlling how various resources are shared. This chapter will discuss basic operating principles and how the operating system manages and shares some of these resources, including the CPU, memory, and I/O subsystem.

7.0 THE CONCEPT OF THE INTERRUPT

Before we discuss how the operating system shares and manages the resource of the CPU, you must have a clear understanding of how a hardware interrupt occurs.

Interrupts occur on behalf of some asynchronous hardware event, such as someone striking a key on the keyboard, completing a disk write operation, or sending the robot to its home docking station. Computers are designed to operate with interrupts. Several mechanisms for dealing with the occurrence of an interrupt are built into the hardware of the system. When an interrupt occurs, the current state of the machine must be preserved and the control transferred to a body of code that will execute on behalf of the interrupt event having occurred. This body of code is referred to as the *interrupt service routine* or the *ISR*. After execution of the ISR is complete, control is transferred back to the point of execution when the interrupt first happened and the system continues running as if nothing had ever happened. How does control get transferred to th
How does the system save the state of th
control get transferred back to the poin
interrupt occurred? All these questions
plaining how the *hardware assists the sof*
tance takes place for a variety of rea
operating systems and handling interrupt

Interrupts are typically associated w
some that transfer data, such as disk driv
not transfer data, such as the time-of-da
interrupt has an *interrupt vector* associate

signed a specific dedicated memory location that contains two pieces of information.

1. The address of the ISR
2. The state of the machine during execution of the ISR

The interrupt vector is where the system is directed to obtain the information it needs to execute the ISR. Before the new program counter is loaded with the ISR address, the system must save the current execution program counter of the program being interrupted along with the state of the machine. This information is *saved on the stack*. A stack is a linear data structure that maintains a LIFO data flow. A stack also contains a *stack pointer (SP)* that indicates the *top of the stack*. As information is added or *pushed* onto the stack, the SP is decremented. A stack grows towards lower memory addresses. As information is removed from the stack, or *popped*, the SP is incremented. The current execution address (current PC) and current machine state are pushed onto the stack. Returning from the ISR involves executing a special instruction that pops the original program counter and machine state off the top of the stack. This pushing and popping manipulation of the SP are all performed by the hardware. A basic stack data structure follows:

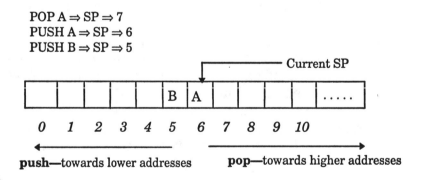

POP A $\Rightarrow$ SP $\Rightarrow$ 7
PUSH A $\Rightarrow$ SP $\Rightarrow$ 6
PUSH B $\Rightarrow$ SP $\Rightarrow$ 5

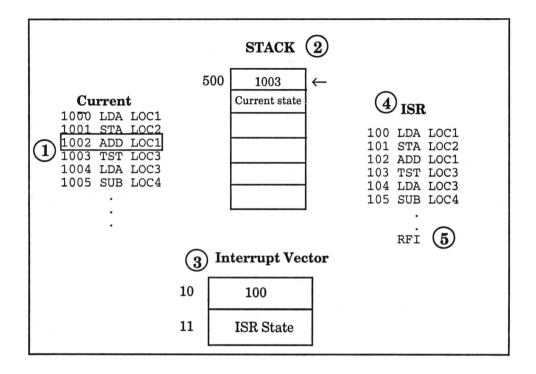

1. Interrupt occurs at this instruction.

2. The system remembers the current PC and machine state and saves this information on the stack.

3. The address of the interrupt service routine is retrieved from the interrupt vector.

4. Execution begins in the interrupt service routine.

5. Control is returned to the point where interrupt first occurred.

Figure 7.1
Steps involved with a hardware interrupt; essential mechanism behind the clock interrupt; basis for a simple scheduler.

7.1 A BASIC SCHEDULER

Understanding the concept of the interrupt is important for understanding the basic nature of the way an operating system scheduler works. The key device involved is the *clock*. The clock produces a regular interrupt many times a second. This interrupt is handled by an ISR, that is, the basic premise of our scheduler. The clock interrupt is how control is transferred from a currently running program to the operating system and then back to the program. The scheduler, or clock ISR, will examine what program is currently running and decide if that program should be allowed to continue executing or if it is another program's turn.

When the scheduler decides that the current program has run long enough and must be preempted to allow another program to execute, the *current state of the system* must be preserved and saved along with the preempted program. This state of the system is also referred to as the *process context*. An operating system scheduler spends a good deal of time saving and restoring process context. Some of the kinds of information that would represent context are:

- The general purpose registers
- Memory management information
- Accounting information
- The program counter
- The state of the machine
- The state of the process

7.1.1 SCHEDULING CHARACTERISTICS

Scheduling can be broken down into several different categories:

- Preemptive and non-preemptive
- Prioritized and non-prioritized
    - Dynamic priority versus static priority

Non-preemptive scheduling means that once a process obtains the CPU, it will not give it up until it is finished. Non-preemptive scheduling is typically used in batch environments where jobs are processed in a serial fashion. *Preemptive* scheduling means a process can be interrupted, or preempted, one or more times before it has completed execution. Time-sharing is a classic example of preemptive scheduling.

Scheduling that utilizes *priorities* assigns a value to a process. This value represents the quality of attention this process will receive by the operating system scheduler. Usually, the higher the priority value, the more priority, and, consequently, the more attention a process will receive. A critical job might be scheduled with a higher priority. The priority scheme can be taken one step further. Some operating system schedulers dynamically adjust the priorities of the processes. This priority adjustment is based on the behavior of the process. For example, a process that has just completed an input I/O would get a priority boost. The rationale being that you want to give the process a better-than-average opportunity to do something with the data it just received. If the process does not perform any acts that deserve a reward of priority boost, the system will continually decrement the priority until it reaches some default level. The operating system scheduler must perform more work to make dynamic scheduling work.

7.1.2 SCHEDULING ALGORITHMS

We will use the terms process, job, and task interchangeably. We will also assume that the jobs are waiting for the CPU in a FIFO queue. We will briefly discuss the following scheduling algorithms:

- First-Come-First-Served (NP)
- Shortest Job First (NP)
- Shortest Remaining Time First (P)
- Highest Response Ratio Next (NP)
- Round-robin (P)
- The Multilevel Feedback Queue (P)

The *First-come-first-served (FCFS)* scheduling algorithm schedules the first process to arrive in the queue waiting for the CPU. Although FCFS is simple to implement, it is not always fair. For instance, consider the situation in which three jobs are waiting to run; the first one to arrive is a very time-consuming program that will take more time to run than the other two waiting jobs combined. Should the other two shorter jobs be made to wait? This is where our next algorithm comes in.

The *Shortest Job First (SJF)* algorithm will pick the next job from the queue that has the lowest amount of CPU time associated with it. How does the system know how much CPU time is involved? Remember that we are discussing a non-preemptive scheduler, and this would most likely be a batch environment. Batch jobs typically require job control language and, in this case, there would be a job card specifying how much CPU time it should get. Actually, this CPU time is a user estimate.

We can modify the SJF algorithm so that it is preemptive. The preemptive version of SJF is called *Shortest Remaining Time (SRT)*. SRT compares the time left to run the current job against the time required to run the next job in the queue. If the amount of time required to run the job waiting in the queue is less than the time left for the currently running job, the currently running job is preempted and the waiting job is scheduled to run. This philosophy is not always the best choice depending on the conditions. If an extremely long job has been running all night, should it be preempted if it is practically finished?

The *Highest Response Ratio Next (HRRN)* algorithm is a non-preemptive scheduling technique conceived by Per Brinch Hansen. HRRN attempts to average the amount of CPU time required to run the job against the amount of time a job has been waiting to use the CPU. HRRN relies on a priority value computed according to the following formula:

$$\text{Priority} = \frac{\text{Service time} + \text{Waiting time}}{\text{Service Time}}$$

The priority is computed as a floating-point value. This formula helps jobs that have been waiting for a long time. The longer the waiting time, the larger the numerator, and hence the value of the priority. The less CPU time (service time) required by a process also causes the priority value to be higher (the denominator is smaller). Therefore, a less CPU intensive job is rewarded by HRRN. The service time is a user estimated value.

Round-robin (RR) scheduling is the essence of time-sharing. All processes are queued FIFO to wait their turn to use the

CPU. A process will be limited in the amount of time it can use the CPU. This time limit is called a *time slice* or *quantum*. Once a process uses up its quantum, it leaves the CPU and goes to the end of the queue to recontend for the processor. A process can leave the CPU for two other situations. It can finish or it can go into a *wait-for-state* for some resource it needs to continue execution. If a process is in a wait-for-state, it no longer needs the CPU and no longer contends for it. A typical wait-for-state would be waiting for an I/O to complete. Once the wait-for-state condition is satisfied, the process is requeued to contend again for the processor. See Figure 7.2.

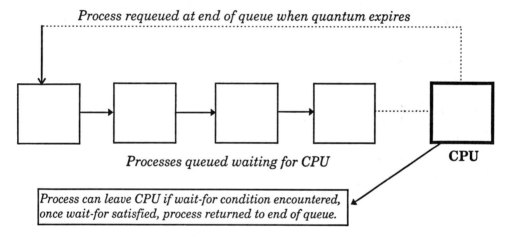

Figure 7.2
Round-robin scheduler.

The *Multilevel Feedback Queue (MLFQ)* provides for a very robust scheduling environment. The MLFQ is a heuristic scheduling mechanism; it learns from its past. The MLFQ uses a series of FIFO queues. The number of these queues involved is a design implementation decision. As new processes are created, they enter the top-most queue level and are received by the CPU. The process can finish, or it can go into a wait-for state. If the process goes into a wait-for state, it leaves the MLFQ mechanism and is placed in a wait-for queue; it no longer needs to contend with the CPU. If the process uses up its entire time slice, it is requeued at the next lower level queue. Unless there are no jobs queued at the top-most level queue, the scheduler will not look at any of the jobs queued at the lower levels. If a process continues to use up its entire quantum at the lower level queues, it keeps on getting requeued at an even lower level queue. If a process is CPU-bound, it will eventually end up at the bottom-most queue. Since there are no more lower level queues, processes are scheduled in a round-robin fashion at this level. What do you do with a process that has just had its wait-for condition satisfied? Do you requeue it at the queue level from which it left for its wait-for condition? Some implementations of MLFQ will queue the process at a queue one higher than when it left the MLFQ environment. Figure 7.4 illustrates how MLFQ works.

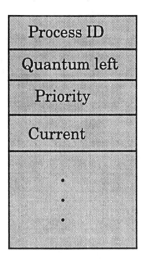

Figure 7.3
Sample process control block.

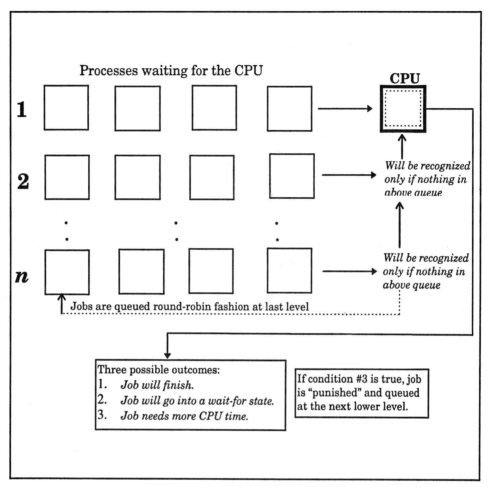

Figure 7.4
Logic flow for multilevel feedback queue.

7.2 PROCESS STATES

A process is manifested to the operating system scheduler as a *process control block (PCB)*. The PCB contains all the information that describes the process. Figure 7.3 shows what kinds of information will be found in the PCB. When we refer to the state of a process, we are referring to where the PCB of that process is queued. Figure 7.5 depicts a *process transition state diagram* and illustrates how the PCBs are moved for the different process states. Notice that once the wait-for condition for a process is satisfied, the process does not go directly to being executed but must be queued up to wait for the CPU with the other processes.

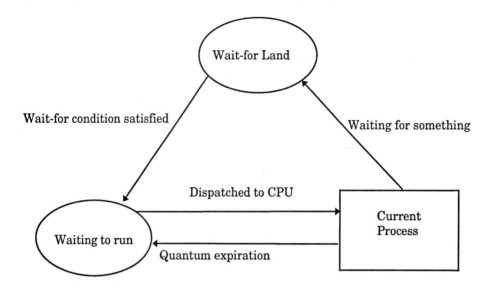

Figure 7.5
A simple process transition state diagram.

7.3 FORMS OF SCHEDULING

Beside all of the scheduling methods we have discussed so far, processes can be scheduled in even more ways:

- Detached (demon) process
- Parent/child
- Threads
- Fork process

Detached processes, sometimes called *demon processes* in the UNIX world, exist as independent entities and do not rely on the existence of any other process or any kind of interaction in the system.

Parent/child processes consist of two processes. In one type, the child depends on the existence of the parent process to endure. In this kind of relationship, once the parent process exits, the child process exits as well. The parent is usually able to determine certain kinds of status relative to the child; for instance, if the child was created successfully or aborted prematurely. This definition is recursive, since the child process can foster one or more other processes and thereby become a parent itself. The hierarchy can exist until system resources are depleted!

Threads are a relatively new concept in program design. The easiest way to understand threads is to imagine the programs you have known and loved, which consist of different subroutines and function calls. Now imagine calling those subroutines and function calls and having them execute as if they were individual tasks running asynchronously with each other. The threads are all running under the context of the *master process* and are sharing the same memory space. Threads are more efficient than full-fledged multitasking; because the context switch involves less work, and they can be used to make a process much more flexible and multifaceted. For example, you might have a process consisting of three threads—one thread is waiting for network I/O, another thread is soliciting input from a user terminal, and a third thread is performing some kind of mathematical analysis. These threads are all part of the same process.

The *fork process* is unique to the world of UNIX. The fork function has been traditionally used to schedule another process to run in conjunction with using another UNIX function exec. The fork routine is interesting, because it causes a complete reincarnation of the calling process to be created; however, execution in the reincarnation *starts at the very same fork call.* How does the fork call know when it is in the copy or the original? In the copy, the system returns a zero, while in the original, a non-zero value is returned.

7.4 MEMORY MANAGEMENT PRINCIPLES

Memory is another resource that an operating system must manage. However, depending on the requirements of the system environment, memory management may involve excess overhead that cannot be tolerated. This condition is possible for certain dedicated real-time processor-based systems that must operate in as streamlined a fashion as possible. Therefore, *no memory management* is a viable, although ironic, choice for a basic memory management technique.

Perhaps the most profound effect of memory management is how it disassociates our logical address perspective from the actual physical memory addressed when we run our programs. Since our program address resolution is all relative zero and, therefore, relocatable, the memory management hardware need only provide us with a means of specifying at what physical address offset we are loaded in memory. As Figure 7.6 illustrates, a *base register* contains the physical address offset value that is added to all of our address references. The effect of the base register is transparent .

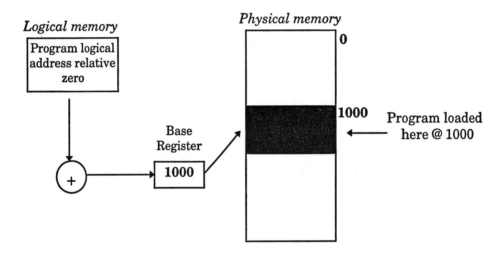

Figure 7.6
Demonstration of disassociation of logical and physical address space.

The most elementary memory managed environment is depicted in Figure 7.7a. Memory is divided into two sections, one for the operating system and another for a user. The most rudimentary environment would pay no regard to the execution behavior of the user program leading to the potential compromise of the operating system.

To protect the operating system, a hardware feature is introduced, the *fence register*. Figure 7.7b illustrates the orientation of the fence register. The fence register is loaded during boot time with the last address occupied by the operating system. Every memory access performed by a user program is compared to the value contained in the fence register. If a user address reference is less than or equal to the contents of the fence register, an address violation trap occurs and the user program is terminated. It is possible to only trap writes since reads are nondestructive.

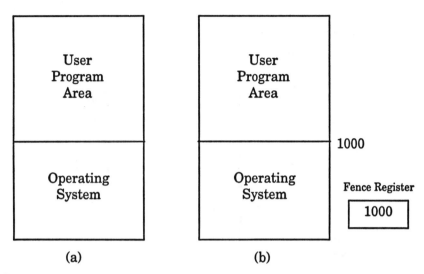

Figure 7.7
(a) Rudimentary memory managed environment; (b) fence registers.

The subsequent evolution of a memory management environment is to support a multiuser/multitasking environment. Memory is now divided into several sections. Besides the operating system, there may be several sections of memory, or *partitions,* to accommodate various processes. Enforcing protection is more important than ever in this kind of environment, and two fence registers are required. These fence registers are loaded as part of the process context and define the lowest and highest addresses of the specific active partition. Figure 7.8 depicts a basic multitasking memory management environment with fence registers. A more formal discussion of multitasking memory management schemes follows in the next section.

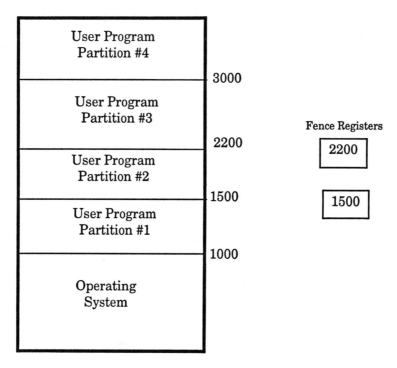

Figure 7.8
Basic multitasking memory management.

Two kinds of memory management are discussed in this chapter: *contiguous style* and *non-contiguous style*. Contiguous style memory management functions under the following conditions:

- The entire process must be in memory.
- The process occupies adjacent memory locations all in one large chunk.

Non-contiguous memory management is also referred to as *paging* and operates according to the following conditions:

- The entire process *does not* have to be in memory.
- The process *does not* have to occupy adjacent memory locations.

7.4.1 CONTIGUOUS MEMORY MANAGEMENT METHODS

Two contiguous memory methods are discussed in this section:

- Multiuser with a fixed number of tasks, MFT.
- Multiuser with a variable number of tasks, MVT.

MFT divides memory into a series of partitions. These partitions are a fixed size, but each partition can be a different size. The size and amount of the partitions are usually determined by the job requirements of the system. MFT can be implemented in several ways. One way is to have a job queue for each partition. Once a job gets queued to a particular partition, it must run in that partition, but this situation is not always efficient. There may be an unoccupied partition available at the same time that a job is needlessly waiting to run in the partition for which it was assigned. One way around this is to have a single queue, a central dispatching mechanism that receives jobs as they enter the system and queues them to whatever partition is available and can accommodate the job. Figure 7.9 illustrates the MFT environment.

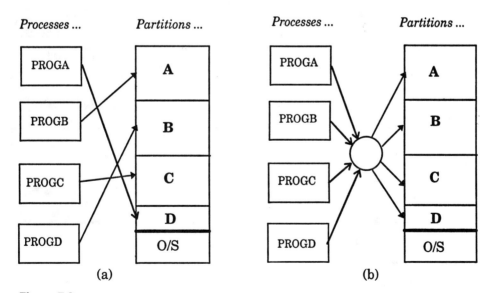

Figure 7.9
(a) MFT memory management with queue per partition; (b) MFT memory management with centralized queue.

MVT memory management is like creating partitions on the fly. MVT attempts to be more efficient than MFT, but memory utilization in MFT is generally not very good since most jobs do not fit integrally into the partitions, and there is a lot of waste. This waste is called *internal fragmentation,* and MVT attempts to lessen its impact. MVT creates partitions as they are required by the system. These partitions are sized to fit the job requirements as closely as possible while minimizing internal fragmentation. This is certainly an improvement over MFT; however, our solution is not without some other costs. Imagine a series of programs in memory and having several to terminate. Memory management is also shown in Figure 7.10.

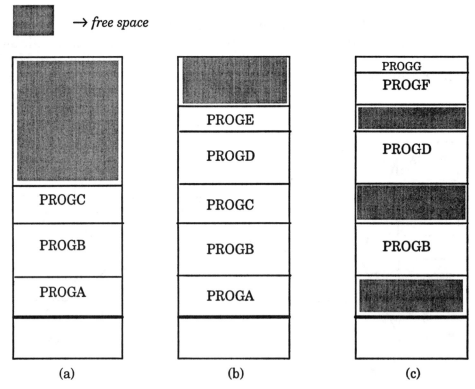

Figure 7.10
MVT memory management.

What is left is a *hole* in memory and is generally not a concern until there are many of them. After the system gets populated with more processes, it is not as straightforward to go out and allocate another partition. MVT performs a hole search to find a hole to best accommodate the process that wants to run. There is an extensive repertoire of *hole fitting* algorithms that are used to make the hole fit as efficiently as possible. Some of the more popularly used ones are:

First Fit   Find the first hole that is big enough to accommodate the process. Drawback is the amount of space left over in the hole if it is too small to be useful and internal fragmentation occurs.

Best Fit   Find the hole that most closely fits the size requirements of the process. Drawback is the overhead involved in investigating every memory hole. Also, internal fragmentation will still occur since the odds of finding an exact memory hole match are slim at best.

Worst Fit   Find the biggest hole for the process. This method appears to be illogical; however, it does have merit since the amount of space left over in the hole can usually be used more readily available than in the First Fit algorithm.

What happens when the system can no longer find any holes to accommodate the process? MVT will perform *hole coalescing*. Processes are moved around in memory to create as much contiguous free space as is currently required. The process movement is usually straightforward, since most modern-day code is relocatable (addressing relative zero), and the memory management hardware takes care of physical addressing details. Care must be taken not to move processes involved in certain kinds of I/O operations, such as DMA, where the hardware has been given a physical memory address as to where to place the data. If a process involved in this kind of operation moved, and the DMA I/O took place, the data would be lost and another innocent process might get overwritten! If even hole coalescing does not work, MVT resorts to swapping selected processes out of memory to secondary storage in order to give another process a turn at using memory. Once swapping begins, a major performance degredation occurs because we are involving a slow, mechanical device—the disk—as part of the context switch.

7.4.2 NON-CONTIGUOUS MEMORY MANAGEMENT

Non-contiguous memory management is commonly called *paging*. The name paging is derived from the manner in which processes are allocated in memory. Processes are divided into equal sized segments called *pages*. The size of a page varies from system to system, but it is usually some integral value of a disk block, such as 512 or 8192 bytes. As we will learn, secondary storage plays a crucial role in making paging work. Physical memory is also divided into the same sized pages, only here, the pages are referred to as *frames*. The system reads a process into memory a page at a time, not necessarily placing these pages in memory contiguously. How then does the system execute such a process with a piece placed here and another piece placed there? We need another data structure and a mechanism that will translate our logical view of the process to where the parts of the process are actually situated in memory. The data structure is the *page table*. A page table consists of a series of *page table entries,* or *PTEs*, which describe where the logical pages of a program are actually located in physical memory. A PTE exists for each process logical page. Any reference to a certain logical page will involve its PTE entry in the page table. Figure 7.11 begins to illustrate how this translation takes place.

Logical   Physical
Address   Page   Address
Space   Table   Space

	A
1	B
2	C
3	D
4	E
5	F
6	G
7	H
8	I
9	J

0	2
1	5
2	0
3	!
4	3
5	6
6	!
7	!
8	!
9	9

0	C
1	?
2	A
3	E
4	?
5	B
6	F
7	?
8	?
9	J

Figure 7.11
The role of the page table.

The logical and physical pages are numbered relative zero. Use the page number as an index into the page table. Therefore, any references to logical page 2 will result in consulting PTE two. The PTE contains the physical frame address of the page in actual memory.

7.4.3 DEMAND PAGING

At this point, we are still requiring that all of our program be in memory before execution can begin. However, we are going to describe *demand paging* where not all of our program need be in memory before execution begins. In this environment, we need to specify more information in the PTE, specifically, if the page is in memory or out! We will steal another bit from the PTE to specify that a page is *valid* (in memory) or *invalid* (out of memory).

In a demand paging system, as execution of a program begins, references will generally be made to program pages that are in memory. However, eventually, execution will occur in a page that is not in memory, whose PTE has the invalid bit set. Upon encountering this situation, the operating system performs a *page fault*. A page fault is a kind of interrupt condition. Remember how the current program counter and system state

were preserved when we discussed interrupts earlier in this
chapter? The same applies here, and control is transferred to a
page fault interrupt service routine. Another example of the
hardware assisting a software function is when the page fault
interrupt handler must retrieve the desired page from secondary
storage, find space for it in memory, update the page tables, and
resume execution of the instruction during which the page fault
happened. Figure 7.12 illustrates the sequence of events that
occur during a page fault. Imagine this occurring for every program instruction! Some poorly designed applications do. Excessive page faulting consumes CPU time and can degrade the
performance of a program. The term used to describe excessive
page faulting is *thrashing*, which can become so bad that the operating system is doing nothing but handling page faults.
Thrashing will be discussed in more detail later in this section.

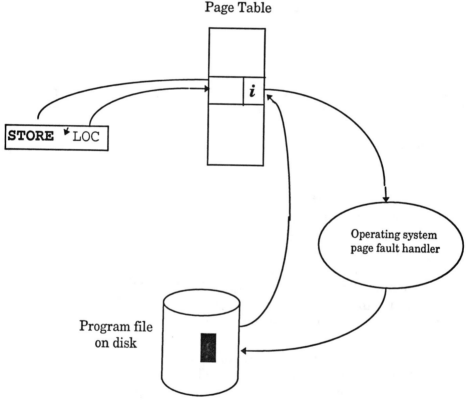

Figure 7.12
Sequence of operations involved in a page fault.

7.4.4 PAGE REPLACEMENT ALGORITHMS

In a demand paging environment, programs grow as their memory requirements increase to accommodate their execution needs. As all the other programs in the system grow, it is apparent that memory is a limited resource. Programs will be able to grow only so large and then a decision has to be made. The decision is to pick whatever page or pages that are currently in memory and are no longer required. This is a crucial decision and the quality of execution performance depends on it. The pages in memory will be replaced with new pages required by the program. How do we know what pages to remove? We do not want to discard a page that is required by the very next instruction execution and would immediately incur a page fault. We need a *page replacement algorithm*. The best page replacement policy is the *optimal* page replacement algorithm. Optimal relies on predicting the future! If you understand the execution behavior of a program before it begins to run, you know what pages to discard and when to discard them.

Unfortunately, we cannot predict the future, but we can build algorithms that approximate a good attempt. The algorithms are heuristic and function based on observing past behavior. This past behavior is related to how often a certain page has been used. If a page has not been used recently, we consider it game for elimination. We will be discussing the following four page replacement algorithms.

- FIFO   First-In First Out
- NUR   Not Used Recently
- LFU   Least Frequently Used
- LRU   Least Recently Used   } Approximate optimal

Two of these algorithms attempt to keep track of page utilization and approximate the optimal replacement policy. The premise for describing how all of these page replacement algorithms work requires a finite set of physical page frames.

The FIFO algorithm merely cycles pages through the page frames in a first-in first-out manner. FIFO does not discriminate page utilization. Figure 7.13 illustrates how the FIFO page replacement algorithm works. Since FIFO pays no regard to page utilization, it is very likely that a busy page will get replaced and an extra page fault is incurred. The FIFO algorithm demonstrates an interesting anamoly. Intuition tells us that providing more physical page frames will decrease the amount of page faulting. Consider Belady's Anomaly in Figure 7.13. In 7.13a, three page frames are used incurring nine faults to process the page reference string. In 7.13b, ten faults occur for the same reference string using four page frames!

Page reference string	FIFO replacement with 3 frames				FIFO replacement with 4 frames				
1	1	-	-	**F**	1	-	-	-	**F**
2	2	1	-	**F**	2	1	-	-	**F**
3	3	2	1	**F**	3	2	1	-	**F**
4	4	3	2	**F**	4	3	2	1	**F**
1	1	4	3	**F**	4	3	2	1	
2	2	1	4	**F**	4	3	2	1	
5	5	2	1	**F**	5	4	3	2	**F**
1	5	2	1		1	5	4	3	**F**
2	5	2	1		2	1	5	4	**F**
3	3	5	2	**F**	3	2	1	5	**F**
4	4	3	5	**F**	4	3	2	1	**F**
5	4	3	5		5	4	3	2	**F**

Figure 7.13
Demonstration of Belady's Anomaly; **F** = fault.

The FIFO algorithm can be enhanced by adding a *reference bit* to the page. If the reference bit is set, it means the page was recently referenced and should not be replaced. The algorithm will look for a page without the reference bit set. If no such pages can be found, the pages are cycled in the former first-in first-out fashion. The reference bits are reset periodically by the system.

The *Not Used Recently* (NUR) page replacement algorithm utilizes an additional bit. Besides a reference bit, NUR also uses a *modified bit*. One aspect of page replacement that has not been mentioned yet is that pages containing modified data must be preserved in a special place. Pages with modified data are also called *dirty* pages. The data contained in these pages must be preserved. Dirty pages are typically kept in a *paging file*. NUR is based on a hierarchy of page types. These page types indicate the kind of pages NUR will attempt to replace first. NUR attempts to initially replace pages that require the least amount of maintenance. Table 7.1 lists the page types from the most preferred to the least preferred for replacement:

Table 7.1 The Not Used Recently page replacement algorithm page classifications

Type	Reference Bit	Modified Bit	Meaning
I	0	0	Not referenced, not modified
II	1	0	Referenced recently, not modified
III	0	1	Not referenced, dirty*
IV	1	1	Referenced recently and dirty

*This page category seems impossible but is explained below.

NUR is going to attempt to deal with Category I type pages first. If none of those are found, it will go on to Category II types, and so on. Category III type pages seem impossible but what is happening here is that the system periodically resets all the referenced bits. A recently modified page would not exhibit this characteristic.

The last two-page replacement algorithms that will be mentioned are *Least Recently Used* (LRU) and *Least Frequently Used* (LFU). LRU is time-based while LFU is frequency-based. These algorithms require that extra information be maintained in the page tables. For LRU, a time stamp of the last reference is kept. When it is time to perform a page replacement, the system will look for pages with the oldest time stamps as candidates for replacement. The assumption is that the page has not been referenced for so long that it is most likely not needed. This is no guarantee! LRU relies on a counter maintained for each page. Every time a page is referenced, the counter is incremented. The pages with the lowest counts are candidates for replacement. Notice that a program performing extensive initialization might have artificially high counts for pages it no longer requires. However, at page replacement time, the system will not choose those pages since it appears they have high utilization. To avoid this dilemma, some implementations increment the high-order bit of the counter.

7.4.5 THE WORKING SET

The concept of the working set is one model to follow for approximating optimal page replacement. Well-behaved programs will intensely page fault to get started and then stabilize. Figure 7.14 illustrates this characteristic.

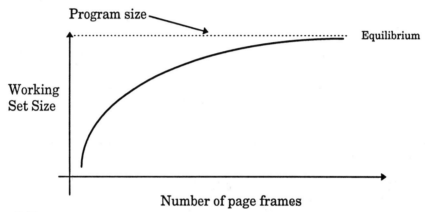

Figure 7.14
Demonstration of the effect of a working set.

A well-behaved program will attain an equilibrium in that it has all of the available pages it needs to execute it in memory. This set of pages is called the *working set*. The idea of the working set is based on taking periodic snapshots of what pages have been recently referenced by a program. Perhaps at time interval t_1 the working set consists of pages {3, 4, 7,10} and at interval t_2 the working set is observed as {4, 10, 16, 20}. At the second interval, pages 3 and 4 were not referenced and would be considered candidates for page replacement. The interval of the snapshot is arbitrary, but it should not be too short nor too long. Also, there is an implied use of reference bits. The algorithm can be made more accurate by maintaining more than one reference bit, such as for each interval. Then the system could tell during which interval or for how many intervals a particular page was referenced and consequently judge that page for replacement.

7.5 THE I/O SYSTEM

The I/O subsystem encompasses the following:

Peripheral devices (hardware)
>   Disks, tapes terminals, et cetera.
>   Communications devices.
>   Special devices, such as instrumentation or robots.

The file system (software)
>   Gives us a high-level logical view of our system storage
>   environment so that we can manage data easier.

I / O drivers and handlers (software)
>   This code, part of the operating system, is intimate with
>   the hardware characteristics of the interfaced devices.

Most of the devices connected to the computer system generate interrupts when they have completed transferring data. For example, the disk controller will generate an interrupt upon completion of a write operation. A terminal device generates an interrupt every time a key on the keyboard is pressed. The interrupt service routines for these devices are written as part of an I/O handler or I/O driver. There is an I/O driver for every hardware device connected to the system. These drivers are considered part of the operating system because they have to perform housekeeping relative to other operating system functions. I/O drivers are the lowest level of software to which system users can communicate to the hardware. Most programmers rarely communicate directly to a terminal driver unless there is some special I/O function that cannot be performed any other way. I/O drivers are a very complicated topic and beyond the scope of this book.

Users are more accustomed to performing I/O requests at a higher level through the file system. File systems allow us to have a logical view of data and not be concerned about physical details of data access. How does the file system convert our logical I/O request to a physical I/O request? First we must understand how physical I/O takes place to a very common file system device, the disk. Data transfer to and from a disk is in terms of blocks. A block is usually 512 bytes or a multiple thereof. If you write 1 byte of data to a disk, an entire block is still written. If you read 5 bytes from a disk, an entire block is still input. Now consider a program that analyzes data represented in 80 byte records. A loop in the program contains an I/O request that sequentially inputs each 80-byte record from a file on disk. What is actually occurring in the program is the file system is performing a read of a single disk block-worth of the file for the very first pass through the loop. The block contains six plus a small portion of a seventh 80-byte record. The file system then passes the first 80-byte segment of the block back to the program. As the program continues executing into the loop a second time, no physical I/O is performed since the second 80-byte segment is already in memory. This condition exists through a sixth iteration of the loop. On the seventh iteration, the file system realizes that the remaining data is an incomplete segment and that a physical I/O is now required. Figure 7.15 illustrates how the file system translates from physical I/O to logical I/O.

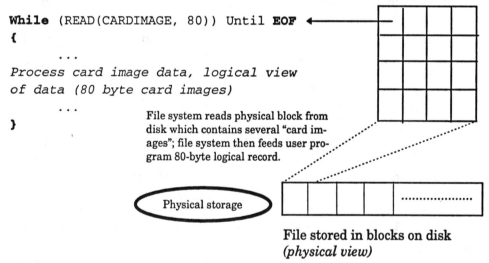

```
While (READ(CARDIMAGE, 80)) Until EOF
{
        . . .
Process card image data, logical view
of data (80 byte card images)
        . . .
}
```

File system reads physical block from disk which contains several "card images"; file system then feeds user program 80-byte logical record.

Physical storage

File stored in blocks on disk
(physical view)

Figure 7.15
File system logical view versus a physical view of data.

File systems use directories as an important data structure for keeping track of files. Directories are special files that are maintained exclusively by the file system. A directory contains all the information there is to know about a file, including:

- File name
- File type
- Date file was created
- Date file was last accessed
- Date file was last changed
- Size
- Protection
- Location of file on disk

The directory is consulted for every kind of file operation; therefore, directory organization can be crucial to system performance. Also, directory organization can determine what kind of security environment can be accomplished. For performance, directories can be organized as follows:

Linear   Directory is searched sequentially; can be time-consuming if many files.

Sorted   Directory is sorted alphabetically to make searching more efficient; has no overhead of sorting. Question: When and how often to sort?

Hashed   Use mathematical function f(filename) = index; function must be robust enough so as not to produce duplicate indices.

For security reasons, directories can be organized as follows:

Single Level   Simple to implement; all file names must be unique; no protection, all files on disk are available.

Two Level   Have a directory of directories, called a Master File Directory; one directory area for each user; each directory is protected from the other.

Tree   File system represented hierarchically with several levels; file specification based on following path from the *root* directory through the different levels until the file is reached; UNIX file system environment.

File systems manage disk space by using a *bit vector map*. Each bit of this map stands for one or more blocks on a disk. Because modern disks are so large, a *cluster factor* is determined and that is what a bit in the vector map represents. Bit vector maps take up little storage space and are easy to manipulate. When a disk block is allocated to a file, the corresponding bit in the vector map is set to one. Block 40 would be bit 40 in the map. To indicate that a file has been deleted, all that is required is to reset the appropriate bits in the vector map that represents the blocks of the file. Note that this is a security loophole. Since only the vector bits are being reset, the original file contents still exist on the disk until they are reallocated to another file.

File system security is accomplished by identifying which entities can have access to the file and specifying what operations these entities are allowed to perform. A typical entity list is:

- The operating system
- A specific user
- The owner of the file
- A group of users
- The world

Operations could be any of the following:

- Reading the file (R)
- Writing to the file (W)
- Deleting the file (D)
- Executing the file (E)
- Changing file protection (C)

The security attributes specified for a file might include the following specification:

The operating system	RWDEC
A specific user	RE
File owner	RWEC
Specific group	RE
World	*None*

The world would be denied access completely in this case. This information would be maintained in the file directory as security attribute information.

7.6 WRAP-UP AND FURTHER READING

This chapter discussed basic operating systems' principles. The operating system was described as a resource manager, and this chapter discussed several of those resources, including the CPU, memory, and the file system. We began with the concept of the interrupt as the foundation for how CPU scheduling is performed. Using a clock device to produce interrupts allows the operating system to time-slice between all the tasks it has to perform. A review of various scheduling algorithms was performed next, demonstrating the difference between preemptive and non-preemptive techniques. The heuristic Multilevel Feedback Queue (MLFQ) was discussed as the culmination of scheduling technology. The design implementation variability of MLFQ makes it suitable for most scheduling purposes. Our next resource was memory and several memory management techniques were discussed. Both contiguous and non-contiguous methods were reviewed. The memory management discussion led to demand paging that is the most prevalent technique in use today. Our last resource was the file system. Here we discussed the concept of physical versus logical I/O and investigated the role of the file directory and how file information could be protected.

A few books are listed here for additional reading. A good overall review of operating systems can be found in [Silberschatz 1994] and [Deitel 1990]. For a comprehensive discussion about distributed environments [Tanenbaum 1992] and [Tanenbaum 1995] are highly recommended. Another book that introduced the world to the Minix operating system is still a good source of operating system principles [Tanenbaum 1987]. Finally, a good basic text that has some very interesting examples not found in many other books is [Flynn 1991].

REFERENCES

[Silberschatz 1994] Silberschatz, Abraham, Peter B. Gavin, *Operating System Concepts Fourth Edition,* Reading, MA: Addison Wesley, 1994.

[Tanenbaum 1992] Tanenbaum, Andrew S., *Modern Operating System*, Englewood Cliffs, NJ: Prentice Hall, Inc., 1992.

[Tanenbaum 1987] Tanenbaum, Andrew S., *Operating Systems Design and Implementation*, Englewood Cliffs, NJ: Prentice Hall Software Series, 1987.

[Tanenbaum 1995] Tanenbaum, Andrew S., *Distributed Operating Systems*, Englewood Cliffs, NJ: Prentice Hall, 1995.

[Flynn 1991] Flynn, Ida M., Ann McIver McHoes, *Understanding Operating Systems,* Pacific Grove, CA: Brooks/Cole Publishing Co., 1991.

[Deitel 1990] Deitel, H. M., *Operating Systems Second Edition*, Reading MA: Addison Wesley Publishing Co., 1990.

CHAPTER 8

UNIX and Win32 API Concurrency Facilities

This chapter will discuss what programming facilities are available under Sun Solaris, Digital UNIX, and the Win32 API environment to perform concurrency operations.

8.0 INTRODUCTION TO THREADS

A prerequisite to learning the concurrency examples in this chapter is an understanding of *threads*. Threads are a relatively new concept in program design and only recently implemented because of advances in computer systems technology. A simple program is composed of a single thread of execution while a complex program is composed of many threads of execution. Most contemporary operating systems contain service calls that allow a programmer to easily create threads. Digital UNIX and the Win32 API (available in Windows NT and Windows 95) environment are two of these operating system environments. One easy way to conceive how threads work is to think of them as subroutine calls. However, once the subroutine is called, it begins execution *concurrently* with the rest of the program. Furthermore, all threads share the same memory address space. These "subroutines" can be called producing a great deal of concurrent activity. Threads allow for more robust program behavior. For example, a program can contain three threads where one thread is receiving data from a modem, another thread is waiting for a user to enter information on a CRT screen, and the third thread is sorting data in a disk file. All these operations can be ongoing simultaneously. Threads are a form of multitasking within the context of a single process. The context switch for threads occurs much more expediently than between processes, since threads share the same process address space.

8.1 COMMON CONCURRENCY FACILITIES IN UNIX

Most versions of UNIX provide the following concurrency functions:

- `fork` call

- `exec` call

- Semaphores

The `fork` and `exec` functions allow one process to schedule another process. Semaphores are used to enforce mutual exclusion and require the use of several calls:

- `semget`   Create semaphores

- `semop`   Perform sophisticated operations on semaphore sets

- `semctl`   Change or query permissions, owner, or value of a semaphore or semaphore set

Fork calls are unusual. At the point in a program where `fork` is called, a complete reincarnation of the calling process is produced. Two copies of the process now exist; however, in the newly created process, execution begins at the point of the `fork` call. The return value from the `fork` call indicates whether you are in the original program or a reincarnate—a zero return value says you are in the reincarnate. Traditionally, in UNIX, the very next call after a `fork`, if you are in the reincarnate, is a call to function exec. Exec actually causes a different program to run. In fact, upon calling exec, the target program is loaded into memory over the calling program, in our case, the `fork`ed reincarnate. A typical `fork`/`exec` call sequence is as follows:

```
if (fork() == 0)
        execlp("newprog", "newprog", (char *) 0);
```

In the reincarnate, the return value would be zero and the exec call would be performed causing the program `newprog` to be loaded on top of the reincarnate. In the original process, the return value from the fork call would be non-zero and the exec would not be performed.

UNIX semaphores are designed to provide a great deal of functionality and are not straightforward enough to understand. We will simplify their use by demonstrating how to produce simple WAIT and SIGNAL semaphore functions. UNIX semaphores must first be created by calling semget, which has the following calling sequence:

```
semid = semget (
            key_t key,    /* Key, usually set to IPC_PRIVATE */
            int nsems,    /* Number of semaphores to create */
            int flags );  /* Option flags */
```

The argument key is assigned a value that uniquely identifies the semaphore set and can be a unique numeric value other than zero. If the semaphore is not going to be shared globally, the value IPC_PRIVATE is passed. You have the option of creating more than one semaphore by specifying the number in argument nsems. Be aware that all semop functions are performed atomically on the semaphore set. The semaphore set is identified in all subsequent semaphore calls by specifying the value semid that is returned from this call. Argument flags is used to indicate protection characteristics and various other creation options.

Function semop is used to perform operations on the entire semaphore set and has the following calling sequence:

```
semop (
        int semid,            /* Id of semaphore set */
        struct sembuf (*ops), /* Semaphore operations array */
        int nops );           /* Number of operations to perform */
```

Argument semid is derived from calling function semget. The operations array defines an array of 3-element structures that contain the following information:

```
struct sembuf sops;

sops.sem_num  /* Semaphore # to perform operation */
sops.sem_op   /* Specifies a value to be added or subtracted */
sops.sem_flg  /* Operation options */
```

Function `semop` is used to acquire or release a semaphore. If `sops.sem_op` is equal to −1 (wait), the calling process blocks until the semaphore specified in argument `sops.sem_num` can be decremented by 1. If sops.sem_op is equal to 1 (signal), the semaphore is incremented by one. We will ignore the operation options and set it to zero.

Function `semctl` performs many functions including querying or changing the permissions, owner, or value associated with a semaphore or semaphore set. `Semctl` is also used in a housekeeping role to remove a semaphore set from the system. UNIX semaphores are part of the IPC family of routines and a semaphore set will remain until explicitly removed. The following call to `semctl` will remove the semaphore set specified by `semid`:

```
semctl (
     semid,       /* Semaphore set identifier */
     0,           /* Semaphore number not applicable */
     IPC_RMID,    /* Command: remove semaphore set */
     Null);       /* No semaphore variable value */
```

We will now demonstrate the use of these semaphore routines by implementing basic WAIT/SIGNAL functions, which exhibit the basic Djikstra semaphore functionality. As a reminder, the mathematical representation of functions WAIT and SIGNAL on a semaphore variable S is:

WAIT(S):
> If S ≤ 0 then *wait here;*
>   else
>   S ⇐ S - 1;
>   *Enter critical section;*

SIGNAL(S):
$$S \Leftarrow S + 1;$$

The following code fragment demonstrates the implementation of WAIT and SIGNAL.

```
#include <sys/sem.h>
#include <sys/ipc.h>
#include <sys/types.h>

int key = 98989;
int sem_id;

struct sembuf sem_ops;

{
  if (sem_id = semget(IPC_PRIVATE,1,0666|IPC_CREATE)) == -1)
        { perror("error with semget");
                exit(-1); }

  sem_ops.sem_num = 0;
  sem_ops.sem_flg = 0;

}


    ..............

wait(sem_id)
{
  sem_ops.sem_op = -1;

  if (semop(sem_id, &sem_ops, 1) == -1)
        { perror("error with semop");
                exit(-2);}
}
```

```
signal(sem_id)
{
  sem_ops.sem_op = 1;

  if (semop(sem_id, &sem_ops, 1) == -1)
        { perror("error with semop");
               exit(-3);}
}
```

These modules would be combined with some other more complete code.

8.2 DIGITAL UNIX

Digital UNIX provides support for DCE threads (DECthreads library) and all the affiliated synchronization facilities. The pthread interface is based on Draft 4 of the Proposed IEEE standard for multithreaded programming, POSIX 1003.4a. The routines are categorized as follows:

- Threads

- Mutexes

- Condition variables

Example 8.1 demonstrates the use of the thread and synchronization routines. In this example, several worker threads are created to compute a series of prime numbers.

8.2.1 THREAD OPERATIONS

The following routines are used to manage threads:

Starting a thread:

```
pthread_create (
        thread_id,      /* Id of created thread */
        thread_attrs,   /* Set to pthread_attr_default */
        entry_point,    /* Thread routine */
        thread_arg );   /* Optional argument to pass */
```

Terminating a thread:

```
pthread_exit (
        *status);     /* Exit status of thread */
```

Waiting for a thread to terminate:

```
pthread_join (
        thread_id,    /* Id of thread to wait for */
        *status );    /* Status of terminating thread */
```

Deleting a thread:

```
pthread_detach (
        thread_id ); /* Id of thread marked for deletion */
```

A comprehensive discussion of all thread routines is beyond the scope of this book.

8.2.2 SYNCHRONIZATION OPERATIONS

Digital UNIX provides two synchronization objects—*mutexes* and *condition variables*. Mutexes can be locked or unlocked. When a mutex is locked, it is *owned* by a thread. When a thread requires access to shared data, a request is made to lock a specific mutex. This mutex is mutually agreed upon by all participating threads. If the mutex is already locked, the requesting thread must wait. The following mutex routines are available:

Creating a mutex:

```
pthread_mutex_init (
        *mutex,       /* Id of created mutex */
        mutex_attr ); /* Set to pthread_mutexattr_default */
```

Locking a mutex:

```
pthread_mutex_lock (
        *mutex );     /* Id of mutex to lock */
```

Try locking a mutex:

```
pthead_mutex_trylock (
        *mutex );      /* Id of mutex to try to lock */
```

This routine will attempt to lock the specified mutex. If the mutex is already locked, the calling thread does not wait for the mutex to become unlocked.

Unlocking a mutex:

```
pthread_mutex_unlock (
        *mutex );      /* Id of mutex to unlock */
```

If more than one thread is waiting for the mutex, only one will be allowed to obtain ownership.

Deleting a mutex:

```
pthread_mutex_destroy (
        *mutex );      /* Id of mutex to eliminate */
```

A condition variable is a synchronization construct used with a mutex. The mutex is used to guarantee access to shared data. Once a mutex lock is obtained, the process evaluates the shared data. If the data is not in a usable state, the process waits on a condition variable. During the condition variable wait, the mutex is released to allow other threads to gain access to the shared data and put it in a usable state. Whatever thread puts the data in a usable state will signal the condition variable. Only one waiting thread will react to the signal. The mutex is also relocked causing other threads waiting on the wait. The data validity should be determined even after returning from a conditional variable wait. It is possible that the data could become invalid during the wait completion time. Figure 8.1 illustrates the proper logic for using condition variables. The condition variable routines available are as follows:

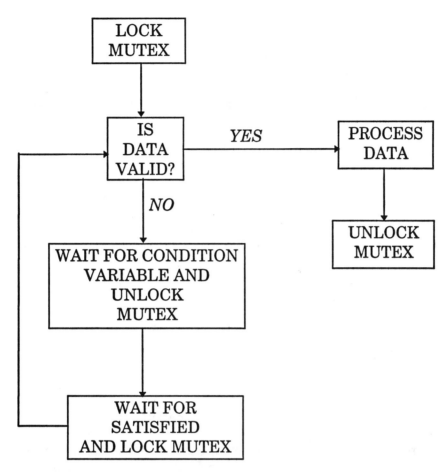

Figure 8.1
Condition variable logic.

Signal all threads waiting on this condition variable:

```
pthread_cond_broadcast (
      pthread_cond_t *condv);
```

Eliminate this condition variable from the system:

```
pthread_cond_destroy (
      pthread_cond_t *condv);
```

Signal the condition variable:

```
pthread_cond_signal (
        pthread_cond_t *condv);
```

Time based condition variable wait. Time specifies when wait expires:

```
pthread_cond_timedwait (
        pthread_cond_t *condv,
        pthread_mutex_t *mutex,
        struct timespec *timeabs);
```

Wait for condition variable to be signaled:

```
pthread_cond_wait (
        pthread_cond_t *condv,
        pthread_mutex_t *mutex);
```

Create a condition variable:

```
pthread_cond_init (
        pthread_cond_t *condv,
        pthread_condattr_t pthread_condattr_default);
```

Example 8.1 is a sample program that demonstrates the use of threads, mutexes, and condition variables. Several other routines are also used in this example, which are explained in more detail in the comments. The `main()` routine creates several threads, all of which execute a single worker routine. The worker routine checks to see if a number is prime. When it finds a prime number, it stores it away in an array. The threads use mutexes to synchronize access to shared variables. In this way, no two threads are checking the same number, and no two threads will try to store their prime in the array at the same time. When all the threads have completed or been canceled, the program prints out the list of primes that were found. Next to each prime listed is the number of the thread that found that particular prime number. Example 8.2 is a Win32 rendition of this program.

Example 8.1 Demonstrating the use of Digital UNIX concurrency functions.

```
/* Decthreads example program conducting a prime number search */
#include <pthread.h>
#include <stdio.h>
#include <stdlib.h>

#define WORKERS 5        /* threads to perform prime check */
#define REQUEST 500      /* Number of primes to find */
#define check(status, string) if (status == -1) perror(string)

/*
 * This structure is used to store the prime numbers found, and which
 * thread they were found by.
 */
typedef struct {
  int prime_number;
  int thread;
} primeRec;

pthread_mutex_t prime_list,     /* Mutex for use in accessing the prime */
        current_mutex,          /* Mutex associated with the current number */
        cond_mutex;             /* Mutex used for ensuring CV integrity */
pthread_cond_t cond_var;        /* Condition variable (CV) for thread start */
int current_num = 1,            /* Next number to be checked, start odd */
        thread_hold = 1,        /* Number associated with condition state */
        count = 0;              /* Count of primes - index to primes */
primeRec primes[REQUEST];       /* Store prime numbers - synchronize access */
pthread_t threads[WORKERS];     /* Array of worker threads */

/* Worker thread routine. Worker threads start with this routine, which begins
   with a condition wait designed to synchronize the workers and the parent.
   Each worker thread then takes a turn taking a number for which it will
   determine whether or not it is prime.
*/
void prime_search(pthread_addr_t arg)
{
    div_t div_results;          /* DIV results: quot and rem */
    int numerator,              /* Used for determining primeness */
        denominator,            /* Used for determining primeness */
        cut_off,                /* Number being checked div 2 */
        notifiee,               /* Used during a cancelation */
        prime,                  /* Flag used to indicate primeness */
        my_number,              /* Worker thread identifier */
        status,                 /* Hold status from pthread calls */
        not_done = 1;           /* Work loop predicate */

    my_number = (int) arg;

    /* Synchronize threads and the parent using a condition variable, of
       which the predicate (thread_hold) will be set by the parent. */
    status = pthread_mutex_lock(&cond_mutex);
    check(status, "1:Mutex_lock bad status\n");

    while (thread_hold)
    {
        status = pthread_cond_wait(&cond_var, &cond_mutex);
        check(status, "3:Cond_wait bad status\n");
    }

    status = pthread_mutex_unlock(&cond_mutex);
    check(status, "4:Mutex_unlock bad status\n");

    /*
     * Check to see how many primes have been found at the time
     * this thread starts executing.
     */
    printf("Entering thread %d, primes found = %d\n",my_number,count);

    /*
     * Perform checks on ever larger integers until the requested number
     * of primes is found.
     */
    while(not_done)
```

```
    {
        /* cancelation point */
        pthread_testcancel();

        /*
         * Get next integer to be checked.  We need to take out
         * a lock around access to 'current_num', since all threads
         * will be modifying this variable
         */
        status = pthread_mutex_lock(&current_mutex);
        check(status, "6:Mutex_lock bad status\n");

        current_num = current_num + 2;          /* Skip even numbers */
        numerator = current_num;

        /* Release lock for 'current_num' */
        status = pthread_mutex_unlock(&current_mutex);
        check(status, "9:Mutex_unlock bad status\n");

        /* Only need to divide in half of number to verify not prime */
        cut_off = numerator/2 + 1;
        prime = 1;

        /* check for prime; exit if something evenly divides */
        for (denominator = 2; ((denominator < cut_off) && (prime));
                denominator++)
                        prime = numerator % denominator;

        if (prime !=0)      /* Found a prime number! */
        {
            /* Explicitly turn off all cancels */
            pthread_setcancel(CANCEL_OFF);

            /*
             * Lock a mutex and add this prime number to the list. Also,
             * if this fulfills the request, cancel all other threads
             */
            status = pthread_mutex_lock(&prime_list);
            check(status, "10:Mutex_lock bad status\n");

            /* Have we found all the primes we were asked to find? */
            if (count < REQUEST)
            {
                primes[count].prime_number = numerator;
                primes[count].thread = my_number;
                count++;
            }
            else if (count == REQUEST)
            {
                not_done = 0;
                count++;

                printf("Thread %d is canceling other threads\n",my_number);
                for (notifiee = 0; notifiee < WORKERS; notifiee++)
                    if (notifiee != my_number)
                    {
                        status = pthread_cancel(threads[notifiee]);
                        check(status, "12:Cancel bad status\n");
                    }

            }
            /* Release lock for 'primes' and 'count' */
            status = pthread_mutex_unlock(&prime_list);
            check(status, "13:Mutex_unlock bad status\n");

            /* Explicitly turn on all cancels */
            pthread_setcancel(CANCEL_ON);
        } /* end if */
        pthread_testcancel();  /* Check to see if this thread was canceled */
    } /* end while */
    pthread_exit(my_number);
}

main()
{
    int worker_num,                 /* Counter used when indexing workers */
```

```
        exit_value,              /* Individual worker's return status */
        list,                    /* Used to print list of primes found */
        status,                  /* Hold status from pthread calls */
        index1,                  /* Used in sorting prime numbers */
        index2,                  /* Used in sorting prime numbers */
        not_done;                /* Indicates swap mode in sort */
    primeRec temp;               /* Used in a swap; part of sort */

    /* Create mutexes */
    status = pthread_mutex_init(&prime_list, pthread_mutexattr_default);
    check(status, "15:Mutex_init bad status\n");
    status = pthread_mutex_init(&cond_mutex, pthread_mutexattr_default);
    check(status, "16:Mutex_init bad status\n");
    status = pthread_mutex_init(&current_mutex, pthread_mutexattr_default);
    check(status, "17:Mutex_init bad status\n");

    /* Create condition value */
    status = pthread_cond_init(&cond_var, pthread_condattr_default);
    check(status, "45:Cond_init bad status\n");

    /* Create worker threads */
    for (worker_num = 0; worker_num < WORKERS; worker_num++)
    {
        status = pthread_create(&threads[worker_num], pthread_attr_default,
                 prime_search, (pthread_addr_t) worker_num);
        check(status, "19:Pthread_create bad status\n");
    }

    /*
     * Set the predicate thread_hold to zero, and broadcast on the condition
     * variable that the worker threads may proceed.
     */
    status = pthread_mutex_lock(&cond_mutex);
    check(status, "20:Mutex_lock bad status\n");

    thread_hold = 0;
    status = pthread_cond_broadcast(&cond_var);

    status = pthread_mutex_unlock(&cond_mutex);
    check(status, "21:Mutex_unlock bad status\n");

    /*
     * Join each of the worker threads in order to obtain their summation
     * totals, and to ensure each has completed successfully.
     * Mark thread storage free to be reclaimed upon termination by detaching
     * it.
     */
    for (worker_num = 0; worker_num < WORKERS; worker_num++)
    {
        status = pthread_join(threads[worker_num], &exit_value);
        check(status, "23:Pthread_join bad status\n");

        if (exit_value == worker_num)
          printf("Thread %d terminated normally\n", worker_num);

        /*
         * Upon normal termination, the exit_value is equivalent to
         * worker_num.
         */
        status = pthread_detach(&threads[worker_num]);
        check(status, "25:Pthread_detach bad status\n");
    }

    /*
     * Take the list of prime numbers found by the worker threads and sort
     * them from lowest value to the highest. The worker threads work
     * concurrently; there is no guarantee that the prime numbers will be
     * found in order. Therefore, a sort is performed.
     */
    not_done = 1;
    for (index1 = 1; ((index1 < REQUEST) && (not_done)); index1++)
        for (index2 = 0; index2 < index1; index2++)
            if (primes[index1].prime_number < primes[index2].prime_number)
            {
                temp = primes[index2];
                primes[index2] = primes[index1];
```

```
                    primes[index1] = temp;
                    not_done = 0;
          }

    /* Print out the list of prime numbers that the worker threads found. */
    printf("The list of %d prime numbers follows:\n", REQUEST);
    printf("%8d(%d)", primes[0].prime_number, primes[0].thread);
    for (list = 1; list < REQUEST; list++)
        printf(",%c%8d(%d)", list % 5 != 0 ? ' ' : '\n',
            primes[list].prime_number, primes[list].thread);
    printf("\n");
}
```

8.3 SUN SOLARIS

Sun Microsystem's Solaris operating system also supports two kinds of thread environments, POSIX threads and Solaris threads. All of the POSIX calls discussed in the previous section are supported. The threads program depicted in Example 8.1 will successfully run under Solaris. The Solaris threads environment provides certain features not found in POSIX.

Threads can be resumed and suspended. By using the routines thr_continue() and thr_suspend(), the specified thread can be made to suspend execution or to resume execution. The calling sequence to these routines is as follows:

```
    thr_suspend(thread_t threadID);

    thr_continue(thread_t threadID);
```

Threads can use reader/writer mutex locking. Solaris provides an entire family of reader/writer mutexes. These mutexes allow shared access to data. When a thread requests and is granted a write lock on the data (rw_wrlock), all threads making lock requests are made to wait. However, many threads can request a read access lock (rw_rdlock) simultaneously. If a thread requests a write lock, it will wait until all other read and write locks are released. The reader/write mutex routines are as follows:

```
rwlock_init(rwlock_t *rwlockp, int rwtype, void * param);
rwlock_destroy(rwlock_t *rwlockp);
rwlock_wrlock(rwlock_t *rwlockp);
rwlock_rdlock(rwlock_t *rwlockp);
rwlock_trywrlock(rwlock_t *rwlockp);
rwlock_tryrdlock(rwlock_t *rwlockp);
```

The "try" versions of these routines allow the user to experience the ritual of determining if the lock request would be granted if a regular call would have been made. The "try" technique is also found in various other Solaris and POSIX thread calls.

Users can control the degree of concurrency. In the Solaris threads library, routine `thr_setconcurrency()` can be used to establish the degree of concurrency desired. This routine controls the number of *light-weight process (LWP)* resources available to your environment. Although a pool of LWPs is available to your process by default, a caller can explicitly request an LWP when a thread is created by using the `the_create()` routine.

Solaris threads are created with the `thr_create()` call. This routine has the following calling sequence:

```
thr_create (
        void *stackbase,               /* Default = NULL
        size_t stacksize,              /* Default = NULL
        void *(*startfcn)(void *),     /* Thread entry point
        void *param,                   /* NULL = no arguments
        long flags,                    /* Flags
        thread_t *threadID);           /* Will receive identifier
```

The calling argument of interest is `flags`. This argument can be set to `THR_NEW_LWP`, ensuring the availability of an LWP resource,

Users can create threads for which the master process does not wait. By specifying `THR_DAEMON` for the flags argument in `thr_create()`. Daemon threads do not affect the exit conditions of a process. A process will not wait for a daemon thread to exit. Furthermore, other synchronization routines such as `thr_join()` are ineffective against daemon threads.

Many of the Solaris thread calls have corresponding POSIX thread calls, just the names of the routines are different. Consult the Solaris threads man page for more information about what thread routines exist between POSIX and Solaris threads.

Example 8.2 is a version of the program from Example 8.1, implemented using Solaris threads. Notice the use of the THR_NEW_LWP setting for the flags argument in the thr_create() routine. This program was contributed by Patrick Burton, a student from the Hartford Graduate Center.

Example 8.2 Solaris threads version of the prime numbers program.

```
/* ****************************************************************** */
/*   Programmer: Patrick Burton                                       */
/*   Date:       06/16/96                                             */
/*   Course:     Unix and Win32 Application Programming Interface     */
/*   Course No.: 166696144                                            */
/*   Instructor: Don Merusi                                           */
/* ****************************************************************** */

/* ****************************************************************** */
/* Solaris-Threads implementation of a prime number searching program */
/* that uses conditions and mutexes for true concurrent worker thread */
/* synchronization.                                                    */
/* ****************************************************************** */
#include <signal.h>
#include <thread.h>
#include <stdio.h>
#include <stdlib.h>
#include <string.h>

#define WORKERS 5    /* Number of Threads to perform prime check */
#define REQUEST 500  /* Number of primes to find */

/* ****************************************************************** */
/* This structure is used to store the prime numbers found, and which */
/* thread found them.                                                 */
/* ****************************************************************** */

typedef struct _PrimeRec {
    int i_Prime;
    int i_Thread;
} sPrimeRec;

/* ****************************************************************** */
/* Synchronization, worker thread and other global declarations to be */
/* used by the threads during the prime number processing.            */
/* ****************************************************************** */
mutex_t   m_Primes,
          m_Current,
          m_Condition;

cond_t    cond_Variable;

int       i_CurrentNum = 1,
          i_ThreadHold = 1,
          i_Count = 0;

sPrimeRec s_Primes[REQUEST];

thread_t  t_Threads[WORKERS];

/* *********************************************************** */
/* Prototype for the Prime Number Search Thread routine */
/* *********************************************************** */
void *PrimeSearch(void *);

int main(int argc, char **argv)
{
    int       i_Done = 0, i, j;
    int       i_ThreadNum[WORKERS];
    void      *v_Status;
    sPrimeRec s_Prime;

    memset(t_Threads, '\0', WORKERS * sizeof(thread_t));
```

```
memset(&m_Primes, '\0', sizeof(mutex_t));
memset(&m_Current, '\0', sizeof(mutex_t));
memset(&m_Condition, '\0', sizeof(mutex_t));
memset(&cond_Variable, '\0', sizeof(cond_t));

/* ********************************* */
/*         Create mutexes           */
/* ********************************* */
mutex_init(&m_Primes, USYNC_THREAD, 0);
mutex_init(&m_Condition, USYNC_THREAD, 0);
mutex_init(&m_Current, USYNC_THREAD, 0);

/* ********************************* */
/*       Create Condition Value     */
/* ********************************* */
cond_init(&cond_Variable, USYNC_THREAD, 0);

/* ***************************************** */
/* Create Worker Threads as THR_NEW_LWP so  */
/* that the they can be run concurrently.   */
/* ***************************************** */

for (i = 0; i < WORKERS; i++) {
    i_ThreadNum[i] = i;
    thr_create(NULL, 0, PrimeSearch, (void *)&i_ThreadNum[i],
        THR_NEW_LWP, &t_Threads[i]);
}

/* ********************************************* */
/* Set the predicate i_ThreadHold to zero, and  */
/* broadcast on the condition variable that the  */
/* worker threads may proceed.                   */
/* ********************************************* */
mutex_lock(&m_Condition);

i_ThreadHold = 0;

cond_broadcast(&cond_Variable);

mutex_unlock(&m_Condition);

/* ********************************************* */
/* Join each of the worker threads in order to   */
/* ensure each has completed successfuly.        */
/* ********************************************* */

while (thr_join(0, NULL, &v_Status) == 0)
    ;

/* ********************************************* */
/*        Sort the prime numbers found.          */
/* ********************************************* */

for (i = 1; ((i < REQUEST) && (!i_Done)); i++) {
    for (j = 0; j < i; j++) {
        if (s_Primes[i].i_Prime < s_Primes[j].i_Prime) {
            memcpy((char *)&s_Prime, (char *)&s_Primes[j],
                sizeof(sPrimeRec));
            memcpy((char *)&s_Primes[j], (char *)&s_Primes[i],
                sizeof(sPrimeRec));
            memcpy((char *)&s_Primes[i], (char *)&s_Prime,
                sizeof(sPrimeRec));

            i_Done = 1;
        }
}
```

```
        }
    }

    /* ********************************************** */
    /* Print out the list of prime numbers that the */
    /* worker threads found.                        */
    /* ********************************************** */
    printf("The Solaris Concurrent Thread list of %d prime numbers after 2
is as follows:\n", REQUEST);
    printf("%8d(%d)", s_Primes[0].i_Prime, s_Primes[0].i_Thread);
    for (i = 1; i < REQUEST; i++)
        printf(",%c%8d(%d)", i % 5 != 0 ? ' ' : '\n',
               s_Primes[i].i_Prime, s_Primes[i].i_Thread);
    printf("\n");
}

/* ********************************** */
/* Prime Number Thread Search Routine */
/* ********************************** */
void *PrimeSearch(void *v_Number)
{
    int i_Number = *(int *)v_Number;
    int i_Numerator, i_Denominator, i_CutOff, i_Prime;

    /* ****************************** */
    /* Threads when started will wait */
    /* until i_ThreadHold is set to 1. */
    /* ****************************** */

    mutex_lock(&m_Condition);

    while (i_ThreadHold)
        cond_wait(&cond_Variable, &m_Condition);

    printf("Entering thread %d, primes found = %d\n", i_Number,
           i_Count);

    mutex_unlock(&m_Condition);

    while (i_Count < REQUEST) {

        /* *************************** */
        /* Get the next number to test */
        /* *************************** */

        mutex_lock(&m_Current);

        i_CurrentNum += 2;
        i_Numerator = i_CurrentNum;

        i_CutOff = i_Numerator / 2 + 1;
        i_Prime = 1;
        for (i_Denominator = 2; ((i_Denominator < i_CutOff && i_Prime));
i_Denominator++)
            i_Prime = i_Numerator % i_Denominator;

        mutex_unlock(&m_Current);

        if (i_Prime != 0) {


            /* *************************** */
            /* Store the prime number found */
            /* *************************** */
```

```
            mutex_lock(&m_Primes);

            if (i_Count < REQUEST) {
                s_Primes[i_Count].i_Prime  = i_Numerator;
                s_Primes[i_Count].i_Thread = i_Number;
                i_Count++;
            }

            if (i_Count == REQUEST) {
                printf("Thread %d is canceling other threads\n", i_Number);
                i_Count++;
            }

            mutex_unlock(&m_Primes);

            if (i_Count >= REQUEST)
                break;
        }
    } /* end While Loop */

    thr_exit(v_Number);

    return(v_Number);
}
```

8.4 THE WIN32 APPLICATION PROGRAM INTERFACE

The Win32 API is an extremely comprehensive repertoire of routines that can be used to perform a vast number of system services and functions. The idea of a synchronization primitive goes beyond what is normally thought of as a concurrency mechanism. The Win32 API considers many other elements, such as processes, threads, and files, as synchronization objects. The basic concept is understanding whether a particular object is *signaled* or *not signaled*. Whether an object is signaled or not causes the particular wait-for functions to behave differently. We will discuss two such routines in this chapter, `WaitForSingleObject` and `WaitForMultipleObjects`. It is possible to wait for more than one instance of the same kind of object or for more than one kind of object. If the object is not signaled, the wait-for functions will cause the caller to suspend. Table 8.1 is a list of the Win32 API objects along with a description of what causes them to be signaled or not.

Table 8.1 Win32 Synchronization Objects Signal Implications

Object	When is it signaled?
event	Set exclusively with SetEvent or PulseEvent function
mutex	When not owned by a thread
semaphore	When semaphore variable count is > 0
process	Final thread terminates
thread	Thread terminates
timer	Timer expires
file	File I/O operation finishes

The calling sequence for the Win32 API wait-for functions are as follows:

```
Status = WaitForSingleObject (
      HANDLE Object,     /* Handle of object for which to wait */
      DWORD Timeout );   /* Set to INFINITE or a timeout value */

Status = WaitForMultipleObjects (
      DWORD Objects,     /* Number of objects to check */
      LPHANDLE Handles,  /* Array of handles of objects */
      BOOL Waitflag,     /* Wait for 1 or all objects */
      DWORD Timeout );   /* Set to INFINITE or a timeout value */
```

These wait-for functions return statuses as follows:

WAIT_OBJECT_0	Wait completed successfully
WAIT_TIMEOUT	Object did not reach signaled state in specified timeout period
WAIT_ABANDONED_0	Mutex owning thread terminated before releasing mutex
WAIT_FAILED	Error occurs, call GetLastError

All Win32 objects have *handles* affiliated with them. A handle is a unique identifier used by the system to refer to the object. A handle is produced when the object is created. These wait-for functions can be used to wait for any of the objects listed in Table 8.1. We will focus on mutexes, semaphores, and events, as well as one other synchronization function not listed in Table 8.1, the critical section.

8.4.1 MUTEXES

The successful use of a mutex to enforce mutual exclusion depends on threads following a protocol. When a thread desires to enter its critical section, it requests ownership of a particular mutex. Once this mutex is owned by a thread, other threads that request ownership of it are made to wait. When a thread is leaving its critical section, it releases the mutex, at which time another waiting thread is granted ownership of the mutex.

Mutexes are known throughout the system. All a thread need do is refer to the mutex by its unique name. So a thread in any process can affiliate with a particular mutex. Mutexes are created via the CreateMutex API, as follows:

```
Handle = CreateMutex (
            LPSECURITY_ATTRIBUTES mutexscrty,   /* Set to NULL */
            BOOL InitialOwner,   /* Creating thread should be owner */
            LPTSTR MutexName );        /* Unique name of mutex */
```

The first argument to CreateMutex deals with a security attributes structure and is not within the scope of this book. This argument specifies security information pertinent to a Windows NT environment only and is not available in Windows 95. For the purposes of discussion in this chapter, this argument is set to NULL. The next argument, InitialOwner, indicates whether the creating thread is the owner of the mutex. If set to TRUE, the mutex is created nonsignaled, if set to FALSE, the mutex is created signaled. If a mutex is nonsignaled, other threads that request it will be made to wait. The last argument specifies a zero-terminated string, assigning a unique name to the mutex.

The first thread to create the mutex calls CreateMutex. Once the mutex has been created, other processes that need to affiliate with it call `OpenMutex`, which has the following calling sequence:

```
Handle = OpenMutex (
            DWORD Access,          /* Set to MUTEX_ALL_ACCESS */
            BOOL Inherit,          /* Allow children to inherit */
            LPTSTR, MutexName );/* Name of mutex */
```

When a thread is finished with a mutex, it releases it by calling `ReleaseMutex`, as follows:

```
ReleaseMutex ( HANDLE MutexHandle );
```

The idea then is for a thread to wait for a mutex to become signaled, and that is accomplished by calling `WaitForSingleObject` or `WaitForMultipleObjects`. The return status from these routines indicate whether the mutex was acquired successfully (`WAIT_OBJECT_0`) or because a thread that had owned the mutex terminated before the mutex was released (`WAIT_ABANDONED_0`).

8.4.2 SEMAPHORES

Unlike mutexes, semaphores are not owned by any threads. Semaphores are known system wide and threads can affiliate with them by specifying the name of the semaphore. Semaphore operation is discussed in Chapter 7. The Win32 API semaphore routines Djikstra equivalent are as follows:

```
WAIT(S)            WaitForSingleObject ( … Semaphore handle … )
                   WaitForMultipleObjects (… Semaphore handle … )

SIGNAL(S)          ReleaseSemaphore (… Semaphore handle … )
```

A semaphore is created by calling the `CreateSemaphore` routine, as follows:

```
Handle = CreateSemaphore (
            LPSECURITY_ATTRIBUTE semaphore_scrty,  /* Set to NULL */
                LONG InitVal,          /* Initial semaphore value */
                LONG MaxVal,           /* Maximum semaphore value */
                LPTSTR SemaphoreName ); /* Unique semaphore name */
```

InitVal represents how many instances of a resource are available. MaxVal represents the total number of instances of a resource that exist.

Once a semaphore is created, other threads need only affiliate with it by name by calling routine OpenSemaphore, as follows:

```
Handle = OpenSemaphore (
          DWORD Access,
          BOOL Inherit,
          LPTSTR SemaphoreName );
```

This call looks familiar to the OpenMutex call and indeed its arguments have the same implications. The calling sequence to routine ReleaseSemaphore is as follows:

```
ReleaseSemaphore (
      HANDLE Semaphore,
      LONG Release,
      LPLONG Previous );
```

The Release argument indicates by how much the semaphore variable count should be incremented. The other argument, Previous, contains the value of the semaphore variable count *before* Release is added to it. NULL can be passed for this argument.

8.4.3 EVENTS

While mutexes and semaphores are used to control access to shared information, events are used to signal that some operation has been completed. Events are created by calling the CreateEvent API, as follows:

```
Handle = CreateEvent (
          LPSECURITY_ATTRIBUTES eventsec, /* Set to NULL */
          BOOL EventType,     /* Manual-reset or auto-reset */
          BOOL InitState,     /* Initialize as signaled? */
          LPTSTR EventName ); /* Name of event object */
```

There are two types of event objects, as indicated by the second argument EventType. An event can be either a *manual-reset* type or an *auto-reset* type. Manual-reset events are not automatically reset to nonsignaled by the wait-for API routines. Auto-reset events stay signaled just long enough to give a *single* waiting thread a chance to wake up from having called one of the wait-for API routines.

Events, both manual-reset and auto-reset types, can be manipulated by calling the following API routines (single argument is the event object handle):

SetEvent	Set event object to the signaled state
ResetEvent	Reset event object to the non-signaled state
PulseEvent	Makes a manual-reset event behave like an auto-reset event

8.4.4 CRITICAL SECTIONS

The Win32 API also provides a concurrency function that is specific to a particular process. The *critical section* APIs are only valid within a single process and are not effective systemwide. A critical section structure is established as follows:

```
CRITICAL_SECTION MyCriticalSection;
```

This critical section is used as an argument in the other four related calls:

```
InitializeCriticalSection(&MyCriticalSection);
DeleteCriticalSection(&MyCriticalSection);
EnterCriticalSection(&MyCriticalSection);
LeaveCriticalSection(&MyCriticalSection);
```

When a thread calls EnterCriticalSection, any other thread that attempts to use that call will be made to wait, until LeaveCriticalSection is called. See Example 8.3 for a demonstration of the use of critical sections.

8.4.5 SAMPLE WIN32 PROGRAM

The program in Example 8.3 was contributed by Patrick Burton, a student from the Hartford Graduate Center. This is the Win32 version of the Digital UNIX program depicted in Examples 8.1 and 8.2. In Example 8.3, after REQUEST prime numbers are determined and stored in memory at sPrimeRec, they are displayed. Mutexes are used to coordinate the worker thread activity.

Example 8.3 Program that demonstrates the use of Win32 API concurrency using mutex functions.

```
/* ********************************************************************* */
/* Win32-Threads implementation of a prime number searching program    */
/* that uses mutexes for worker thread synchronization.                 */
/* ********************************************************************* */
#include <windows.h>
#include <stdio.h>
#include <stdlib.h>
#include <string.h>

#define WORKERS 5     /* Number of Threads to perform prime check */
#define REQUEST 500   /* Number of primes to find */

/* ********************************************************************* */
/* This structure is used to store the prime numbers found, and which   */
/* thread found them.                                                   */
/* ********************************************************************* */

typedef struct _PrimeRec {
    DWORD dw_Prime;
    DWORD dw_Thread;
} sPrimeRec;

/* ********************************************************************* */
/* Synchronization, worker thread and other global declarations to be   */
/* used by the threads during the prime number processing.              */
/* ********************************************************************* */

HANDLE    h_Primes,
          h_Current;

DWORD     dw_CurrentNum = 1,
          dw_Count = 0;

sPrimeRec s_Primes[REQUEST];

HANDLE  h_Threads[WORKERS];

/* ************************************************** */
/* Prototype for the Prime Number Search Thread routine */
/* ************************************************** */
DWORD PrimeSearch(LPVOID v_Number);

void main(int argc, char **argv)
{
    DWORD      dw_Done = 0, i, j;
    DWORD      dw_ThreadNum[WORKERS];
        DWORD     thr_Id;
```

```
sPrimeRec s_Prime;

memset(h_Threads, '\0', WORKERS * sizeof(HANDLE));
memset(&h_Primes, '\0', sizeof(HANDLE));
memset(&h_Current, '\0', sizeof(HANDLE));

/* ******************************** */
/*         Create Mutexes           */
/* ******************************** */
h_Primes = CreateMutex(NULL, FALSE, "PRIMES");
    h_Current = CreateMutex(NULL, FALSE, "CURRENT");

/* ***************************************** */
/* Create Worker Threads that are suspended */
/* at startup.                              */
/* ***************************************** */
for (i = 0; i < WORKERS; i++) {
    dw_ThreadNum[i] = i;
    h_Threads[i] = CreateThread(NULL, 0,
                (LPTHREAD_START_ROUTINE)PrimeSearch,
                (LPVOID)&dw_ThreadNum[i],
                CREATE_SUSPENDED, &thr_Id);
}

/* ********************************************* */
/* Resume worker threads, so that they start at */
/* the same time.                               */
/* ********************************************* */
    for (i = 0; i < WORKERS; i++)
        ResumeThread(h_Threads[i]);

/* ********************************************* */
/* Wait for each of the worker threads in order */
/* to ensure each has completed successfuly.    */
/* ********************************************* */

WaitForMultipleObjects(WORKERS, h_Threads, TRUE, INFINITE);

/* ********************************************* */
/*        Sort the prime numbers found.         */
/* ********************************************* */

for (i = 1; ((i < REQUEST) && (!dw_Done)); i++) {
    for (j = 0; j < i; j++) {
        if (s_Primes[i].dw_Prime < s_Primes[j].dw_Prime) {
            memcpy((char *)&s_Prime, (char *)&s_Primes[j],
                sizeof(sPrimeRec));
            memcpy((char *)&s_Primes[j], (char *)&s_Primes[i],
                sizeof(sPrimeRec));
            memcpy((char *)&s_Primes[i], (char *)&s_Prime,
                sizeof(sPrimeRec));

            dw_Done = 1;
        }
    }
}

/* ********************************************* */
/* Print out the list of prime numbers that the */
/* worker threads found.                        */
/* ********************************************* */
printf("The Win32 Mutex list of %d prime numbers after 2 is as
    follows:\n", REQUEST);
printf("%8d(%d)", s_Primes[0].dw_Prime, s_Primes[0].dw_Thread);
for (i = 1; i < REQUEST; i++)
```

```
        printf(",%c%8d(%d)", i % 5 != 0 ? ' ': '\n',
                s_Primes[i].dw_Prime, s_Primes[i].dw_Thread);
    printf("\n");
}

/* ********************************* */
/* Prime Number Thread Search Routine */
/* ********************************* */
DWORD PrimeSearch(LPVOID v_Number)
{
    DWORD dw_Number = *(DWORD *)v_Number;
    DWORD dw_Numerator, dw_Denominator, dw_CutOff, dw_Prime;
    DWORD dw_Cresult, dw_Presult;

/* ************************************ */
/* The Threads are started suspended    */
/* when resumed, print out the entry    */
/* thread number and current count.     */
/* ************************************ */

        dw_Cresult = WaitForSingleObject(h_Current, INFINITE);

    printf("Entering thread %d, primes found = %d\n", dw_Number,
            dw_Count);

    ReleaseMutex(h_Current);

    while (dw_Count < REQUEST) {

                /* *************************** */
                /* Get the next number to test */
                /* *************************** */

        dw_Cresult = WaitForSingleObject(h_Current, INFINITE);

        dw_CurrentNum += 2;
        dw_Numerator = dw_CurrentNum;

        dw_CutOff = dw_Numerator / 2 + 1;
        dw_Prime = 1;
        for (dw_Denominator = 2; ((dw_Denominator < dw_CutOff &&
                dw_Prime)); dw_Denominator++)
            dw_Prime = dw_Numerator % dw_Denominator;

        ReleaseMutex(h_Current);

        if (dw_Prime != 0) {

                /* *************************** */
                /* Store the prime number found */
                /* *************************** */

            dw_Presult = WaitForSingleObject(h_Primes, INFINITE);

            if (dw_Count < REQUEST) {
                s_Primes[dw_Count].dw_Prime  = dw_Numerator;
                s_Primes[dw_Count].dw_Thread = dw_Number;
                dw_Count++;
            }

                if (dw_Count == REQUEST) {
                printf("Thread %d is canceling other threads\n",
                        dw_Number);
                dw_Count++;
            }
```

```
        ReleaseMutex(h_Primes);

        if (dw_Count >= REQUEST)
            break;
        }
    } /* end of While Loop */

        /* Exit Thread to free allocated resources */
    ExitThread(dw_Number);

    return(dw_Number);
}
```

Example 8.4 is another version of the same program, also provided by HGC student Patrick Burton, implemented with critical sections.

Example 8.4 The prime numbers program implemented with critical sections.

```
/* ********************************************************************* */
/* Programmer: Patrick Burton                                          */
/* Date:       06/16/96                                                */
/* Course:     Unix and Win32 Application Programming Interface        */
/* Course No.: 166696144                                               */
/* Instructor: Don Merusi                                              */
/* ********************************************************************* */

/* ********************************************************************* */
/* Win32-Threads implementation of a prime number searching program    */
/* that uses critical sections for worker thread synchronization.       */
/* ********************************************************************* */
#include <windows.h>
#include <stdio.h>
#include <stdlib.h>
#include <string.h>

#define WORKERS 5    /* Number of Threads to perform prime check */
#define REQUEST 500  /* Number of primes to find */

/* ********************************************************************* */
/* This structure is used to store the prime numbers found, and which  */
/* thread found them.                                                   */
/* ********************************************************************* */

typedef struct _PrimeRec {
    DWORD dw_Prime;
    DWORD dw_Thread;
} sPrimeRec;

/* ********************************************************************* */
/* Synchronization, worker thread and other global declarations to be  */
/* used by the threads during the prime number processing.             */
/* ********************************************************************* */

CRITICAL_SECTION    cs_Primes,
                    cs_Current;

DWORD    dw_CurrentNum = 1,
         dw_Count = 0;
```

```
sPrimeRec s_Primes[REQUEST];

HANDLE  h_Threads[WORKERS];

/* ******************************************************** */
/* Prototype for the Prime Number Search Thread routine */
/* ******************************************************** */
DWORD PrimeSearch(LPVOID v_Number);

void main(int argc, char **argv)
{
    DWORD       dw_Done = 0, i, j;
    DWORD         dw_ThreadNum[WORKERS];
      DWORD        thr_Id;
    sPrimeRec s_Prime;

    memset(h_Threads, '\0', WORKERS * sizeof(HANDLE));
    memset(&cs_Primes, '\0', sizeof(CRITICAL_SECTION));
    memset(&cs_Current, '\0', sizeof(CRITICAL_SECTION));

    /* ******************************** */
    /*     Create Critical Sections         */
    /* ******************************** */
    InitializeCriticalSection(&cs_Primes);
    InitializeCriticalSection(&cs_Current);

    /* ****************************************** */
    /* Create Worker Threads that are suspended */
    /* at startup.                              */
    /* ****************************************** */
    for (i = 0; i < WORKERS; i++) {
       dw_ThreadNum[i] = i;
       h_Threads[i] = CreateThread(NULL, 0,
                 (LPTHREAD_START_ROUTINE)PrimeSearch,
                 (LPVOID)&dw_ThreadNum[i],
              CREATE_SUSPENDED, &thr_Id);
    }

    /* ******************************************** */
    /* Resume worker threads, so that they start at */
    /* the same time.                               */
    /* ******************************************** */
       for (i = 0; i < WORKERS; i++)
          ResumeThread(h_Threads[i]);

    /* ********************************************** */
    /* Wait for each of the worker threads in order */
    /* to ensure each has completed successfuly.    */
    /* ********************************************** */

    WaitForMultipleObjects(WORKERS, h_Threads, TRUE, INFINITE);

    /* ************************************** */
    /* Delete Critical Sections to release any */
    /* allocated resources.                    */
    /* ************************************** */
       DeleteCriticalSection(&cs_Primes);
       DeleteCriticalSection(&cs_Current);

    /* ********************************************** */
    /*        Sort the prime numbers found.           */
    /* ********************************************** */

    for (i = 1; ((i < REQUEST) && (!dw_Done)); i++) {
       for (j = 0; j < i; j++) {
```

```
            if (s_Primes[i].dw_Prime < s_Primes[j].dw_Prime) {
                memcpy((char *)&s_Prime, (char *)&s_Primes[j],
                        sizeof(sPrimeRec));
                memcpy((char *)&s_Primes[j], (char *)&s_Primes[i],
                        sizeof(sPrimeRec));
                memcpy((char *)&s_Primes[i], (char *)&s_Prime,
                        sizeof(sPrimeRec));

                dw_Done = 1;
            }
        }
    }

    /* ********************************************* */
    /* Print out the list of prime numbers that the */
    /* worker threads found.                        */
    /* ********************************************* */
    printf("The Win32 Critical Section list of %d prime numbers after 2 is
        as follows:\n", REQUEST);
    printf("%8d(%d)", s_Primes[0].dw_Prime, s_Primes[0].dw_Thread);
    for (i = 1; i < REQUEST; i++)
        printf(",%c%8d(%d)", i % 5 != 0 ? ' ': '\n',
                s_Primes[i].dw_Prime, s_Primes[i].dw_Thread);
    printf("\n");
}

/* ********************************** */
/* Prime Number Thread Search Routine */
/* ********************************** */
DWORD PrimeSearch(LPVOID v_Number)
{
    DWORD dw_Number = *(DWORD *)v_Number;
    DWORD dw_Numerator, dw_Denominator, dw_CutOff, dw_Prime;

    /* ********************************** */
    /* The Threads are started suspended  */
    /* when resumed, print out the entry  */
    /* thread number and current count.   */
    /* ********************************** */

        EnterCriticalSection(&cs_Current);

    printf("Entering thread %d, primes found = %d\n", dw_Number,
            dw_Count);

    LeaveCriticalSection(&cs_Current);

    while (dw_Count < REQUEST) {

                /* ************************** */
                /* Get the next number to test */
                /* ************************** */

        EnterCriticalSection(&cs_Current);

        dw_CurrentNum += 2;
        dw_Numerator = dw_CurrentNum;

        dw_CutOff = dw_Numerator / 2 + 1;
        dw_Prime = 1;
        for (dw_Denominator = 2; ((dw_Denominator < dw_CutOff &&
            dw_Prime)); dw_Denominator++)
            dw_Prime = dw_Numerator % dw_Denominator;

        LeaveCriticalSection(&cs_Current);
```

```
       if (dw_Prime != 0) {

               /* *************************** */
               /* Store the prime number found */
               /* *************************** */

           EnterCriticalSection(&cs_Primes);

           if (dw_Count < REQUEST) {
               s_Primes[dw_Count].dw_Prime  = dw_Numerator;
               s_Primes[dw_Count].dw_Thread = dw_Number;
               dw_Count++;
           }

                   if (dw_Count == REQUEST) {
               printf("Thread %d is canceling other threads\n",
                       dw_Number);
               dw_Count++;
           }

           LeaveCriticalSection(&cs_Primes);

           if (dw_Count >= REQUEST)
               break;
       }
   } /* end of While Loop */


/* Exit Thread to free allocated resources */
   ExitThread(dw_Number);

   return(dw_Number);
}
```

8.5 WRAP-UP AND FURTHER READING

This chapter was a compare and contrast of how to perform certain operating system services with the Win32 API and UNIX system functions. The UNIX environments focused on Digital UNIX and Solaris. The system services discussed included process and thread scheduling, synchronization, and concurrency control. Threads are a relatively new concept in programming and are a convenient means of writing extremely flexible and robust applications that require synchronization and concurrency control. Both Windows and UNIX provide a wealth of synchronization and concurrency functions, including semaphores, mutexes, critical sections, and condition variables.

A plethora of books exist for describing how to program in Windows with the Win32 API. A good introduction to the philosophy behind the design of Windows NT [Custer 1994] is recommended. For a more intimate discussion about the internal workings of windows environments, [Hallberg 1994], [King

1994], [Custer 1992], and [Ivens 1996] are recommended. [Petzold 1996] continues his excellent series about programming in Windows 95. Microsoft Corporation has produced a good reference for Windows programming [Microsoft 1995]. [Garg 1995] is an excellent reference specifically about threads programming in Windows and [Brain 1996] is an excellent reference for Win32 API programming in Windows NT and Windows 95. A superb book about concurrency and synchronization facilities in UNIX can be found in [Robbins 1996] and [Merusi 1995].

REFERENCES

[Custer 1992] Custer, Helen, *Inside Windows NT*, Redmond, WA: Microsoft Press, 1992.

[Custer 1994] Custer, Helen, *Inside the Windows NT File System,* Redmond, WA: Microsoft Press, 1994.

[Hallberg 1994] Hallberg, Bruce, Forrest Houlette, and Jim Boyce, *Inside Windows*, New Riders Publishers, 1994.

[King 1994] King, Adrian, *Inside Windows 95*, Redmond, WA.: Microsoft Press, 1994.

[Ivens 1996] Ivens, Kathy, Bruce Hallberg, Bob Chronister, Drew Heywood, and George Eckel, New Riders Publishers, 1996.

[Microsoft 1995] Microsoft Corporation, *Programmer's Guide to Windows 95: Key Topics on Programming for Windows from the Microsoft Windows Development Team*, Redmond, WA: Microsoft Press, 1995.

[Petzold 1996] Petzold, Charles, *Programming Windows 95*, Redmond, WA.: Microsoft Press, 1996.

[Garg 1995] Garg, Pankaj K., Thuan Pham, *Multithreaded Programming with Windows NT*, Englewood Cliffs, NJ: Prentice Hall, 1995.

[Brain 1996] Brain, Marshall, *Win32 System Services: The Heart of Windows 95 and Windows NT 2nd Edition*, Englewood Cliffs, NJ: Prentice Hall Technical Series, 1996.

[Merusi 1995] Merusi, Donald E., *Software Implementation Techniques: Writing Software in OpenVMS, OS/2, UNIX and Windows NT 2nd Edition*, Burlington, MA: Digital Press, 1995.

[Robbins 1996] Robbins, Kay A., Steven Robbins, *Practical UNIX Programming: A Guide to Concurrency, Communication and Multithreading*, Englewood Cliffs, NJ: Prentice Hall Technical Reference, 1996.

APPENDIX A

An Overview of C++

Many of the examples shown in this book were compiled with Borland **C++** Version 5.01, which uses the Rogue Wave implementation of the Standard Template Library. This appendix contains an overview of **C++**. The object of this appendix is not to give a detailed description of the language, but rather to describe it on a high enough level to provide a "reading familiarity" with the language. It is assumed that the reader has some familiarity with the **C** language. Anyone wishing a more intensive study of **C++** is invited to pick up any of the many reference books available on the market.

A.1 IMPROVEMENTS TO THE C SYNTAX

C++ has many features that are just modifications to the standard **C** syntax. Some of the more obvious are:

A.1.1 DECLARATION OF NAMED CONSTANTS

C++ adds the "const" keyword to declare constants and give them a name. Thus,

```
const float pi = 3.14159;
```

can be used to replace the former

```
#define pi 3.14159
```

A common problem with the latter form is that the symbol is not defined in the symbol table and is not available to the debugger.

A.1.2 PASS BY REFERENCE PARAMETERS

Usually, **C** passes parameters by value. This means that a copy of the parameter's *value* is passed to the called procedure. This has the advantage that any changes that the called process makes to the parameter will not affect the original value belonging to the process that made the call. This avoids many side effects. There are times when you *do* want to have the values passed to a procedure changed by the procedure. For instance, a procedure to exchange the values would be useful in a sort program. To do this in **C** requires the use of pointers and passing the addresses of the parameters.

```c
void exchange(int *a, int *b)
{
    int *temp = *a;
    *a = *b;
    *b = *temp;
}

void sort()
{
    ... ...
    exchange(&x[i], &x[j]);
    ... ...
}
```

Many find this form to be confusing. It's easier to think of changing the parameters than changing what they are pointing at. **C++** introduced a notation that allows parameters to be passed by reference, that is, the address of the parameter is implicitly passed to the procedure. The notational change is to put the '&' in the declaration instead of the call. The result looks like:

```c
void exchange(int &a, int &b)
{
    int temp = a;
    a = b;
    b = temp;
}

void sort()
{
    ... ...
    exchange(x[i], x[j]);
    ... ...
}
```

Since the function knows that it is using addresses, the manipulation of the variables does not need the "*" in the procedure's code. This indirect referencing form is automatically handled by the compiler. I personally find the new form much more readable and easier to understand. (For those interested in how this "indirection" is handled, refer to the discussion at the end of Section 6.2.)

A.1.3 METHOD OF EXPRESSING EXPLICIT TYPE CONVERSIONS

The expression "type conversions" can refer to one of two possibilities:

- Total change of the internal representation of the data inside the machine.
- Change in the type that the compiler associates with an item (without changing the internal representation). For instance, the integer value 65 and the ASCII character "A" both have the same internal bit representation (although the size may be different).

In **C**, either of the conversions could be requested in the source code with a "type casting" notation, such as the following, which converts an integer into a character:

```
char  ch = (char) 65;
```

C++ has introduced a representation that looks more like a function call.

```
char  ch = char(65);
```

Pointer types still need to be converted using the older format:

```
char  ch_ptr = (char *) int_ptr;
```

A.1.4 SIMPLIFIED INPUT / OUTPUT (I/O) STATEMENTS

The operators "<<" and ">>" were used in **C** to indicate "shift left" and "shift right" respectively. In **C++** they are given additional meanings, "shift to output" and "shift from input." This eliminates the usual assortment of printf, scanf, getc, and putc calls. To output a string and a real value followed by a new line, one simply writes:

```
cout << "The value of pi is " << 3.14 << endl;
```

You can specify format information by inserting predefined manipulators in the sequence. For instance, the following inputs a decimal value and a hexadecimal value:

```
cin >> dec >> decimal_val >> hex >> hex_value;
```

It is also possible to write I/O operations in a functional sort of representation. The following statement mixes both forms. It is used to copy from the input to the output until all characters have been read. The get function returns a value of "true" until the end of input is detected.

```
while (cin.get(c)) cout << c;
```

When using this form of I/O, you must place a statement to "#include <iostream.h>" at the beginning of the program. The manipulators require an "#include <iomanip.h>" if they take an argument.

It is also possible to do similar operations on files. This requires an "#include <fstream.h>" statement. Once this is done you can name the file and use it just like cin or cout. The following copies from a file named "here" to a file named "there":

```
ifstream fin("here");
ofstream fout("there");
while (fin >> c) fout << c;
```

The "fin >> c" form is the same as "fin.get(c)". As such, it also returns "true" until the end of the input is detected. It is also possible to read a complete line using the getline function in much the same way as the get function mentioned above. There is also a close function to use if you need to close a file. (Files close automatically at the end of the program or as soon as they go out of scope. Refer to Section 4.10 for more information on scope.)

A.1.5 AN ALTERNATE FORM OF COMMENTS

C++ introduces an alternate form of comments. Anything from a "//" to the end of the line is considered to be a comment. This helps avoid some of the strange forms of multiline comments using the old "/* ... */" forms. Compare

```
//  This code uses the Rogue Wave implementation of the Standard
//  Template Library.
```

with

```
/*
**  This code uses the Rogue Wave implementation of the Standard
**  Template Library.
*/
```

A.1.6 MEMORY ALLOCATION

C++ has replaced the `malloc` form of memory allocation with simplified forms. If T represents some form of type, then a statement like "*new T*" will allocate enough space for an instance of the type and will return a pointer to the memory. Likewise, there is also a "*delete*" function that deallocates the memory. For instance, the following defines *int_prt* as a pointer to an integer. The call to new allocates the memory for it. The next line stores a value in this space. The last line deallocates the memory.

```
int  *int_ptr = new int;
*int_ptr = 123;
delete int_ptr;
```

A.1.7 OPERATOR OVERLOADING

C++ has a method for operator overloading, that is, adding a new meaning to an operator. I have defined no overloaded operators in the LuxLyk compilers or P-Machine; however, these programs do use overloaded operators. The "<<" and ">>" forms mentioned under simplified I/O are examples of overloaded operators. Another example relates to a special type known as string. The equals sign is used instead of `strcpy`, and the plus is used instead of `strcat`. The following command concatenates "copy" and "right" and copies the result to *cpy_rt*:

```
cpy_rt = "copy" + "right";
```

A.1.8 POLYMORPHIC FUNCTIONS

You've probably seen examples of polymorphism in other languages. Most languages have an `ABS()` function that returns the absolute value of the parameter passed to it. The function returns a value that is the same type as the parameter that was passed to it. Polymorphism refers to functions that act somewhat differently, depending on the type or form of the input parameters. This functionality is usually built into a language for a small set of functions. **C++** allows you to define your own polymorphic functions. As a matter of fact, the two forms of the `exchange` function shown in Section A.1.2 could both be included in the same program. If you use pointers to integers when you call the function, the first form is used. If you use integers in the call, however, the second form will be used. As long as the arguments are unique, the compiler will determine the correct form of the function to call.

The type of the parameter is not the only way to specify different forms. Another method is to use a different number of parameters. This form is particularly useful for extracting data from a dictionary data structure, such as a symbol table. There may be instances when you don't need to examine all of the fields. A form of the `Examine` function that returns fewer parameters could be used.

A.1.9 DEFAULT ARGUMENTS

Along with allowing function forms with different numbers of parameters, **C++** also provides a way of using a default value if a specific argument is not passed to it. Consider the following pointer and function definitions:

```
int  *i_arr;

void mk_arr(int siz = 100)      // 100 is the default
{   i_arr = new int[siz];   }
```

If this is called by "*mk_arr(50)*", an array of 50 integers will be allocated. On the other hand, a call of "*mk_arr()*" will allocate 100 integers. The default value is specified in the parameter list by the "= 100". Any parameter so marked can be omitted in the call and the default value will be substituted.

A.2 OBJECT-ORIENTED CONCEPTS

When designing a large program such as a compiler, it is necessary to break it down into smaller pieces that are easier to manage. In really large programs, this becomes an iterative process; the smaller pieces in turn must be broken down. The question is how to break it down.

In the past, the answer to this question was to break it down procedurally, that is, break it down into a series of things to do. For a compiler, the job might be initially broken into "parse the input." "Parse the input" might be separated into "parse the symbol declarations" and "parse the statements." Eventually, this would lead us down to a series of actions to read the input source and generate the output code. Notice that everything is a *verb*, i.e., "do this...," "do that...."

The object-oriented approach answers the question by saying that the program should be broken up into *objects*, that is, *nouns*. These objects will be expressed in the program as a complete package that contains any data structures necessary to simulate the object and a collection of functions that perform certain operations on the object or report on its status. This changes the whole emphasis of the proram. Instead of looking for what to do, you must look for the objects and then decide how they interact. In the case of a compiler, the primary objects are all of the non-terminals that make up the source code. They must be put together in the form of a parse tree and then the output code must be generated by the structure. Secondary objects include such things as the tokens and the symbol table.

The idea of putting everything related to an object in one package has been around for some time. It's known as *encapsulation*. The LuxLyk monitor is an encapsulation. If you take it a step further and make the unit reusable, it is called an *abstract data type*. The LuxLyk monitor is not an abstract data type; it must be rewritten for each use. A common theme in encapsulation and abstract data types is *data hiding* or *information hid-*

ing. This says that the client, that is, the program (or programmer) who uses the package, does not need to know the form of the data within the package and should not have access to this data. All that matters is that calling the handling functions performs the proper operations on the data. Quite often, dangerous side effects can be avoided by isolating the client from the internal data structures.

Object-oriented design takes abstract data types a step further by introducing the concept of inheritance. The idea here is that if one object is derived from another, it inherits features from the one it is derived from. In the Lil'LuxLyk compiler, all of the non-terminals are derived from the basic parse node. In our case, the only thing the parse node has to inherit are the parse and generate member functions. (Member functions will be explained below.)

A.3 OBJECT-ORIENTED FEATURES IN C++

In **C++**, the package usually used to define an object is known as a *class*. A class is a specialized form of a **C** structure (struct). There are some differences. Part of a class can be used to hold the hidden data and possibly some private functions. This section of the class may be visible, but it can't be accessed by the client code. This section is introduced by the keyword private, however, the first part of the class definition is private by default, and does not require the keyword. Another section of the class contains the data and functions that may be accessed by the client. This section is introduced by the keyword public. Although the functions in this area may be called by other parts of the program, there is no need for the program (or the programmer who writes the code that calls the function) to know how the function actually works. For this reason, a stripped down form of the class is provided in a header file and the actual implementation is kept in a separate file. The header file can be published for anyone who wishes to use the class. The "stripped down" form is known as a *prototype*. The other file is usually used by the implementer(s) only.

Figure A.1 shows a possible header file for the class that represents a stack of integers. The definition starts off with the keyword "class" followed by the name of the class. The initial part of the class is automatically "private", thus the integer pointers are protected from access from outside the class. Most likely, the stack will be implemented as an array and these will be pointing to the top and bottom elements of the active stack. The public section of the class is introduced by the keyword "public". The next line is a special function known as the "constructor." It has the same name as the class. This function is called automatically when an instance of the class is created. (I'll discuss that later.) This function might create a dynamic instance of the stack array (by calling "new") and make *top* and *bot* point to the first element of the array. The size of the array will be determined by the passed parameter. The following line is known as a destructor. It has the same name as the class, but is preceded by a "~". It is called when the stack is terminated. It would call "delete" to deallocate the array used to implement the stack. The last two lines define the prototypes of the functions that push and pop an integer off the stack.

```
class i_stack {
    int *top, *bot;
public:
        i_stack(int siz = 25);
        ~i_stack();
    void push(int x);
    int  pop();
};
```

Figure A.1
The definition of an integer stack class.

A little more terminology is required. The variables of a class, whether private or public, are usually called "*member variables.*" The functions associated with a class are known as "*member functions*" or probably more commonly, "*methods.*" You may notice that I use the former term more frequently. Common object-oriented terminology for calling a member function is "*messaging*" or "*passing a message.*" I work with a couple of middleware products that actually pass messages between processes. In addition, the last section of Chapter 6 was concerned with passing information between processes in the form of a message. For these two reasons, I find it difficult to refer to calling a member function as "passing a message." I feel that "calling" is generally understood, but "messaging" can get to be confusing when there are other types of messages being considered.

Now we must look at the various forms by which the member functions are expressed. The form shown in Figure A.1 is a prototype. It consists of a definition of the function's type, name, and parameters. It does not have a body (where the implementation would be defined). Instead of a body, the declaration is terminated by a semicolon. It is possible to include the body in the class declaration, especially if the body is short. For instance, the push function could be declared inside the class declaration as:

```
void push(int x)   { *tp++ = x; }
```

The terminating ";" is replaced by the body of the function. As I mentioned earlier, the implementation code is usually written in a separate file. Whenever the implementation code is written outside of the class declaration, a special notation is necessary to tell the compiler that the function being defined here is actually the member function of the class declared in the header file. The special notation is to place the name of the class and two colons in front of the name of the member function. If push were defined in a separate file, the form would be:

```
void i_stack::push(int x)
{
   *tp++ = x;
}
```

There also is a special notation when external functions call a member function. In this case, it must reference an instance of the class. First we need to see how an "instance" is produced. Consider the following code fragment.

```
i_stack   stack_a, *stack_b;

stack_b = new i_stack(50);
stack_a.push(100);
stack_b->push( stack_a.pop() );
```

The first line declares two i_stacks, but it only creates one instance of the i_stack. The *stack_a* variable *is* an i_stack. As such, it is immediately created. That means that the constructor is called and the default value of 25 is used as the size of the array. The *stack_b* variable is a pointer to an i_stack. That means it will be created later. This happens in the next line. The "new" function is called to allocate room for the data type. In the case of a class data type, it creates an instance of the class. The constructor is called, but in this case, a value of 50 is passed and an array of that size is created.

The next line shows a value of 100 being pushed onto the stack_a. In this case, the variable's name (i.e., stack_a) is separated from the member function's name (i.e., push) by a period.

The last line shows the value being popped off stack_a and pushed onto the i_stack pointed to by stack_b. Notice that when the variable points to a class instance, the variable's name and the member function's name are separated by "->" instead of a period.

What we've looked at so far is good for a stack of integers. What if we wanted to have a stack of reals or strings? At first it seems like we would have to write a class definition for each type individually. Fortunately, there are several alternatives. The best one is to use a tool called a template. A template for a generic type might look something like Figure A.2.

```
template <class T>
class stack {
    int *top, *bot;
public:
        stack(int siz = 25);
        ~stack();
    void push(T x);
    T    pop();
};
```

Figure A.2
The definition of a stack class template.

In this case, a stack of integers might be declared by a statement such as:

```
stack<int>   stack_a;
```

Further discussion of templates is beyond the scope of this appendix. No templates were defined in this book. On the other hand, the Standard Template Library was used. This library provides many predefined container classes including stacks and queues. There were several queues used throughout the Lil'LuxLyk compiler code. At the places where they were used, the chapter attempted to supply enough insight into the underlying design to make the code readable.

A.4 WRAP-UP AND FURTHER READING

As stated at the beginning of this appendix, the basic goal was to provide a reading familiarity with **C++**. For those wishing a more complete tutorial on **C++**, there are many books available in bookstores. Most should suffice. The original definition of the language was in [Stroustrup 1991]. The **C++** language is presently in the process of being standardized by the American National Standards Institute (ANSI). Some of the draft proposals for the standard can be found in [Plauger 1995]. If you have Internet access, the working paper of the ANSI draft proposals for **C++** can also be found online at http://www.cygnus.com/misc/wp/draft/index.html. The Standard Template Library is part of this proposal. Additional information on the STL can be found in [Musser 1996].

REFERENCES

[Musser 1996] Musser, David R., Atul Saini, *STL Tutorial and Reference Guide: C++ Programming with the Standard Template Library*, Reading, MA: Addison-Wesley Publishing Company 1996.

[Plauger 1995] Plauger, P. J., *The Draft Standard C++ Library*, Englewood Cliffs, NJ: Prentice Hall, Inc., 1995.

[Stroustrup 1991] Stroustrup, Bjarne, *The C++ Programming Language*, Reading, MA: Addison-Wesley Publishing Company 1991.

APPENDIX B

UNIX System Synchronization Functions

This appendix lists some commonly used UNIX system service calls associated with concurrency and synchronization control. The threads routines can be found in Digital UNIX, Solaris, and Linux and are becoming available in more versions of UNIX. The pthread interface is based on Draft 4 of the proposed IEEE standard for multithreaded programming, POSIX 1003.4a. All routine arguments are described in an abbreviated fashion. The reader is urged to consult a more comprehensive source for more detailed information about these calls.

SEMAPHORES

- **Creating semaphores**

```
semid = semget (
          key,
          number_of_semaphores,
          flags );
```

semid	Unique id assigned by system
key	A unique identifier for this semaphore set
number_of_semaphores	How many semaphores in this set
flags	Creating flags, protection, etc.

- ## Perform semaphore control functions

```
semctl (
      semid,
      semaphore_number,
      command,
      param );
```

semid   Identifier returned from semctl
semaphore_number   Specific semaphore involved this call
command   Action to perform to this semaphore
param   Value associated with action

- ## Perform specified number of operations on each semaphore in set

```
semop (
      semid,                          Identifier returned from semget
      semaphore_operation,            Structure defining semaphore operation
      number_semaphore_operations );
                                      Number operation structures
```

PROCESS CREATION

- ## Fork/Wait calls

```
status = fork();
status = vfork();

wait(&status);
```

- ## Exec calls -- v, l & p forms

```
execvp ( filename, argp );
execlp ( filename, command, ...., (char *) 0 );
```

filename   Filename of program files
command   Command line to invoke program

DIGITAL UNIX/SOLARIS/LINUX THREADS—PTHREAD INTERFACE

- ## Creating a thread

```
pthread_create( ThreadID, Attribute, Entry_Point, Arg );
```

ThreadID   Identifier assigned by system to thread
Attribute   Attribute associated with thread (priority,etc.)
Entry_Point   Entry point of thread routine
Arg   Optional argument passed to thread

- ## Deleting/terminating a thread

```
pthread_detach( ThreadID );
```

ThreadID   Identifier assigned by system to thread

- ## Waiting for a thread to terminate

```
pthread_join( ThreadID, status );
```

ThreadID   Identifier assigned by system to thread
status   Termination status of thread

- ## Creating a mutex

```
pthread_mutex_init( mutex, attribute );
```

mutex   Handle assigned to mutex
attribute   Attribute assigned to thread (fast, etc.)

- ## Requesting/releasing mutex ownership

```
pthread_mutex_lock ( mutex );
pthread_mutex_trylock( mutex );
pthread_mutex_unlock ( mutex );
```

mutex   Handle of mutex

• Destroying a mutex

```
pthread_mutex_destroy ( mutex );
```

mutex   Mutex handle

• Initializing a condition variable

pthread_cond_init (cv, attributes);

cv   Condition variable handle
attributes   Attributes assigned to conditional variable

• Wait for a condition variable

```
pthread_cond_wait ( cv );
```

cv   Condition variable handle

• Perform a timed wait for a condition variable

```
pthread_cond_timedwait ( cv );
```

cv   Condition variable handle

• Destroy a condition variable

```
pthread_cond_destroy ( cv );
```

cv   Condition variable handle

• Wake all threads waiting on condition variable

```
pthread_cond_broadcast ( cv );
```

cv   Condition variable handle

APPENDIX C

Win32 API System Synchronization Functions

This appendix lists the Win32 API calls associated with concurrency and synchronization control. All API arguments are described in an abbreviated fashion. The reader is urged to consult a more comprehensive source for more detailed information about these calls.

PROCESSES AND THREADS

- **Creating a Thread**

```
Handle CreateThread (
          LPSECURITY_ATTRIBUTES SecAttrs,
          DWORD Stack,
          LPTHREAD_START_ROUTINE Entry_Point,
          LPVOID Arg,
          DWORD CreateFlag,
          LPDWORD ThreadID);
```

SecAttrs	Security attributes structure
Stack	Local thread stack
Entry_Point	Entry of thread routine
Arg	Optional argument passed to thread
CreateFlag	Thread creation status, suspended, etc.
ThreadID	Receive thread ID upon creation

- **Terminating a Thread**

```
ExitThread ( DWORD ExitCode );
TerminateThread ( HANDLE Thread, DWORD ExitCode);
```

ExitCode	Thread exits with this value as status
Thread	Handle of thread being terminated

- ## Creating a Thread Remotely

```
Handle CreateRemoteThread (
            HANDLE Process,
            LPSECURITY_ATTRIBUTES SecAttrs,
            DWORD Stack,
            LPTHREAD_START_ROUTINE Entry_Point,
            LPVOID Arg,
            DWORD CreateFlag,
            LPDWORD ThreadID);
```

Arguments similar to CreateThread with the exception of the following:

Process   Handle of process in which thread is being created

- ## Setting and Getting a Thread's Priority

```
SetThreadPriority ( HANDLE Thread, INT Priority );
GetThreadPriority ( HANDLE Thread, INT Priority );
```

Thread   Handle of thread involved with priority
Priority   Priority value being assigned or returned

- ## Suspending and Resuming Threads

```
SuspendThread ( HANDLE Thread );
ResumeThread ( HANDLE Thread );
```

Thread   Handle of thread being resumed or suspended

- **Creating a Process**

```
HANDLE CreateProcess (
             LPCTSR Image,
             LPCTSR Command,
             LPSECURITY_ATTRIBUTES Process_SecAttrs,
             LPSECURITY_ATTRIBUTES Thread_SecAttrs,
             BOOL InheritFlag,
             DWORD CreationMode,
             LPVOID Environment,
             LPTSTR CurrentDir,
             LPSTARTUPINFO StartupInfo,
             LPPROCESS_INFORMATION ProcessInfo );
```

Image	Name of program image file
Command	Command to invoke program
Process_SecAttrs	Security attributes associated with process
Thread_SecAttrs	Security attributes with primary thread
InheritFlag	Pass characteristics on to thread prodigy
CreationMode	Process creation mode, suspended, etc.
Environment	Envionment variables (DOS symbols)
CurrentDir	Current directory
StartupInfo	Process startup structure
ProcessInfo	Returned process and thread information

WAIT-FOR FUNCTIONS

- **Waiting for a single object**

```
DWORD WaitForSingleObject (
       HANDLE Object,
       DWORD Timeout );
```

Object	Handle of object for which we are waiting
Timeout	How long to wait for object

- ## Waiting for Multiple Objects

```
DWORD WaitForMultipleObjects (
        DWORD NumberObjects,
        CONST HANDLE * ObjectArray,
        BOOL WaitForAll,
        DWORD Timeout );
```

NumberObjects	Number of objects involved in this wait
ObjectArray	Array of handles of object involved in wait
WaitForAll	Wait for all or any of the objects
Timeout	How long to wait for objects

MUTEXES

- ## Creating a Mutex

```
HANDLE CreateMutex (
            LPSECURITY_ATTRIBUTES SecAttrs,
            BOOL Owner,
            LPTSTR MutexName );
```

SecAttrs	Security attributes structure
Owner	Set to TRUE if caller wants to own mutex
MutexName	Name of mutex

- ## Associating with a Mutex

```
HANDLE OpenMutex (
            DWORD Access,
            BOOL InheritFlag,
            LPTSTR MutexName );
```

Access	SYNCHRONIZE or MUTEX_ALL_ACCESS
InheritFlag	Controls inheritance of mutex handle
MutexName	Name of mutex

- ### Releasing a Mutex

ReleaseMutex (HANDLE Mutex);

```
Mutex              Handle of mutex to be released
```

SEMAPHORES

- ### Creating a Semaphore

```
HANDLE CreateSemaphore (
            LPSECURITY_ATTRIBUTES SecAttrs,
            LONG InitCount,
            LONG MaxRefCount,
            LPTSTR SemaphoreName );
```

```
SecAttrs           Security attributes structure
InitCount          Initial value of semaphore
MaxRefCount        Maximum value of semaphore
SemaphoreName      Name of semaphore
```

- ### Associating with a Semaphore

```
HANDLE OpenSemaphore (
            DWORD Access,
            BOOL InheritFlag,
            LPTSTR SemaphoreName );
```

```
Access             Describe nature of access
InheritFlag        Control inheritance of semaphore handle
SemaphoreName      Name of semaphore
```

- ### Releasing a Semaphore

```
BOOL ReleaseSemaphore (
            HANDLE Semaphore,
            LONG RelCount,
            LPLONG PreRelCount );
```

Semaphore	Semaphore handle
IncCount	Value added to semaphore
PreIncCount	Hold IncCount prior to incrementing

EVENTS

- ### Creating an event object

```
HANDLE CreateEvent (
            LPSECURITY_ATTRIBUTES SecAttrs,
            BOOL ManualReset,
            BOOL InitialState,
            LPTSTR EventName );
```

SecAttrs	Security attributes structure
ManualReset	Set for manual or automatic reset
InitialState	Initial state of event
EventName	Name of event

- ### Associating with an event object

```
HANDLE OpenEvent (
            DWORD Access,
            BOOL InheritFlag,
            LPTSTR EventName );
```

Access	Describe access to event
InheritFlag	Control inheritance of event handle
EventName	Name of event

- **Setting, resetting, & pulsing an event object**

```
BOOL SetEvent   ( HANDLE Event );
BOOL ResetEvent ( HANDLE Event );
BOOL PulseEvent ( HANDLE Event );
```

Event   Handle of event

CRITICAL SECTIONS

- **Define critical section structure**

```
CRITICAL_SECTION cs_structure;
```

- **Initializing a critical section structure**

```
InitializeCriticalSection ( &cs_structure );
```

- **Entering and leaving a critical section**

```
EnterCriticalSection ( &cs_structure );
LeaveCriticalSection ( &cs_structure );
```

APPENDIX D

ICS Instructions & Opcodes

Legend:

R_x	General purpose register (32-bit)
F_x	Floating-point register (48-bit)
T_a	Target address
PC	Program counter
(...)	Contents of
SP	Stack pointer

Instruction Specification	Opcode$_{16}$ & Type	Operation performed
LOAD R_x, T_a	01 *RM*	$R_x \leftarrow (T_a)$
STORE R_x, T_a	02 *RM*	$T_a \leftarrow (R_x)$
ADD R_x, T_a	03 *RM*	$R_x \leftarrow R_x + (T_a)$
SUB R_x, T_a	04 *RM*	$R_x \leftarrow R_x - (T_a)$
DIV R_x, T_a	05 *RM*	$R_x \leftarrow [R_x / (T_a)]$
MUL R_x, T_a	06 *RM*	$R_x \leftarrow (R_x) \times (T_a)$
BEQ* T_a	07 *RM*	If $(R_x) = 0$ then PC $\leftarrow T_a$
BLT* T_a	08 *RM*	If $(R_x) < 0$ then PC $\leftarrow T_a$
BGE* T_a	09 *RM*	If $(R_x) \geq 0$ then PC $\leftarrow T_a$
BGT* T_a	0A *RM*	If $(R_x) > 0$ then PC $\leftarrow T_a$
BLE* T_a	0B *RM*	If $(R_x) \leq 0$ then PC $\leftarrow T_a$
BNE* T_a	0C *RM*	If $(R_x) \neq 0$ then PC $\leftarrow T_a$
CLR R_x	0D *RR*	$R_x \leftarrow 0$
NEG R_x	0E *RR*	$R_x \leftarrow -(R_x)$
TR* R_x	0F *RR*	Evaluate (R_x)
POP R_x	10 *RR*	$R_x \leftarrow (SP)$; SP $\leftarrow$ SP + 4
PUSH R_x	11 *RR*	SP $\leftarrow$ SP - 4; (SP) $\leftarrow (R_x)$
CALL T_a	12 *RM*	SP $\leftarrow$ SP - 4 (SP) $\leftarrow$ PC PC $\leftarrow T_a$

---

* Instruction action based on value loaded into R_X from a preceding instruction.

Instruction Specification	Opcode$_{16}$ & Type	Operation performed
RET	13 *RR*	PC ← (SP); SP ← SP + 4
LOADR R$_x$, R$_y$	14 *RR*	R$_x$ ← R$_y$
ADDR R$_x$, R$_y$	15 *RR*	R$_x$ ← R$_x$ + R$_y$
SUBR R$_x$, R$_y$	16 *RR*	R$_x$ ← R$_x$ - R$_y$
MULR R$_x$, R$_y$	17 *RR*	R$_x$ ← R$_x$ × R$_y$
DIVR R$_x$, R$_y$	18 *RR*	R$_x$ ← [R$_x$ / R$_y$]
INCR R$_x$	19 *RR*	R$_x$ ← R$_x$ + 1
DECR R$_x$	1A *RR*	R$_x$ ← R$_x$ - 1
ADDF F$_x$, T$_a$	1B *RM*	F$_x$ ← F$_x$ + (T$_a$)
SUBF F$_x$, T$_a$	1C *RM*	F$_x$ ← F$_x$ - (T$_a$)
MULF F$_x$, T$_a$	1D *RM*	F$_x$ ← F$_x$ × (T$_a$)
DIVF F$_x$, Y$_a$	1E *RM*	F$_x$ ← [F$_x$ / (T$_a$)]
LODF F$_x$, T$_a$	1F *RM*	F$_x$ ← (T$_a$)
STORF F$_x$, T$_a$	20 *RM*	T$_a$ ← (F$_x$)
JMP T$_a$	21 *RM*	PC ← T$_a$

Addressing modes forms:

Bits 39	38	37	36	Mode	Instruction Form
0	0	0	0	PC-relative TA_{LOC} ← (PC) + Displ Rx ← (TA_{LOO})	LOAD R$_x$, Loc
1	0	0	0	Indirect TA_{LOC} ← (Displ. + (PC)) Rx ← (TA_{LOO})	LOAD R$_x$, @Loc
0	1	0	0	Immediate(literal) Rx ← Literal value Loc	LOAD R$_x$, #Loc
0	0	1	0	Indexed TA_{LOC} ← (PC) + Displ + (R$_y$) Rx ← (TA_{LOO})	LOAD R$_x$, Loc (R$_y$)
0	0	0	1	Absolute Rx ← (Loc)	LOAD R$_x$, %Loc

APPENDIX E

The LuxLyk Compiler

This appendix contains the upper
level and syntax parser for the LuxLyk compiler (which is the
most important part of the compiler). The total compiler can be
found on the CD. The code shown here was compiled with Borland C++ Version 5.01, which uses the Rogue Wave implementation of the Standard Template Library.

E.1 PARSER.H—THE HIGH LEVEL PARSER HEADER

```
#ifndef __PARSE__
#define __PARSE__ 1
#include <queue>                    // defines a queue
#include <list>                     //  ...used by the queue
#include "Symbol.h"                 // Symbol / Token class definition
#include "SymSet.h"                 // Symbol Set class definition

class ParseNode                     // the basic parse tree node
{
public:
                ParseNode() {}      // Constructor
    virtual     ~ParseNode() {}     // Destructor
    virtual void Parse()      {}    // Parse source code for this node
    virtual void Generate()   {}    // Generate output code for node
};


typedef queue<ParseNode *, list<ParseNode *> > parseQ;

struct DeclObj                      // the basic identifier definition
{                                   // (holds definition temporarily)
    string      name;               //    name of symbol
    TokenType   kind;               // type of variable (const, var, etc)
    int         level;              //    nesting level of the symbol
    int         n_value;            //    numeric value of the symbol
    string      value;              //    string form of the number
    int         dimen;              //    dimension if an array
    int         size;               //    size of symbol
    TokenType   typeRef;            //    base type of symbol
};
```

```
typedef queue<DeclObj *, list<DeclObj *> > declQ;

class Block;

class Program:    public ParseNode  // The Program (i.e., root) Node
{
   Block         *block;
public:
                  Program();
   virtual void   Parse();
   virtual void   Generate();
};

class Parameters;
class Declaration;
class Body;

class Block:       public ParseNode  // The Program or Procedure Block
{
   Parameters    *param;
   Declaration   *declar;
   Body          *body;
   int            tbl_x, tbl_x0;
   int            dsp_x;
public:
                  Block(int  tx = 0);
   virtual void   Parse();
   virtual void   Generate();
   virtual void   Update_x(int &tx,  int &dx);
};

class ParDeclar;

class Parameters: public ParseNode  // procedure Parameters Node
{
   ParDeclar     *parDeclar;
   int            tbl_x, tbl_x0;
   int            dsp_x;
   int            pcd_x;
public:
                  Parameters(int  tx);
   virtual void   Parse();
   virtual void   Generate();
```

```
            virtual void    Update_x(int &tx,   int &dx);
       };

       class ConstDeclar;
       class VarDeclar;
       class ProcDeclar;

       class Declaration: public ParseNode   // The Declaration Dispatcher
       {
            ConstDeclar    *constDeclar;
            VarDeclar      *varDeclar;
            ProcDeclar     *procDeclar;
            int             tbl_x;
            int             dsp_x;
       public:
                            Declaration(int  tx);
            virtual void    Parse();
            virtual void    Generate();
            virtual void    Update_x(int &tx,   int &dx);
       };

       class Body:         public ParseNode   // The Program or Procedure Body
       {
            ParseNode      *statementList;
            symSet         *untilSyms;
            int             tbl_x, tbl_x0;
            int             dsp_x;
            int             pcd_x;
       public:
                            Body(int  tx,   int  dx,   int  tx0);
            virtual void    Parse();                                          •
            virtual void    Generate();
            virtual void    Update_x(int &tx,   int &dx);
       };

       class ParDeclar: public ParseNode   // Node for declaring parameters
       {
            declQ          *parameters;
            TokenType       typeRef;
            int             typeSize;
            int             tbl_x;
            int             dsp_x;
       public:
                            ParDeclar(int tx,   int dx);
```

```
   virtual void   Parse();
   virtual void   Generate();
   virtual void   Update_x(int &tx,   int &dx);
};


class ConstDeclar: public ParseNode  // Node for declaring constants
{
   declQ          *constants;
   int            tbl_x;
   int            dsp_x;
 public:
                  ConstDeclar(int tx,   int dx);
   virtual void   Parse();
   virtual void   Generate();
   virtual void   Update_x(int &tx,   int &dx);
};


class VarDeclar:  public ParseNode   // Node for declaring variables
{
   declQ          *variables;
   int            tbl_x;
   int            dsp_x;
 public:
                  VarDeclar(int tx,   int dx);
   virtual void   Parse();
   virtual void   Generate();
   virtual void   Update_x(int &tx,   int &dx);
};


class ProcDeclar: public ParseNode   // Node for declaring procedures
{
   Block          *procedure;
   int            tbl_x;
   int            dsp_x;
public:
                  ProcDeclar(int tx,   int dx);
   virtual void   Parse();
   virtual void   Generate();
   virtual void   Update_x(int &tx,   int &dx);
};


   #endif
```

E.2 Parser.cpp—The High Level Parser

```
#include <stdlib.h>              // defines atoi(), etc
#include <ctype.h>               // defines isdigit(), etc
#include "Parser.h"              // Parser class definition
#include "Statemen.h"            // StatementList class definition
#include "Symbol.h"              // Symbol / Token class definition
#include "SymbolTa.h"            // Symbol Table class definition
#include "Code.h"                // Code class definition
#include "Coproces.h"            // defines monitor

   Symbol          *Sym;         // lex analyser
   SymbolTable     symbolTable;  // symbol table
   Code            code;         // code ADT
   Level           level;        // nesting level
   decl_beg_symbols dclr_beg_sym; // declaration beginning symbols
   stmt_beg_symbols stmt_beg_sym; // statement beginning symbols
   extern  char    file_name[80]; // name of file being compiled
   extern  monitor  monitorBlock; // monitor control

//  Program class  ----------------------------------------------

      Program::Program()
{  Sym = new Symbol();  }

void  Program::Parse()
{
   Token   *token;
   block = new Block;
   block->Parse();
   block->Generate();
   delete block;
   token = Sym->getSymbol();
   if (token->Token != Period)
      Sym->Message("'.' expected");
}

void  Program::Generate()
{
   FunctType   fct;
   int         lev, val, dim, siz, done, i = 0;
   string      name;
   TokenType   kind, typ;
```

```
   do
   {
      done = code.Fetch(fct, lev, val, i);
      if (done)
      {
         cout << i << '\t';
         switch (fct)
         {
            case OPR:   cout << "OPR";   break;
            case LIT:   cout << "LIT";   break;
            case LOD:   cout << "LOD";   break;
            case LODA:  cout << "LODA";  break;
            case LODI:  cout << "LODI";  break;
            case LODX:  cout << "LODX";  break;
            case STO:   cout << "STO";   break;
            case STOI:  cout << "STOI";  break;
            case STOX:  cout << "STOX";  break;
            case CAL:   cout << "CAL";   break;
            case PRC:   cout << "PRC";   break;
            case INT:   cout << "INT";   break;
            case JMP:   cout << "JMP";   break;
            case JPC:   cout << "JPC";   break;
            case CSP:   cout << "CSP";   break;
         }
         cout << '\t' << lev << '\t' << val << endl;
      }
      i++;
   }
   while (done);
   delete Sym;
}


// Block class  -----------------------------------------------------

      Block::Block(int tx)
{  tbl_x = tx;     tbl_x0 = tx;  }

void  Block::Parse()
{
   Token     *token;
   param = new Parameters(tbl_x);
   param->Parse();
   param->Generate();
```

```
      param->Update_x(tbl_x, dsp_x);
      delete param;
      if (level.get() > 0 || monitorBlock.isEnabled())
      {
         token = Sym->getSymbol();
         if (token->Token != Semicol)
            Sym->Message("`;' expected");
      }
      declar = new Declaration(tbl_x);
      declar->Parse();
      declar->Generate();
      declar->Update_x(tbl_x, dsp_x);
      delete declar;
      body = new Body(tbl_x, dsp_x, tbl_x0);
      body->Parse();
      body->Generate();
      body->Update_x(tbl_x, dsp_x);
      delete body;
}


void  Block::Generate()  {}


void  Block::Update_x(int &tx,  int &dx)
{  tx = tbl_x;   dx = dsp_x;  }


//  Parameters class  ---------------------------------------------


      Parameters::Parameters(int  tx)
{  tbl_x = tx;    tbl_x0 = tx;     dsp_x = 0;  }


void  Parameters::Parse()
{
   if (level.get() != 0 || monitorBlock.isEnabled())
   {
      parDeclar = new ParDeclar(tbl_x, 0);
      parDeclar->Parse();
      parDeclar->Generate();
      parDeclar->Update_x(tbl_x, dsp_x);
   }
}


void  Parameters::Generate()
{
   code.Enter (JMP, 0, 0, pcd_x);
```

```
        symbolTable.FixValue ( pcd_x - 1,   tbl_x0 );
}


void  Parameters::Update_x(int &tx,  int &dx)
{  tx = tbl_x;   dx = dsp_x;  }


//  Declaration class  -----------------------------------------

        Declaration::Declaration(int  tx)
{
    tbl_x = tx;        // table storage index
    if (monitorBlock.isEnabled() && level.get() == 0)
        dsp_x = monitorBlock.getDisplacement();
    else
        dsp_x = 3;     // base offset value (room for SL, DL, & RA)
}


void  Declaration::Parse()
{
    Token      *token;
    TokenType  sym;
    token = Sym->getNewSymbol();
    sym   = token->Token;
    while ( dclr_beg_sym.contains(sym) )
    {
        switch (sym)
        {
          case constSym:
              constDeclar = new ConstDeclar(tbl_x, dsp_x);
              constDeclar->Parse();
              constDeclar->Generate();
              constDeclar->Update_x(tbl_x, dsp_x);
              delete constDeclar;
              break;
          case varSym:
              varDeclar   = new VarDeclar(tbl_x, dsp_x);
              varDeclar->Parse();
              varDeclar->Generate();
              varDeclar->Update_x(tbl_x, dsp_x);
              delete varDeclar;
              break;
          case procSym:
          case functSym:
          case Monitor:
```

```
                procDeclar  = new ProcDeclar(tbl_x, dsp_x);
                procDeclar->Parse();
                procDeclar->Generate();
                procDeclar->Update_x(tbl_x, dsp_x);
                delete procDeclar;
                break;
        }
        token = Sym->getSymbol();
        sym   = token->Token;
        if ( ! ( dclr_beg_sym.contains(sym)
              || stmt_beg_sym.contains(sym)
              || sym == Ident) )   // Ident also begins a statement
        {
            Sym->Message("Declaration or statement expected");
            //        try to get back in sync
            while ( ! ( dclr_beg_sym.contains(sym)
                     || stmt_beg_sym.contains(sym)
                     || sym == Ident
                     || sym == Period || sym == Semicol) )
            {
                token = Sym->getNewSymbol();
                sym   = token->Token;
            }
        }
    }
}


void  Declaration::Generate()  {}

void  Declaration::Update_x(int &tx,  int &dx)
{  tx = tbl_x;    dx = dsp_x;  }

// Body class  ---------------------------------------------------------

     Body::Body(int  tx,  int  dx,  int  tx0)
{  tbl_x = tx;        tbl_x0 = tx0;       dsp_x = dx;  }

void  Body::Parse()
{
    Token      *token;
    TokenType  sym;
    token = Sym->getSymbol();
    sym   = token->Token;
    if (sym == beginSym)
```

```
      {
         token = Sym->getNewSymbol();
         sym   = token->Token;
      }
      else
         Sym->Message("`BEGIN' expected");

      untilSyms = new symSet;
      untilSyms->insert(endSym);
      statementList = new StatementList(untilSyms, tbl_x);
      statementList->Parse();
      delete untilSyms;

      token = Sym->getSymbol();
      sym   = token->Token;
      if (sym != endSym)
         Sym->Message("`END' expected");
      token = Sym->getNewSymbol();
      sym   = token->Token;
   }

   void  Body::Generate()
   {
      string      name, gate = "mon$tor";
      TokenType   kind;
      int         lev, val, adr, dim, pos;
      code.Enter(INT, 0, dsp_x, pcd_x);
      symbolTable.Examine(name, kind, lev, val, dim, tbl_x0);
      code.FixValue(pcd_x - 1, val);
      symbolTable.FixValue(pcd_x - 1, tbl_x0);
      if (monitorBlock.isEnabled() && level.get() <= 1)
      {
         pos = symbolTable.Position(gate, tbl_x);
         symbolTable.Examine(name, kind, lev, val, dim, pos);
         if (level.get() == 0)
         {
            code.Enter(LODA, level.get() - lev, val, pcd_x);
            code.Enter( LIT,                 0,   1, pcd_x);
            code.Enter( OPR,                 0,  28, pcd_x);
         }
         else
         {
            code.Enter( LOD, level.get() - lev, val, pcd_x);
            code.Enter( OPR,                 0,  29, pcd_x);
```

```
        }
    }
    statementList->Generate();
    if (level.get() == 0 && monitorBlock.isEnabled())
    {
        code.Enter(INT, 0, -dsp_x, pcd_x);
        code.Enter(JMP, 0,      0, pcd_x);
        symbolTable.Examine(name, kind, lev, adr, dim,      0);
        symbolTable.Examine(name, kind, lev, val, dim, tbl_x0);
        code.FixValue(val, adr);
        symbolTable.FixValue(pcd_x - 1, 0);
    }
    else
        code.Enter(OPR, 0, 0, pcd_x);
}


void  Body::Update_x(int &tx,  int &dx)
{  tx = tbl_x;   dx = dsp_x;  }

//  ParDeclar class  ----------------------------------------------------

    ParDeclar::ParDeclar(int tx,  int dx)
{  parameters = new declQ;   tbl_x = tx;   dsp_x = dx;  }

void  ParDeclar::Parse()
{
    Token     *token;
    TokenType  sym;
    DeclObj   *parDef;
    declQ     *parList;
    string     name;
    TokenType  kind;
    int        lev, val, dim, pos;
    token = Sym->getNewSymbol();
    sym   = token->Token;
    if (sym == lParen)
    {
        if (level.get() == 0 && monitorBlock.isEnabled())
            Sym->Message("Monitor cannot have parameters");
        token = Sym->getNewSymbol();
        sym   = token->Token;
        do
        {
            parList = new declQ;
```

```
if (sym == Ident)
{
   parDef = new DeclObj;
   parDef->name  = *token->Value;
   parDef->kind  = varSym;
   parDef->level = level.get();
   token = Sym->getNewSymbol();
   sym   = token->Token;
   if (sym == lBrkt)     // is an array
   {
      token = Sym->getNewSymbol();
      sym   = token->Token;
      switch (sym)
      {
         case Number:
            parDef->dimen = atoi( token->Value->data() );
            break;
         case Ident:
            pos=symbolTable.Position(*token->Value, tbl_x);
            if (pos == 0)
               Sym->Message("Undefined variable");
            else
            {
               symbolTable.Examine(name,          kind, lev,
                                   parDef->dimen, dim, pos);
               if (kind != constSym)
                  Sym->Message("Constant expected");
            }
            break;
         default:
            Sym->Message("Constant expected");
      }
      token = Sym->getNewSymbol();
      sym   = token->Token;
      if (sym == rBrkt)
      {
         token = Sym->getNewSymbol();
         sym   = token->Token;
      }
      else
         Sym->Message("']' expected");
   }
   else
      parDef->dimen = 1;       // not an array
```

```
                parList->push(parDef);
         }
         else
            Sym->Message("Identifier expected");
         while (sym == Comma)
         {
            token = Sym->getNewSymbol();
            sym   = token->Token;
            if (sym == Ident)
            {
               parDef = new DeclObj;
               parDef->name = *token->Value;
               parDef->kind = varSym;
               parDef->level = level.get();
               token = Sym->getNewSymbol();
               sym   = token->Token;
               if (sym == lBrkt)     // is an array
               {
                  token = Sym->getNewSymbol();
                  sym   = token->Token;
                  switch (sym)
                  {
                     case Number:
                        parDef->dimen = atoi(token->Value->data());
                        break;
                     case Ident:
                        pos = symbolTable.Position(
                        *token->Value, tbl_x);
                        if (pos == 0)
                           Sym->Message("Undefined variable");
                        else
                        {
                           symbolTable.Examine(name,      kind, lev,
                                           parDef->dimen, dim, pos);
                           if (kind != constSym)
                           Sym->Message("Constant expected");
                        }
                        break;
                     default:
                        Sym->Message("Constant expected");
                  }
                  token = Sym->getNewSymbol();
                  sym   - token->Token;
                  if (sym == rBrkt)
```

```
            {
                token = Sym->getNewSymbol();
                sym   = token->Token;
            }
            else
                Sym->Message("']' expected");
        }
        else
            parDef->dimen = 1;    // not an array
        parList->push(parDef);
    }
    else
        Sym->Message("Identifier expected");
}
if (sym == Colon)
{
    token = Sym->getNewSymbol();
    sym   = token->Token;
    switch (sym)
    {
        case intSym:
            typeRef  = intSym;
            typeSize = 1;
            break;
        case charSym:
            typeRef  = charSym;
            typeSize = 1;
            break;
        case realSym:
            typeRef  = realSym;
            typeSize = realSize;
            break;
        case strSym:
            typeRef  = strSym;
            token = Sym->getNewSymbol();
            sym   = token->Token;
            if (sym == lBrkt)
            {
                token = Sym->getNewSymbol();
                sym   = token->Token;
                switch (sym)
                {
                    case Number:
                        typeSize = atoi(token->Value->data());
```

```
                              break;
                        case Ident:
                            pos = symbolTable.Position(
                            *token->Value, tbl_x);
                            if (pos == 0)
                                Sym->Message("Undefined variable");
                            else
                            {
                                symbolTable.Examine(name,   kind, lev,
                                                    typeSize, dim, pos);
                                if (kind != constSym)
                                    Sym->Message("Constant expected");
                            }
                            break;
                        default:
                            Sym->Message("Constant expected");
                    }
                    token = Sym->getNewSymbol();
                    sym   = token->Token;
                    if (sym != rBrkt)
                        Sym->Message("']' expected");
                }
                else
                    Sym->Message("String size expected");
                break;
            default:
                Sym->Message("Type reference expected");
                break;
        }
        token = Sym->getNewSymbol();
        sym   = token->Token;
    }
    else
    {
        typeRef  = intSym;
        typeSize = 1;
    }
    while ( ! parList->empty() )
    {
        parDef = parList->front();
        parList->pop();
        parDef->typeRef = typeRef;
        parDef->size    = typeSize;
        parameters->push(parDef);
```

```
      }
      if (sym == rParen || sym == Semicol)
      {
         token = Sym->getNewSymbol();
         sym   = token->Token;
      }
      else
         Sym->Message("`)' expected");
      delete parList;
   }
   while (sym == Ident);
}
if (sym == Colon)
{
   symbolTable.Examine(name, kind, lev, val, dim, tbl_x);
   if (kind != functSym)
      Sym->Message("Use 'function' to return a type");
   token = Sym->getNewSymbol();
   sym   = token->Token;
   switch (sym)
   {
      case intSym:
         typeRef  = intSym;
         typeSize = 1;
         break;
      case charSym:
         typeRef  = charSym;
         typeSize = 1;
         break;
      case realSym:
         typeRef  = realSym;
         typeSize = realSize;
         break;
      case strSym:
         typeRef  = strSym;
         token = Sym->getNewSymbol();
         sym   = token->Token;
         if (sym == lBrkt)
         {
            token = Sym->getNewSymbol();
            sym   = token->Token;
            switch (sym)
            {
               case Number:
```

```
                        typeSize = atoi(token->Value->data());
                        break;
                    case Ident:
                        pos = symbolTable.Position(
                        *token->Value, tbl_x);
                        if (pos == 0)
                            Sym->Message("Undefined variable");
                        else
                        {
                            symbolTable.Examine(name,      kind, lev,
                                                 typeSize,  dim, pos);
                            if (kind != constSym)
                                Sym->Message("Constant expected");
                        }
                        break;
                    default:
                        Sym->Message("Constant expected");
                }
                token = Sym->getNewSymbol();
                sym   = token->Token;
                if (sym != rBrkt)
                    Sym->Message("']' expected");
            }
            else
                Sym->Message("String size expected");
            break;
        default:
            Sym->Message("Type reference expected");
            break;
        }
        token = Sym->getNewSymbol();
        sym   = token->Token;
    }
    else
    {
        typeRef  = intSym;
        typeSize = 1;
    }
}


void  ParDeclar::Generate()
{
    DeclObj    *parDef;
    string      name;
```

```
TokenType    kind;
int          lev, val, dim;
int          entries, size, i;

if ( ! parameters->empty() )
{
   entries = parameters->size();
   size = 0;
   for (i = 0;  i < entries;  i++)
   {
      parDef = parameters->front();
      parameters->pop();
      size += parDef->dimen * parDef->size;
      parameters->push(parDef);
   }
   dsp_x = - size;
}
else
   dsp_x = 0;
symbolTable.Examine(name, kind, lev, val, dim, tbl_x);
if (kind == functSym)
{
   symbolTable.Enter(name,      kind,      lev,    val,
                          1, typeSize, typeRef, tbl_x);

   name = "ret$val";
   symbolTable.Enter(name,    varSym, lev + 1, dsp_x - typeSize,
                          1, typeSize, typeRef,            ++tbl_x);
}
if ( ! parameters->empty() )
{
   while ( ! parameters->empty() )
   {
      parDef = parameters->front();
      parameters->pop();
      symbolTable.Enter(parDef->name, parDef->kind, parDef->level,
                          dsp_x,         parDef->dimen, parDef->size,
                          parDef->typeRef, ++tbl_x);
      dsp_x += parDef->dimen * parDef->size;
      delete parDef;
   }
}
}
```

```
void  ParDeclar::Update_x(int &tx,  int &dx)
{  tx = tbl_x;   dx = dsp_x;  }


//  ConstDeclar class  -------------------------------------------

      ConstDeclar::ConstDeclar(int tx,  int dx)
{  constants = new declQ;   tbl_x = tx;   dsp_x = dx;  }

void  ConstDeclar::Parse()
{
    Token      *token;
    TokenType  sym;
    DeclObj    *constDef;
    token = Sym->getNewSymbol();
    sym   = token->Token;
    do
    {
       if (sym == Ident)
       {
          constDef = new DeclObj;
          constDef->name  = *token->Value;
          constDef->kind  = constSym;
          constDef->level = level.get();
          token = Sym->getNewSymbol();
          sym   = token->Token;
          if (sym == Equal || sym == Becomes)
          {
             if (sym == Becomes)
                Sym->Message("Replace `:=' by `='");
             token = Sym->getNewSymbol();
             sym   - token->Token;
             constDef->n_value = +1;
             if (sym == Plus || sym == Minus)
             {
                if (sym == Minus)                    // save sign information
                   constDef->n_value = -1;
                else
                   constDef->n_value = +1;
                token = Sym->getNewSymbol();
                sym   = token->Token;
             }
             if (sym -- Number || sym == Ident)
             {
                constDef->value = *token->Value;
```

```
            constants->push(constDef);
            token = Sym->getNewSymbol();
            sym   = token->Token;
          }
          else
            Sym->Message("Number or Ident expected");
        }
        else
          Sym->Message("`=' expected");
      }
      else
        Sym->Message("Identifier expected");
      if (sym == Semicol)
      {
        token = Sym->getNewSymbol();
        sym   = token->Token;
      }
      else
        Sym->Message("`;' expected");
    }
    while (sym == Ident);
}


void  ConstDeclar::Generate()
{
    DeclObj    *constDef;
    char       ch;
    int        numb, dim;
    string     name;
    TokenType  kind;
    int        pos, lev;
    while ( ! constants->empty() )
    {
      constDef = constants->front();
      constants->pop();
      ch = constDef->value[0];
      if (isdigit(ch))
        numb = atoi(constDef->value.data());
      else
      {
        pos = symbolTable.Position(constDef->value, tbl_x);
        symbolTable.Examine(name, kind, lev, numb, dim, pos);
      }
      numb *= constDef->n_value;        // restore sign information
```

```
      symbolTable.Enter(
              constDef->name, constDef->kind, constDef->level,
                        numb,                0,            ++tbl_x);
      delete constDef;
   }
}


void  ConstDeclar::Update_x(int &tx,  int &dx)
{  tx = tbl_x;   dx = dsp_x;  }


//  VarDeclar class  -------------------------------------------------

      VarDeclar::VarDeclar(int tx,  int dx)
{  variables = new declQ;   tbl_x = tx;   dsp_x = dx;  }

void  VarDeclar::Parse()
{
   Token      *token;
   TokenType  sym;
   DeclObj    *varDef;
   declQ      *varList;
   string     name;
   TokenType  kind, typeRef;
   int        lev, dim, typeSize, pos;
   token = Sym->getNewSymbol();
   sym  = token->Token;
   do
   {
      varList = new declQ;
      if (sym == Ident)
      {
         varDef = new DeclObj;
         varDef->name    = *token->Value;
         varDef->kind    =  varSym;
         varDef->level   =  level.get();
         token = Sym->getNewSymbol();
         sym   = token->Token;
         if (sym == lBrkt)    // is an array
         {
            token = Sym->getNewSymbol();
            sym   = token->Token;
            switch (sym)
            {
```

```
            case Number:
               varDef->dimen = atoi( token->Value->data() );
               break;
            case Ident:
               pos = symbolTable.Position(*token->Value, tbl_x);
               if (pos == 0)
                  Sym->Message("Undefined variable");
               else
               {
                  symbolTable.Examine(name,         kind, lev,
                                       varDef->dimen, dim,  pos);
                  if (kind != constSym)
                     Sym->Message("Constant expected");
               }
               break;
            default:
               Sym->Message("Constant expected");
         }
         token = Sym->getNewSymbol();
         sym   = token->Token;
         if (sym == rBrkt)
         {
            token = Sym->getNewSymbol();
            sym   = token->Token;
         }
         else
            Sym->Message("']' expected");
      }
      else
         varDef->dimen = 1;      // not an array
      varList->push(varDef);
   }
   else
      Sym->Message("Identifier expected");
   while (sym == Comma)
   {
      token = Sym->getNewSymbol();
      sym   = token->Token;
      if (sym == Ident)
      {
         varDef = new DeclObj;
         varDef->name  = *token->Value;
         varDef->kind  = varSym;
         varDef->level = level.get();
```

```
token = Sym->getNewSymbol();
sym   = token->Token;
if (sym == lBrkt)     // is an array
{
    token = Sym->getNewSymbol();
    sym   = token->Token;
    switch (sym)
    {
        case Number:
            varDef->dimen = atoi( token->Value->data() );
            break;
        case Ident:
            pos = symbolTable.Position(
            *token->Value, tbl_x);
            if (pos == 0)
                Sym->Message("Undefined variable");
            else
            {
                symbolTable.Examine(name,          kind, lev,
                                    varDef->dimen,  dim, pos);
                if (kind != constSym)
                    Sym->Message("Constant expected");
            }
            break;
        default:
            Sym->Message("Constant expected");
    }
    token = Sym->getNewSymbol();
    sym   = token->Token;
    if (sym == rBrkt)
    {
        token = Sym->getNewSymbol();
        sym   = token->Token;
    }
    else
        Sym->Message("']' expected");
}
else
    varDef->dimen = 1;    // not an array
varList->push(varDef);
}
else
    Sym->Message("Identifier expected");
}
```

```
if (sym == Colon)
{
   token = Sym->getNewSymbol();
   sym   = token->Token;
   switch (sym)
   {
      case intSym:
         typeRef  = intSym;
         typeSize = 1;
         break;
      case charSym:
         typeRef  = charSym;
         typeSize = 1;
         break;
      case realSym:
         typeRef  = realSym;
         typeSize = realSize;
         break;
      case strSym:
         typeRef  = strSym;
         token = Sym->getNewSymbol();
         sym   = token->Token;
         if (sym == lBrkt)
         {
            token = Sym->getNewSymbol();
            sym   = token->Token;
            switch (sym)
            {
               case Number:
                  typeSize = atoi( token->Value->data() );
                  break;
               case Ident:
                  pos = symbolTable.Position(
                  *token->Value, tbl_x);
                  if (pos == 0)
                     Sym->Message("Undefined variable");
                  else
                  {
                     symbolTable.Examine(name,     kind, lev,
                                      typeSize,  dim, pos);
                     if (kind != constSym)
                        Sym->Message("Constant expected");
                  }
                  break;
```

```
                                default:
                                    Sym->Message("Constant expected");
                            }
                            token = Sym->getNewSymbol();
                            sym   = token->Token;
                            if (sym != rBrkt)
                                Sym->Message("']' expected");
                        }
                        else
                            Sym->Message("String size expected");
                        break;
                    default:
                        Sym->Message("Type reference expected");
                        break;
                }
                token = Sym->getNewSymbol();
                sym   = token->Token;
            }
            else
            {
                typeRef  = intSym;
                typeSize = 1;
            }
            while ( ! varList->empty() )
            {
                varDef = varList->front();
                varList->pop();
                varDef->typeRef = typeRef;
                varDef->size    = typeSize;
                variables->push(varDef);
            }
            if (sym == Semicol)
            {
                token = Sym->getNewSymbol();
                sym   = token->Token;
            }
            else
                Sym->Message("`;' expected");

            delete varList;
        }
        while (sym == Ident);
    }
```

```
void  VarDeclar::Generate()
{
   DeclObj   *varDef;
   string    gate = "mon$tor";

   if ( level.get() == 0 && monitorBlock.isEnabled()
        && (monitorBlock.getDisplacement() == dsp_x) )
      symbolTable.Enter(
             gate, varSym, 0, dsp_x++,  1, 1, intSym, ++tbl_x);
   while ( ! variables->empty() )
   {
      varDef = variables->front();
      variables->pop();
      symbolTable.Enter(
             varDef->name, varDef->kind, varDef->level,   dsp_x,
             varDef->dimen, varDef->size, varDef->typeRef, ++tbl_x);
      dsp_x += varDef->dimen * varDef->size;
      delete varDef;
   }
}

void  VarDeclar::Update_x(int &tx,  int &dx)
{  tx = tbl_x;   dx = dsp_x;  }

//  ProcDeclar class  ---------------------------------------------

      ProcDeclar::ProcDeclar(int tx,  int dx)
{  tbl_x = tx;   dsp_x = dx;  }

void  ProcDeclar::Parse()
{
   Token      *token;
   TokenType  sym, procType, kind, typ;
   string     name, blank = " ", gate = "mon$tor";
   int        tbl_x0, tx, lev, val, dim, siz;
   token    = Sym->getSymbol();      // determine if
   procType = token->Token;          // PROCEDURE, FUNCTION or MONITOR
   token    = Sym->getNewSymbol();
   sym      = token->Token;
   if (sym == Ident)
   {
      symbolTable.Enter(
          *token->Value, procType, level.get(), 0, 0, ++tbl_x);
      if (procType == Monitor)
```

```
        {
           tbl_x0 = tbl_x;
           monitorBlock.Enable(dsp_x);
        }
        else
           level.inc();
        procedure = new Block(tbl_x);
        procedure->Parse();
        procedure->Generate();
        if (procType == Monitor)
        {
           procedure->Update_x(tbl_x, dsp_x);
           for (tx = tbl_x0;  tx <= tbl_x;  tx++)
           {
              symbolTable.Examine(
                  name, kind, lev, val, dim,  siz, typ, tx);
              if (kind == constSym || kind == varSym
                                   || kind == Monitor)
                 symbolTable.Enter(
                     blank, kind, lev, val, dim,  siz, typ, tx);
           }
           monitorBlock.Disable();
        }
        else
           level.dec();
     }
     else
        Sym->Message("Identifier expected");
     token = Sym->getSymbol();
     sym   = token->Token;
     if (sym == Semicol)
     {
        token = Sym->getNewSymbol();
        sym   = token->Token;
     }
     else
        Sym->Message("`;' expected");
}

void ProcDeclar::Generate()  {}

void ProcDeclar::Update_x(int &tx,  int &dx)
{   tx = tbl_x;    dx = dsp_x;   }
```

E.3 STATEMENT.H—THE STATEMENT PARSER HEADER

```
#ifndef __STATEMENT__
#define __STATEMENT__ 1
#include "Parser.h"        // Parser class definitions
#include "Expressi.h"      // Condition class definitions

struct ReadObj            // used for reading indexed variables
{
    DeclObj     var;
    Condition  *index;
};

typedef queue<ReadObj *, list<ReadObj *> > readobjQ;

class Statement: public ParseNode
{
    ParseNode      *statement;
    symSet         *untilSyms;
    int             tbl_x;
    int             dsp_x;
    int             pcd_x;
public:
                Statement(symSet *UntilSyms, int tx);
                ~Statement();
    virtual void  Parse();
    virtual void  Generate();
};

class StatementList: public ParseNode
{
    parseQ         *statements;
    symSet         *untilSyms;
    int             tbl_x;
    int             dsp_x;
    int             pcd_x;
public:
                StatementList(symSet *UntilSyms, int tx);
                ~StatementList();
    virtual void  Parse();
    virtual void  Generate();
};
```

```
class assignStatement:  public ParseNode
{
   Condition     *index;
   Condition     *expression;
   symSet        *untilSyms;
   symSet        *indexSyms;
   TokenType      typ;
   int            lev, val, dim, siz;
   int            tbl_x;
   int            dsp_x;
   int            pcd_x;
public:
                  assignStatement(symSet *UntilSyms, int tx);
                  ~assignStatement();
   virtual void   Parse();
   virtual void   Generate();
};


class callOrAssign:  public ParseNode
{
   ParseNode     *statement;
   symSet        *untilSyms;
   symSet        *endSyms;
   int            tbl_x;
   int            dsp_x;
   int            pcd_x;
public:
                  callOrAssign(symSet *UntilSyms, int tx);
                  ~callOrAssign();
   virtual void   Parse();
   virtual void   Generate();
};


class callStatement:  public ParseNode
{
   ParseNode     *procedure;
   symSet        *untilSyms;
   symSet        *endSyms;
   int            tbl_x;
   int            dsp_x;
   int            pcd_x;
public:
                  callStatement(symSet *UntilSyms, int tx);
                  ~callStatement();
```

```
   virtual void   Parse();
   virtual void   Generate();
};


class cobegStatement:  public ParseNode
{
   symSet          *untilSyms;
   int             tbl_x;
public:
                   cobegStatement(symSet *UntilSyms, int tx);
                   ~cobegStatement();
   virtual void   Parse();
   virtual void   Generate();
};


class coendStatement:  public ParseNode
{
   symSet          *untilSyms;
   int             tbl_x;
   int             pcd_x;
public:
                   coendStatement(symSet *UntilSyms, int tx);
                   ~coendStatement();
   virtual void   Parse();
   virtual void   Generate();
};


class conditStatement:  public ParseNode
{
   Condition       *index;
   symSet          *untilSyms;
   symSet          *indexSyms;
   int             lev, val, dim;
   int             tbl_x;
   int             dsp_x;
   int             pcd_x;
public:
                   conditStatement(symSet *UntilSyms, int tx);
                   ~conditStatement();
   virtual void   Parse();
   virtual void   Generate();
};


class delayStatement:  public ParseNode
```

```
{
    Condition      *index;
    symSet         *untilSyms;
    symSet         *indexSyms;
    int             lev, val, dim;
    int             tbl_x;
    int             dsp_x;
    int             pcd_x;
public:
                    delayStatement(symSet *UntilSyms, int tx);
                    ~delayStatement();
    virtual void   Parse();
    virtual void   Generate();
};


class forStatement:  public ParseNode
{
    Condition      *expression1;
    Condition      *expression2;
    ParseNode      *statementList;
    symSet         *untilSyms1;
    symSet         *untilSyms2;
    symSet         *endSyms;
    int             pos;
    int             lev, val, dim;
    int             tbl_x;
    int             dsp_x;
    int             pcd_x;
  public:
                    forStatement(symSet *UntilSyms, int tx);
                    ~forStatement();
    virtual void   Parse();
    virtual void   Generate();
};


class ifStatement:  public ParseNode
{
    Condition      *condition;
    ParseNode      *t_statementList;
    ParseNode      *e_statementList;
    symSet         *untilSyms1;
    symSet         *untilSyms2;
    symSet         *endSyms;
    int             tbl_x;
```

```
    int             dsp_x;
    int             pcd_x;
public:
                    ifStatement(symSet *UntilSyms, int tx);
                    ~ifStatement();
    virtual void    Parse();
    virtual void    Generate();
};


class initStatement:  public ParseNode
{
    Condition       *index;
    Condition       *expression;
    symSet          *untilSyms;
    symSet          *indexSyms;
    int             lev, val, dim;
    int             tbl_x;
    int             dsp_x;
    int             pcd_x;
public:
                    initStatement(symSet *UntilSyms, int tx);
                    ~initStatement();
    virtual void    Parse();
    virtual void    Generate();
};


class procedureCall:  public ParseNode
{
    conditQ         *exprList;
    symSet          *untilSyms;
    symSet          *endSyms;
    TokenType       kind;
    int             lev, val, dim;
    int             tbl_x;
    int             dsp_x;
    int             pcd_x;
public:
                    procedureCall(symSet *UntilSyms, int tx);
                    ~procedureCall();
    virtual void    Parse();
    virtual void    Generate();
};


class readStatement:  public ParseNode
```

```
{
    readobjQ        *varList;
    symSet          *untilSyms;
    int             tbl_x;
    int             dsp_x;
    int             pcd_x;
public:
                    readStatement(symSet *UntilSyms, int tx);
                    ~readStatement();
    virtual void    Parse();
    virtual void    Generate();
};


class repeatStatement:  public ParseNode
{
    Condition       *condition;
    ParseNode       *statementList;
    symSet          *untilSyms;
    symSet          *endSyms;
    int             tbl_x;
    int             dsp_x;
    int             pcd_x;
public:
                    repeatStatement(symSet *UntilSyms, int tx);
                    ~repeatStatement();
    virtual void    Parse();
    virtual void    Generate();
};


class returnStatement:  public ParseNode
{

    Condition       *expression;
    symSet          *untilSyms;
    TokenType       typ;
    int             lev, val, dim, siz;
    int             tbl_x;
    int             dsp_x;
    int             pcd_x;
public:
                    returnStatement(symSet *UntilSyms, int tx);
                    ~returnStatement();
    virtual void    Parse();
    virtual void    Generate();
```

```
    };

    class sendStatement: public ParseNode
    {
        Condition      *index;
        symSet         *untilSyms;
        symSet         *indexSyms;
        int            lev, val, dim;
        int            tbl_x;
        int            dsp_x;
        int            pcd_x;
    public:
                       sendStatement(symSet *UntilSyms, int tx);
                       ~sendStatement();
        virtual void   Parse();
        virtual void   Generate();
    };

    class signalStatement: public ParseNode
    {
        Condition      *index;
        symSet         *untilSyms;
        symSet         *indexSyms;
        int            lev, val, dim;
        int            tbl_x;
        int            dsp_x;
        int            pcd_x;
    public:
                       signalStatement(symSet *UntilSyms, int tx);
                       ~signalStatement();
        virtual void   Parse();
        virtual void   Generate();
    };

    class suspendStatement: public ParseNode
    {
        symSet         *untilSyms;
        int            tbl_x;
        int            pcd_x;
    public:
                       suspendStatement(symSet *UntilSyms, int tx);
                       ~suspendStatement();
        virtual void   Parse();
        virtual void   Generate();
```

```
    };

    class waitStatement:  public ParseNode
    {
        Condition      *index;
        symSet         *untilSyms;
        symSet         *indexSyms;
        int            lev, val, dim;
        int            tbl_x;
        int            dsp_x;
        int            pcd_x;
    public:
                       waitStatement(symSet *UntilSyms, int tx);
                       ~waitStatement();
        virtual void   Parse();
        virtual void   Generate();
    };

    class whileStatement:  public ParseNode
    {
        Condition      *condition;
        ParseNode      *statementList;
        symSet         *untilSyms;
        symSet         *endSyms;
        int            tbl_x;
        int            dsp_x;
        int            pcd_x;
    public:
                       whileStatement(symSet *UntilSyms, int tx);
                       ~whileStatement();
        virtual void   Parse();
        virtual void   Generate();
    };

    class writeStatement:  public ParseNode
    {
        conditQ        *exprList;
        symSet         *untilSyms;
        symSet         *endSyms;
        int            tbl_x;
        int            dsp_x;
        int            pcd_x;
    public:
                       writeStatement(symSet *UntilSyms, int tx);
```

```
                    ~writeStatement();
    virtual void   Parse();
    virtual void   Generate();
};


#endif
```

E.4 STATEMENT.CPP—THE STATEMENT PARSER

```
#include "Statemen.h"    // Statement Parser class definitions
#include <stdlib.h>      // defines atoi(), etc
#include <ctype.h>       // defines isdigit(), etc
#include "Parser.h"      // Parser class definition
#include "Expressi.h"    // Condition Parser class definition
#include "Symbol.h"      // Symbol / Token class definition
#include "SymbolTa.h"    // Symbol Table class definition
#include "Code.h"        // Code class definition
#include "Coproces.h"    // Coprocessing / Monitor class definitions

    extern Symbol           *Sym;           // lex analyser
    extern SymbolTable      symbolTable;     // symbol table
    extern Code             code;            // code ADT
    extern Level            level;           // nesting level
    extern decl_beg_symbols dclr_beg_sym;    // declaration symbols
    extern stmt_beg_symbols stmt_beg_sym;    // statement symbols
    extern fctr_beg_symbols fctr_beg_sym;    // factor symbols
           coprocess        coprocess;       // co-processing control
           monitor          monitorBlock;    // Monitor control

//  Statement class  -------------------------------------------------

    Statement::Statement(symSet *UntilSyms, int tx)
{  untilSyms = new symSet(*UntilSyms);    tbl_x = tx;  }


    Statement::~Statement()
{  delete untilSyms;  }


void  Statement::Parse()
{
    Token    *token;
    TokenType sym;
    token = Sym->getSymbol();
```

```
sym    = token->Token;
if (sym == beginSym)
{
    Sym->Message("delete `BEGIN'");
    token = Sym->getNewSymbol();
    sym    = token->Token;
}
switch (sym)
{
    case Ident:
        statement = new callOrAssign(untilSyms, tbl_x);       break;
    case callSym:
        statement = new callStatement(untilSyms, tbl_x);      break;
    case cobegSym:
        statement = new cobegStatement(untilSyms, tbl_x);     break;
    case coendSym:
        statement = new coendStatement(untilSyms, tbl_x);     break;
    case Condit:
        statement = new conditStatement(untilSyms, tbl_x);    break;
    case Delay:
        statement = new delayStatement(untilSyms, tbl_x);     break;
    case forSym:
        statement = new forStatement(untilSyms, tbl_x);       break;
    case ifSym:
        statement = new ifStatement(untilSyms, tbl_x);        break;
    case Init:
        statement = new initStatement(untilSyms, tbl_x);      break;
    case readSym:
        statement = new readStatement(untilSyms, tbl_x);      break;
    case returnSym:
        statement = new returnStatement(untilSyms, tbl_x);    break;
    case repeatSym:
        statement = new repeatStatement(untilSyms, tbl_x);    break;
    case Send:
        statement = new sendStatement(untilSyms, tbl_x);      break;
    case Signal:
        statement = new signalStatement(untilSyms, tbl_x);    break;
    case Suspend:
        statement - new suspendStatement(untilSyms, tbl_x);   break;
    case Wait:
        statement = new waitStatement(untilSyms, tbl_x);      break;
    case whileSym:
        statement = new whileStatement(untilSyms, tbl_x);     break;
    case writeSym:
```

```
                statement = new writeStatement(untilSyms, tbl_x);    break;
          default:    // fubar, try next symbol (this one is no good!)
             Sym->Message("Improper symbol beginning statement");
             statement = NULL;
             token = Sym->getNewSymbol();
             sym   = token->Token;
             return;
       }
       statement->Parse();
       token = Sym->getSymbol();
       sym   = token->Token;
       if ( ! (  stmt_beg_sym.contains(sym)
              || dclr_beg_sym.contains(sym)
              || untilSyms->contains(sym)
              || sym == Ident   // Ident also begins a statement
              || sym == Period || sym == Semicol) )
       {
          Sym->Message("Improper symbol before statement");
          //          try to get back in sync
          while ( ! (  stmt_beg_sym.contains(sym)
                    || dclr_beg_sym.contains(sym)
                    || untilSyms->contains(sym)
                    || sym == Ident
                    || sym == Period || sym == Semicol) )
          {
             token = Sym->getNewSymbol();
             sym   = token->Token;
          }
       }
}


void  Statement::Generate()
{
    if (statement != NULL)
    {  statement->Generate();    delete statement;  }
}


//  StatementList class  -----------------------------------------

     StatementList::StatementList(symSet *UntilSyms, int tx)
{
    statements = new parseQ;
    untilSyms  = new symSet(*UntilSyms);
    tbl_x = tx;
```

```
}

        StatementList::~StatementList()
{  delete statements;   delete untilSyms;  }

void  StatementList::Parse()
{
   ParseNode *statement;
   Token     *token;
   TokenType  sym;
   statement = new Statement(untilSyms, tbl_x);
   statement->Parse();
   statements->push(statement);
   token = Sym->getSymbol();
   sym   = token->Token;
   while (  sym == Semicol
         || stmt_beg_sym.contains(sym))
   {
      if (sym != Semicol)
         Sym->Message("insert `;'");
      else
      {
         token = Sym->getNewSymbol();
         sym   = token->Token;
      }
      statement = new Statement(untilSyms, tbl_x);
      statement->Parse();
      statements->push(statement);
      token = Sym->getSymbol();
      sym   = token->Token;
   }
}


void  StatementList::Generate()
{
   ParseNode *statement;
   while ( ! statements->empty() )
   {
      statement = statements->front();
      statements->pop();
      statement->Generate();
      delete statement;
   }
}
```

```
// assignStatement class  ------------------------------------------

      assignStatement::assignStatement(symSet *UntilSyms, int tx)
{
   untilSyms = new symSet(*UntilSyms);
   indexSyms = new symSet(*UntilSyms);
   tbl_x = tx;
}


      assignStatement::~assignStatement()
{ delete untilSyms;   delete indexSyms;  }

void  assignStatement::Parse()
{
   Token      *token;
   TokenType  sym, kind;
   string     name;
   int        pos;
   token = Sym->getSymbol();
   sym   = token->Token;
   pos = symbolTable.Position(*token->Value, tbl_x);
   symbolTable.Examine(name, kind, lev, val, dim, siz, typ, pos);
   token = Sym->getNewSymbol();
   sym   = token->Token;
   if (dim > 1)
   {
      if (sym != lBrkt)
      {
         siz = dim;
         dim = 1;
      }
      else
      {
         token = Sym->getNewSymbol();
         sym   = token->Token;
         indexSyms->insert(rBrkt);
         index = new Condition(indexSyms, tbl_x);
         index->Parse();
         token = Sym->getSymbol();
         sym   = token->Token;
         if (sym != rBrkt)
            Sym->Message("`]' expected");
         else
```

```
        {
            token = Sym->getNewSymbol();
            sym   = token->Token;
        }
    }
}
if (sym != Becomes)
    Sym->Message("`:=' expected");
else
{
    token = Sym->getNewSymbol();
    sym   = token->Token;
}
expression = new Condition(untilSyms, tbl_x);
expression->Parse();
}


void  assignStatement::Generate()
{
    TokenType  type;
    int        size;
    if (dim > 1)
    {
        index->Generate(size, type);
        if (typ != intSym && typ != charSym)
        {
            code.Enter(LIT,                    0, siz, pcd_x);
            code.Enter(OPR,                    0,   4, pcd_x);
            code.Enter(LODA, level.get() - lev, val, pcd_x);
            code.Enter(OPR,                    0,   2, pcd_x);
        }
    }
    else if ((typ != intSym && typ != charSym) || siz != 1)
        code.Enter(LODA, level.get() - lev,     val, pcd_x);
    expression->Generate(size, type);
    delete expression;
    if (   (typ != type || siz != size)
        && (type != strSym  || typ != charSym || size != siz)
        && (type != charSym || typ != strSym  || size != siz) )
        Sym->Message("Incompatible types");
    if ((typ != intSym && typ != charSym) || siz != 1)
        code.Enter(STOI, level.get() - lev, siz - 1, pcd_x);
    else if (dim > 1)
        code.Enter(STOX, level.get() - lev,     val, pcd_x);
```

```
   else
      code.Enter( STO, level.get() - lev,     val, pcd_x);
}

// callOrAssign class ------------------------------------------

      callOrAssign::callOrAssign(symSet *UntilSyms, int tx)
{  untilSyms = new symSet(*UntilSyms);    tbl_x = tx;   }

      callOrAssign::~callOrAssign()
{  delete untilSyms;   }

void  callOrAssign::Parse()
{
   Token       *token;
   TokenType    sym;
   int          pos;
   int          lev, val, dim;
   string       name;
   TokenType    kind;
   token = Sym->getSymbol();
   sym   = token->Token;
   pos   = symbolTable.Position(*token->Value, tbl_x);
   if (pos == 0)
   {
      Sym->Message("Undefined variable");
      statement = NULL;
   }
   else
   {
      symbolTable.Examine(name, kind, lev, val, dim, pos);
      switch (kind)
      {
         case varSym:
            statement = new  assignStatement(untilSyms, tbl_x);
            break;
         case procSym:
            statement = new  procedureCall(untilSyms, tbl_x);
            break;
         default:
            Sym->Message("Procedure or variable expected");
            statement = NULL;
      }
      if (statement != NULL)
```

```
            statement->Parse();
      }
}


void  callOrAssign::Generate()
{
   if ( statement != NULL)
   {   statement->Generate();   delete statement;  }
}


//  callStatement class -----------------------------------------------

      callStatement::callStatement(symSet *UntilSyms, int tx)
{  untilSyms = new symSet(*UntilSyms);   tbl_x = tx;  }

      callStatement::~callStatement()
{  delete untilSyms;  }

void  callStatement::Parse()
{
   Token      *token;
   TokenType  sym;
   int        pos;
   int        lev, val, dim;
   string     name;
   TokenType  kind;
   token = Sym->getNewSymbol();
   sym   = token->Token;
   if (sym != Ident)
   {
      Sym->Message("Ident expected");
      procedure = NULL;
   }
   else
   {
      pos   = symbolTable.Position(*token->Value, tbl_x);
      if (pos == 0)
      {
         Sym->Message("Undefined variable");
         procedure = NULL;
      }
      else
      {
         symbolTable.Examine(name, kind, lev, val, dim, pos);
```

```
            if (kind != procSym)
            {
                Sym->Message("call to non-procedure");
                procedure = NULL;
            }
            else
            {
                procedure = new procedureCall(untilSyms, tbl_x);
                procedure->Parse();
            }
        }
    }
}


void  callStatement::Generate()
{  if (procedure != NULL)  procedure->Generate();  }


//  cobegStatement class  ------------------------------------------

        cobegStatement::cobegStatement(symSet *UntilSyms, int tx)
{  untilSyms = new symSet(*UntilSyms);   tbl_x = tx;  }


        cobegStatement::~cobegStatement()
{  delete untilSyms;  }


void  cobegStatement::Parse()
{  Token  *token = Sym->getNewSymbol();  }


void  cobegStatement::Generate()
{  coprocess.Enable();  }


//  coendStatement class  ------------------------------------------

        coendStatement::coendStatement(symSet *UntilSyms, int tx)
{  untilSyms = new symSet(*UntilSyms);   tbl_x = tx;  }


        coendStatement::~coendStatement()
{  delete untilSyms;  }


void  coendStatement::Parse()
{  Token  *token = Sym->getNewSymbol();  }


void  coendStatement::Generate()
{  code.Enter(OPR, 0, 26, pcd_x);   coprocess.Disable();  }
```

```
//   conditStatement class  -----------------------------------------

      conditStatement::conditStatement(symSet *UntilSyms, int tx)
{
   untilSyms = new symSet(*UntilSyms);
   indexSyms = new symSet(*UntilSyms);
   tbl_x = tx;
}


      conditStatement::~conditStatement()
{ delete untilSyms;   delete indexSyms;  }

void  conditStatement::Parse()
{
   Token       *token;
   TokenType   sym;
   int         pos;
   string      name;
   TokenType   kind;
   token = Sym->getNewSymbol();
   sym   = token->Token;
   if (sym != lParen)
      Sym->Message("`(' expected");
   else
   {
      token = Sym->getNewSymbol();
      sym   = token->Token;
      if (sym != Ident)
         Sym->Message("Ident expected");
      else
      {
         pos = symbolTable.Position(*token->Value, tbl_x);
         if (pos == 0)
            Sym->Message("Undefined variable");
         else
         {
            symbolTable.Examine(name, kind, lev, val, dim, pos);
            if (kind != varSym)
               Sym->Message("CONDITION on a non-variable");
            token = Sym->getNewSymbol();
            sym   = token->Token;
            if (dim > 1)
            {
```

```
              if (sym != lBrkt)
                 Sym->Message("`[' expected");
              else
              {
                 token = Sym->getNewSymbol();
                 sym   = token->Token;
              }
              indexSyms->insert(rBrkt);
              index = new Condition(indexSyms, tbl_x);
              index->Parse();
              token = Sym->getSymbol();
              sym   = token->Token;
              if (sym != rBrkt)
                 Sym->Message("`]' expected");
              else
              {
                 token = Sym->getNewSymbol();
                 sym   = token->Token;
              }
           }
        }
     }
  }
  if (sym != rParen)
     Sym->Message("`)' expected");
  else
  {
     token = Sym->getNewSymbol();
     sym   = token->Token;
  }
}


void  conditStatement::Generate()
{
  TokenType  type, kind;
  string     name, gate = "mon$tor";
  int        levl, value, dimen, size, pos;

  pos = symbolTable.Position(gate, tbl_x);
  symbolTable.Examine(name, kind, levl, value, dimen, pos);
  code.Enter(   LOD, level.get() - levl, value, pcd_x);
  if (dim > 1)
  {
     index->Generate(size, type);
```

```
        code.Enter(LODA,   level.get() - lev,   val, pcd_x);
        code.Enter( OPR,                    0,    2, pcd_x);
        delete index;
    }
    else
        code.Enter(LODA,   level.get() - lev,   val, pcd_x);
    code.Enter(   OPR,                   0,   31, pcd_x);
}

//  delayStatement class  -------------------------------------------

    delayStatement::delayStatement(symSet *UntilSyms, int tx)
{

    untilSyms = new symSet(*UntilSyms);
    indexSyms = new symSet(*UntilSyms);
    tbl_x = tx;
}


    delayStatement::~delayStatement()
{ delete untilSyms;   delete indexSyms;  }

void  delayStatement::Parse()
{
    Token       *token;
    TokenType   sym;
    int         pos;
    string      name;
    TokenType   kind;
    token = Sym->getNewSymbol();
    sym  = token->Token;
    if (sym != lParen)
        Sym->Message("`(' expected");
    else
    {
        token = Sym->getNewSymbol();
        sym  = token->Token;
        if (sym != Ident)
            Sym->Message("Ident expected");
        else
        {
            pos = symbolTable.Position(*token->Value, tbl_x);
            if (pos == 0)
                Sym->Message("Undefined variable");
```

```
        else
        {
            symbolTable.Examine(name, kind, lev, val, dim, pos);
            if (kind != varSym)
                Sym->Message("DELAY on a non-variable");
            token = Sym->getNewSymbol();
            sym   = token->Token;
            if (dim > 1)
            {
                if (sym != lBrkt)
                    Sym->Message("`[' expected");
                else
                {
                    token = Sym->getNewSymbol();
                    sym   = token->Token;
                }
                indexSyms->insert(rBrkt);
                index = new Condition(indexSyms, tbl_x);
                index->Parse();
                token = Sym->getSymbol();
                sym   = token->Token;
                if (sym != rBrkt)
                    Sym->Message("`]' expected");
                else
                {
                    token = Sym->getNewSymbol();
                    sym   = token->Token;
                }
            }
        }
    }
    if (sym != rParen)
        Sym->Message("`)' expected");
    else
    {
        token = Sym->getNewSymbol();
        sym   = token->Token;
    }
}


void delayStatement::Generate()
{
    TokenType  type;
```

```
FunctType  fct;
int        size, cx1, cx2, loc, levl, valu;
if (dim > 1)
{
   cx1 = code.CurrentLoc();
   index->Generate(size, type);
   cx2 = code.CurrentLoc();
   code.Enter(   LODX, level.get() - lev, val, pcd_x);
   delete index;
}
else
   code.Enter(   LOD, level.get() - lev,  val, pcd_x);
code.Enter(        OPR,                 0,   35, pcd_x);
if (dim > 1)
{
   for (loc = cx1;  loc < cx2;  loc++)
   {
      code.Fetch(fct, levl, valu, loc);
      code.Enter(fct,              levl, valu, pcd_x);
   }
   code.Enter(   LODX, level.get() - lev,  val, pcd_x);
}
else
   code.Enter(   LOD, level.get() - lev,  val, pcd_x);
code.Enter(        OPR,                 0,   32, pcd_x);
if (dim > 1)
{
   for (loc = cx1;  loc < cx2;  loc++)
   {
      code.Fetch(fct, levl, valu, loc);
      code.Enter(fct,              levl, valu, pcd_x);
   }
   code.Enter(   LODX, level.get() - lev,  val, pcd_x);
}
else
   code.Enter(   LOD, level.get() - lev,  val, pcd_x);
code.Enter(        OPR,                 0,   33, pcd_x);
if (dim > 1)
{
   for (loc = cx1;  loc < cx2;  loc++)
   {
      code.Fetch(fct, levl, valu, loc);
      code.Enter(fct,              levl, valu, pcd_x);
   }
```

```
      code.Enter(  LODX, level.get() - lev,  val, pcd_x);
   }
   else
      code.Enter(   LOD, level.get() - lev,  val, pcd_x);
   code.Enter(       OPR,               0,   36, pcd_x);
}


//  forStatement class  ---------------------------------------------

      forStatement::forStatement(symSet *UntilSyms, int tx)
{
   untilSyms1 = new symSet(*UntilSyms);
   untilSyms2 = new symSet(*UntilSyms);
   endSyms    = new symSet(*UntilSyms);
   tbl_x = tx;
}


      forStatement::~forStatement()
{ delete untilSyms1;   delete untilSyms2;   delete endSyms;  }

void  forStatement::Parse()
{
   Token      *token;
   TokenType  sym;
   string     name;
   TokenType  kind;
   token = Sym->getNewSymbol();
   sym   = token->Token;
   if (sym != Ident)
   {
      Sym->Message("Ident expected");
      pos = 0;
   }
   else
   {
      pos = symbolTable.Position(*token->Value, tbl_x);
      if (pos == 0)
         Sym->Message("Undefined variable");
      else
      {
         symbolTable.Examine(name, kind, lev, val, dim, pos);
         if (kind != varSym)
         {
            Sym->Message("Assignment to a non-variable");
```

```
            pos = 0;
         }
      }
   }
   token = Sym->getNewSymbol();
   sym  = token->Token;
   if (sym != Becomes)
      Sym->Message("`:=' expected");
   else
   {
      token = Sym->getNewSymbol();
      sym  = token->Token;
   }
   untilSyms1->insert(toSym);
   expression1 = new Condition(untilSyms1, tbl_x);
   expression1->Parse();
   token = Sym->getSymbol();
   sym  = token->Token;
   if (sym != toSym)
      Sym->Message("TO expected");
   else
   {
      token = Sym->getNewSymbol();
      sym  = token->Token;
   }
   untilSyms2->insert(doSym);
   expression2 = new Condition(untilSyms2, tbl_x);
   expression2->Parse();
   token = Sym->getSymbol();
   sym  = token->Token;
   if (sym != doSym)
      Sym->Message("DO expected");
   else
   {
      token = Sym->getNewSymbol();
      sym  = token->Token;
   }
   endSyms->insert(endSym);
   statementList = new StatementList(endSyms, tbl_x);
   statementList->Parse();
   token = Sym->getSymbol();
   sym  = token->Token;
   if (sym == endSym)
   {
```

```
      token = Sym->getNewSymbol();
      sym   = token->Token;
   }
   else
      Sym->Message("`END' expected");
}


void  forStatement::Generate()
{
   TokenType  type;
   int        size;
   int        cx1, cx2;
   expression1->Generate(size, type);
   delete expression1;
   if (pos != 0)
      code.Enter(STO, level.get() - lev, val, pcd_x);
   expression2->Generate(size, type);
   delete expression2;
   code.Enter(   OPR,              0,  21, pcd_x);
   cx2 = pcd_x - 1;
   if (pos != 0)
      code.Enter(LOD, level.get() - lev, val, pcd_x);
   code.Enter(   OPR,              0,  11, pcd_x);
   code.Enter(   JPC,              0,   0, pcd_x);
   cx1 = pcd_x - 1;
   statementList->Generate();
   delete statementList;
   if (pos != 0)
   {
      code.Enter(LOD, level.get() - lev, val, pcd_x);
      code.Enter(OPR,                0,  19, pcd_x);
      code.Enter(STO, level.get() - lev, val, pcd_x);
   }
   code.Enter(   JMP,              0, cx2, pcd_x);
   code.FixValue(code.CurrentLoc(), cx1);
   code.Enter(   INT,              0,  -1, pcd_x);
}


//  ifStatement class  --------------------------------------------------

      ifStatement::ifStatement(symSet *UntilSyms, int tx)
{
   untilSyms1 = new symSet(*UntilSyms);
   untilSyms2 = new symSet(*UntilSyms);
```

```
   endSyms    = new symSet(*UntilSyms);
   tbl_x = tx;
}


    ifStatement::~ifStatement()
{  delete untilSyms1;    delete untilSyms2;    delete endSyms;  }


void  ifStatement::Parse()
{
   Token      *token;
   TokenType  sym;
   token = Sym->getNewSymbol();
   sym   = token->Token;
   untilSyms1->insert(thenSym);
   untilSyms1->insert(elseSym);
   untilSyms1->insert(doSym);
   untilSyms1->insert(endSym);
   condition = new Condition(untilSyms1, tbl_x);
   condition->Parse();
   token = Sym->getSymbol();
   sym   = token->Token;
   t_statementList = NULL;
   e_statementList = NULL;
   if (sym == thenSym || sym == doSym)
   {
      if (sym == doSym)
         Sym->Message("Replace `DO' with `THEN'");
      token = Sym->getNewSymbol();
      sym   = token->Token;
      untilSyms2->insert(elseSym);
      untilSyms2->insert(endSym);
      t_statementList = new StatementList(untilSyms2, tbl_x);
      t_statementList->Parse();
      token = Sym->getSymbol();
      sym   = token->Token;
      if (sym == elseSym)
      {
         token = Sym->getNewSymbol();
         sym   = token->Token;
         endSyms->insert(endSym);
         e_statementList = new StatementList(endSyms, tbl_x);
         e_statementList->Parse();
      }
      token = Sym->getSymbol();
```

```
      sym   = token->Token;
      if (sym == endSym)
      {
          token = Sym->getNewSymbol();
           sym   = token->Token;
      }
      else
          Sym->Message("`END' expected");
   }
   else
      Sym->Message("`THEN' expected");
}


void  ifStatement::Generate()
{
   TokenType   type;
   int         size;
   int         cx1;
   condition->Generate(size, type);
   delete condition;
   if (type != intSym && type != charSym)
   Sym->Message("Bad condition type");
   code.Enter(   JPC, 0, 0, pcd_x);
   cx1 = pcd_x - 1;
   if (t_statementList != NULL)
   {
      t_statementList->Generate();
      delete t_statementList;
   }
   if (e_statementList !- NULL)
   {
      code.Enter(JMP, 0, 0, pcd_x);
      code.FixValue(pcd_x, cx1);
      cx1 = pcd_x - 1;
      e_statementList->Generate();
      delete e_statementList;
   }
   code.FixValue(code.CurrentLoc(), cx1);
}


// initStatement class ------------------------------------------+----------+--

      initStatement::initStatement(symSet *UntilSyms, int tx)
   {
```

```
     untilSyms = new symSet(*UntilSyms);
     indexSyms = new symSet(*UntilSyms);
     tbl_x = tx;
}


     initStatement::~initStatement()
{ delete untilSyms;   delete indexSyms;  }

void  initStatement::Parse()
{
   Token       *token;
   TokenType   sym;
   int         pos;
   string      name;
   TokenType   kind;
   token = Sym->getNewSymbol();
   sym   = token->Token;
   if (sym != lParen)
      Sym->Message("`(' expected");
   else
   {
      token = Sym->getNewSymbol();
      sym   = token->Token;
      if (sym != Ident)
         Sym->Message("Ident expected");
      else
      {
         pos = symbolTable.Position(*token->Value, tbl_x);
         if (pos == 0)
            Sym->Message("Undefined variable");
         else
         {
            symbolTable.Examine(name, kind, lev, val, dim, pos);
            if (kind != varSym)
               Sym->Message("SEMAPHORE on a non-variable");
            else
            {
               token = Sym->getNewSymbol();
               sym   - token->Token;
               if (dim > 1)
               {
                  if (sym != lBrkt)
                     Sym->Message("`[' expected");
                  else
```

```
            {
                token = Sym->getNewSymbol();
                sym   = token->Token;
            }
            indexSyms->insert(rBrkt);
            index = new Condition(indexSyms, tbl_x);
            index->Parse();
            token = Sym->getSymbol();
            sym   = token->Token;
            if (sym != rBrkt)
                Sym->Message("`]' expected");
            else
            {
                token = Sym->getNewSymbol();
                sym   = token->Token;
            }
        }
        if (sym != Comma)
            Sym->Message("`,' expected");
        else
        {
            untilSyms->insert(rParen);
            token = Sym->getNewSymbol();
            sym   = token->Token;
            expression = new Condition(untilSyms, tbl_x);
            expression->Parse();
            token = Sym->getSymbol();
            sym   = token->Token;
        }
      }
     }
   }
  }
  if (sym != rParen)
     Sym->Message("`)' expected");
  else
  {
     token = Sym->getNewSymbol();
     sym   = token->Token;
  }
}

void  initStatement::Generate()
{
```

```
    TokenType  type;
    int        size;
    if (dim > 1)
    {
        index->Generate(size, type);
        code.Enter(LODA, level.get() - lev, val, pcd_x);
        code.Enter( OPR,                 0,   2, pcd_x);
        delete index;
    }
    else
        code.Enter(LODA, level.get() - lev, val, pcd_x);
    if (expression != NULL)
    {
        expression->Generate(size, type);
        code.Enter( OPR,                 0,  28, pcd_x);
        delete expression;
    }
}


// procedureCall class -------------------------------------------

    procedureCall::procedureCall(symSet *UntilSyms, int tx)
{
    untilSyms = new symSet(*UntilSyms);
    exprList  = new conditQ;
    tbl_x = tx;
}


    procedureCall::~procedureCall()
{ delete untilSyms;   delete exprList;  }

void procedureCall::Parse()
{
    Token      *token;
    TokenType  sym;
    int        pos;
    string     name;
    Condition *expression;
    token = Sym->getSymbol();
    sym   = token->Token;
    pos   = symbolTable.Position(*token->Value, tbl_x);
    symbolTable.Examine(name, kind, lev, val, dim, pos);
    token = Sym->getNewSymbol();
    sym   = token->Token;
```

```
if (sym == lParen)
{
   untilSyms->insert(Comma);
   untilSyms->insert(rParen);
   do
   {
      token = Sym->getNewSymbol();
      sym   = token->Token;
      expression = new Condition(untilSyms, tbl_x);
      expression->Parse();
      exprList->push(expression);
      token = Sym->getSymbol();
      sym   = token->Token;
   }
   while (sym == Comma);

   if (sym != rParen)
      Sym->Message("`)' expected");
   else
   {
      token = Sym->getNewSymbol();
      sym   = token->Token;
   }
}
}


void procedureCall::Generate()
{
   Condition *expression;
   TokenType  type;
   int        size;
   int        argCount = 0;
   if ( kind == procSym && coprocess.isEnabled() )
   {
      code.Enter(  OPR,                 1000,       24, pcd_x);
      code.Enter(  OPR,                 0,         25, pcd_x);
   }
   while ( ! exprList->empty() )
   {
      expression = exprList->front();
      exprList->pop();
      expression->Generate(size, type);
      argCount += size;
      delete expression;
```

```
      }
      if ( kind == procSym && coprocess.isEnabled() )
         code.Enter(   PRC, level.get() - lev,          val, pcd_x);
      else
      {
         code.Enter(   CAL, level.get() - lev,          val, pcd_x);
         if (argCount != 0)
            code.Enter(INT,                   0, - argCount, pcd_x);
      }
   }


// readStatement class -----------------------------------------------

      readStatement::readStatement(symSet *UntilSyms, int tx)
{
   untilSyms = new symSet(*UntilSyms);
   varList   = new readobjQ;
   tbl_x = tx;
}


      readStatement::~readStatement()
{ delete untilSyms;   delete varList;  }

void  readStatement::Parse()
{
   Token     *token;
   TokenType  sym, kind, typ;
   int        lev, val, dim, siz, pos;
   string     name;
   ReadObj   *variable;
   token = Sym->getNewSymbol();
   sym   = token->Token;
   if (sym != lParen)
      Sym->Message("`(' expected");
   else
   {
      do
      {
         token = Sym->getNewSymbol();
         sym   = token->Token;
         if (sym != Ident)
            Sym->Message("Ident expected");
         else
         {
```

```
pos = symbolTable.Position(*token->Value, tbl_x);
if (pos == 0)
   Sym->Message("Undefined variable");
else
{
   symbolTable.Examine(
       name, kind, lev, val, dim, siz, typ, pos);
   if (kind != varSym)
      Sym->Message("READ to a non-variable");
   else
   {
      variable = new ReadObj();
      variable->var.level   = lev;
      variable->var.n_value = val;
      variable->var.dimen   = dim;
      variable->var.size    = siz;
      variable->var.typeRef = typ;
      if (dim > 1)
      {
         token = Sym->getNewSymbol();
         sym   = token->Token;
         if (sym != lBrkt)
            Sym->Message("`[' expected");
         else
         {
            token = Sym->getNewSymbol();
            sym   = token->Token;
         }
         untilSyms->insert(rBrkt);
         variable->index = new Condition(
         untilSyms, tbl_x);
         variable->index->Parse();
         token = Sym->getSymbol();
         sym   = token->Token;
         if (sym != rBrkt)
            Sym->Message("`]' expected");
      }
      varList->push(variable);
   }
   token - Sym->getNewSymbol();
   sym   - token->Token;
}
}
}
```

```
        while (sym == Comma);
        if (sym != rParen)
          Sym->Message("`)' expected");
        else
        {
          token = Sym->getNewSymbol();
          sym   = token->Token;
        }
      }
    }
}


void  readStatement::Generate()
{
    ReadObj    *variable;
    TokenType  type, typ;
    int        size, lev, val, dim, siz;
    while ( ! varList->empty() )
    {
      variable = varList->front();
      varList->pop();
      lev = variable->var.level;
      val - variable->var.n_value;
      dim = variable->var.dimen;
      siz = variable->var.size;
      typ = variable->var.typeRef;
      if (dim > 1)
      {
        variable->index->Generate(size, type);
        if (typ !- intSym && typ != charSym)
        {
          code.Enter( LIT,                     0,     siz, pcd_x);
          code.Enter( OPR,                     0,       4, pcd_x);
          code.Enter(LODA, level.get() - lev,  val, pcd_x);
          code.Enter( OPR,                     0,       2, pcd_x);
        }
      }
      else if (typ != intSym && typ != charSym)
        code.Enter(  LODA, level.get() - lev,   val, pcd_x);
      switch (typ)
      {
        case charSym:
          code.Enter( CSP,                     0,       0, pcd_x);
          break;
        case intSym:
```

```
         code.Enter( CSP,                0,      2, pcd_x);
         break;
      case realSym:
         code.Enter( CSP,                0,      6, pcd_x);
         break;
      default:
         Sym->Message("Cannot read this variable type");
   }
   if (typ != intSym && typ != charSym)
      code.Enter(  STOI, level.get() - lev, siz - 1, pcd_x);
   else if (dim > 1)
      code.Enter(  STOX, level.get() - lev,     val, pcd_x);
   else
      code.Enter(   STO, level.get() - lev,     val, pcd_x);
   delete variable;
   }
}


// repeatStatement class  -----------------------------------------

    repeatStatement::repeatStatement(symSet *UntilSyms, int tx)
{
   untilSyms = new symSet(*UntilSyms);
   endSyms   = new symSet(*UntilSyms);
   tbl_x = tx;
}


    repeatStatement::~repeatStatement()
{ delete untilSyms;   delete endSyms;  }

void  repeatStatement::Parse()
{
   Token     *token;
   TokenType  sym;
   token = Sym->getNewSymbol();
   sym   = token->Token;
   untilSyms->insert(untilSym);
   statementList = new StatementList(untilSyms, tbl_x);
   statementList->Parse();
   token = Sym->getSymbol();
   sym   = token->Token;
   if (sym != untilSym)
      Sym->Message("`UNTIL' expected");
   else
```

```
      {
          token = Sym->getNewSymbol();
          sym   = token->Token;
      }
      condition = new Condition(endSyms, tbl_x);
      condition->Parse();
   }


   void  repeatStatement::Generate()
   {
      TokenType  type;
      int        size;
      int        cx1 = code.CurrentLoc();
      statementList->Generate();
      delete statementList;
      condition->Generate(size, type);
      delete condition;
      if (type != intSym && type != charSym)
         Sym->Message("Bad condition type");
      code.Enter(JPC, 0, cx1, pcd_x);
   }


   //  returnStatement class  ----------------------------------------

         returnStatement::returnStatement(symSet *UntilSyms, int tx)
   {  untilSyms = new symSet(*UntilSyms);   tbl_x = tx;  }


         returnStatement::~returnStatement()
   {  delete untilSyms;  }


   void  returnStatement::Parse()
   {
      Token      *token;
      TokenType  sym, kind;
      string     name = "ret$val";
      int        pos;
      token = Sym->getNewSymbol();
      sym   = token->Token;
      if (fctr_beg_sym.contains(sym))
      {
          expression = new Condition(untilSyms, tbl_x);
          expression->Parse();
          pos = symbolTable.Position(name, tbl_x);
          if (pos == 0)
```

```
      {
         Sym->Message("Procedure cannot return a value");
         expression = NULL;
      }
      else
      {
         symbolTable.Examine(
            name, kind, lev, val, dim, siz, typ, pos);
         if (lev != level.get())
         {
            Sym->Message("Procedure cannot return a value");
            expression = NULL;
         }
      }
   }
   else
      expression = NULL;
}


void   returnStatement::Generate()
{
   TokenType  type;
   int        size;
   if (expression != NULL)
   {
      if ((typ != intSym && typ != charSym) || siz != 1)
         code.Enter(LODA, level.get() - lev,    val, pcd_x);
      expression->Generate(size, type);
      if (  (typ != type || siz != size)
         && (type != charSym || typ != strSym  || size != siz) )
         Sym->Message("Incompatible types");
      if ((typ != intSym && typ != charSym) || siz != 1)
         code.Enter(STOI,                0, siz - 1, pcd_x);
      else
         code.Enter( STO, level.get() - lev,    val, pcd_x);
      delete expression;
   }
   code.Enter(        OPR,                0,       0, pcd_x);
}


//  sendStatement class  ---------------------------------------

      sendStatement::sendStatement(symSet *UntilSyms, int tx)
   {
```

```
        untilSyms = new symSet(*UntilSyms);
        indexSyms = new symSet(*UntilSyms);
        tbl_x = tx;
    }


        sendStatement::~sendStatement()
    {  delete untilSyms;    delete indexSyms;  }

    void  sendStatement::Parse()
    {
        Token       *token;
        TokenType   sym;
        int         pos;
        string      name;
        TokenType   kind;
        token = Sym->getNewSymbol();
        sym   = token->Token;
        if (sym != lParen)
        .  Sym->Message("`(' expected");
        else
        {
            token = Sym->getNewSymbol();
            sym   = token->Token;
            if (sym != Ident)
                Sym->Message("Ident expected");
            else
            {
                pos = symbolTable.Position(*token->Value, tbl_x);
                if (pos == 0)
                    Sym->Message("Undefined variable");
                else
                {
                    symbolTable.Examine(name, kind, lev, val, dim, pos);
                    if (kind != varSym)
                        Sym->Message("SEND to a non-variable");
                    token = Sym->getNewSymbol();
                    sym   = token->Token;
                    if (dim > 1)
                    {
                        if (sym != lBrkt)
                            Sym->Message("`[' expected");
                        else
                        {
                            token = Sym->getNewSymbol();
```

```
                    sym   = token->Token;
                }
                indexSyms->insert(rBrkt);
                index = new Condition(indexSyms, tbl_x);
                index->Parse();
                token = Sym->getSymbol();
                sym   = token->Token;
                if (sym != rBrkt)
                    Sym->Message("`]' expected");
                else
                {
                    token = Sym->getNewSymbol();
                    sym   = token->Token;
                }
            }
        }
    }
    if (sym != rParen)
        Sym->Message("`)' expected");
    else
    {
        token = Sym->getNewSymbol();
        sym   = token->Token;
    }
}


void  sendStatement::Generate()
{
    TokenType  type;
    int        size;
    if (dim > 1)
    {
        index->Generate(size, type);
        code.Enter(LODX, level.get() - lev, val, pcd_x);
        delete index;
    }
    else
        code.Enter( LOD, level.get() - lev, val, pcd_x);
    code.Enter(    OPR,                 0,  30, pcd_x);
}


//  signalStatement class  -----------------------------------------
```

```
      signalStatement::signalStatement(symSet *UntilSyms, int tx)
{
   untilSyms = new symSet(*UntilSyms);
   indexSyms = new symSet(*UntilSyms);
   tbl_x = tx;
}


      signalStatement::~signalStatement()
{ delete untilSyms;    delete indexSyms;  }

void  signalStatement::Parse()
{
   Token       *token;
   TokenType   sym;
   int         pos;
   string      name;
   TokenType   kind;
   token = Sym->getNewSymbol();
   sym   = token->Token;
   if (sym != lParen)
      Sym->Message("`(' expected");
   else
   {
      token = Sym->getNewSymbol();
      sym   = token->Token;
      if (sym != Ident)
         Sym->Message("Ident expected");
      else
      {
         pos = symbolTable.Position(*token->Value, tbl_x);
         if (pos == 0)
            Sym->Message("Undefined variable");
         else
         {
            symbolTable.Examine(name, kind, lev, val, dim, pos);
            if (kind != varSym)
               Sym->Message("SIGNAL to a non-variable");
            token = Sym->getNewSymbol();
            sym   = token->Token;
            if (dim > 1)
            {
               if (sym != lBrkt)
                  Sym->Message("`[' expected");
               else
```

```
                {
                    token = Sym->getNewSymbol();
                    sym   = token->Token;
                }
                indexSyms->insert(rBrkt);
                index = new Condition(indexSyms, tbl_x);
                index->Parse();
                token = Sym->getSymbol();
                sym   = token->Token;
                if (sym != rBrkt)
                    Sym->Message("`]' expected");
                else
                {
                    token = Sym->getNewSymbol();
                    sym   = token->Token;
                }
            }
        }
    }
}
if (sym != rParen)
    Sym->Message("`)' expected");
else
{
    token = Sym->getNewSymbol();
    sym   = token->Token;
}
}


void  signalStatement::Generate()
{
    TokenType  type;
    FunctType  fct;
    int        size, cx1, cx2, cx3, loc, levl, valu;
    if (dim > 1)
    {
        cx1 = code.CurrentLoc();
        index->Generate(size, type);
        cx2 = code.CurrentLoc();
        code.Enter( LODX, level.get() - lev,  val, pcd_x);
        delete index;
    }
    else
        code.Enter(  LOD, level.get() - lev,  val, pcd_x);
```

```
      code.Enter(        OPR,                0,   37, pcd_x);
      code.Enter(        LIT,                0,    0, pcd_x);
      code.Enter(        OPR,                0,   12, pcd_x);
      cx3 = pcd_x;
      code.Enter(        JPC,                0,    0, pcd_x);
      if (dim > 1)
      {
         for (loc = cx1;  loc < cx2;  loc++)
         {
            code.Fetch(fct, lev1, valu, loc);
            code.Enter(fct,             lev1, valu, pcd_x);
         }
         code.Enter(  LODX, level.get() - lev,  val, pcd_x);
      }
      else
         code.Enter(  LOD, level.get() - lev,  val, pcd_x);
      code.Enter(        OPR,                0,   34, pcd_x);
      code.Enter(        JMP,                0,    0, pcd_x);
      code.FixValue(pcd_x, cx3);
      cx3 = pcd_x - 1;
      if (dim > 1)
      {
         for (loc = cx1;  loc < cx2;  loc++)
         {
            code.Fetch(fct  lev1, valu, loc);
            code.Enter(fct,             lev1, valu, pcd_x);
         }
         code.Enter(  LODX, level.get() - lev,  val, pcd_x);
      }
      else
         code.Enter(  LOD, level.get() - lev,  val, pcd_x);
      code.Enter(        OPR,                0,   32, pcd_x);
      code.FixValue(pcd_x, cx3);
}


//  suspendStatement class  --------------------------------------------

      suspendStatement::suspendStatement(symSet *UntilSyms, int tx)
{  untilSyms = new symSet(*UntilSyms);    tbl_x = tx;  }

      suspendStatement::~suspendStatement()
{  delete untilSyms;  }

void  suspendStatement::Parse()
```

```
{  Token  *token = Sym->getNewSymbol();  }

void  suspendStatement::Generate()
{  code.Enter(OPR, 0, 27, pcd_x);  }

//  waitStatement class  --------------------------------------------

     waitStatement::waitStatement(symSet *UntilSyms, int tx)
{
   untilSyms = new symSet(*UntilSyms);
   indexSyms = new symSet(*UntilSyms);
   tbl_x = tx;
}


     waitStatement::~waitStatement()
{  delete untilSyms;    delete indexSyms;  }

void  waitStatement::Parse()
{
   Token       *token;
   TokenType    sym;
   int          pos;
   string       name;
   TokenType    kind;
   token = Sym->getNewSymbol();
   sym   = token->Token;
   if (sym != lParen)
      Sym->Message("`(' expected");
   else
   {
      token = Sym->getNewSymbol();
      sym   = token->Token;
      if (sym != Ident)
         Sym->Message("Ident expected");
      else
      {
         pos = symbolTable.Position(*token->Value, tbl_x);
         if (pos == 0)
            Sym->Message("Undefined variable");
         else
         {
            symbolTable.Examine(name, kind, lev, val, dim, pos);
            if (kind != varSym)
               Sym->Message("WAIT on a non-variable");
```

```
                    token = Sym->getNewSymbol();
                    sym   = token->Token;
                    if (dim > 1)
                    {
                        if (sym != lBrkt)
                            Sym->Message("`[' expected");
                        else
                        {
                            token = Sym->getNewSymbol();
                            sym   = token->Token;
                        }
                        indexSyms->insert(rBrkt);
                        index = new Condition(indexSyms, tbl_x);
                        index->Parse();
                        token = Sym->getSymbol();
                        sym   = token->Token;
                        if (sym != rBrkt)
                            Sym->Message("`]' expected");
                        else
                        {
                            token = Sym->getNewSymbol();
                            sym   = token->Token;
                        }
                    }
                }
            }
        }
        if (sym != rParen)
            Sym->Message("`)' expected");
        else
        {
            token = Sym->getNewSymbol();
            sym   = token->Token;
        }
    }


    void  waitStatement::Generate()
    {
        TokenType  type;
        int        size;
        if (dim > 1)
        {
            index->Generate(size, type);
            code.Enter(LODX, level.get() - lev, val, pcd_x);
```

```
      delete index;
   }
   else
      code.Enter( LOD, level.get() - lev, val, pcd_x);
   code.Enter(    OPR,               0,  29, pcd_x);
}


//  whileStatement class  -----------------------------------------

      whileStatement::whileStatement(symSet *UntilSyms, int tx)
{
   untilSyms = new symSet(*UntilSyms);
   endSyms   = new symSet(*UntilSyms);
   tbl_x = tx;
}


      whileStatement::~whileStatement()
{ delete untilSyms;   delete endSyms;  }

void  whileStatement::Parse()
{
   Token     *token;
   TokenType  sym;
   token = Sym->getNewSymbol();
   sym   = token->Token;
   untilSyms->insert(doSym);
   untilSyms->insert(endSym);
   condition = new Condition(untilSyms, tbl_x);
   condition->Parse();
   token = Sym->getSymbol();
   sym   = token->Token;
   statementList = NULL;
   if (sym == doSym)
   {
      token = Sym->getNewSymbol();
      sym   = token->Token;
      endSyms->insert(endSym);
      statementList = new StatementList(endSyms, tbl_x);
      statementList->Parse();
      token = Sym->getSymbol();
      sym   = token->Token;
      if (sym =- endSym)
      {
         token = Sym->getNewSymbol();
```

```
            sym     = token->Token;
        }
        else
            Sym->Message("`END' expected");
    }
    else
        Sym->Message("`DO' expected");
}


void  whileStatement::Generate()
{
    TokenType   type;
    int         size;
    int         cx1 = code.CurrentLoc();
    int         cx2;
    condition->Generate(size, type);
    delete condition;
    if (type != intSym && type != charSym)
        Sym->Message("Bad condition type");
    code.Enter(JPC, 0,    0, pcd_x);
    cx2 = pcd_x - 1;
    if (statementList != NULL)
    {
        statementList->Generate();
        delete statementList;
    }
    code.Enter(JMP, 0, cx1, pcd_x);
    code.FixValue(pcd_x, cx2);
}


//  writeStatement class -------------------------------------------

        writeStatement::writeStatement(symSet *UntilSyms, int tx)
{
    untilSyms = new symSet(*UntilSyms);
    exprList  = new conditQ;
    tbl_x = tx;
}


        writeStatement::~writeStatement()
{ delete untilSyms;   delete exprList;   }

void  writeStatement::Parse()
{
```

```
Token      *token;
TokenType  sym;
Condition *expression;
token = Sym->getNewSymbol();
sym   = token->Token;
if (sym != lParen)
   Sym->Message("`(' expected");
else
{
   untilSyms->insert(Comma);
   untilSyms->insert(rParen);
   do
   {
      token = Sym->getNewSymbol();
      sym   = token->Token;
      expression = new Condition(untilSyms, tbl_x);
      expression->Parse();
      exprList->push(expression);
      token = Sym->getSymbol();
      sym   = token->Token;
   }
   while (sym == Comma);
   if (sym != rParen)
      Sym->Message("`)' expected");
   else
   {
      token = Sym->getNewSymbol();
      sym   = token->Token;
   }
}
}

void  writeStatement::Generate()
{
   Condition  *expression;
   TokenType  type;
   int        size;
   while ( ! exprList->empty() )
   {
      expression = exprList->front();
      exprList->pop();
      expression->Generate(size, type);
      if (type == charSym && size != 1)
         type = strSym;
```

```
        switch (type)
        {
          case charSym:
              code.Enter(CSP,         0, 1, pcd_x);
              break;
          case intSym:
              code.Enter(CSP,         0, 3, pcd_x);
              break;
          case realSym:
              code.Enter(CSP,         0, 7, pcd_x);
              break;
          case strSym:
              code.Enter(CSP, size - 1, 8, pcd_x);
              break;
        }
        delete expression;
    }
    if (type != charSym)
    {
        code.Enter(LIT, 0, 13, pcd_x);
        code.Enter(CSP, 0,  1, pcd_x);
        code.Enter(LIT, 0, 10, pcd_x);
        code.Enter(CSP, 0,  1, pcd_x);
    }
}
```

APPENDIX F

The Concurrent P-Machine

This appendix contains the complete code for the Full Bodied P-Machine (P-Machine / FB). The code shown here was compiled with Borland C++ Version 5.01 that uses the Rogue Wave implementation of the Standard Template Library.

F.1 PMACHINE.CPP—THE MAIN PROGRAM

```
#include <stdlib.h>
#include <string.h>
#include <iostream.h>
#include <fstream.h>
#include "Code.h"        // defines the Code segment
#include "PSymbol.h"     // defines the P-Code input parser
#include "PInterp.h"     // defines the P-Code interpreter

    ifstream in;
    int     chance = 2;

int main(int argc,  char *argv[])
{
    Code      *code;
    PSymbol   *Lex;
    PInstr    *pcode;
    PInterp   *Pmachine;
    FunctType fct;
    int       level, value;
    int       cx_max;
    char      file_name[80];

    code     = new Code();
    Lex      = new PSymbol();
    Pmachine = new PInterp();
    if (--argc == 0)
    {
        cerr << "\n   usage:    PMachine       <input file>" << endl;
        cerr << "      --or--   PMachine  -n <input file>"  << endl;
        cerr << "    (where there is 1 chance in `n' that"  << endl;
```

```
      cerr << "     concurrent processes will switch)\n"    << endl;
      exit(EXIT_FAILURE);
   }
   else
   {
      strcpy(file_name, *++argv);
      if (file_name[0] == '-')    // woops, this one was an option
      {
         file_name[0] = ' ';
         chance = atoi(file_name);
         strcpy(file_name, *++argv);    // get the real filename
      }
   }
   cout << "Loading P-Code" << endl;
   in.open(file_name);
   do {
      pcode = Lex->getInstr();
      if (pcode != NULL)
      {
         fct   = pcode->fnctn;
         level = pcode->level;
         value = pcode->value;
         code->Enter(fct, level, value, cx_max);
      }
   } while (pcode != NULL);
   in.close();
   cout << "Executing P-Code" << endl;
   Pmachine->Execute(code);
   cout << "End of program" << endl;
   return (EXIT_SUCCESS);
}
```

F.2 PSYMBOL.H—THE P-CODE SCANNER

```
#ifndef __PSYMBOL__
#define __PSYMBOL__ 1

#include <map>
#include <string>
#include "PCode.h"        // defines FunctType and PInstr
using namespace std;

typedef map<string, FunctType, less<string> > fct_dict;
```

```
    typedef fct_dict::iterator                    location;

    class PSymbol
    {
       static fct_dict  op_codes;
       static string    PLine;
       static int       PFilled;
              char       getChar();
              void       ungetChar(char ch);
              void       ignoreComnt();
    public:
                         PSymbol();       // Lex analyzer constructor
              PInstr    *getInstr();      // returns the next instruction
    };

    #endif
```

F.3 PCODE.H—DEFINITION OF THE P-CODES

```
    #ifndef __PCODE__
    #define __PCODE__ 1

    enum FunctType { OPR,      // operation
                     LIT,      // load immediate  (i.e., literal)
                     LOD,      // load value
                     LODA,     // load address
                     LODI,     // load indirect value
                     LODX,     // load indexed value
                     STO,      // store value
                     STOI,     // store value indirectly
                     STOX,     // store indexed value
                     CAL,      // call subroutine
                     PRC,      // call process
                     INT,      // increment T register
                     JMP,      // jump  (unconditional)
                     JPC,      // conditional jump
                     CSP  };   // call special procedure
    struct PInstr
    {
       FunctType fnctn;        // op_code of the instruction
       int       level;        // level (difference) value
       int       value;        // value of the instruction
    };
```

```
// the following defines the size of a REAL WRT an INTEGER

const  realSize = (sizeof(float) + sizeof(int) - 1) / sizeof(int);

#endif
```

F.4 PSYMBOL.H—TOKEN ANALYZER IMPLEMENTATION

```
#include <stdlib.h>
#include <ctype.h>
#include <iostream.h>
#include <fstream.h>
#include "PSymbol.h"                    // class definition header

    extern ifstream  in;               // input source file

    fct_dict  PSymbol::op_codes;
    string    PSymbol::PLine;
    int       PSymbol::PFilled = 0;

    PSymbol::PSymbol() // constructor -- saves op_codes in dictionary
{
    if (PFilled) return;
    op_codes["OPR"]  = OPR;      op_codes["LIT"]  = LIT;
    op_codes["LOD"]  = LOD;      op_codes["LODA"] = LODA;
    op_codes["LODI"] = LODI;     op_codes["LODX"] = LODX;
    op_codes["STO"]  = STO;      op_codes["STOI"] = STOI;
    op_codes["STOX"] = STOX;     op_codes["CAL"]  = CAL;
    op_codes["PRC"]  = PRC;      op_codes["INT"]  = INT;
    op_codes["JMP"]  = JMP;      op_codes["JPC"]  = JPC;
    op_codes["CSP"]  = CSP;
    PFilled = 1;
}


char PSymbol::getChar()  // returns a single ch from the input
{
    char  ch, readLine[80];
    if (PLine.empty())
    {
       if (in.getline(readLine, 80)) // read in new PLine (unless EOF)
       {
          PLine - readLine;   // convert to string
```

```
            PLine += " ";           // add blank at end of line
        }
        else
            return '\0';            // return NUL for end of file
    }
    ch     = PLine[0];              // extract 'ch' from beginning of PLine
    PLine = PLine.remove(0, 1);
    return ch;
}


void PSymbol::ungetChar(char ch) // puts a ch back in the input
{
    string  prepend;     // add 'ch' back at beginning of PLine
    prepend = ch;        PLine   = prepend + PLine;
}


void PSymbol::ignoreComnt()      // skips rest of PLine
{ while ( ! PLine.empty())  PLine = PLine.remove(0, 1);  }

PInstr *PSymbol::getInstr()   // returns the next PInstr from input
{
    PInstr    *nextPInstr;
    location  key;
    string    val;
    char      ch;

    nextPInstr = new PInstr;
    do {
        if ((ch = getChar()) == '\0')    // get a character
            return (NULL);               // unless end of file
        if (ch == '!') ignoreComnt();    // or comment
    } while ( ! isalpha(ch));            // skip till alpha character

    val =  char(toupper(ch));     // convert character to a string
    do {
        ch = getChar();               // then convert to FunctType (fnctn)
        if ( isalpha(ch) ) val += char( toupper(ch) );
    } while  ( isalpha(ch) );
    ungetChar(ch);
    key = op_codes.find(val);
    if (key != op_codes.end())
        nextPInstr->fnctn = (*key).second;
    else
    { cerr << "Bad PCode " << val << endl;   exit(EXIT_FAILURE);   }
```

```
    do ch = getChar();            // skip till digit or sign
    while ( ! (isdigit(ch) || ch == '-' || ch == '+'));

    val = ch;             // convert character to a string
    do {
       ch = getChar();   // then convert to integer (level)
       if (isdigit(ch)) val += ch;
    } while (isdigit(ch));
    ungetChar(ch);
    nextPInstr->level = atoi(val.data());
    do ch = getChar();     // skip till digit or sign
    while ( ! (isdigit(ch) || ch == '-' || ch == '+'));
    val   = ch;           // convert character to a string
    do {
       ch = getChar();    // then convert to integer (value)
       if (isdigit(ch)) val += ch;
    } while (isdigit(ch));            ungetChar(ch);
    nextPInstr->value = atoi(val.data());
    ignoreComnt();         // skip rest of line
    return nextPInstr;
}
```

F.5 PINTERP.H—P-MACHINE DEFINITION

```
#ifndef __PINTERP__
#define __PINTERP__ 1
#include "Code.h"          // defines the Code segment
#include "PCode.h"         // defines the P-Code basics
#include "Process.h"       // defines a process (control block)
#include "Semaphor.h"      // defines a (general) semaphore
#include "Conditio.h"      // defines a condition

const  stacksize  = 10000;
const  procsize   = 1000;
const  max_sema4  = 25;
const  max_condit = 15;
const  Imax       = realSize;

extern int    chance;

union equiv
{
```

```
    float       Flt;
    int         Int[Imax];
};


class PInterp
{
    int         P;                      // program counter
    int         T;                      // top of stack
    int         B;                      // base of stack-frame
    int         H;                      // top of heap
    PInstr      I;                      // instruction register
    equiv       Rstk[2];                // Real stack
    int         stk[stacksize];         // system stack (int)
    Process     *proc, *main;           // processes (PCBs)
    ProcQ       *ready;                 // the queue of ready processes
    Semaphore *semaphore[max_sema4];    // semaphores
    int         next_semaphore;         // next unused semaphore
    Condition *condition[max_condit];   // conditions
    int         next_condition;         // next unused condition
    int         concur;                 // concurrency enabler
    int         active_processes;       // active process count
    void        pop2();                 // pop 2 floats off Real stack
    void        pop1();                 // pop 1 float off Real stack
    void        push1();                // push 1 float on Real stack
    int         power(int   m, int   n); // integer power function
    float       power(float m, float n); // real power function
    int         base(int lev);          // base finder
public:
                PInterp();              // constructor
    void        Execute(Code *code);    // execute (interpret) the code
};

#endif
```

F.6 PINTERP.CPP—THE P-MACHINE INTERPRETER

```
#include <stdlib.h>
#include <sys/types.h>
#include <time.h>
#include <math.h>
#include <iostream.h>
#include "PInterp.h"      // defines the P Machine
```

```
      PInterp::PInterp()
{
   T      = -1;    B     = 0;      P     = 0;     H = stacksize;
   stk[0] =  0;    stk[1] = 0;     stk[1] = 0;
   main   = new Process;
   ready  = new ProcQ;
   next_semaphore   = 0;           // no semaphores assigned
   next_condition   = 0;           // no conditions assigned
   concur           = 0;           // disable concurrency
   active_processes = 0;           // active processes
   srand( int( time(NULL) ) );     // seed random number generator
}

void  PInterp::pop1()
{ for (int i = 0;  i < Imax;  i++)    Rstk[0].Int[i] = stk[T--];    }

void  PInterp::pop2()
{ pop1();     Rstk[1].Flt = Rstk[0].Flt;     pop1();                }

void  PInterp::push1()
{ for (int i = 0;  i < Imax;  i++)    stk[++T] = Rstk[0].Int[i];    }

int   PInterp::power(int m, int n)
{
   if (n && 1)
      return ( m * power(m, n-1) );
   else if (n == 0)
      return (1);
   else
   {
      int i = power(m, n / 2);


   }
}


float PInterp::power(float m, float n)
{ return ( exp( log(m) * n ) );      }

int   PInterp::base(int lev)
{
   int  b1 = B;
   while (lev > 0)  {  b1 = stk[b1];    --lev;  }
   return (b1);
}
```

```
void  PInterp::Execute(Code *code)
{
   int   level = 0;
   int   i, j, k;
   int   s4, con, gate;
   char  ch, str[80];

   do
   {
      if ( ! code->Fetch(I.fnctn, I.level, I.value, P))
      {
         cerr<<"Fetch violation at location "<<P<<endl;
         exit(EXIT_FAILURE);
      }
      else          // execute
      {
         P++;

         switch (I.fnctn)
         {
            case OPR:                          // OPeRation
               switch (I.value)
               {
                  case 0:                      // RETURN
                     if (concur && (level == 1))
                     {
                        active_processes--;
                        if ( ! ready->empty() )
                        {
                           proc = ready->front();
                           ready->pop();
                           proc->Get(P, B, T, level);
                        }
                        else if (active_processes > 0)
                        {
                           cerr << "SYSTEM DEADLOCK !!" << endl;
                           exit (EXIT_FAILURE);
                        }
                        else
                        {
                           main->Get(P, B, T, level);
                           concur = 0;
                        }
```

```
       }
       else
       {
          T = B - 1;
          P = stk[T+3];
          B = stk[T+2];
          level--;
       }
       break;
    case 1:                          // NEGATE
       if (I.level)
       {
          pop1();
          Rstk[0].Flt = - Rstk[0].Flt;
          push1();
       }
       else   stk[T] = - stk[T];
       break;
    case 2:                          // ADD
       if (I.level)
       {
          pop2();
          Rstk[0].Flt += Rstk[1].Flt;
          push1();
       }
       else   {  stk[T-1] += stk[T];   T--;   }
       break;
    case 3:                          // SUBTRACT
       if (I.level)
       {
          pop2();
          Rstk[0].Flt -= Rstk[1].Flt;
          push1();
       }
       else   {  stk[T-1] -= stk[T];   T--;   }
       break;
    case 4:                          // MULTIPLY
       if (I.level)
       {
          pop2();
          Rstk[0].Flt *= Rstk[1].Flt;
          push1();
       }
       else   {  stk[T-1] *= stk[T];   T--;   }
```

```
        break;
case 5:                          // DIVIDE
    if (I.level)
    {
        pop2();
        Rstk[0].Flt /= Rstk[1].Flt;
        push1();
    }
    else   {  stk[T-1] /= stk[T];   T--;  }
    break;
case 6:                          // isODD
    stk[T] &= 1;
    break;
case 7:                          // MODULO
    stk[T-1] %= stk[T];   T--;
    break;
case 8:                          // isEQUAL
    if (I.level)
    {
        pop2();
        stk[++T] = (Rstk[0].Flt == Rstk[1].Flt);
    }
    else   {  stk[T-1] = stk[T-1] == stk[T];   T--;  }
    break;
case 9:                          // isNOT_EQUAL
    if (I.level)
    {
        pop2();
        stk[++T] = (Rstk[0].Flt != Rstk[1].Flt);
    }
    else   {  stk[T-1] = stk[T-1] != stk[T];   T--;  }
    break;
case 10:                         // isLESS
    if (I.level)
    {
        pop2();
        stk[++T] = (Rstk[0].Flt < Rstk[1].Flt);
    }
    else   {  stk[T-1] = stk[T-1] < stk[T];   T--;  }
    break;
case 11:                         // isNOT_LESS
    if (I.level)
    {
        pop2();
```

```
          stk[++T] = (Rstk[0].Flt >= Rstk[1].Flt);
        }
        else {  stk[T-1] = stk[T-1] >= stk[T];  T--;  }
        break;
case 12:                           // isGREATER
    if (I.level)
    {
        pop2();
        stk[++T] = (Rstk[0].Flt > Rstk[1].Flt);
    }
    else   {  stk[T-1] = stk[T-1] > stk[T];  T--;  }
    break;
case 13:                           // isNOT_GREATER
    if (I.level)
    {
        pop2();
        stk[++T] = (Rstk[0].Flt <= Rstk[1].Flt);
    }
    else {  stk[T-1] = stk[T-1] <= stk[T];  T--;  }
    break;
case 14:                           // AND
    stk[T-1] &= stk[T];  T--;
    break;
case 15:                           // OR
    stk[T-1] |= stk[T];  T--;
    break;
case 16:                           // NOT
    stk[T] = ~ stk[T];
    break;
case 17:                           // LSHIFT
    stk[T] <<= 1;
    break;
case 18:                           // RSHIFT
    stk[T] >>= 1;
    break;
case 19:                           // INC
    stk[T] += 1;
    break;
case 20:                           // DEC
    stk[T] -= 1;
    break;
case 21:                           // COPY
    stk[T+1] = stk[T];  T++;
    break;
```

```
case 22:                          // m ^ n
   if (I.level)
   {
      pop2();
      Rstk[0].Flt =power(Rstk[0].Flt, Rstk[1].Flt);
      push1();
   }
   else
   { stk[T-1] = power(stk[T-1], stk[T]);  T--;  }
   break;
case 23:                          // CONVERT
   if (I.level)
   {
      pop1();
      stk[++T] = Rstk[0].Flt;
   }
   else
   {
      Rstk[0].Flt = stk[T--];
      push1();
   }
   break;
case 24:                          // NEW (size)
   H -= I.level;
   stk[++T] = H;
   break;
case 25:                          // CO-INIT
   proc = new Process;
   active_processes++;
   proc->Put(0, 0, T-1, level);
   T = stk[T] - 1;
   break;
case 26:                          // CO-START
   main->Put(P, B, T, level);
   proc = ready->front();
   ready->pop();
   proc->Get(P, B, T, level);
   concur = 1;      // enable concurrency
   break;
case 27:                          // SUSPEND
   if (concur)
   {
      proc->Put(P, B, T, level);
      ready->push(proc);
```

```
                proc = ready->front();
                ready->pop();
                proc->Get(P, B, T, level);
            }
            break;
        case 28:                         // SEMAPHORE (s4, expr)
            semaphore[next_semaphore++] = new Semaphore;
            j = stk[T--];    // value of expr
            stk[ stk[T--] ] = next_semaphore;
            s4 = next_semaphore - 1;
            for (i = 0;  i < j;  i++)
                semaphore[s4]->IncCount();
            break;
        case 29:                         // WAIT (s4)
            s4 = stk[T--] - 1;
            if (concur)
            {
                if ( semaphore[s4]->Count() > 0 )
                    semaphore[s4]->DecCount();
                else if ( ready->empty() )
                {
                    cerr << "SYSTEM DEADLOCK !!" << endl;
                    exit (EXIT_FAILURE);
                }
                else
                {
                    proc->Put(P, B, T, level);
                    semaphore[s4]->insert(proc);
                    proc = ready->front();
                    ready->pop();
                    proc->Get(P, B, T, level);
                }
            }
            break;
        case 30:                         // SEND (s4)
            s4 = stk[T--] - 1;
            if (concur)
            {
                if ( semaphore[s4]->isWaiting() )
                {
                    proc->Put(P, B, T, level);
                    ready->push(proc);
                    proc = semaphore[s4]->get();
                    proc->Get(P, B, T, level);
```

```
            }
            else
            {
                semaphore[s4]->IncCount();
                if ( ! ready->empty() )
                {
                    proc->Put(P, B, T, level);
                    ready->push(proc);
                    proc = ready->front();
                    ready->pop();
                    proc->Get(P, B, T, level);
                }
            }
        }
        break;
    case 31:                       // CONDITION(gate, con)
        semaphore[next_semaphore]   = new Semaphore;
        s4   = next_semaphore++;
        i    = stk[T--];       // addr of condition
        gate = stk[T--] - 1;   // number of sema4 gate
        condition[next_condition++] =
            new Condition(s4, gate);
        stk[ i ] = next_condition;
        break;
    case 32:                        // SEND (gate)
        con = stk[T--] - 1;
        if (concur)
        {
            gate = condition[con]->GetGate();
            if ( semaphore[gate]->isWaiting() )
            {
                proc->Put(P, B, T, level);
                ready->push(proc);
                proc = semaphore[gate]->get();
                proc->Get(P, B, T, level);
            }
            else
            {
                semaphore[gate]->IncCount();
                if ( ! ready->empty() )
                {
                    proc->Put(P, B, T, level);
                    ready->push(proc);
                    proc - ready->front();
```

```
            ready->pop();
            proc->Get(P, B, T, level);
        }
    }
}
break;
case 33:                    // WAIT (con)
    con = stk[T--] - 1;
    if (concur)
    {
        s4 = condition[con]->GetSema4();
        if ( semaphore[s4]->Count() > 0 )
            semaphore[s4]->DecCount();
        else if ( ready->empty() )
        {
            cerr << "SYSTEM DEADLOCK !!" << endl;
            exit (EXIT_FAILURE);
        }
        else
        {
            proc->Put(P, B, T, level);
            semaphore[s4]->insert(proc);
            proc = ready->front();
            ready->pop();
            proc->Get(P, B, T, level);
        }
    }
break;
case 34:                    // SEND (con)
    con = stk[T--] - 1;
    if (concur)
    {
        s4 = condition[con]->GetSema4();
        if ( semaphore[s4]->isWaiting() )
        {
            proc->Put(P, B, T, level);
            ready->push(proc);
            proc = semaphore[s4]->get();
            proc->Get(P, B, T, level);
        }
        else
        {
            semaphore[s4]->IncCount();
            if ( ! ready->empty() )
```

```
                        proc->Put(P, B, T  level);
                        ready->push(proc);
                        proc = ready->front();
                        ready->pop();
                        proc->Get(P, B, T, level);
                    }
                }
            }
            break;
        case 35:                    // INCR (con)
            con = stk[T--] - 1;
            if (concur) condition[con]->IncCount();
            break;
        case 36:                    // DECR (con)
            con = stk[T--] - 1;
            if (concur) condition[con]->DecCount();
            break;
        case 37:                    // GET (con)
            con = stk[T] - 1;
            if (concur) stk[T] = condition[con]->Count();
            break;
        case 38:                    // DELAYED (con)
            con = stk[T] - 1;
            if (concur)
            {
                s4 = condition[con]->GetSema4();
                stk[T] = semaphore[s4]->isWaiting();
            }
            else stk[T] = 0;
            break;
    }
    break;
case LIT:                           // load LITeral
    stk[++T] = I.value;
    break;
case LOD:                           // LOaD (i.e. push)
    stk[++T] = stk[base(I.level) + I.value];
    break;
case LODA:                          // LOaD Address
    stk[++T] = base(I.level) + I.value;
    break;
case LODI:                          // LOaD Indirect
    T += I.value;
```

```
     for (i = 0;  i <= I.value;  i++)
        stk[T - i] = stk[ stk[T - I.value] + I.value - i ];
     break;
  case LODX:                          // LOaD indeXed
     stk[T] = stk[ base(I.level) + I.value + stk[T] ];
     break;
  case STO:                           // STOre (i.e. pop)
     stk[base(I.level) + I.value] = stk[T  ];
     break;
  case STOI:                          // STOre Indirect
     T -= (I.value + 2);
     for (i = 0;  i <= I.value;  i++)
     {  stk[ stk[T+1] + i ] = stk[ T+2 + i ];  }
     break;
  case STOX:                          // STOre indeXed
     T -= 2;
     stk[ base(I.level) + I.value + stk[T+1] ] = stk[T+2];
     break;
  case CAL:                           // CALl procedure
     stk[T+1] = base(I.level);
     stk[T+2] = B;    B = T + 1;
     stk[T+3] = P;    P = I.value;
     level++;
     break;
  case PRC:                           // PRocess Call
     stk[T+1] - base(I.level);
     stk[T+2] = B;
     stk[T+3] = 1;               // illegal process return
     proc->Get(i, j, k, level); // k = saved T value
     proc->Put(I.value, T+1, T, 1);
     ready->push(proc);          // put in ready queue
     T = k;
     break;
  case INT:                           // INcrement T-reg
     T += I.value;
     break;
  case JMP:                           // JuMP
     P = I.value;
     break;
  case JPC:                           // JumP on Condition
     if (stk[T--] == I.level)  P = I.value;
     break;
  case CSP:                           // Call Spec. Procedure
     switch (I.value)
```

```
    {
       case 0:                          // READ char
          ch = char(cin.get());
          stk[++T] = int(ch);
          break;
       case 1:                          // WRITE char
          ch = char(stk[T--]);
          cout.put(ch);
          if (ch == '\n')
             cout << flush;
          break;
       case 2:                          // READ integer
          cout << "d> " << flush;
          cin >> dec >> stk[++T];
          break;
       case 3:                           // WRITE integer
          cout << dec << stk[T--] << ' ';
           break;
       case 4:                          // READ hex
          cout << "x> " << flush;
          cin >> hex >> stk[++T];
          break;
       case 5:                          // WRITE hex
          cout << hex << stk[T--] << ' ';
          break;
       case 6:                          // READ real
          cout << "f> " << flush;
          cin >> Rstk[0].Flt;
          push1();
          break;
       case 7:                          // WRITE real
          pop1();
          cout << Rstk[0].Flt << ' ';
          break;
       case 8:                          // WRITE string
          T -= (I.level + 1);
          for (i = 0;  i <= I.level;  i++)
             str[i] = char( stk[T+1+i] );
          str[I.level+1] = '\0';
          cout << str;
          break;
    }
    break;

}
```

```
        if (concur)                           // context switch
        {
           int r = int( rand() % 16384 );
           int d = (16383 + chance) / chance;
           if (r / d >= chance - 1)
           {
              proc->Put(P, B, T, level);
              ready->push(proc);
              proc = ready->front();
              ready->pop();
              proc->Get(P, B, T, level);
           }
        }
     }
  }
  while (P > 0);
  if (P == -1)
     cout << "Illegal return from process" << endl;
}
```

F.7 CODE.H—CODE HEADER FILE

```
#ifndef __CODE__
#define __CODE__ 1

#include <map>
#include  "PCode.h"          //defines FunctType
using namespace std;

typedef map< int, PInstr, less<int> > code_dict;

class Code
{
   static  code_dict  code;
   static  int        c_loc;
public:
        Code();                         // constructor
   void Enter     (FunctType  fct, // type of function (e.g. OPR...)
                   int        level, // nesting level of code
                   int        value, // value of the code
                   int        &cx); // location for next instr
   int  Fetch     (FunctType &fct,   // type of function
                   int        &level, // nesting level of instr
                   int        &value, // value of code
```

```
                        int     cx);      // code location to examine
    int   FixValue  (int        value,   // new value for the instr
                        int     cx);      // location of instr to be
                                          // modified
    int   CurrentLoc();                   // return current location
};


class Level
{
   static int  level;
   static int  defed;
  public:
         Level();                         // constructor
   void  inc();                           // raise the nesting level
   void  dec();                           // lower the nesting level
   int   get();                           // get the nesting level
};


#endif
```

F.8   CODE.CPP—THE CODE CLASS IMPLEMENTATION

```
#include "Code.h"               // defines the Code class

code_dict  Code::code;          // the static variables
int        Code::c_loc;         //  "     "         "

Code::Code()                    // constructor
{  c_loc = 0;  }                // set to beginning of dictionary

void Code::Enter (FunctType  fct, int  level, int  value, int &cx)
{
   PInstr  entry;

   entry.fnctn = fct;           // load the entry
   entry.level = level;
   entry.value = value;
   code[c_loc] = entry;         // store entry in dictionary
   cx = ++c_loc;                // return pointer to next entry
}


int Code::Fetch (FunctType &fct, int &level, int &value, int  cx)
{
```

```
    PInstr   entry;

    if (code.find(cx) != code.end())
    {
       entry = code[cx];              // get the entry
       fct   = entry.fnctn;           // extract the field values
       level - entry.level;
       value = entry.value;
       return TRUE;
    }
    else
       return FALSE;
}

int Code::FixValue (int value, int cx)
{
    PInstr   entry;

    if (code.find(cx) != code.end())
    {
       entry = code[cx];              // get old entry
       entry.value = value;           // change the value
       code[cx] - entry;              // store back in dictionary
       return TRUE;
    }
    else
       return FALSE;
}

int Code::CurrentLoc()
{ return c_loc;   }

int   Level::level;                   // the static variables
int   Level::defed = 0;               // "       "       "

Level::Level()
{
    if (defed)  return;
    level = 0;   defed = 1;
}

void  Level::inc  ()     { level ++ ;          }

void  Level::dec  ()     { level -- ;          }
```

```
int   Level::get ()    {  return (level);   }
```

F.9 PROCESS.H—PROCESS DEFINITION

```
#ifndef __PROC__
#define __PROC__ 1

class Process
{
   int   P;                  // latest program counter for process
   int   B;                  // latest current base for process
   int   T;                  // latest top of stack for process
   int   Level;              // current nesting level of process
public:
         Process();          // constructor

   void  Put(                // put values into process control block
            int  p,          // current program counter
            int  b,          // current base
            int  t,          // current top of stack
            int  level);     // current nesting level

   void  Get(                // get values from process control block
            int  &p,         //    new program counter
            int  &b,         //    new base
            int  &t,         //    new top of stack
            int  &level);    //    new nesting level
};

#endif
```

F.10 PROCESS.CPP—PROCESS OPERATIONS

```
#include "Process.h"

      Process::Process()  { }

void  Process::Put(int  p,  int  b,   int  t,   int  level)
{     P = p;    B = b;    T = t;    Level = level;    }

void  Process::Get(int  &p,  int  &b,   int  &t,   int  &level)
```

```
{    p = P;    b = B;    t = T;    level = Level;    }
```

F.11 SEMAPHORE.H—SEMAPHORE DEFINITION

```cpp
#ifndef __SEMI4__
#define __SEMI4__ 1

#include <queue>
#include <list>
#include "Process.h"
using namespace std;

typedef queue<Process *, list<Process *> > ProcQ;

class Semaphore
{
    int     count;
    ProcQ   *waiting;
public:
            Semaphore();        // constructor
    void    insert(            // insert process onto Semaphore queue
                Process *proc); //    the process to insert
    Process *get();            // get process from Semaphore queue
    int     Count();           // returns value of semaphore count
    int     isWaiting();       // returns 1 if processes waiting
    void    IncCount();        // increment the semaphore count
    void    DecCount();        // decrement the semaphore count
};

#endif
```

F.12 SEMAPHORE.CPP—SEMAPHORE IMPLEMENTATION

```cpp
#include "Semaphor.h"

    Semaphore::Semaphore()
{   waiting = new ProcQ;   count  = 0;  }

void  Semaphore::insert(Process *proc)
{   waiting->push(proc);   }

Process *Semaphore::get()
```

```
{
    Process *temp;

    temp = waiting->front();   waiting->pop();
    return (temp);
}

int   Semaphore::Count()
{  return (count);   }

int   Semaphore::isWaiting()
{  return( ! waiting->empty());   }

void  Semaphore::IncCount()
{  count++;   }

void  Semaphore::DecCount()
{  count--;   }
```

F.13 CONDITION.H—MONITOR CONDITION DEFINITION

```
#ifndef __MONITOR__
#define __MONITOR__ 1

#include "Process.h"
#include "Semaphor.h"

class Condition
{
    int    count;
    int    Sema4;
    int    Gate;
public:
            Condition(int sema4,  int gate);  // constructor
    int    Count();                // returns value of monitor count
    void   IncCount();             // increment the monitor count
    void   DecCount();             // decrement the monitor count
    int    GetSema4();             // returns the semaphore number
    int    GetGate();              // returns the gate semaphore number
};

#endif
```

F.14 CONDITION.CPP—MONITOR CONDITION IMPLEMENTATION

```cpp
#include "Conditio.h"

    Condition::Condition(int sema4,  int gate)
{
   Sema4 = sema4;
   Gate  = gate;
   count = 0;
}

int   Condition::Count()
{  return (count);   }

void  Condition::IncCount()
{  count++;   }

void  Condition::DecCount()
{  count--;   }

int   Condition::GetSema4()
{  return (Sema4);   }

int   Condition::GetGate()
{  return (Gate);   }
```

INDEX

LICENSE AGREEMENT AND LIMITED WARRANTY

READ THE FOLLOWING TERMS AND CONDITIONS CAREFULLY BEFORE OPENING THIS SOFTWARE MEDIA PACKAGE. THIS LEGAL DOCUMENT IS AN AGREEMENT BETWEEN YOU AND PRENTICE-HALL, INC. (THE "COMPANY"). BY OPENING THIS SEALED SOFTWARE MEDIA PACKAGE, YOU ARE AGREEING TO BE BOUND BY THESE TERMS AND CONDITIONS. IF YOU DO NOT AGREE WITH THESE TERMS AND CONDITIONS, DO NOT OPEN THE SOFTWARE MEDIA PACKAGE. PROMPTLY RETURN THE UNOPENED SOFTWARE MEDIA PACKAGE AND ALL ACCOMPANYING ITEMS TO THE PLACE YOU OBTAINED THEM FOR A FULL REFUND OF ANY SUMS YOU HAVE PAID.

1.   **GRANT OF LICENSE:** In consideration of your payment of the license fee, which is part of the price you paid for this product, and your agreement to abide by the terms and conditions of this Agreement, the Company grants to you a nonexclusive right to use and display the copy of the enclosed software program (hereinafter the "SOFTWARE") on a single computer (i.e., with a single CPU) at a single location so long as you comply with the terms of this Agreement. The Company reserves all rights not expressly granted to you under this Agreement.

2.   **OWNERSHIP OF SOFTWARE:** You own only the magnetic or physical media (the enclosed SOFTWARE) on which the SOFTWARE is recorded or fixed, but the Company retains all the rights, title, and ownership to the SOFTWARE recorded on the original SOFTWARE copy(ies) and all subsequent copies of the SOFTWARE, regardless of the form or media on which the original or other copies may exist. This license is not a sale of the original SOFTWARE or any copy to you.

3.   **COPY RESTRICTIONS:** This SOFTWARE and the accompanying printed materials and user manual (the "Documentation") are the subject of copyright. You may not copy the Documentation or the SOFTWARE, except that you may make a single copy of the SOFTWARE for backup or archival purposes only. You may be held legally responsible for any copying or copyright infringement which is caused or encouraged by your failure to abide by the terms of this restriction.

4.   **USE RESTRICTIONS:** You may not network the SOFTWARE or otherwise use it on more than one computer or computer terminal at the same time. You may physically transfer the SOFTWARE from one computer to another provided that the SOFTWARE is used on only one computer at a time. You may not distribute copies of the SOFTWARE or Documentation to others. You may not reverse engineer, disassemble, decompile, modify, adapt, translate, or create derivative works based on the SOFTWARE or the Documentation without the prior written consent of the Company.

5.   **TRANSFER RESTRICTIONS:** The enclosed SOFTWARE is licensed only to you and may not be transferred to any one else without the prior written consent of the Company. Any unauthorized transfer of the SOFTWARE shall result in the immediate termination of this Agreement.

6.   **TERMINATION:** This license is effective until terminated. This license will terminate automatically without notice from the Company and become null and void if you fail to comply with any provisions or limitations of this license. Upon termination, you shall destroy the Documentation and all copies of the SOFTWARE. All provisions of this Agreement as to warranties, limitation of liability, remedies or damages, and our ownership rights shall survive termination.

7.   **MISCELLANEOUS:** This Agreement shall be construed in accordance with the laws of the United States of America and the State of New York and shall benefit the Company, its affiliates, and assignees.

8.   **LIMITED WARRANTY AND DISCLAIMER OF WARRANTY:** The Company warrants that the SOFTWARE, when properly used in accordance with the Documentation, will operate in substantial conformity with the description of the SOFTWARE set forth in the Documentation. The Company does not warrant that the SOFTWARE will meet your requirements or that the operation of the SOFTWARE will be uninterrupted or error-free. The Company warrants that the

media on which the SOFTWARE is delivered shall be free from defects in materials and workmanship under normal use for a period of thirty (30) days from the date of your purchase. Your only remedy and the Company's only obligation under these limited warranties is, at the Company's option, return of the warranted item for a refund of any amounts paid by you or replacement of the item. Any replacement of SOFTWARE or media under the warranties shall not extend the original warranty period. The limited warranty set forth above shall not apply to any SOFTWARE which the Company determines in good faith has been subject to misuse, neglect, improper installation, repair, alteration, or damage by you. EXCEPT FOR THE EXPRESSED WARRANTIES SET FORTH ABOVE, THE COMPANY DISCLAIMS ALL WARRANTIES, EXPRESS OR IMPLIED, INCLUDING WITHOUT LIMITATION, THE IMPLIED WARRANTIES OF MERCHANTABILITY AND FITNESS FOR A PARTICULAR PURPOSE. EXCEPT FOR THE EXPRESS WARRANTY SET FORTH ABOVE, THE COMPANY DOES NOT WARRANT, GUARANTEE, OR MAKE ANY REPRESENTATION REGARDING THE USE OR THE RESULTS OF THE USE OF THE SOFTWARE IN TERMS OF ITS CORRECTNESS, ACCURACY, RELIABILITY, CURRENTNESS, OR OTHERWISE.

IN NO EVENT, SHALL THE COMPANY OR ITS EMPLOYEES, AGENTS, SUPPLIERS, OR CONTRACTORS BE LIABLE FOR ANY INCIDENTAL, INDIRECT, SPECIAL, OR CONSEQUENTIAL DAMAGES ARISING OUT OF OR IN CONNECTION WITH THE LICENSE GRANTED UNDER THIS AGREEMENT, OR FOR LOSS OF USE, LOSS OF DATA, LOSS OF INCOME OR PROFIT, OR OTHER LOSSES, SUSTAINED AS A RESULT OF INJURY TO ANY PERSON, OR LOSS OF OR DAMAGE TO PROPERTY, OR CLAIMS OF THIRD PARTIES, EVEN IF THE COMPANY OR AN AUTHORIZED REPRESENTATIVE OF THE COMPANY HAS BEEN ADVISED OF THE POSSIBILITY OF SUCH DAMAGES. IN NO EVENT SHALL LIABILITY OF THE COMPANY FOR DAMAGES WITH RESPECT TO THE SOFTWARE EXCEED THE AMOUNTS ACTUALLY PAID BY YOU, IF ANY, FOR THE SOFTWARE.

SOME JURISDICTIONS DO NOT ALLOW THE LIMITATION OF IMPLIED WARRANTIES OR LIABILITY FOR INCIDENTAL, INDIRECT, SPECIAL, OR CONSEQUENTIAL DAMAGES, SO THE ABOVE LIMITATIONS MAY NOT ALWAYS APPLY. THE WARRANTIES IN THIS AGREEMENT GIVE YOU SPECIFIC LEGAL RIGHTS AND YOU MAY ALSO HAVE OTHER RIGHTS WHICH VARY IN ACCORDANCE WITH LOCAL LAW.

ACKNOWLEDGMENT

YOU ACKNOWLEDGE THAT YOU HAVE READ THIS AGREEMENT, UNDERSTAND IT, AND AGREE TO BE BOUND BY ITS TERMS AND CONDITIONS. YOU ALSO AGREE THAT THIS AGREEMENT IS THE COMPLETE AND EXCLUSIVE STATEMENT OF THE AGREEMENT BETWEEN YOU AND THE COMPANY AND SUPERSEDES ALL PROPOSALS OR PRIOR AGREEMENTS, ORAL, OR WRITTEN, AND ANY OTHER COMMUNICATIONS BETWEEN YOU AND THE COMPANY OR ANY REPRESENTATIVE OF THE COMPANY RELATING TO THE SUBJECT MATTER OF THIS AGREEMENT.

Should you have any questions concerning this Agreement or if you wish to contact the Company for any reason, please contact in writing at the address below.

Robin Short
Prentice Hall PTR
One Lake Street
Upper Saddle River, New Jersey 07458